# Cinema and Landscape

# Cinema and Landscape

Graeme Harper & Jonathan Rayner (eds)

**intellect** Bristol, UK / Chicago, USA

First published in the UK in 2010 by
Intellect, The Mill, Parnall Road, Fishponds, Bristol, BS16 3JG, UK

First published in the USA in 2010 by
Intellect, The University of Chicago Press, 1427 E. 60th Street,
Chicago, IL 60637, USA

A catalogue record for this book is available from the
British Library.

Cover designer: Holly Rose
Copy-editor: Rebecca Vaughan-Williams
Typesetting: Mac Style, Beverley, E. Yorkshire

ISBN 978-1-84150-309-7

Printed and bound by 4edge Limited. Hockley. www.4edge.co.uk

FSC Mixed Sources
SA-COC-001695
FSC © 1996 FSC A.C.

2012.0295

# Contents

# The Editors

**Prof. Graeme Harper** is a Fellow of the Royal Geographical Society (FRGS) and of the RSA, Director of the National Institute for Excellence in the Creative Industries at Bangor University, co-editor of *Studies in European Cinema* (Intellect) and of the new *Journal of Popular European Culture* (Intellect, 2010). He is also Honorary Professor at the University of Bedfordshire, and a panel member of the national Arts and Humanities Research Council (AHRC).

**Dr Jonathan Rayner** is a Reader in Film Studies, Convenor of the MA in International Cinema at the University of Sheffield, a recent Caird Senior Research Fellow at The National Maritime Museum at Greenwich (UK), a member of the AHRC Peer Review college, and an Editorial Board member of *Studies in Australasian Cinema* and *Studies in European Cinema*.

# Foreword

David Desser

Béla Belázs's lyrical paeans to the power of the close up in cinema remain vital components to our understanding of how movies work their magic. And whatever Roland Barthes meant when he wrote, 'The face of Garbo is an Idea, that of Hepburn an Event', he still knew that close ups account for much of the pleasures of the cinematic text. Yet surely the Lumière Brothers knew equally well that the long shot, the landscape, could excite the artistic imagination as much as the intimate portrait. Not for nothing do we see a train arriving at a station, workers leaving the factory – the landscape existing in space yet shifting in time. While it is doubtful that people ran screaming from the Grand Café at the sight of a train hurtling toward them, a genuine excitement was indeed experienced when a landscape, at once familiar and now made strange, came alive before their eyes. The cinema's debt to photography is abundantly clear in the Lumière Brothers' films; they were, after all, the purveyors of photographic equipment. Yet is not photography equally suited to the landscape as much as the portrait? And who, moreover, living in France in the second half of the nineteenth century could be unaware and unaffected by Impressionism? For all the documentary value in their films, we find marvellous touches of Impressionism: are we excited at the image of Monsieur and Madam Lumière feeding their baby – the very portrait of the nineteenth-century bourgeoisie – or is the sight of the rustling of the leaves behind them that truly engages our sensibilities? This is both the birth of cinema and of cinephilia.

It is perhaps the 'impressionism' of the cinematic landscape that so strongly commands our attention. Like the Lumière films existing on the boundary between the documentary and the experimental, the marvellous, yet perhaps increasingly forgotten 'city symphonies' such as *Rien que les heures* (Alberto Cavalcanti, 1926), *Berlin: Symphony of a Big City* (Walther Ruttman, 1927) and the two transcendent masterpieces of the genre, *A propos de Nice* (Jean Vigo, 1929) and Dziga Vertov's *Man with a Movie Camera* (1929), reveal the power of the cinema to animate space that both freezes it in time yet endows it with timeless mobility. No surprise, then, that so many cinematic movements that followed understand the impressionism of the city. What is the French New Wave without Paris? What are the films of Sidney Lumet, Woody Allen, Martin Scorsese and Spike Lee, without New York? And think of the masterpiece, *Tokyo Story* (1953). Though not a director of long shots and vistas, Ozu surely has something in mind with those few shots of the sad old couple amid the anonymous megalopolis compared with the graceful sense of home conveyed by the film's famous opening and closing sequences. The 'painterly' associations that landscape inevitably brings to bear have not escaped the greatest of Hollywood's filmmakers, either: John Ford painted a portrait of the Old West as much with the buttes of Monument Valley as he did the increasingly careworn face of John Wayne.

The notion of 'landscape' is a complex one, of course, but however it is defined it has been central to the art and artistry of the cinema and to the cinephilia that goes into the creation of a book like this one.

# Acknowledgements

The Editors would like to sincerely thank each and every one of the contributors to *Cinema and Landscape* for their terrific contributions.

These contributions are not only a wonderful reflection of the laudable commitment displayed here by the authors, but also reflect some considerable challenges faced along the way – all of which makes this book the result of what can be achieved by an international community of scholars.

Sincere thanks also go to our publishers, the very fine Intellect, to Sam King and the wonderful Intellect team, for their ongoing commitment, their lively ideas and their fabulous creative support.

*Graeme Harper & Jonathan Rayner*

# Chapter 1

## Introduction – Cinema and Landscape

Graeme Harper and Jonathan Rayner

14th May 1930: American actor Johnny Mack Brown (1904–1974) surveys the rugged landscape of the Grand Canyon in Arizona in a scene from 'Billy the Kid' (aka 'The Highwayman Rides'), directed by King Vidor. (Photo by John Kobal Foundation/Getty Images)

Photographs are not *hand*-made; they are manufactured. And what is manufactured is an image of the world.[1]

## Cartography

This book is a cinematic circumnavigation. Though extensive, it is not exhaustive. The journey's impetus here, in comparison to the treks of Arctic explorers, the voyages of ocean navigators or the conquests of mountaineers, is not concerned so much with physical exertion, or with the possession of tangible space, but with the examining of the evidence of cultural production – in this case, specifically, the cinema. This book provides a map. All maps involve stories, in which there is both a narrative and a discourse. All maps involve selection, inclusion, omission, observation and, on occasions, invention. Maps are predicated on the use of specific techniques and, therefore, specific technologies. Ptolemy's eight-volume *Geography* showed the Earth as flat, and disc-shaped. Medieval exploration offered alternate views of where, and how, land and sea, mountains and valleys, might be depicted, and raised questions about the notion of location, the place of the individual, in both the natural and constructed worlds. The earliest surviving terrestrial globe, a representation of the Earth in its true spherical form, was made by the German geographer Martin Behaim in 1492, and may well have directly reassured Christopher Columbus of the potential of his explorations.

European efforts to discover what became known as the 'New World' brought about new techniques in cartography. Maps exist in time, and they raise questions that are equally spatial *and* temporal. They have a shape and form, and suggest an order. Maps can be the product of an individual, or of many individuals working together, or sequentially, over time. In this way, map-making is analogous to the cinematic endeavour, where communal effort and singular vision often meet. The role of the film director could be seen as similar to the role of the individual map-maker; while the role of the actors and film crew could, indeed, be compared to the role of the ship's crew or mountaineering team. Both maps and films assume and position audiences, ideologically as well as geographically. The interaction between map-makers/filmmakers and their audiences can be akin to a shared pilgrimage, in which the individual, or the group, or a culture, moves through a familiar or newly discovered landscape. This relationship with landscape, temporal and spatial as it is, can even form the basis of a rite of passage, in which the depth or breadth of what is known is enhanced or acquaintance made with that which was previously unknown. Landscape then – in a particularly useful application of the term – offers a cartographic receptacle to assist the acquisition of further human understanding.

## Defining landscape

Landscape involves isolation of a certain spatial extent and a certain temporal length. That is, all notions of landscape are produced by human interpretation which, simply due to human physiology or due to political or cultural bias, is selective. Subsequent aesthetic treatments of landscape, whether in painting, photography or film, involve further selection, interpretation and omission, whether by an individual or group. Landscapes can be comforting or daunting, challenging or reassuring. The newly discovered landscapes found on the world journeys of European adventurers in the seventeenth and eighteenth centuries often brought forth highly emotive texts, with discoverers engaging in personal as well as scientific recollection. But landscapes are not always discovered, they can also be created. Reproduced, or even invented landscapes, landscapes created largely in the imagination of painters or filmmakers, often initiate similar responses to the discovered or recorded landscapes of the real world. Landscapes, therefore, are not only selective but are never neutral in intention or reception. Depicted landscapes are often symbolic, and frequently contribute to social formation, impacting upon human associations and societal norms. In the sense of landscape as illusionistic space, in which invented features are foregrounded and the topographical is secondary to the evocative, the relationship between individual or group disposition and landscape depiction is even further heightened.

A definition of landscape, therefore, needs to acknowledge different kinds of environments, from the rural to the urban, from the macro-environment of expansive ecology to the micro-environment of human habitation. Depictions of landscapes can incorporate the manifestations of modernity or be entirely composed of occurrences of nature. While it is possible to narrow landscape definitions on the basis of human intervention, absence or presence of natural features or, indeed, the impact of conspicuous characteristics, the key point about landscapes is that they are composed of many elements and that these elements interact to create our overall conception and reception.

Like a map, the cinematic landscape is the imposition of order on the elements of landscape, collapsing the distinction between the found and the constructed. Like a map, the cinematic landscape has involved technologies and techniques which have evolved. Through the twentieth century, the association of new film technologies with the formation of cinematic landscapes worked to enhance the ways in which the communication and interpretation of landscape was shared. Cinema, as the twentieth century's most successful art form, worked in an analogous way to the globe produced by Behaim in the fifteenth century, in that it delineated and disseminated images and ideas about landscape, and promoted them for further discovery.

Cinema reached a key developmental point in the latter twentieth century with the arrival of digital film technologies. Digital technologies, progressing swiftly on the domestic front with such hardware as the Apple Mac, the first readily accessible home computer, arriving in the later 1970s, software such as the CD-ROM, arriving in the early 1980s, offering convenient data storage and the DVD of the 1990s, with its supplementary platforms of filmic information, have already asked us to reconsider such things as visual veracity and aural truth.

The arrival of digital film technologies has coincided with a reorientation of our understanding of what constitutes a nation, or nation state, with a reevaluation of the idea of community, corresponding to the rise of communities founded on the world wide web and facilitated by the internet, and with the increased significance of the global, supported by this digitally enhanced communication. However, concepts and ideas that currently inform our understanding of film, and of cinematic landscapes, are those concepts and ideas formed in the analogue era of the twentieth century.

In the future, those born in the emerging digital age may have a different response to cinematic landscapes, founded on the coherence of the image and sound, perhaps, rather than on the correspondence of the film to a sense of pre-existing form, or verisimilitude connected with experience. But here, at the end of the analogue age, cinematic landscapes relate to the analogous nature of representation, whether this representation is produced by selection or construction, or an amalgam of these, and these landscapes have corresponding degrees of authenticity and originality.

## Framing landscape

Film, composed of frames of reference as well as frames of composition, largely presents its art as a serial choice. Depictions of landscapes, as complex combinations of found or chosen features, emphasize the incredible variety of possible interrelations that make up the world; cinematic landscapes, most often further complicated by movement, rely on the frame to both suggest a reading and limit the range of interpretations. While it might be possible to envisage a film in which the line between one frame and the next might be seen as entirely continuous, and the frames themselves given the appearance of being devoid of boundaries, the technologies of the cinema have been used to provide encapsulated pictures that, rather than limit human perception, have the ability to enhance it. That is, the importance of the cinematic frame is in its ability to make possible interpretation and understanding by conferring form. This formal structure, related as it is to the historical context of pictorial art, is an enabling device, much as the formal structures of certain kinds of poetry enable the poet to better construct poetic argument.

As Ross Gibson points out:

the camera is not a machine designed for expressing sublimity – either of the Romantic Pantheistic kind or the post-modernist, supra-systemic kind before which the cohesive, centralized self begins to disintegrate. The camera does not express inexpressibility. Quite the opposite. It is designed not to warp the perspectival codes which were installed in art practice during the Renaissance.[2]

The role of framing in the cinema, using the camera to record or select scenery, is different, however, to the role of the frame in painting in that within the cinematic frame movement is most often one of the substantive indicators of meaning. The frame, most often, is a contributor to movement (that is, it is known to be one portion of a continuum); it often contains movement, but suggests that this movement goes beyond its limits. Within the frame, camera movement can occur, through the use of deep and rack focus; shots can pan or zoom; a filmmaker can present and pull back from an object or person; the frame can appear to expand of contract, through shifts from medium to wide shot. Not all of this occurs in the staging of action or the setting-up of a scene, much occurs in the edit suite, and in the application of editorial emphasis in relation to speed, juxtaposition, contrast and rhythm. The frame allows for, or even encourages, the audience to move over, or scan, the image; and the overall effect of a film is to place the audience in a dynamic and extensive experience.

Within any given frame, or in the entirety of any cinematic landscape, not only movement but colour and shape play a part. Colour and shape in the cinema have natural precedents. We only need look at the animal or plant kingdoms to recognize the role of colour and shape in declarations of danger or safety, in the formation of patterns of behaviour and in the cycles of seasonal activity. The natural world, informing our own practical and instinctive senses, has impacted on our constructive nature, suggesting to us ways in which we might compose and orchestrate visual art. Given the expansive quality of the cinema, the range of potential tonal and configural alternatives is considerable, and the role of individual filmmakers, or creative contributors in a film team, is enhanced. In many cases, cinematic landscapes involve a group or shared vision; in some cases they are the product of a strong individual sense, nevertheless related to a cultural or societal history. Yet, in all cases, tonal and configural alternatives rest on communal conventions of reference. These work as mnemonics, recalling for us our natural understanding, and referring us back to associations and origins which, in many ways, are pre-linguistic. Film language, therefore, and the language of cinematic landscapes, are portrayals that connect filmmakers and audiences with an innate and primal sense of self and of the world.

Cinematic landscapes are not simply of the moment, but can recall both our own and a general condition prior to their representation. This mnemonic offering, founded on the complexity of such a framing and such a juxtaposing of framing, and on the place of elements of the composition in our innate understanding, is atemporal in that it does not necessarily correspond to the day-to-day time that is imposed on human life. Rather, in the way discussed by Henri Bergson, this time is pure or actual and the memories stimulated interweave with the surface actions of day-to-day existence. Bergson's suggestions have particular reference here because, in analysing cinematic landscapes, it is possible to observe a set of referential characteristics that are as much meta-physical as physical. Bergson once wrote:

> Everything, then, must happen as if an independent memory gathered images as they successively occur along the course of time; and as if our body, together with its surroundings, was never more than one among these images, the last is that which we obtain at any movement by making an instantaneous section in the general stream of becoming.[3]

So cinematic landscapes, while obviously part of a continuum, and equally composed of frames, can also be considered conduits to memories, and a form of time, that transcends the cinema itself.

It would be incorrect, however, to suggest that cinematic landscapes are composed only of images, and the careful arrangement, or the collection, or the construction of these images. What of the aural landscape? Sound and music are integral to cinematic landscapes. Whether these work as naturalist reinforcements of the image, or whether they are complementary, their contribution is considerable. Of course, this has not always been the case: cinema's history, and the earliest examples of pre-sound cinema being enamoured of the pictorial, reveal a set of relations with aural understanding that bear further examination from the point of view of the connotative as well as the denotative. Film's acoustic environments reveal a set of relations with sound as well as offering a variety of associations for film narrative, the responses of film audiences and the compositional possibilities available to directors and editors.

As with movement, colour and shape, cinematic landscapes use film sound as an attribute, but not as a discrete, concrete element; rather, film sound is experienced in relation to what we *see* on screen; what we *hear* adds, questions, progresses, extends, completes or challenges the action, image, movement, colour or shape. Sound, or music, can foreground – signalling forthcoming action or event, suggesting character traits or potential narrative turns. Sound can mark a place, or time – history, or a specific moment or movement in history, for example, can be indicated in the cinematic landscape as much through the incorporation of sound and music as by the use of costume or setting. Sound also, or in particular music, stresses the performative nature of film, and the theatrical aspects of the cinematic landscape can be augmented by the use of sound and/or music.

Whereas visual space is almost exclusively solid or opaque, aural space is transparent. Interestingly, were we to reverse ideas of this relationship in terms of the visual and the aural in the cinema, we could even view film as a transparent map for its sound. Maps represent, and endeavour to embody the physical. They are successful if they become transparent; no longer objects themselves, rather they are the canvas on which the representation finds form. Sound and music, as with image, have a perspective. They can add a mimetic depth to a frame, or film sequence. They can also be purely evocative, and this is often the case with film music. The cross-sensory aspects of cinematic landscapes are considerably evaluated in any consideration of the aural, and in differentiating between sound, music and, indeed, noise. Noise, which tends to denote unexpected or unpleasant sound, interrupts a cinematic landscape, suggesting a disturbance to the equilibrium of the image or sound track.

The framing of a cinematic landscape involves a complex combination of found or chosen features – some visual, some aural, some relating to movement, some based in innate understanding. The variety of interrelations between these features is infinite, and dependent not only on individual creativity or individual interpretation, but also on group or cultural comprehension. Framing the cinematic landscape is both formal and conceptual and our reading of cinematic landscapes asks us to be complicit with both filmmakers and our fellow film viewers.


## Typology of landscape perceptions

When considering cinematic landscapes, we don't necessarily construct doctrinal classifications but we do enter realms of agreement. So, for example, agreement on what constitutes interior or exterior space, agreement on the relationship between foreground and background, agreement on how we perceive height, width and length and their relevance to such concepts as status, distance, duration, longevity, and even beauty. Film, being a complex collection of movement, colour, shape and sound, needs such agreements to allow its ordering to have coherent or relatively consensual meaning. This can include reference to geographic locale, to culture or historical period. Such things can, of course, be manipulated: take the role of costume in some Science Fiction cinema in both referencing an alien world and, as is in the case of *Star Wars* (1977) or *Blade Runner* (1982), providing consciously anachronistic allusion to earlier periods of history. Personal as well as public typologies relating to cinematic landscapes assist in conveying subject and theme by variant uses of recognizable tropes. Film can be both metaphoric in its depictions, as well metonymic.

The majority of film is metonymic in nature, and is based on an identifiable range of designations. So, for example, in a cinematic landscape in which a skyscraper is depicted, we have transference of the idea of a city, of the ideas of business and commerce, of the ideas of capitalism and wealth, and of the ideas of ambition and aspiration. Alternately, in the framing of a ramshackle farmer's hut, perhaps of the nineteenth century, we have the transference of the idea of labour, of pastoralism, of the pre-industrial or agrarian existence. Metonymic landscapes do not suggest their completion; rather they indicate further and larger concepts and relevance and they encapsulate rather than suggest inclusivity. But not all film is metonymic.

The metaphoric cinematic landscape is the landscape of suggestion. Metaphor entails the transference to an alternate plain of reference. The purpose of metaphor is to deepen our understanding of a subject or theme and, as with its use in literature, in film metaphor enables the audience to extend its relationship with the text. In *The Day After Tomorrow* (2004), Jack Hall's (Dennis Quaid) trek across a frozen landscape is representative of his renewed commitment to a parental role, in relation to his estranged son Sam (Jake Gyllenhaal). *The Day After Tomorrow* uses the easily identifiable apocryphal story of climate change to investigate wider themes of responsibility, commitment, leadership, belief and faith. The film's cinematic landscapes alter the actual landscape of New York, while at the same time referring to New York as it is exists in its old form. The film presents both an *actual* New York, an altered but recognizable meeting place for the protagonists, and a *thematic* New York, a meeting place of values and interpretations. In doing so, the metaphoric nature of the film's landscapes is constantly renewed, and the 'thawing' conclusion returns the audience to the question of how to prevent a scenario of climatic disaster but also how to renew their sense of responsibility on matters well beyond those referred to in the film.

Cinematic landscapes, drawing not only on the literal, but also on the metonymic and metaphoric, can articulate the unconscious as well as the conscious. Cinematic landscapes can therefore be landscapes of the mind, offering displaced representations of desires and values, so that these can be expressed by the filmmakers and shared by audiences. Such signification, and the substitutions that operate, assist in exploration of these spaces in a way not less significant than that seen in the human exploration of actual geographic space. Cinematic landscapes are thus both material and mediated. They are places of discovery.

## Mapping cinematic landscapes

Mapping landscapes involves quantitative and qualitative measurement. Quantitative measurement relates to the selection of points on the map that have significance – these can often be determined, in map-making, by the frequency of usage or reference, or by their prominence, or by the extent of their distinctiveness. Quantitative data is a measurement of magnitude, expressed largely in physical terms, but can also relate to personal characteristics. Quantitative measurement often uses correspondences or similarities to suggest rules of analysis or particular groupings. However, mapping also involves qualitative measurement.

Qualitative analysis emphasizes meaning, and discusses inherent or distinctive characteristics. Qualitative measurement is not necessarily about proving what is superior or more important; rather, qualitative measurement aims to distinguish examples and to recognize innate properties. Measurement here relates to essential attributes, and the origins of qualitative measurement arise from our experience of natural phenomena. Empathy plays a role in qualitative measurement, and those engaged in such measurement are themselves subjects positioned within a historical and socio-cultural context.

In the case of mapping cinematic landscapes at the beginning of the twenty-first century, commentators are located in an analogue film history; they are engaged in an increasingly globalized yet still nationalized sense of cinematic production, and they are aware of, though not necessarily born into, the collapse of boundaries between varieties of media, the convergence of an Old World notion of the cinema with a New World ideal of media multivalence.

Mapping is not solely a mathematical occupation. While mapping landscapes in ancient times involved degrees of speculation in terms of defining dimensions and accurately locating features, cinematic landscape mapping in the contemporary sense privileges a specialized knowledge of over a century of filmic evolution, and an acknowledgement of the compelling nature of navigating an increasingly dynamic landscape between film production and film consumption and a now almost boundary free milieu of film dissemination.

## Nation and aesthetics

A film's settings, its range of image-captured locations, might appear as the only unequivocal, genuine element incorporated in an inconspicuously engineered spectacle. Found cinematic landscapes, natural and urban, physical and social, have existences independent of their depictions and uses in filmic images. Their persistence in the frame embodies a realism that belies the contrived placement and inescapable artificiality of the human performances in the more sharply focused foreground.

We cannot state with confidence that a found cinematic landscape appears purely as a realist record, when it is as subject as any other cinematic element to aesthetic manipulation, technological enhancement and ideological indoctrination. Its prominent and articulate presence draws attention to itself as a conscious inclusion, a bearer of meanings relevant to the refinement of a visual aesthetic, a communal cultural contact between filmmaker and audience and/or the maintenance, questioning and propagation of national identity.

Cinematic landscapes can also be constructed – that is, formed from the conscious and intentional isolation and emphasis of topographic detail, and/or the application of medium-specific techniques and technologies (choices of perspectives and lenses, editing, optical filters, computer-generated or -enhanced imagery). The realist sway of motion pictures, and the formal and ideological properties of the cinematic apparatus itself, may betray or obscure this work of construction. What is contained in the frame can assume the status of the real simply from its presence within it. Yet the authenticity of the cinematic landscape is not indisputable: the critical concentration in discussions of cinematic realism on the film medium's technologies of reproduction ahead of what is *selected* for reproduction alerts us to the landscape's presence as a role, as another performative element. The quotation from Cavell at the head of this introduction incorporates and acknowledges this paradox inherent in the medium: the apparent realist certainty of the unmediated, mechanical reproduction on film of whatever falls within the boundaries of the frame, and the interpretative truth of the inevitably partial selection, construction and inclination of an image, serving implicit or explicit purposes. Also key within the recognition of selection is the identification of an individual who can be credited with artistic creation. This isolation of the film auteur as solitary map-maker for cinematic landscape may be particularly prevalent and tempting within national cinema contexts, in which the aura of art is co-opted by motivations of national, ideological and aesthetic value. Scandinavian cinema of the 1920s gives us the poles of Victor Sjöstrom's rural morality plays and Mauritz Stiller's urban/urbane comedies. British filmmaking of the 1950s and 1960s oscillates between documentary-influenced features with dour, realist, northern working-class settings and brash, colorful, equally (more?) authentic depictions of 'swinging London'. The prominent Scottishness of Bill Forsyth's feature films, in terms of settings, characters and a superficial quaintness of tone, obscures a stylistic and metaphoric engagement with the shooting and editing of images of the landscape which is integral, not coincidental, to their narrative, emotional and intellectual force.[4] Although zealously committed to the use of real, unaltered and unadulterated locations, documentary filmmaker Paul Rotha conceded that 'creation lies not in the arrangement of the setting but in the interpretation of it'.[5] Few cinematic landscapes are as eloquent as the Rome of *Ladri di Biciclette* (Vittorio De Sica, 1948): images of the Italian capital are more communicative of the social deprivation and urban alienation of the post-war environment than the protagonist who experiences them firsthand. Very few have been as ambivalent as Jacques Tati's *Playtime* (1967), in mixing humour and pathos, complex physical gags and human folly, nostalgic whimsy and present pessimism, in the depiction of a traditional French identity and a recognizable Paris becoming lost within a clinical, modernist reconstruction.[6] Fewer are as grandiloquent as the French capital displayed in *Diva* (Jean-Jacques Beineix, 1982): its inhabitants partake of a Paris advertised as another consumer item, apparently unaware of the irony in their assertions of individuality via the acquisition and deification of mass-produced items and simulacra, which implicitly deride and destroy originality. While the surface realism in *La Haine* (Mathieu Kassovitz, 1995) is credited with demanding the cultural and political recognition of the contested Parisian suburbs (the *banlieue*), its 'discovery' of contemporary social circumstances in the extensive use of locations competes with the stylized editing and cinematography of action films.[7] Despite the cultural continuities which co-exist among the burgeoning new buildings, more than the passage of time makes Yasujiro Ozu's Tokyo different from Akira Kurosawa's, Kurosawa's different from Juzo Itami's, and Itami's from Takeshi Kitano's, for the directors and protagonists as much as for audiences. The apparently uninflected 'still life' observation of interior and exterior landscape in Ozu's *Tokyo Story* (1953) hides a pervasive stylistic commentary upon the interdependence of the traditional and the modern. Kurosawa's post-war urban landscapes operate as overtly metaphorical and moral arenas, in *Drunken Angel* (1948), *Stray Dog* (1949), *Ikuru* (1952) and *High and Low* (1963). While Itami's Tokyo in *Tampopo* (1986) is a truly post-modern, multi-cultural and -textual environment in which no value, occurrence, stereotype or eccentricity can be ruled out, Kitano's in *Violent Cop* (1989) and *Sonatine* (1993) is almost a desert of value, recorded with a camera as dispassionate as Ozu's. For some filmed landscapes, interpretational license becomes the offer of such representational flexibility that any cultural aspect of the national environment committed to film is negated by the economic potential of offshore production. The Film New Zealand Production Guide, published in 1999, to attract overseas filmmakers to use New Zealand locations took the title *The World in One Country*, implying a geographical inter-changeability in representative-ness to match the contemporary film's international complexities of funding and personnel.[8]

The inescapable truth that cinema has itself contributed to the imagining and definition of national landscapes and communities provides some of the motivations and parameters for papers in this collection. The cinema's power in the depiction of the landscape, be it rural, metropolitan, industrial, urban or suburban, has driven or led filmmakers of every nationality and political viewpoint, has fed and fed upon definitions of national identity and been read by cinema audiences as one of the most conspicuous and eloquent elements in the idiom of the film culture from which it emanates. With the presence in the frame of a significant, interpretable landscape, the products of national cinemas come to 'represent' their countries of origin in ways which are at once realist, physical and tangible, and artistic, imaginative and metaphorical. Film images of the landscape, therefore, have as much to offer the cultural geographer as they do the film critic or cinema historian.[9] To the acknowledgement of the landscape's potential fluidity of cultural meaning must be added the recognition of interpretative filters linked to modes (feature, short and documentary filmmaking), genres (the road movie, the thriller, the horror film) and auteurs (in all their national, industrial and critical manifestations) which inform the approaches, readings and conclusions contained in this collection.

## Navigating from cinematic maps

This book has presented numerous conceptual, structural and methodological challenges to its makers, and we hope it will challenge readers in a similar fashion. The contributors to this volume have striven to interpret the significance of landscapes occurring within the multifarious industrial and cultural contexts of world cinema. The editors have endeavoured to place and connect these individual examinations in mutually beneficial ways: rather than group them on their continents, in their hemispheres or through their climates and geographies, our circumnavigation details and distinguishes the subjects of study, and recognizes their sense of 'place' both nationally and internationally. Their critical placement requires further elucidation.

Every chapter in this book begins at the same junction: the meeting point of discourses of national cinematic representation, the aesthetics, techniques and technologies of cinema, and the concerns and expressions of outstanding filmmakers. Each analysis and argument draws from (and contributes to) existing scholarship in these areas, but also subsumes, synthesizes and outstrips its precedents and influences, by virtue of this book's wider intention: to acknowledge, instigate and integrate theorizations of landscapes on film. The mapping undertaken in the collection as a whole fulfils the cartographic requirements of quantitative and qualitative measurement: it selects and highlights the significant, the prominent and the representative, but it also strives to delineate the essential and innate properties of each example, and account for the historically, and socially and culturally meaningful within it.

The contributors to this volume cannot be called navigators or explorers themselves. Existing as experts of the cinematic territories they describe here, they are more properly seen as pathfinders or pilots, who possess a unique acquaintance and knowledge of the national cinemas which this book traverses, and who as a consequence are qualified to guide others through them. As editors, we have acted at a further remove, more as map-makers of these lands, which have been skilfully surveyed by others. So it is our readers who must be the explorers, ranging in historical time as much as in geographical space, and who must steer a course of their own choosing through this more or less familiar terrain. All roads will be new for some, and well known and documented for others, but even for those on home ground there will be some less-travelled paths to investigate. Each writer and scholar contributing to this volume has had to find their own path, and has identified individual, salient points as the landmarks relevant to their discussion of a particular national cinema. Various political, historical, geographical and cultural connections link the cinemas under consideration, and other themes, aspects of nationhood and aesthetic consistencies provide the borders (but not the boundaries) to these analyses. Although our circumnavigation may follow one course, the same cannot be said of the individual contributors, or of their detours within the journey. A single path is not inevitable, and certainly not implied.

Tom Gunning's 'Landscape and the fantasy of moving pictures: Early cinema's phantom rides', which serves as an exciting pre-cursor to the chapters in this book, as well as an exploration focused at the point of invention of film, is an investigation of the nature of landscape, North American landscape, 'panoramic views', visual representation and, most significantly of all, the filmic technologies and attitudes that have intersected and impacted notably upon these. Starting from a foundation in nineteenth-century principles, contexts and media for landscape representation, Gunning takes us through a consideration of the work of creators, whose framing and transmuting of landscapes was considerable, to the makers and audiences of cinema whose interaction with these new filmic depictions of landscape changed the relationship between humanity and landscape so significantly. Gunning considers such things as 'the sensation of immersion into a represented space' and 'an almost obsessive goal of total spectator involvement'. The result is a chapter that sets its sight on the nature of film's relationship with the physicality of our world.

Landscapes, often involving journeys, are recalled in Emma Widdis's chapter, 'One foot in the air?': Landscape in the Soviet and Russian road movie', where thoughts on scale and flatness, stylization and sometimes hidden folklore prevail. In this context, largely uninvestigated to date, Widdis tracks through the 'reclaiming' of a physical world, a potential new landscape contained in the old. In extracting Werner Herzog's films from their context in the New German cinema, Brad Prager's chapter not only seeks to revise the relationship between the filmmaker and his national cinema (and other examples of German visual art), but also to show how Herzog seeks to defamiliarize a range of international settings at risk from media-imperialist homogenization. In Herzog's cinema, Prager argues, there are landscapes and protagonists that go beyond national limits, which are pro-cinema as much as they are anti-television, which are as pro-international as they are anti-globalization. In contrast to this one filmmaker's denial or re-orientation of the 'national' in filmic representation, William Hope considers the individualistic and post-modern treatment of landscapes in two notable Italian films. By concentrating on the contemporary urban environment (as seen in *Caro Diario* (Nanni Moretti, 1994), Hope reveals how the director's apparently omnipotent subjectivization of the cityscape actually belies the loss of empowerment and erosion of social value experienced by the politicized individual. In his chapter, 'Landscape in Spanish Cinema', Marvin D'Lugo considers the notion of the evolving nation represented in film, the spaces of tradition, the spaces of modernity and the spaces of change.

There are often links in a discussion of filmic landscapes with ideas about 'beauty'. Indeed, if there is a most frequently used word in this volume it might well be 'beauty', though with the word 'stark' following closely behind. This discussion often finds form in consideration of national identity or even nationalism. Such a discussion informs Martin McLoone's chapter on Irish cinematic landscapes, where traditional landscape balances restorative qualities with consumerism, trouble and calm and, in that sense asks questions about the notion of an Irish 'grand narrative'. In her analysis of the filmed landscapes of the British Isles, Sue Harper details a production history of British cinema which separates and succeeds the World Wars. This history embraces variety in studio ethos, in genre and mode (documentary, horror and melodrama) and in personnel (Britons, Europeans and Americans), which translate into myriad and distinctive uses of deceptively familiar landscapes.

Susan Hayward's fine chapter on French filmic landscapes focuses on the post-colonial, highlighting the ways in which the idea of owned landscape might extend to the changing circumstances of ownership. She notes that much of this representation relates to the 'after-effects of the colonial moment' and, in her close study of the work of Claire Denis, returns the reader to the idea of what might be contained in landscape that might also be contained in a sense of 'belonging'. Bob Britton's consideration of the Cuban cinema examines the union of documentary, drama and political filmmaking in the country's post-revolutionary history. Britton argues that, as the landscape is used to stand for national principles and histories, and as those histories are articulated consciously by observant, politicized filmmakers, so the Cuban landscape on film has become a repository for and visual account of the island nation's brief existence.

As familiar as they were to their director, the landscapes of India of Satyajit Ray's *Apu* trilogy are rendered new in the director's images via the child's perspective assumed by his camera. In his chapter, Wimal Dissayanake offers an assessment of the director's influences, and a reassessment of the subjective and objective landscape images which characterize Ray's masterpiece. Martin Mhando looks at the construction of meaning, the impact on cinema audiences and the imperatives engendered in Zimbabwean film. As a case study located on the African continent, Mhando's chapter also considers the pedagogic dimensions involved in connections between film and geography, and the clashes that can occur between different cultural perspectives and the appropriation of landscape through film. Kate Taylor's chapter picks up the tension between people and landscape in Chinese films, ranging from the cityscapes of Hong Kong in *Seung Sing* to the multitude of Taiwanese landscapes shown in *Zui hao de shi guang* to consider the nature of disenfranchised space. She particularly calls into question the fixity of ideas of time and space, giving consideration to the nature of

Chinese filmic landscapes which show a widening of the divide between urban and rural, based on a clash between the time of history and the space of change. Paul Spicer's chapter on Japanese cinema matches history to representation, and closely considers the production techniques that match the individual interests of Japanese filmmakers, the period in which the films were made and political circumstances these filmic landscapes encapsulate.

Spicer's approach has some key links to the circumstances Harper investigates in 'A version of beauty and terror: Australian cinematic landscapes'. Here, however, it is the notion of an indigenous landscape encapsulated in settler film history that forms the basis of a discussion of potential new visions, whose origins are in a much longer indigenous cultural history. Similarly, in addressing the output of the revived New Zealand film industry, Jonathan Rayner groups together some landmark features and filmmakers, and extracts several key thematic and auteurist nodes for analysis. Characterizing the New Zealand cinema as defined by conflict and division along lines of race, gender and belief, Rayner's survey plots the crucial role of the landscape in delineating the complexities of colonial culture.

Perhaps not unexpectedly, Jim Leach's consideration of Canadian film begins with a reference to nature, not dissimilar to that seen in the work of Harper and Rayner. What marks out Leach's chapter, however, is his discussion of a depiction 'before it becomes landscape'. One of the joys of editing a volume of essays is discovering new ideas and this was certainly a revelatory notion. Leach explores the 'tensions and contradictions' that inform the representation of landscape in the cinema, and concludes in relation to Canadian film that 'both nature and nation are increasingly experienced as obliterated' – a point that is as significant as it is provocative.

Finally, returning to the United States through their survey of avowedly escapist genres (horror and science fiction), Christina, Tianna and Mèlisa Kennedy pursue pervasive filmic images of the contemporary American landscape, and its attendant ideological terrain. They identify certain enduring socio-political trends and beliefs in American culture, and determine their inseparability from recurrent, romanticized representations of natural, rural, suburban and metropolitan environments. Under their scrutiny, the union of the horror and documentary in *The Blair Witch Project* (Daniel Myrick and Eduardo Sanchez, 1999) and the exaggeration of the modern metropolis in the megalopolis seen in *The Fifth Element* (Luc Besson, 1997), connects cinematic popular culture with underlying, conservative valuations of and relationships with the contemporary American landscape. The final chapter takes us to a fitting location for our conclusion, in acknowledging in its examples the acculturated and conventionalized cinematic landscapes of contemporary popular film. In ending with an unequivocally constructed cinematic landscape, one determined by formulaic and culturally embedded encoding and decoding, we stress the complexity, communality, relevance and pervasiveness of the cinematic landscape even as we acknowledge its fabrication, its controlled and mapped eloquence.

## Notes

1. Stanley Cavell, *The World Viewed*, enlarged ed. (London: Harvard University Press, 1979), 20.
2. Ross Gibson, 'Camera natura: landscape in Australia feature films', *Framework* 22/23 (1983), 47–51 (50).
3. Henri Bergson, *Matter and Memory* (London: Zone, 1991), 77.
4. Stuart C. Aitken, 'A Transactional Geography of the Image-Event: The Films of Scottish Director, Bill Forsyth', *Transactions of the Institute of British Geographers*, New Series, vol.16 n.1 (1991), 105–118 (111).
5. Paul Rotha, *Documentary Film* (London: Faber, 1936), 187.
6. Lee Hilliker, 'In the modernist mirror: Jacques Tati and the Parisian landscape', *The French Review* 76(2) (2002), 318–329.
7. Ginette Vincendeau, 'Designs on the *Banlieue*: Mathieu Kassovitz's *La Haine* (1995)', in Susan Hayward and Ginette Vincentia (eds), *French Film: Texts and Contexts*, 2nd ed. (London: Routledge, 2000), 310–311.
8. Ian Conrich 'In God's own country: Open spaces and the New Zealand road movie', in Ian Conrich and David Woods (eds), *New Zealand – A Pastoral Paradise?* (Nottingham: Kakapo, 2000), 32.
9. Brian J. Godfrey, 'Regional depiction in contemporary film', *Geographical Review* 83(4) (1993), 428–440.

# PART I

The Invention of the Cinematic Landscape

Conway Castle (courtesy of the Netherlands Filmmuseum, with sincere thanks)

# Chapter 2

Landscape and the Fantasy of Moving Pictures: Early Cinema's Phantom Rides

Tom Gunning

Haverstraw Tunnel (courtesy of the Netherlands Filmmuseum, with sincere thanks)

*For Iris Cahn who started me thinking, Scott McDonald who focused my argument and Claribel Cone, the painter.*

## Placing the world in a frame: The technologies of landscape

> Da nun alles, ales sich bewegte,
> Baume, Fluß und Blumen und der Schleier
> Und der zarte Fuß der Allerschönsten,
> Glaubt ihr wohl, ich sei auf meinen Felsen
> Wie ein Felsen still und fest geblieben?
>
> Now everything, but everything was moving,
> Trees, the flowers, filmy robe, the river
> Delicate feet of the girl in all her beauty –
> Do you think I sat so calm and steadfast
> Rocklike on my rock a moment longer?
>
> Goethe, 'Amor as Landscape Painter' (1787)
>
> Landscape is not a genre of art, but a medium
>
> W. J. T. Mitchell, 'Imperial Landscape'

What makes nature into a landscape? What aesthetic and technical processes transform the formal possibilities of natural surroundings into images? Alberti inaugurated the theory of Western painting by defining a picture as something traced within a quadrilateral that served as a window onto the world. Placing a view of nature within a frame, fixing that view within a geometrical frame of reference, defined landscape as an art form. A frame that organizes a composition geometrically, while simultaneously opening a view into a depth – this describes the double aspects of the landscape. As Renzo Dubbini puts it,

In Western Europe the invention of landscape painting coincided with the elaboration of the *veduta* or 'view' as a space contained within a picture, but which opened up the setting to the world beyond. The discovery of an adequate technique for framing and defining depth signalled the invention of landscape as a cultural space, visible in all its aspects.'[1]

Landscape painting displayed the mastery of perspective and composition that defined Western easel painting as an aesthetic form. The work of seventeenth-century landscapist Claude Lorrain (as well as the work of Gaspar Poussin) provided an archetype for landscape, balancing compositional frame and recessive depth – containment and distance. Claude created synthetic ideal landscapes, artistic visions that never claimed to be records of actual topographies (as Edgar Poe said in his landscape fantasy 'The Domain of Arnheim', 'No such paradises are to be found in reality as have glowed on the canvass of Claude.')[2]

This 'Ideal Landscape' schema provided painters with a structure for centuries. In a Claude landscape, towering trunks of backlit trees crowned by fan-like foliage framed a recessive arrangement of space, theatrical in effect. These powerfully vertical trees served as *coulisse* (a theatrical term for the flats that conceal and naturalize the off-stage space of the wings), or *repoussoirs*, darker elements framing the foreground, setting off the landscape's glowing central depth, and drawing the viewer's gaze into a distance dissolved in a luminous blur of aerial perspective.[3] Claude created a clearly marked succession of planes, based in an ordered presentation of natural elements. A darkened, largely empty, horizontal foreground came first, often populated by fairly small human figures or *staffage*. Towering trees provided the vertical frame, while streams or lakes led the viewer's gaze into a middle distance where water shimmered with reflected light. An atmospherically diffused vista of mountains defined the distance, outlining a horizon dominated by a luminous sky. Ideal Landscapes wove together these clearly marked stages of recession with a harmonic gradation and variety of light that unified the image.

By the late eighteenth century such visual schemata served not only as a template for landscape painting, but as a new model for viewing and experiencing nature, finding its clearest articulation in England in the concept of the 'picturesque'. As both a new mode of aesthetic experience and a means of defining what constituted a proper landscape, the picturesque not only served as a guide to creating and viewing painting, it also directed the gaze of tourists and inspired the ground plans of gardeners. In 1734 poet Alexander Pope had declared that 'all gardening is landscape-painting', and gardens in the eighteenth century provided optical experiences as much as spaces for wandering or the display of plant life.[4] Even in the seventeenth century formal French gardens applied perspectival and visual effects taken from theatrical designers, while somewhat later the more 'natural' English gardens frequently took Claude's landscapes as their model.[5] British landscape artists even added the 'prime ingredient of picturesque view', crumbling ruins made to order, to satisfy the 'love for broken and rough surfaces' so praised by James Gilpin, chief theorist of the picturesque.[6] The picturesque defined gardens as a succession of images, carefully ordered and artificially created by the gardener's construction, employing colours and textures as well as devices of framing and (often forced) perspective.

'The picturesque moment' – the passion for experiencing nature as a picture that reached a climax in the late eighteenth century – also introduced the 'Claude Glass', a device used by artists, artistic amateurs and simple tourists to transform the natural world into a source of endless images.[7] Named for the landscapist (who most likely never used one), the Claude Glass consisted of a hand-held mirror, usually darkly tinted and convex, most often oval, but sometimes rectangular. As Hunt puts it, 'the use of the mirror…concentrated for its owner all picturesque possibilities:[8]

> To the picturesque tourist and amateur artist [the Claude Glass] reflected the real world, yet also collected carefully chosen images within the oval or rectangular frame and colored them with its one coordinating tint.[9]

More than earthmoving, fake ruins or even carefully arranged belvederes and observation towers, the Claude Glass exemplified the process of turning nature into landscape through a technology of vision. Arnaud Maillet describes the subtle but essential optical transformations the mirror accomplished: 'The sensible reduction of objects reflected in the mirror occurs on two levels: one concerns colors, the other involves the visual field.'[10] The tinting of the mirror lowered the level of light, 'reducing not only the lights and shadows but also the colors to a tonal unity,' casting the scene into an artificial twilight in which the values of disparate colours merged.[11] The convex mirror (like a wide-angle camera lens) creates an artificial sense of distance, reducing the scene, as Maillet puts it, 'in order to unify'.[12] Gilpin claimed this allowed viewers 'to grasp the landscape in a single glance, like a painting'.[13] The Claude Glass processed nature optically, yielding an epitome of the visual qualities valorized by the picturesque: an image carefully framed and optically lifted out of an undifferentiated visual field – automatically creating a landscape.

While the 'picturesque' landscape model encountered challenges in the nineteenth century from, successively, the romantic sublime, the less ideal compositional schemata emerging from the Barbizon school of *plein air* painting, and – eventually – the Impressionists, the Ideal Landscape remained the model against which innovations in landscape painting were measured. The schema's longevity depended on balancing landscape's essential tension between geometrical framing and illusionistic depth. The Claudean recessive landscape solicits a voyage of both eye and body into the depth of the scene, inviting spectator fantasies of entrance and exploration into this bounded and avowedly artificial space.

How does cinema relate to this landscape tradition? Too often, discussions of landscape in cinema simply assume films, at least certain films, contain landscapes, positing a simple transfer of visual principles and effects from canvas to cinema screen. I believe we must first ask what the concepts of the landscape and the picturesque offered to cinema as it emerged at the end of the nineteenth century. Perhaps even more vitally, we should ask in what ways cinema transformed the possibilities of landscape, both as a form of imagery and as a way of experiencing nature. In this essay I will attempt to sketch aspects of this question, focusing primarily on nineteenth-century American landscapes and their interaction with technology.

## Landscape and technology: The railroad

…this admirable invention of the railroad…is destined to do away with those stale ideas of home and fireside, and substitute something better.

Nathaniel Hawthorne, *The House of Seven Gables* (1851)

In a footnote buried in perhaps the most serious discussion of the inspiration landscape painting has offered American cinema, *The Garden in the Machine*, historian of American avant-garde cinema Scott McDonald seems to question the relation between landscape and early cinema that he explores in the body of the work. Referring to a pioneering essay by Iris Cahn that related early American films to the 'Great Picture' tradition of Frederic Church, McDonald notes:

The Library of Congress lists dozens of titles that claim as their central focus not only American landscapes but also, in a good many instances, precisely those landscapes made so popular by the Hudson River and Rocky Mountain painters of the mid-nineteenth century: The Catskill Mountains, Niagara Falls, Yosemite Valley, Yellowstone.

But McDonald then demurs:

However, while titles of many of these early films identify landscapes as their subject, it must be said that many of the films are really about railway travel through landscapes and are more fully focused on the railroad tracks into the landscapes than on the landscapes themselves.[14]

While I might question what it means to 'really' make a landscape 'the subject' of a film, I take seriously McDonald's sense that these early films of famous tourist landscapes project a different experience of place than the nineteenth-century painting that may have inspired them. While this difference needs to be explored rather than assumed, I believe it opens essential questions about landscape's relation to modern space and technology as exemplified by the cinema.

Seemingly off-handedly, McDonald contrasts 'landscapes themselves' with films 'fully focused on railroads tracks *into* the landscapes' [my emphasis]. A true landscape, it would seem, maintains a certain distance from the viewer, an invisible barrier to actual penetration. Early films, shot by cameras mounted on the fronts of locomotives tracking into famous landscapes, violated the barrier that defines contemplative beauty. As opposed to the carefully framed, distanced and *static* picture offered by Claudean Ideal Landscape, early landscape films actually moved into the landscape via technology. Not only do the tracks travel into the frame, but the camera that rides upon them as well, transporting the viewer as an ersatz passenger, rather than framing a view for a transfixed and immobilized viewer. In doing so these films make explicit a fantasy of penetration and visual voyage implied in the Claudean model, described by Rachel DeLue: 'Nothing obstructs the passage of the eye from zone to zone; indeed, its traversal is made easy by alternating strips of light and dark, Claudean in origin, that ferry it from foreground to depth in an orderly fashion.'[15] But to literalize and actually achieve such transit – indeed to industrialize it, as in early train films – involves an extreme transformation in the landscape tradition. This essay will explore this transformation in spectatorship and the transformations in landscape technology that made it possible.

The title of McDonald's book wittily inverts another famous title: Leo Marx's 1964 *The Machine in the Garden: Technology and the Pastoral Ideal in America*. Marx analysed the encounter of American culture with the machine, typified by the intense experience of the invasion of the American landscape by the locomotive, which he described as a 'sense of the machine as a sudden, shocking intruder upon a fantasy of idyllic satisfaction.'[16] Henry David Thoreau's description of a locomotive passing by Walden Pond captured the vulnerability of the American wilderness (and the pastoral ideal it represented) to the onslaught of industrialism. McDonald claims American avant-garde film and video-makers as Thoreau's ideological heirs, creating a reservation of wildness and pastoral contemplation in opposition to the industrial filmmaking of Hollywood. These often avowedly pastoral or ecological motion pictures, McDonald claims, ultimately owe inspiration to the visionary tradition of the American landscape exemplified by Thomas Cole, Frederic Church and Albert Bierstadt. McDonald and Marx avoid an inert dichotomy between nature and culture in favour of a dialectical narrative of the way landscape depends on technology, even as it is threatened by it. Extending this intricate and often traumatic interaction between nature and technology to early cinema, I would claim landscape must be viewed not simply as a refuge from technology, but, in a complex manner, as its product.

The railroad initially carried the freight of this encounter between wilderness and technology. As a mode of transportation, as a business dependent partly on tourism and as the beneficiary of the greatest federal land grants in US history, the railroad literally opened up the American countryside to appropriation as landscape. The railroad used aestheticized images of American nature (including landscape paintings commissioned by the railroads themselves) as tools of commerce. Thus, rather than posing polar opposites, technology and the industrial expansion of American business simultaneously generate and exploit the idea of natural landscape. Indeed, as Richard Grusin argues in *Culture, Technology and America's National Parks*, even the wilderness reserves of national parks:

need to be understood as technologies for the reproduction of that very nature which is being threatened and destroyed…Neither gardens in the machine nor machines in the garden, national parks are machines that are made up of gardens, or gardens that function as machines.[17]

Marx's work outlined a uniquely American conception, a faith that a pastoral ideal could be realized, not as a mythical Golden Age nostalgically contemplated, but as a national ideal charting plans for future development. Envisioned by such figures as Thomas Jefferson, a pastoral state could be attained through cooperation with technology, rather than in opposition to it. In this vision, to quote Marx, 'the railroad is the chosen vehicle of bringing America into its own as a pastoral utopia'.[18] However, the harmony initially imagined by this pastoral vision gave way to a growing sense of ambivalence and danger, embodied in Thoreau's warning, 'we do not ride upon the railroad; it rides upon us'.[19] But even within this minatory mode, the convergence between landscape as the redeeming force of natural energy (what Thoreau called 'wildness') and the force of technology remains. The modern American landscape envisioned a new 'technological sublime' that cast its spell even over Thoreau as the harbinger of a new mythology: '...when I hear the iron horse make the hills echo with his snort like thunder, shaking the earth with his feet, and breathing fire and smoke from his nostrils...it seems as if the earth had got a race now worthy to inhabit it'.[20] This dialectic between the seemingly pastoral landscape and modern technology penetrates deeply into the history and concept of American landscape painting. To understand the transformation the railroad brought to this tradition, we need to trace the long-standing fantasy of entering into a landscape painting.

Ideal Landscapes, including American versions, frequently place diminutive *staffage* figures in the foreground in postures of beholding (backs to the viewer, facing into the scene and occasionally gesturing reactions of delight or pointing into the depth) strongly evoking a mood of contemplation and its religious connotations of awe. While these figures posed on the threshold of the composition maintain a certain distance from the view, beholding the wonders of nature, they also inaugurate imagined narratives of entrance into the represented space. Landscape as a form did not wait for the cinema to provide an image of entrance into the landscape, although the new medium certainly transformed both the means and meaning of doing so. The pronounced perspective of the Ideal Landscape and such compositional devices as streams, pathways or minute travellers traditionally lead the viewer's eye into the distance, generating fantasy of penetration and exploration.

Denis Diderot in his description of the Salon of 1763 had first verbalized this fantasy of entering into a landscape in response to a painting by Philippe-Jacques de Loutherbourg (whose optical device the Eidophusikon offered an early mechanical form of motion pictures), imagining lingering among grazing herds and then wandering into the distance.[21] As Rachael DeLue points out, 'for Diderot the success of specific types of landscape representations could depend on the encouragement of this fiction'.[22] With its display of perspective as an invitation to voyage, the landscape seduces the gaze into fantasies of physical entrance.

In American landscape painting these imagined trajectories into the distance increasingly manifested a national sense of destiny in the westward course of the empire.[23] Albert Boime calls the view from a height into the distance characteristic of American landscapes 'the magisterial gaze' in which the fantasy of penetration takes on a national imperative and spatial expansion and historical progress:

> taking us rapidly from an elevated geographical zone to another below and from one temporal zone to another locating progress synchronically in time and space. Within this fantasy of domain and empire gained from looking out and down over broad expanses is the subtext of metaphorical forecast of the future.[24]

The image of the locomotive impinging on a natural landscape that Marx traced through American literature also infiltrated modern American landscape painting. Images produced by artists associated with America's first great school of landscape painting, the Hudson River School, portrayed the ideal pastoral vision of technology that Marx described, with trains and railroads integrated into Claudean views framed by foreground trees, with waterways or pathways snaking towards the distant horizon where luminous skies meet mountains blurred by aerial perspective (see Thomas Cole, *River in the Catskills*, 1843; Thomas Doughty, *A View of Swampscott*, 1847; Jasper Cropsey, *Starrucca Viaduct, Pennsylvania*, 1865; George Inness, *Delaware Water Gap*, 1861). However, as Barbara Novak claims, trains and railways hardly dominate these compositions: '…how remote and insignificant are the trains that discreetly populate the American landscape paintings of the mid-century!'[25] Placed in the middle distance, Thoreau's titanic locomotive appears miniaturized and firmly integrated into an ordered and hierarchy schema, its trail of smoke or steam, as Novak pointed out, blending with the billowing clouds.[26] Marx notes that 'these artists were bent on making the new machine blend as inconspicuously as possible into its natural surroundings.'[27]

However, these seemingly harmonic Ideal Landscapes also interwove ambivalence into their celebration of America's errand into the wilderness, typified by the complex composition of *The Oxbow* painted in 1836 by Thomas Cole, dean of American landscape painters. A view from Mount Holyoke in Massachusetts of a point where the Connecticut River takes on an 'oxbow' shape, circling in on itself, the composition divides between untamed nature on the craggy mountain on the left and an agricultural landscape, with fields and villages viewed below along the riverbanks on the right. While the nearly allegorical composition seems to reflect the westward trek of civilization, clearing the land and making it fertile, it also reflects Cole's own questioning of the *Course of Empire* (the title of a sequence of five allegorical paintings he was working on at the same time as this landscape, chronicling a pessimistic view of man – and America's? – progress from savage and pastoral states to decadence and destruction).[28] Angela Miller convincingly reads the curve of the oxbow as forming a question mark, posing Cole's own uncertainty about American expansion into the wilderness (the painting includes a minuscule self-portrait of Cole as contemplative figure, a painter sketching at his easel, firmly placed on the wilderness side of the image).

America's greatest and most complex landscape painter, George Inness, supplied a similar riddling image in his *The Lackawanna Valley* from 1856 or 1857. In contrast to Inness's extraordinary experimental paintings of the decades to come, this landscape basically follows the Claudean formula, including a *repoussoir* tree framing the left of the image, mountains dissolving in aerial perspective in the distance and a recumbent *staffage* figure in the foreground gazing towards the horizon. However, in the middle distance a medium-sized locomotive steams towards the foreground, leaving behind a marked trail of smoke and steam, with the industrial structure of a railway roundhouse visible beyond. While still not dominating the foreground, nonetheless this locomotive breaches the discretion maintained by trains in most landscapes of the era. Novak draws our attention to the manner that tree stumps mark the foreground edge of the painting and dominate the zone of middle distance that bridges the contemplative figure and the locomotive. While the tree stump served as a recognized symbol of the march of civilization into the wilderness, clearing the land for future planting and building, this field of stumps seems excessive.[29] Not all critics share Novak's critical reading of technology in Inness's painting and Inness himself indicated his preference for 'the civilized landscape' that bore the signs of 'every act of man, everything of labor, effort, suffering, want, anxiety, necessity, love,' over 'the savage and untamed'.[30] The fact that the painting was commissioned by the Delaware and Lackawanna Railway indicates its sponsors felt it celebrated their achievements (although that Inness found it years later in a curiosity shop in Mexico and bought it for a few dollars may indicate something else!). I feel that what Novak calls the 'shocking' quality of the painting comes from the mismatch between the contemplative Claudean schema and the new dynamics of motion and transformation in the subject. The recumbent figure seems to have wandered in from another painting as he gazes into this new realm of speed and energy.

Inness's commission from the Lackawanna Railway was hardly unique. The railroad industry, which completed a transcontinental network during the greatest period of American landscape painting, forged commercial alliances with landscape painters. Boime claims the 'magisterial gaze' he isolates in landscape paintings was 'converted into the diagonal of a line of tracks and speeding locomotive'.[31] The railroad industry understood that, while their major commerce was freight transportation, tourism could form an important side business. To encourage the traffic in tourists searching for picturesque landscapes, tours for painters were arranged by railroad companies even before the Civil War, and became a common practice for the next decades.[32] Landscapes were produced that depended on railroads to carry painters to their sites, and were commissioned by the companies in order to incite a desire to see such views on the part of potential passengers. Railway magnates were major patrons of such painters as Inness, Church, Bierstadt and most gloriously Thomas Moran. Train travel extended the tradition of the picturesque tour, with guidebooks describing the most picturesque locations railroads could reach, and indicating the sights available to the train passenger from her window.[33] Even when railroads or trains were not featured in American landscapes, the railroad stands outside the frame as a major motivation for the vision they created.

But the new technology of the railroad did more than appropriate the older landscape tradition; as in Inness's painting, tensions inherent in the encounter led to visible transformations and the rise of new media. Susan Danly points out:

Painters tended to include the railroad as a small compositional detail fully integrated into the overall format of their landscape, while photographers more often monumentalized railroad structures and emphasized innovative building techniques rather than the natural world.[34]

Mass-produced chromolithographs aimed at a popular audience often placed the dramatic locomotive at the centre of compositions, belching smoke and flame and speeding through the landscape.[35] Was the Ideal Landscape, amazingly stable for centuries, irrevocably challenged by new technological modes of travel, new spaces defined by industrial appropriation, and new media better suited to portray these transformations? Would this convergence of technology end in the elimination of landscape both as form and as experience? Historian and theorist of the transformations the railway brought to the nineteenth century, Wolfgang Schivelbusch claims the experience of train travel transformed perceptions of space and time. The traditional experience of landscape deriving from other forms of travel changed with train travel, as the train's velocity diminished visual perception of the passing countryside, blurring the foreground, eliminating detail and abolishing the stasis of contemplation.

But rather than simply erasing the view, Schivelbusch claims, 'The railroad creates a new landscape'.[36] For detail it substituted variety and transformation, the pleasures of speed and rapid succession replaced contemplation. Schivelbusch dubs this new mode of viewing landscapes 'panoramic perception'. Seated unmoving in her upholstered seat, watching the landscape roll by through the glass window of her compartment, the train observer simultaneously seemed physically immobilized, but perceptually mobile. Thus as Schivelbusch describes it, 'Panoramic perception, in contrast to traditional perception, no longer belongs to the same space as the perceived objects: the traveler sees the objects, landscapes, etc. *through* the apparatus which moves him through the world.'[37]

But as important as this transformation in landscape perception might be, it may pose less a radical break with the model of the Ideal Landscape than a shift along the gamut of the picturesque. Not only had the Claude Glass already set up the essential mediation of an apparatus of viewing mediating between observer and nature, but the charm of picturesque gardens and the reflections captured in the glass derived as much from motion and changing viewpoints as from the contemplation of fixed compositions. In his 1770 essay 'On modern gardening', Horace Walpole had described the enjoyment of a garden as mobile, claiming, 'every journey is made through a succession of pictures'.[38] Gilpin used his Claude Glass while travelling in a chaise, savouring not only the singularity of an image but its transformation: 'Forms, and colours in brightest array, fleet before us, and if the transient glance of a good composition happen to unite with them, we should give any price to fix and appropriate the scene.'[39] The fixed image and its contemplation still provided the privileged mode of landscape viewing, but the pleasures of transience, motion, variety, succession and, especially, mediation through an apparatus of viewing already played a key role. Throughout the nineteenth century, fascination in the mobile view of a landscape gave rise to new technologies of motion pictures and mobile viewpoints, transforming the picturesque model by radicalizing its implication of motion and penetration.

## Technology of landscape: Panorama

> To reflect rigorously on the particular pathos that lies hidden in the art of the panoramas.
> On the particular relation of this art to nature, but also, and above all, to history.
>
> Walter Benjamin, Passagenwerke, Convolute Q

Schivelbusch took the term 'panoramic', of course, from a major technological transformation in the nature of landscape in the nineteenth century, one which rivalled photography in innovation and popularity: the panorama. This form of visual entertainment was once so omnipresent and its name so popular (historian Stephan Oettermann calls it 'the first visual mass medium'), it became absorbed into common language and is generally used today with little sense (and rarely any direct experience) of its original reference.[40] The nearly total eclipse of the panorama in the twentieth century has led to a lack of acknowledgement of its very great influence over the way landscapes were conceived. A technical device first and foremost, the panorama was patented in 1787 by Robert Barker in its original form: a painted canvas of such unaccustomed scale and shape, housed in such a manner as to create effect of an image without limits – *tableau sans bornes*.[41] The panorama brought the landscape image to a crisis, destroying its defining aspect – the frame. As historian of panoramas Bernard Comment comments, 'Abolishing the frame was the only way of transcending the limits of traditional representation.'[42] Displayed in a specially designed building whose unique construction constituted the core of Barker's invention, the panorama depended as much on architecture as painting for its effect. As in garden landscaping, the panorama functioned as an environmental, rather than simply a representational, form, creating a new space as much as it represented one. (As Comment puts it, 'the aim of the panorama was to produce – using all available means – the illusion of another space.')[43] From the moment of entrance, the design of the panorama space determined the spectator's experience as much as (or more than) the composition of the canvas, truly becoming an apparatus of vision. Comment summarizes the control of the viewing process through control of point of view and lighting:

> To gain access to a panorama canvas, the spectator had to walk along a darkened corridor so as to forget the reality of the world outside and so that the effect of being plunged into the total illusion of the representation would have more impact. Viewers were confined to an observation platform and could not approach the canvas. A canopy concealed the overhead lighting that entered from behind a glass panel.[44]

The viewer was completely surrounded by the circular painting, while architectural design concealed upper and lower limits of the image, giving the illusion of a boundless view. The construction of the building carefully controlled the lighting, filtering the daylight that shone on the painting and leaving the viewers in relative shadow. As in the panorama of the Battle of Navarino in 1831 (in which the audience stood on a realistic mock-up of the deck of a naval man of war), the viewing area and the space situated between it and the canvas frequently became the site of three-dimensional props (and even figures) that merged into the two-dimensional images of the canvas.

As Stephen Oettermann points out, the panorama liberated landscape vision from the constraint of the frame, delivering a complete view of the encompassing horizon. However, the observer was completely subject to the exhibition schema, a 360-degree space that confined the observer in 'a complete prison for the eye'.[45] A German aesthetician, J. A. Eberhardt described this sensation as 'this ghastly dream from which I have to wrench myself against my will'.[46] But the drive towards this panoramic viewpoint remained a product of the picturesque impulse. Oettermann relates the panorama to a late eighteenth-century passion for viewing the horizon evident in the observation towers constructed in picturesque gardens and landscapes, as well as the popularity of balloon ascents as a means of viewing landscapes. The picturesque certainly sought to confine a view within a frame, but it passionately desired to extend that frame into new unexplored spaces and into greater and more expansive dimensions, 'surrounding and seizing the whole', as Oettermann puts it.[47] More than any previous form, the panorama realized Diderot's fantasy of the viewer's entrance into a fictive world, but it also transformed it.

Instead of the single perspective of Claude's theatrical space with its enframed central view into the depth, the panorama embraced the viewer, or more properly, the viewers, offering what Oettermann describes as a 'democratic perspective' as 'the infinite number of points of view are matched – theoretically – by an infinite number of viewing points from which observer can look at the picture without distortion'.[48] Rather than a single observer regarding the scene in isolated contemplation, the panorama attracted an 'audience', a commercial mass made up of varied classes, who wandered from viewing point to viewing point to obtain the full effect of the image. The German explorer and scientist Alexander von Humboldt whose epic account of his global travels, *Cosmos*, greatly influenced American landscape painters, praised the totalizing effect of the panorama which surrounded 'the spectator, inclosed [sic] as it were, within a magic circle, and wholly removed from all the disturbing influences of reality'.[49] Viewers attested to the realistic effect of the panorama on a number of levels. Panoramas featuring the sea, for instance, caused seasickness in a number of viewers, reportedly even Queen Charlotte of England.[50] Some decades later, a large Newfoundland dog supposedly tried to leap into the sea in a panorama of Malta.[51]

These stories indicate two aspects of panorama spectatorship that challenge the tradition of landscape contemplation. First, they were the responses of an audience rather than a single viewer withdrawn into himself. The panorama audience was not only multiple, but varied, made up of not only connoisseurs but of gawkers from the middle and even the working class.[52] Further, whether attributed to Queens or dogs, physical sensations and reactions rather than intellectual contemplation emanated from the panorama. Although the panorama might seem an absolute fulfilment of the fantasies of being absorbed into a representation, for many observers it crossed the line that separated art from popular spectacle and modern technology.

Jacques-Louis David told his students to attend Prevost's panorama 'to study nature'. David's purported comment carries a double edge; if he praised the panorama's verisimilitude, he did not claim it to be the best place to study art. A triumph of perceptual realism, to the neoclassical ideal, the panorama was too real.[53] Britain's great landscape painter John Constable declared after visiting Daguerre's diorama: 'it is without the pale of art, because its object is deception. Art pleases by reminding, not deceiving'.[54] The panorama's verisimilitude, art critics repeated throughout the nineteenth century, aimed at fooling the eye, not the true blending of realism and idealism that art should aspire to. A critic praising the effect of a German panorama in 1880 still had to add parenthetically, 'the fundamental aim of the whole – to create the greatest possible illusion and confound appearances with reality – is not artistic'.[55]

The panorama had many predecessors and successors, from Loutherbourg's Eidophusikon to Daguerre's diorama, all of which offered what I have called elsewhere the supplement of realism, the addition to traditional representations of something felt to be 'missing' for the achievement of total verisimilitude, whether the scale and circular format of the panorama, lighting effects of the diorama or the movement given to the Eidophusikon.[56] These technologies exemplify a new anxiety about the limits of representation that was repressed as beyond the pale of aesthetics by academic discourse, but exerted a fascination over the broader public. In the United States the influence of the panorama was pervasive, but the greatest enthusiasm was reserved for a native variation, the moving panorama. The vast lengths of these panoramas were measured in miles (Banville's panorama of the Mississippi was advertised as three miles in length, while Smith's rival panorama was claimed to measure four miles). Mounted on twin sets of rollers and, like a gargantuan version of a Chinese scroll painting, the moving panorama unrolled bit by bit before theatrical audiences, accompanied by music and a spoken lecture commenting on the views.[57] Eschewing the effect of total immersion via the 360-degree format, the moving panorama instead emphasized an ever-expanding image, presenting a succession of views for a seated audience, an experience whose duration simulated the impression of a condensed journey by train or railway.

This literalization of the temporal and spatial expanse of the imaginary journey, endowed with epic portions far beyond the Claudean horizon promised by the Ideal Landscape, strikes many critics as a peculiarly American response to the landscape tradition (Oettermann dubs it 'an art form for American tastes').[58] As Angela Miller claims, 'The vehicle of the grand plot embedded within American landscape was the road, or it fluid counterpart, the river, connecting the incidents of the landscape in a unified whole'.[59] From the pioneering treks of Western expansion to the counter-journeys of Huck and Jim down the Mississippi, or Ahab and crew across the ocean, the sense of movement and journey offered a central image of the protean American identity.

Perhaps pressured by the popularity of moving and static panoramas as new stage in the portrayal landscape, American landscape painters seemed to respond (or in some cases anticipate) the new forms within their work. Most obviously Fredric Church's display of his massive canvas *The Heart of the Andes* as an elaborately stage-managed quasi-theatrical event, complete with paid admission recalled the viewer address of the panorama. Iris Cahn describes the exhibition of this and similar 'Great Pictures':

> Viewers would pay admission, enter a *darkened* room and sit on benches to stare at one single enormous, *illuminated* canvas. The frame surrounding the painting was often dark wood (unlike the prevailing gilt of the day) and so blended into walls draped with light absorbing fabrics. Gaslight and skylight controlled by draperies created illusion that light was emanating from the canvas itself, that one was looking, perhaps, onto a real scene. Opera glasses were used, allowing the observer to enlarge and reframe the parts of the larger canvas. Pamphlets were distributed, their words functioning much like slide lecture narrations, or, as film intertitles would later. The words traced a visual path for the eye through the various planes of the painting, explaining exotic locations, unfamiliar plants, animals and geographic formations.[60]

The Great Pictures of the American landscape painters of the middle of the nineteenth century aspired to the domains of high art. But in their pursuit of the more expansive form of the picturesque, the romantic sublime and a unique sense of American terrain, like the panorama, they pushed against the limits of the Ideal Landscape, creating new attitudes toward framing and spectatorship. Perhaps ironically (or perhaps inevitably) these experiments converged with the commercial technological modes of emerging mass media.

Gilpin had theorized that the titanic scale of the American landscape might exceed the possibilities of the picturesque. The lakes of Switzerland or Italy could serve as material for picturesque landscapes, but Gilpin claimed, 'the *larger* lakes, like those of America, are disproportioned to their accompaniments: the water occupies too large a space, and throws the scenery too much into the distance'.[61] Thomas Moran's sublime Turneresque portrayal of the Great Lakes, Longfellow's 'shining Big-Sea-Water' in his series of paintings based on *Hiawatha*, demonstrate the inspiration such scale could provide in expanding, if not exploding, the concept of the picturesque. Thomas Cole in his famous essays on American scenery admitted there were those who claimed that the American landscape was 'rude without picturequesness, and monotonous without sublimity'.[62] Cole's own attempts to blend the Ideal Landscape with the sublime show the dynamics of American landscape, tensions that he manages to hold in equilibrium, while the next generation found it necessary to seek new solutions. Cole's tendency to create series of paintings in which action unfolded through a succession of canvases also seems related to the panorama tradition. Scott McDonald has beautifully detailed the proto-cinematic flow of action and meaning in Cole's 1840 series *The Voyage of Life*, moving from one canvas to the next, the river providing a constant pathway for the voyage, even as the apparent 'screen direction' of the boat reverses from 'shot' to 'shot'.[63] Likewise the five canvases of his *Course of Empire* fix the same basic geographical spot (the distant mountain with its precarious balanced boulder providing a point of reference for each view, shifting a bit, but never radically switching viewpoint). Such stable spatial reference underscores the temporal transformations of each scene, as the course of empire runs through its historical cycle. This practice particularly recalls Daguerre's diorama, in which a change in lighting radically transformed a scene of a single location – from day to night, from spring to winter.

Using a variety of means – scale, a use of seriality or theatrical modes of presentation – American landscape painters in the nineteenth century absorbed the challenges to framing and spectatorship exemplified by the various forms of panorama entertainments. We see in these landscapes the mastery of framing contending with an energy striving to burst them asunder in pursuit of a new relation to the spectator. The location of the spectator, increasingly addressed as an embodied physical presence with physiological sensations, became a contested site.

## How can a landscape experience be framed?

I long for the return of the dioramas, whose brutal and enormous magic has the power to impose on me a useful illusion. I would rather go to the theater and feast my eyes on the scenery, in which I find my dearest dreams treated with consummate skill and tragic conclusions. These things, because they are false, are infinitely closer to the truth, whereas the majority of our landscape painters are liars, precisely because they fail to lie.

Charles Baudelaire, 'Salon of 1859'

In the nineteenth-century American landscape painting confronted a series of challenges: new subject matter – such as the titanic proportions of the expanses of American nature; technological transformations – such as the railroad; and new models of spectatorship – such as those offered by the panorama. While the picturesque tried to maintain the balance of framing and recession exemplified by the Ideal Landscape, these new challenges pushed the landscape increasingly towards a companion concept: the sublime, the romantic experience of the infinite, of experience itself pushed beyond limits, which appeared both as the intensification of the picturesque and its explosion. However, the older models of the sublime, supplied by Salvatore Rosa and his landscapes of wild trees and stormy mountains populated by banditti, hardly seemed adequate for a new technological age, which could be satisfied only with a new technological sublime. The sublime supplied less a model for new compositions than an impulse to explore new technical options, pursuing new effects for the viewer. The increased canvas size introduced by Moran, Church and Bierstadt did more than simply contain the scale of the American landscape; massive paintings sought to convey the overwhelmingly sublime effect of the American landscape on the observer, especially as the Rockies replaced the White Mountains and the Colorado superseded the Hudson.

In this respect the tradition of the Great Painting took up the challenge of the panorama, aspiring to its power over a spectator. New concepts of spectatorship were emerging – yet these

Circa 1929: Director Ernst Lubitsch (1892–1947) wearing a cap, behind the camera, directing Camilla Horn (1906–) and John Barrymore (1882–1942) during the filming of 'Eternal Love' (aka 'Der Koenig der Bernina') in the Canadian Rocky Mountains for United Artists. (Photo by Hulton Archive/Getty Images)

concepts do not so much reverse the traditional stance of the viewer as force artists and viewers to confront contradictions inherent in the sublime form of landscape. Andrew Wilton, speaking of J. M. W. Turner's massive and sublime landscapes (which exerted a decisive influence on the American landscape) claimed, 'Landscape was no longer to be contemplated from afar, but participated in an immediate experience'.[64] In fact, the nineteenth-century landscape spectator seems torn between several positions: the traditional distanced contemplation called for by the Ideal Landscape; Diderot's fantasy of lingering penetration and transversal; the domineering and surveying magisterial gaze of exploration and appropriation; the intense sensual subjection to the overwhelming sublime experience of nature (in Turner, Friedrich or Church); the technological illusion of being engulfed by the image of the panorama; and the fascinated, but distanced, mobile gaze of the panoramic train traveller.

The affinity between the Great Paintings and the panorama did not pass unnoticed, or uncensored, since the panoramas themselves were considered outside the bounds of art. The subtlest American critic of the era, James Jackson Jarvies, satirically invoked the country bumpkin who, seeing Bierstadt Great Painting from 1863, *The Rocky Mountain*, 'mistook [the painting] for a panorama, and after waiting a while asked when the thing was going to move'. The rube, Jarvies claimed, 'was a more sagacious critic than he knew himself to be'.[65] Jarvies himself criticized the painting: 'all this quality of painting is more or less panoramic from being so material in its artistic features as always to keep the spectator at a distance. He can never forget his point of view, and that he is looking at a painting'.[66] We find here a contradictory welter of metaphors, like Baudelaire's oxymoron of truthful illusions, that reveal the contested nature of landscape spectatorship at the middle of the nineteenth century. Did the Ideal Landscape or did the panorama keep the spectator at a distance? Was this distance a good or a bad thing, a product of artistic contemplation or the inevitable disillusioned reaction to a spectacle aimed at deception? In what sense could a spectator 'forget his view point?' Did panoramic perception bring one into the landscape, fulfilling a longstanding fantasy, or did it further separate viewer and spectacle by affirming the power of the apparatus through which things were viewed?

This series of nearly irresolvable contradictions points, I believe, to a anxiety about the nature of direct experience in the modern era, a desire for modes of representation intended to reproduce not simply a landscape, but the full sensual experience of being there, often employing sensual supplements (late panoramas added simulations of breezes, smells and kinesthetic experiences such as the pitching of a boat).[67] But the pursuit of direct experience need not take such a literal path in its final manifestation. In preparing for perhaps the greatest nineteenth-century painting of the new technology of the locomotive, Turner's 1843 *Rain, Steam, Speed*, the artist reportedly stuck his head out a train window during torrential downpour for some nine minutes, then sat soaked in streaming water, contemplating his experience with closed eyes for another quarter of an hour.[68] A similar story is told about Turner being lashed to a ship's mast during a storm.[69] Whether the artist directly experienced seasickness beforehand or the observer felt nauseous as a result, the forms of aesthetic experience were reaching for a new identification with bodily sensation.

But we encounter again the paradox of the panoramic. Did the new technology such as train travel bring one closer to a more intense, more sublime experience of 'rain, steam and speed', or did it remove one from the world it travelled through? Recall that Schivelbusch defined panoramic perception not in terms of being environmentally engulfed by a represented space to the point of physical reaction – enclosed in Humboldt's 'magic circle', forgetful of all else – but, rather, in terms of separation, as the viewer 'no longer belongs to the same space as the perceived objects: the traveller sees the objects, landscapes, etc. *through* the apparatus…' and he cites numerous nineteenth-century descriptions of train travel to support this view.[70] As if confirming Schivelbusch's definition, American poet Bayard Taylor described a trip on the Eire Railroad as,

> a rapidly unrolling panorama…We sped along…in a warm and richly furnished chamber, lounging on soft seats, half arm-chair and half couch. Apparently as disconnected from the landscape as a loose leaf blown over it by the winds.[71]

One technology, an apparatus of representation, the panorama, strove to represent an experience so intensely it could trigger nausea. Another technology, a mode of transportation, the train journey, became an apparatus of vision that transformed real landscapes into virtual ones, and travellers into spectators. Travelling becomes a frictionless form of transportation typified by the fictional global traveller of record-breaking speed Phileas Fogg, whom Jules Verne describes as 'not travelling, but only describing a circumference...he was a solid body traversing an orbit around the terrestrial globe, according to the laws of rational mechanics'.[72] No wonder Turner felt compelled to stick his head out the window!

Focusing once again on the frame may help us gain a handle on this contradiction. The panorama appeared almost simultaneously with another new medium whose history ultimately lasted longer: photography. Photography also posed a challenge to the tradition of the Ideal Landscape. The American landscapes from Cole and Durand through Church and Bierstadt, while drawing on sketches from nature understood their relation to nature to be synthetic, aestheticizing and idealizing, composing landscapes that never claimed to correspond precisely to the views that originally inspired them. Photography, by contrast, according to aestheticians seemed unlikely to become a true art form precisely because it was condemned to an accurate portrayal of the scene it photographed, the 'hand maiden' rather than the master of nature. As Peter Galassi puts it, 'the camera's inability to compose rendered the old standards nearly obsolete from the outset'.[73]

However Galassi's pioneering essay on the relation between photography and the composition of 'views' explored the complexity of the relation between technology and aesthetics. The breakdown of the Ideal Landscape in certain forms of landscape views and sketches can by no means be attributed simply to the invention of photography. Galassi claims the invention of photograph (or at least it aesthetic use) should instead be understood in relation to changes in artistic composition that occurred before it. Almost from its origins the picturesque carried an impulse towards the casual and aleatory that seems to contradict its investment in carefully framed pictures. While the picturesque favoured the rearrangement of nature into more balanced composition, the very tools it used in venturing into nature, the *camera obscura* and the Claude Glass, directly anticipate the fragmentary, 'taken directly from nature' aspect of both the photography and new models of landscape composition.

It is useful to return to the Claude Glass. This capturing of reflections also raises the complex question of what it means to 'frame'. The German Romantic painter Carus criticized the Claude Glass from the point of view of composition in a letter to Caspar David Friedrich:

Look at a natural landscape in a mirror! You will see it reproduced with all its charms, all its colours and shapes; but if you capture this reflection and compare it to the effect a finished work of art representing a landscape has on you, what do you notice? – It is obvious that the work of art falls short of the truth; for whatever it is that makes the beautiful natural shapes so charming, the colours so luminous, it is never entirely achieved in the painting. You experience at the same time the feeling that the authentic work of art constitutes a whole, a little world (microcosm) in itself; a reflection in retrospect will always appear to be a fragment, a part of infinite nature, detached from its organic links and circumscribed within its limits from nature.[74]

The Ideal Landscape pursued through its balanced composition the creation of a fragment that seemed self-contained. But the very genre of the landscape, with its invitation to voyage introduced the leaven that would undermine this illusion self-containment. The landscape implied a voyage inside its frame, soliciting other view points, like the succession of images the Claude Glass gave to the tourist, which Gilpin claimed he would give any price to fix and appropriate. In spite of Carus' objection, in the nineteenth century both Realism and Romanticism (to invoke two massive concepts) encouraged a taste for the fragmentary and rooted aesthetics less in ideal models than in the selection of a point of view. From Friedrich to Degas (or from Church to Inness) painting explored what Galassi calls 'the formative role of the vantage point', implicit already in perspective, but increasingly wandering away from the architectonic composition that theatricalized the space viewed.[75]

Various technological responses to this tension loomed, including the chemical fixing of *camera obscura* images that Daguerre, Niecpe and Fox Talbot sought and achieved before the middle of the nineteenth century – photography. But the photograph seemed condemned to the fragmentary, if not the random. The panorama offered another response, combining photography's detailed accuracy and adherence to nature with a form that aspired less to a microcosm, than to imaging Humboldt's totalizing *Cosmos*.[76] While the contrast between photography and the panorama might seem as absolute as that between fragment and whole, in their common purpose of conveying accurate topographical information, each overthrow the Ideal Landscape, abolishing synthetic ideal composition in favour of an image of a place determined by the apparatus of view. As Comment put it, 'The panorama therefore had no composition other than that implied by the chosen vanishing point.'[77] Fundamentally, both media exploit the 'formative role of the vantage point'. Photographs soon served panorama artists as guides in the preparation of their massive canvases, and photographic panoramas appeared, including Eadweard Muybridge's two versions of a photographic panorama of San Francisco.[78]

The panorama seems to embody the imperial ambitions inherent in the 'magisterial gaze', a role recognized in its use as a tool of nationalist propaganda from Napoleon's plan to establish a series of rotundas displaying the military victories of the Revolution and Empire through to the twentieth-century panoramas of the defence of Stalingrad, the (still existing?) Battle of Al-Qadissiyah installed by Sadam Hussein outside of Baghdad, or the Battle of Tetshou in North Korea, or celebrating colonial ambitions as in the massive 1913 Belgium panorama of the Congo.[79] Evoking on the one hand visual and physical mastery, the panorama also provoked a feeling of being physically overwhelmed, of vertigo, rather than mastery, as Comment describes it, 'an exquisite switching from feelings of dominance to those of dissolution, of loss'.[80] One might claim the ideological effect of identification with a masterful gaze is dependent upon an experience of disorientation, but I would agree with Comment that this simplifies the dialectical nature of the experience, ignoring the panorama's essential relation to the sublime tradition of Turner, Friedrich and Church, 'to destabilize their viewers, to make them lose their bearings, to destructure the background so that they could be sucked into the vertigo of the image, to be as it were immersed in the forces of nature and painting'.[81]

The panorama underwent a commercial climax around 1900 with a dramatic proliferation and new technological sophistication evident in the variety of panoramas offered at the 1900 Universal Exposition at Paris.[82] Then, as a mass medium, it died a lingering death. The history of the emergence of cinema, while acknowledging cinema's debt to several centuries of visual entertainments, unfortunately often adopts a Darwinian arc of ascent in which the cinema fulfils, as it abolishes, a series of predecessors, including the panorama. Approached more broadly, the proliferation of mechanically produced images readily available through a complex modern visual culture ended the commercial possibility of an artisan product like the panorama, however industrialized its production had attempted to become. But modern landscape painting was undoubtedly shaped by this rival in more ways than imitation of scale and mode of presentation by the Great Paintings. Barbara Novak subtly shows that the American luminists while absolutely avoiding the theatricality and monumentality of the Great Picture worked out their own appropriation of the lessons of the panorama. While the landscapes of Kensett and Heade made no attempt to rival the panorama's scale, they also abandoned the classic proportions of the Ideal Landscape, producing horizontally extensive canvases:

> Significantly the luminist artists duplicated the horizontal extensions of the panorama in their picture's proportions. I say significantly because I am suggesting that they had a profound understanding of the structural means whereby the popular panorama could be transformed back into high art.[83]

Likewise, Comment reminds us that Monet's conception of *The Waterlilies* originally envisioned display within a circular panorama type structure which would maximize the experience Monet described as, 'a whole without end, of a wave without horizon and without shore'.[84] Even if it disappeared as a medium, the panorama pioneered a new relation to the frame and the viewer whose influence on modern art and new media endured.

## An unseen energy

> As we become accustomed to the gloom, we see an EYE, far ahead; a half-closed eye, growing larger and larger as we approach, It glistens on the converging rails; it grows larger; it grows brighter. We see a delicate picture outlined in that tiny space; a picture of a station, a tower, bright trees, shining meadows; and suddenly we're right in the midst of it all.

> Edison, 1900 Catalogue Description of *Running Through Gallitzen Tunnel, Penna., R.R*

The relation between landscape and cinema must be understood in relation to a long history of transformations in framing, the view framed and the role of the spectator. Approaching landscape and *early* cinema also demands attention to transformations in film history. I have argued that, in contrast to later cinema, for at least the first decade of film history narrative played a secondary role.[85] Rather than primarily telling stories, early films displayed things, placing a variety of attractions on display for curious audiences. These attractions included vaudeville acts, magical camera tricks (disappearances and transformations), brief gags and views of various sights, both man-made (famous buildings, World Fairs, city streets) and natural (rivers, waterfalls, mountains, canyons – the sort of things panoramas initially featured). This cinema of attraction, with its emphasis on the 'view', showed a greater affinity with the genre of landscape painting than we find in later films. Films presenting landscape 'views' formed a major genre of early cinema, gradually transforming into the travelogues of the classical cinema programme, lasting until the end of the studio system.[86] Filmed views of natural landscapes recall more directly the still photographic views printed on postcards, magic lantern slides and pasted in tourist albums, yet these fairly recent practices had absorbed lessons in composition and a canon of worthwhile sights from landscape painting – even as the photograph introduced new models of framing.

Travel films composed a major genre of early cinema, fitting in seamlessly with such popular traditions as lantern slide travel lectures and illustrated guidebooks. All these forms presented to audiences views of sights and sites that either they were thinking of visiting, enjoyed recalling – or knew they would never be able to afford to see and therefore particularly valued through this ersatz form of tourism.[87] Like landscape painting and landscape photography (such as the work of William Henry Jackson and Eadweard Muybridge), early films were often sponsored by railroads in the hope these cinematic views would spawn the curiosity of tourists when they were shown. At the turn of the century, American railroads sponsored filmmaking tours along their routes, just as they had (and continued to) sponsored tours for painters and photographers. Edison made films with the cooperation of the Lehigh Valley Railroad and the Southern Pacific Railroad. The Mutoscope and Biograph Company made a series of films in cooperation with the New York Central, the Union Pacific, the Canadian Pacific and the Sante-Fe Railways. Travel had become an industry in which the technologies of transportation and image-making were mutually beneficial.

The affinity between the railroad and the cinema as emblems of modernity has been widely commented on.[88] Film capturing the dynamic speed of the locomotive, especially when filmed from an angle so that the train moves rapidly towards the camera, formed a major genre of the novelty phase of film exhibition in the 1890s. Starting with Lumière's famous *Arrival of a Train at Ciotat*, shown at the premiere projection of the Lumière Cinématographe in Paris 1895, the image of a locomotive apparently charging out from the screen became a defining image of the new medium internationally. Edison filmed the world's fastest locomotive, the Lehigh Valley's Black Diamond Express, while its rival film company Biograph filmed the New York Central's rival contender for fastest locomotive, The

Empire Express.[89] More than simply a choice of dynamic subject matter, filming locomotives in this manner implied new attitudes towards the frame and the spectator.

These forward-charging trains gave birth at some later point to an enduring myth, a sort of cinematic primal scene, in which audiences, mistaking the moving images for reality and the train's motion for a violent assault upon them, ran out of the theatre. No one has ever documented an instance of such behaviour among the first cinema audiences.[90] But if not literally true, such stories raise important issues for the newly forming film spectatorship. The legend confuses sensory experience and intellectual belief. If we keep these separate, we can better describe the spectator address of panoramas and cinema, in which conventions of representation took second place to the delivering of sensual experiences.

When the *New York Telegraph* covered the premiere projection of Biograph films in 1896 New York City it reported that two women in the audience 'screamed and fainted' during the projection of the Biograph film of the Empire Express (a claim later modified to read 'screamed and *nearly* fainted');[91] this reaction recalls Queen Charlotte's seasickness at the panorama, or the report of an attack of the hysterics by anonymous woman at Langlois's panorama of the Naval Battle of Naravino.[92] Even if these reports are reliable, they tell us little about spectator belief in the reality of the illusion, but rather indicate that sensual stimulation can trigger psychophysical reactions. While no one probably ever ran from such a screening in fear of a train wreck, spectators undoubtedly screamed, made sudden reflex motions or had other physical reactions in reaction to the movement on the screen (as they continue to do during highly kinetic scenes in movies, especially when shown in such exhibition situations as three-dimensional movies or the semi-panoramic Cinerama).

Like the panorama, moving pictures also redefined the interaction of frame and spectator. The poster Albert Truchet designed for the 1896 Lumière Cinématographe exhibitions shows fashionably dressed ladies watching an arrival of a train on the screen in front of them.[93] But as Klaus-Jurgen Sembach points out, the train track emerges irrationally from the left corner of the screen frame extending into the space of the audience. The anomaly reflects more than a stylistic flourish. A British commentator writing under the name O. Winter described the effect of the Lumière film, 'And a train, running (so to say) out of the cloth, floats upon our vision.'[94] The fantasy of the train's emergence from the screen was omnipresent and powerful in the novelty era, attested to by numerous journalists, including Maxim Gorky who in 1896 sadistically imagined the Lumière train 'plunge into the darkness in which you sit, turning you into a ripped sack full of lacerated flesh and splintered bone and crushing into dust and into broken fragments this hall...', a fantasy he then deflated by adding, 'But this too is but a train of shadows'.[95]

Cinema simultaneously maintains the frame (the screen rectangle fixed and visible in the front of the auditorium) and ruptures it. The quadrilateral on which the film is projected does not vary, but, as the Truchet's poster illustrates and as the fantasies of emergence testify, movement extends beyond the frame, 'out of the cloth' – or seems to. The creation of off-screen space fascinated and confused early film spectators. Yuri Tsivian describes the effect of what he calls the 'disappearing figure', as moving figures came to the edge of the frame

– and then seemingly disappeared.[96] Reviewers of the premiere of Biograph films, which included a film of presidential candidate William McKinley, noticed with confusion that when McKinley 'came to the edge of the curtain' he vanished.[97] The moving panorama had mimed landscapes slipping past a viewer seated in a train or boat and disappearing from view, anticipating the lateral displacement of movement through a film frame. But the arrival of the train, or similar films featuring motion aimed at the camera (such as the delightful 1900 film by Cecil Hepworth, *How It Feels to Be Run Over*), opened up a new space beyond the frame, not simply on either side. This novel movement towards the camera – that is, *towards the spectator* – prompted cries of alarm and fantasies of collision. The panorama, moving or fixed, maintained a constant and safe distance between spectator and the spectacle.[98] Movement toward the camera seemed to undermine that traditional separation, collapsing the contemplative distance in the anticipation of collision, and heightening the physical sensations evoked in the panorama to an intense shock. Did the cinema therefore abolish the sense of separation between observer and scene that Schivelbusch calls 'panoramic perception', attested to by so many nineteenth-century train travellers? Or did it simply redefine its effects?

The symbiosis between the panorama and the cinema that occurred at the turn of the century, strongly transformed the effects of the older medium, rather than simply absorbing it. The cinematic 'pan' – short for 'panoramic shot' – a pivoting camera movement as the camera turns on a stationary tripod – marks one of the terms of this merging of the forms. This camera movement was introduced quite early. Barry Salt claims Robert Paul designed the first pivoting camera in order to cover Queen Victoria's Diamond Jubilee in 1897, and the manufacture of camera-heads that could pan smoothly and steadily institutionalized its place in the cinema's vocabulary to the present day.[99] Although also used to follow the action of an event (a parade or a sporting event), its earliest uses tended to acknowledge the pan's derivation from the panorama. Early film companies offered 'panoramas' or 'panoramic views' of sites, natural and man-made. Not all early films that included the term 'panorama' in their title used such 'panning' motion, and likewise not all films that used a pan mentioned it in their title, but a large number did, often modifying the term to 'circular panorama' to indicate a sweeping view (occasionally, but not always, a full 360 degrees). Edison made circular panoramas of the Niagara Falls (one of the many examples Cahn noted of early cinema picking up the locations familiar from American landscape painting)[100] as well as of 360-degree views of the 1900 Paris Universal Exposition.

But the term 'panorama' or 'panoramic view' also described another sort of landscape film, undoubtedly the most popular and most dynamic visually. These panoramas did not simply show locomotives moving towards the camera, but instead mounted a camera on a train, capturing a mobile view of a landscape. Edison first shot such a film in June of 1896, *View from Gorge Railroad*, which the *Boston Herald* described as 'a panoramic picture obtained from the rear end of a swiftly-moving train on the Niagara Gorge railway'.[101] The term 'panoramic' first designated an Edison train film in 1897, with *Panoramic Scene, Susquehanna River*. Titles like Biograph's 1902 *Panorama from Incline Railway* (shot from

Mt Beacon, NY), or Edison's 1901 *Panoramic View, Kicking Horse Canyon* all refer to films shot from the front of moving trains. These films deliver an experience of movement more extensive and dynamic than the pivoting pans. Whereas the arc of vision in a pan presents a sweeping circular view of a scene from a fixed centre, with the camera mounted on the front of a train these films actually travel through space, like the train itself, moving through the landscape. Thus the films realize the centuries-old fantasy of penetration that had remained literally impossible in landscape painting. Besides 'panoramic views', catalogues and exhibitors called such films 'phantom rides', a term richly evoking the uncanny effect of ghostly movement that I feel was central to their popularity.

Many historians see these films simply as simulacra of train travel or other sorts of tourist journeys (some were filmed from other forms of transportation, such as boats, trolley cars or automobiles). As such they seem to provide the ultimate form of Schivelbusch's panoramic perception, with the distance between traveller and unfolding landscape now become the ontological difference between live audience and filmed image on the screen. Certainly the essence of this genre resides in what Charles Musser has called the 'viewer as passenger' convention.[102] But most of these films show a strong deviation from the tourist experience, firmly embodied in point of view. As the Edison catalogue stressed in their description of their 1903 film *Phantom Ride on the Canadian Pacific*, 'the view taken from the front of the train running at high speed is one even tourists riding over the line are not privileged to enjoy'.[103] The viewpoint of the train traveller primarily remained lateral, looking through the train window as it moved past the landscape. The moving panoramas mimed this lateral motion with the most elaborate versions, such as the panorama of the Trans Siberian Express at the Paris 1900 Exposition, providing mockups of the compartment windows for spectator to gaze through (and, in this case, an elaborate system of multiple rolls of canvas to simulate the apparently different rates of speed that objects at various distances move past the viewer, more rapidly for the foreground fields, more slowly for the distant vista of mountains).[104] But the cinematic phantom rides dove straight into the landscape and presented this plunging point of view directly to the viewer.

Some contemporary descriptions of such films recall Diderot's imaginary itinerary into an Ideal Landscape, as in the Edison catalogue description of *Panorama of Susquehanna River Taken from the Black Diamond Express*:

There is hardly a lovelier spot along the whole Lehigh Valley railroad than this stretch of road. We are on a gently curving bit of track, mountains on both sides. We glide beneath a slender bridge, pass a crossing and a wayside station and run out on a steep embankment. Suddenly the road dips into the hills, then out again, round a point, and the valley of the Susquehanna bursts out upon our view. Far away in the blue distance the river glistens like a silver thread. There are bridges and houses and barns and steeples. There are checkerboard farms, and broad patches of virgin forest. All calm and serene in the glory of God's sunshine.[105]

Thus films of 'panoramic views' seemed to fulfil desires inherent in the Ideal Landscape, exploring a new literal portrayal of motion into the landscape.

However, other films (or perhaps other marketing strategies) promoted spectator experiences that contrasted sharply with contemplative visual voyages. The Edison Company in 1902 advertised their film *Panoramic View of Lower Kicking Horse Canyon* for its physical thrills and the appearance of danger: 'of all panoramic mountain pictures this is the most thrilling, as the audience imagines while they are being carried along with the picture the train will be toppled over thousands of feet into the valley below'. Of a companion film of the same canyon the catalogue claimed: 'the train seems to be running into the mountains of rock as each curve is reached and rounded, making the scene exciting from start to finish'. The key attraction of Edison's *Panoramic View of Mt Tamalpias, Cal.* according to their publicity lay in 'the sensation of momentarily expecting to be hurled into space'.[106]

These films fully exploit the dynamics of their unique frontal point of view, driving a wedge between the 'phantom ride' and the distanced panoramic perception of the train tourist. The view from the front of the train created a more thrilling perspective, allowing the suspenseful anticipation of collisions and derailments described in the Edison catalogue for their *Lower Kicking Horse Canyon* panoramas. Far from a contemplative mode, this viewpoint summoned up the possibility of shock and intense sensual involvement that had migrated from the painted panorama and intensified as it found its home in the new electrical fairground with its thrill rides, such as the Leap Frog Railway which threatened passengers with a direct collision between train cars – only to have the cars 'leap over' each other at the last moment. Such fairground attractions strove to create a sense of physical danger while passengers were actually nestled in a device guaranteed to keep physical collision and injury in abeyance.[107]

If the panorama films shot from the front of the train seem to abolish the traditional reception of landscapes by accelerating the fantasy of travel into a landscape with a vengeance, one might note that the early excursions mounted by railway companies for artists also frequently featured rides on the front of the locomotive.[108] Whatever inspiration such rides provided artists, they do not seem to have literally inspired the viewpoint of any canvas. Like Turner sticking his head out from the train compartment window, such experiences might deepen an artist's experience of a landscape, but were unlikely to inspire a choice of compositional viewpoint. But in the early films taken from camera mounted on the front of the train the effect of this viewpoint often becomes nearly overwhelming, to my mind the richest and most dialectical experience offered by early cinema in its exploration of movement and point of view. Such phantom rides substitute sensation for contemplation, overcoming effects of distance in a rush of visual motion.

The longevity of phantom rides filmmaking testifies to the inherent power of its effect. I have found examples as early as 1896 and many exist as late as 1907, when the cinema of attractions had become increasingly seduced by the tasks of narrative. Indeed, there are similar tracking shots from the front of locomotives integrated into later narrative films that deal with the railway (and viewers of European television will recognize the final survival of the form in long-lasting videos of train rides broadcast on certain channels in the wee hours of the morning apparently for the pleasure of trainspotters, insomniacs and a few sleepless devotees of the power of visual kinesis). Intuiting the energy slumbering within the form, a number of panoramic train films have also been reworked by avant-garde filmmakers, most gloriously by Ernie Gehr and Ken Jacobs.

From 1905 to about 1907, towards the end of era of the cinema of attractions, this genre was renewed by George C. Hale, who returned it to its roots in the panorama and brought it closer to the new electric amusement parks. Hale adopted the exhibition strategy of many panoramas by fashioning a viewing area that imitated an aspect of panorama's then, such as the Trans-Siberian Express Panorama. In Hale's Tours and Scenes of the World, the audience was seated in a mock-up of a train car, complete with sound effects of the clickety-clack of the wheels running over the rails and the hiss of the air brakes, as they watched the films projected in the front of the car, narrated by lecturers dressed as train conductors. These theatres were briefly very popular, and films taken from the front of trains are often referred to as Hale's Tours Films, somewhat anachronistically, since the genre had been in existence for nearly a decade before Hale introduced his specialized theatres.[109]

The increased mimesis of train travel that these theatres offered reaffirm their role as ersatz tourism, like the panoramas themselves, a new technological version of what Comment refers to as 'a dream that had been prevalent since the beginning of the nineteenth century, to travel without having to move'.[110] But the intensity of this experience, as I have argued, exceeded a simple reproduction of travel and transformed the experience of landscape. Only a thick description of this experience, both phenomenological and historical, reveals its radical transformation of the landscape tradition. With their front-on viewpoint, the phantom rides provide a unique realization of the fantasy of penetrating a landscape, of chasing the horizon into the depth of an ever-unfolding image. The displacement from the lateral view provided by the train (and the moving panoramas) to a head-on plunge into the centre of the image fundamentally transforms the distance Schivelbusch described as inherent in panoramic perception.

In previous essays I have quoted an anonymous journalist's account of his experience of one of the Biograph earliest phantom rides.[111] I find it such a rich description of the experience of a film travelling down the train tracks I feel compelled to return to it once again in this new context:

The way in which the unseen energy swallows up space and flings itself into the distances is as mysterious and impressive as an allegory. A sensation is produced akin to that which Poe in his 'Fall of the House of Usher' relates was communicated to him by his doomed companion when he sketched the shaft in the heart of the earth, with an unearthly radiance thrilling through it. One holds his breath instinctively as he is swept along in the rush of the phantom cars. His attention is held almost with the vise of a fate.[112]

The terms of comparison that journalist offers probe deeply into the novelty of this experience of spectatorship. The locomotive, which never appears on the screen, but is present only in its motive force, literally embodies an unseen energy that compels the camera, the film and the viewer down the track. Since it remains off-screen and invisible, the locomotive takes on a basic characteristic of a phantom, a presence evident in its effects, while remaining unseen. Although we *know* the camera was perched on the front of a train, the film delivers a fantasy of total visual dominance. It is *our eyes*, liberated from any visible body, that fly down the track, 'swallowing up space', like the film spectator described by Christian Metz decades later as 'taking everything in with their eyes, nothing with their bodies'.[113]

The head-on confrontation between the viewer's vantage point and the direction of movement into space evoke the possibility of shock and collision, in contrast to the lateral view of the traditional train rider that created the sense of separation essential to panoramic perception. Nonetheless, a fundamental fissure between viewer and spectacle remains, dependent less on visual viewpoint, yet physically more absolute. As much as the expectation, even the sensation, of collision may be evoked by such film, no collision is ever possible. As with the fantasy of emergence of the train from the screen, we remain in a realm of shadow, not substance. No physical shock is possible, no meeting between our bodies and the space on screen can occur, however much we may seem to penetrate into it.

This ultimately ontological separation between viewer and screen therefore posits a new form of the distance characteristic of panoramic perception, the return of the unreality of the image repressed by the apparent sensual immediacy delivered by the cinematic experience of motion. As film viewers, we seem to be there, to actually fulfil the desire for entrance into an illusionary landscape. Space streams right at us – yet, it only invites our eyes to enter, our bodies remain seated, on the other side of the screen. We experience our exile from this represented space, like a phantom hovering over our seeming participation. In an uncanny way, as film viewers, we experience that transcendent experience that Emerson described in his essay 'Nature' and that has become an emblem not only for American Transcendentalism, but for the experience of the nineteenth-century American landscape: 'Standing on the bare ground – my head bathed by the blithe air, and uplifted into infinite space – all mean egotism vanishes. I become a transparent eye-ball; I am nothing; I see all…'[114] In a more concrete (but not less extraordinary manner) in these films the spectator vanishes physically, leaving only the energy of travel, the sensation of movement through the landscape. Yet this all-seeing eye is also a physiological eye, one alert for the possibility of collision and ready to flinch at the sensation of danger, even as it is protected by its very medium from physical contact. In spite of its fulfilment of the centuries old fantasy of penetration it remains, what Benjamin describes as modern 'protective eye', alert of potential dangers, rather than 'daydreaming surrender to distance and faraway things'. As Benjamin speculates the magic of distance maybe broken.[115]

The convergence of tracks in the distance, the ultimate image of perspective in our culture – parallel lines merging at the vanishing point of infinity – sets up the dynamic balance of the visible and the invisible in these films. The energy forcing us down the tracks remains unseen. The space we travel through, once we have moved past it, slides around the frame, and vanishes as well, forming an invisible wake of remembered space trailing behind us.

As we move towards the ever-receding horizon, new bits of landscape seem to come into existence at the limits of our vision; hills, bridges, train stations, towns, cliffs and forests burst into sight. An ever-renewed landscape emerges from the distance that remains continuously bisected by the tracks in front of us, which hold steady not only our trajectory but, as the journalist cannily observes, our *attention*, as in a vice of fate. Our track cannot deviate, nor can we look in any other direction than straight ahead, any more than we can retain a sight of the passing landscape that we only catch a glimpse of. All space is in constant motion; all is continuously both approaching us and slipping away from us. Diderot's fantasy of a voyage into a landscape becomes a nightmare of infinite regress, impelled by a fate-like irresistible resistible force.

Noel Burch in his influential and pioneering work on early cinema figured the spectator in the phantom rides as an anticipation of the classical spectator of later cinema around whom all space is organized – the coherent subject of ideology sutured into a continuous narrative of illusory domination.[116] This interpretation fits, just as the panoramic viewpoint corresponds to the magisterial gaze of manifest destiny. However, as Comment claimed with the panorama, another experience seems dominant, one prompted by physical sensations of vertigo, perhaps even more powerful than the relation the panorama had to dissolution and loss. The vanishing point, the fixed convergence of classical perspective, its point of coherence, becomes in the phantom ride a point of constant transformation and instability. From it new vistas emerge like ants swarming up from an unseen anthill. Instead of the point where things vanish, the far distance becomes the point of entrance into visibility. Our point of view, as stand-ins for the camera, becomes the point at which everything converges and then disappears, reversing the traditional schema of perspective. The reversal reworks perspective's inherent sense of visual dominance into an experience of an abject subjection to the course of movement and the logic of the track. As shaped by the camera lens, instead of offering the broad and inviting foreground, a stable viewing point on which traditional landscape *staffage* figures can loll at ease to gaze into the distance, the foreground of a phantom ride represents the narrowest point of the image, as well as the point of greatest velocity, the anticipated site of collision. To watch a phantom ride film, I find, provokes not only a crisis within the spectator's relation to space and landscape, but a heightened awareness of perception and consciousness itself, its temporal protentions and retentions, its constant reach into the distance, balanced by its sense of passing by and leaving behind. If the phantom ride is 'a mysterious and impressive allegory' one might describe it as an allegory of spatial perception itself.[117] Yet this one-tracked mind flies obsessively in a nightmare inversion of the contemplative gaze Diderot imagined picking its leisurely way through the varied zones of the Ideal Landscape.

In one of his papers on technique Freud advised patients beginning analysis to imagine 'you were a traveller next to a window of the railway carriage and describing to someone inside the carriage the changing views which you see outside'.[118] Access to the unconscious unfolds like a sightseeing trip. But the phantom ride's direct stare down the track seems to invoke more closely the hypnotic state that Freud increasingly rejected as a means of reaching unconscious experience. In the opening of his film *Zentropa*, Lars von Trier has the voice of Max von Sydow address the audience as a hypnotist, inducting them into a trance that will be the film, entered into by following the camera movement down these train tracks. The tracks appear gleaming within darkness, passing through no visible landscape, other than the abstract pathway they lay down. We could see this prologue as cinema's ultimate anti-landscape, the nightmare armature on which fantasies of domination and of being dominated are carried.

## Ghost dances

After I had looked at five or six of them, they gradually began to separate themselves from their surroundings, and I was no longer able to see them as moons. They became holes in the canvas, apertures of whiteness looking onto another world. Blakelock's eye perhaps. A blank circle suspended in space, gazing down at things that were no longer there.

Paul Auster, *Moon Palace*

In describing the uncanny effect of the Biograph train film the journalist compared it to the painting produced by Roderick Usher in Poe's 'The Fall of the House of Usher'. Poe's description could stand, I believe, as the exemplar of an anti-landscape:

A small picture presented the interior of an immensely long and rectangular vault or tunnel, with low walls, smooth, white, and without interruption or device. Certain accessory points of the design served well to convey the idea that this excavation lay at an exceeding depth below the surface of the earth. No outlet was observed in any portion of its vast extent, and no torch, or other artificial source of light was discernible; yet a flood of intense rays rolled throughout, and bathed the whole in a ghastly and inappropriate splendor.[119]

While the American landscapes tradition more immediately brings to mind as a literary correlative a figure like James Fenimore Cooper whose description of the Adirondacks inspired a major painting by Thomas Cole, I would claim no major American author thought as deeply or wrote as profoundly about the composition of landscape than Poe. Two of his most obscure late works, 'The Domain of Arnheim' (1846) and 'Landor's Cottage' consist entirely of descriptions of the composition of landscapes and discussions of the art of landscape architecture. His sketch 'The Island of the Fay' performs an imaginary exploration of an Ideal Landscape based on an engraving, while his article 'Morning on the Wissahiccon' provides a gentle satire on the passion for picturesque landscapes.

But we properly associate Poe more with interior spaces (as Charles Olson said, Poe's response to the American landscape was to dig in).[120] Poe, we might claim, turned American space inside out (in his amazing fantasy of landscape gardens, 'The Domain of Arnheim', Poe imagines a garden whose configuration could only be appreciated and understood by a perspective beyond the human and terrestrial).[121] The interior portrayed in Usher's picture empties out our consciousness of space and place. Usher's painting has sometimes been described (anachronistically) as an exercise in abstract art. More accurately, it performs an act of ascesis, a landscape sunk beneath the surface, composed exclusively of formal aspects of framing and depth, illuminated by a light whose deathly quality and lack of source invert Claude's golden varied sunlight and shade. Walter Benjamin called Poe's story 'The Man of the Crowd' 'the x-ray' of a detective story.[122] I believe we could call Usher's picture the x-ray of a landscape.

Is it too far a flight of speculation, spurred by a journalist's comparison, but also by the uncanny experience generated by most of the scores of phantom rides I have seen from film archives around the world, to identify early cinema's seemingly realistic genre of mobile landscapes with Poe's picture that strips landscape of all spatial and temporal moorings? I feel it is greatly significant that phantom ride films appear around the time that artists such as Monet, Cezanne and Seurat crafted a new era in painting partly by rethinking the form of the landscape. But rather than rehearse a well-known European-based narrative, I want to return to the American tradition, and consider two final heirs of the Hudson River School and its gradual reworking and dismantling of the Claudean Ideal Landscape: George Inness and Ralph Blakelock.

Both painters could be described as heirs of the original school of American landscape painting, the Hudson River School of Cole, Durand, Cropsey, Gifford and others which had revivified the Claudean Ideal Landscape by giving it an American urgency. Working primarily in the later half of the nineteenth century, both Inness and Blakelock were aware of the later development in European landscape painting, of first the Barbizon school and then the Impressionists.[123] While each acknowledged an influence from these movements, they also maintained their distance from them, especially in regard to painting from nature. With only a few exceptions, neither attempted to paint existing landscapes, remaining faithful to the ideal of the Claudean landscape as a synthesis of various elements, recalled and reassembled.[124] Blakelock's landscape seem to recycle a nocturnal shadow of the Claudean Ideal Landscape, the golden sunlight given over to a pale moonlight that seems more like a dark melancholic sun than a nocturnal view. I am certainly not claiming that these artists, perhaps the least photographic of American landscape painters, produced 'cinematic images'. But I feel they both bring the American landscape tradition to a culmination, in ways that recall (but never actually resemble visually) the uncanny aspect of the phantom rides, especially seen through the filter of Usher's anti-landscape.

Rachael DeLue reminds us that the original reception of Inness's landscapes found them violent and shocking, even describing them as seeming to rush toward the viewer from off the wall.[125] Partly because Inness still makes reference to the schemata of the Ideal Landscape, less ignoring its constraints than contradicting them, his late paintings seem to me to recall the phantom ride's reversal of spectator position from the Ideal Landscape through its extreme fulfilment of its fantasy of penetration. Using painterly means rather than contradictory psychophysical sensations of motion, Inness too transforms our sense of horizon and foreground, disorienting our relation to the imaginary scene. As DeLue describes it, some of his paintings seem to stack multiple horizons on top of each other.[126] Likewise Inness frequently transfers the blurring, which as atmospheric perspective gave the Ideal Landscape an effect of distance, to the foreground.[127] Rather than a stable foreground providing an inviting entrance way and place for contemplation to the viewer, DeLue sees Inness's foregrounds as 'expanding and recalcitrant' and in his later landscapes describes them as 'sliding'.[128] These reversals, DeLue argues powerfully, 'compromise any fantasy of entrance and traversal'.[129] DeLue demonstrates that in his engagement with and undermining of the conventions of the Ideal Landscapes, 'Inness's landscapes are ever in process, are ever engaged in working out a proper way to conceive of the relation between self and world, eye and truth'.[130] Inness's work challenges viewers to renegotiate their sense of space and image, a process keenly aware of its own stages of development, as DeLue puts it 'creating an effect of gradual unfolding and continual flux'.[131] As such, they both recall the irresistible motion of the phantom ride and offer a response, reclaiming a form of contemplation proper to a world in dissolution.

The dissolution one senses in Ralph Blakelock's Moonlights, the series of almost obsessively similar nocturnal landscapes he produced in the 1880s through the 1890s seems to chronicle a more personal struggle with the coherence of the landscape, whether one relates it directly to the artist's growing madness or more generally with a sense of a crisis of subjectivity attempting to define a stance in the face of not only incoherent space but disillusioning history.[132] The usually minuscule Native American figures that populate many of Blakelock's landscapes recall a long tradition of Indian *staffage* figures contemplating the landscape, providing a recognizable allegory not only of wilderness, but of a vanishing past. These Native American figures cast a wistful gaze at the landscape inevitably evoking their ultimate displacement from their homeland as one of the consequences of the magisterial gaze. These images sentimentalize the Indians even as compositional schemes naturalize their vanishing, like the brilliant coloured foliage of a Hudson Valley autumn. Blakelock, while clearly drawing as much on romantic clichés as on his own direct experience of Native American life in his youthful trips to the West, rarely sentimentalizes his figures, yet the sense of their transience extends to every aspect of the canvas.[133] It is not simply the Indians that are being displaced here: a whole world appears to be fading, growing darker and paler in moonlight.

Compared to Inness's constant experimentation with spatial effects, his demand on the viewer to find new ways of orienting oneself to his montage of compositional schemes, Blakelock seems fixated on an inflexible version of the Ideal Landscape, almost schematic in form. Particularly in the Moonlight canvases, Blakelock's skein of spiky-leaved trees punctured by irregular patches of moonlight seem highly theatrical in effect, recalling the two-dimensional coulisses of the baroque theatre that inspired Claude. These arboreal frames, protective in their embracing gesture and yet carrying a sinister overtone in their prickly form, sharpened by the impasto of Blakelock's paint, seem to frame a fairyland set, both enchanted and haunted. Fantasies here derive less from imagined voyages into a depth that appears too blurred to ever be physically navigable, than from the almost hallucinatory varied textures and colours that Blakelock built up through his fanatically worked-over surface, applying layer upon layer of paint, and then scrapping, polishing and gauging it with palate knife and pumice stone and even subjecting the canvas to running water.[134] The effect is not only deeply tactile, creating a modernist push-pull between surface and depth, but sparkles with points of colour and a variety of textures, evoking the experience of sight at low light levels in which the physiology of the eye competes with the forms of the world in creating a swim and play of colours, phosphemes and optical eccentricities. In complete contrast to the sunlit vision of the Impressionists, Blakelock evokes a uniquely beautiful night-vision, uncanny in its familiarity, surprising in its continually renewing variations.

One of Blakelock's last canvases before his decades-long institutionalization for dementia praecox bears the title *Ghost Dance* or alternatively *The Vision of Life*. Blakelock's trees framing a moonlit distance provide a theatrical backdrop to the image. The foreground, made up of a field of variegated colours and textures, provides a stage for a cluster of midground figures primarily on the right of the canvas. A fairly uniform yellowish brown defines all these figures whose outlines are impossibly blurred and vague, but human forms and postures are recognizable, even if individual features remain effaced. The composition recalls to some extent Blakelock's *Pipe Dance* and this resemblance (along with the title) encourages the viewer to see these hardly identifiable figures as Native Americans performing a dance. Scrutiny of the figures can only yield Rorschach-like projections, but to my eye they are not exclusively Native Americans, as some forms recall figures in evening wear, creating an allegorical *danse macabre*, rather than an ethnographic image.

Nonetheless, I strongly believe that Blakelock intended the canvas to recall his Native American landscapes. Although it has been questioned whether Blakelock intended the title *Ghost Dance*, it opens the painting to a rich series of associations.[135] The image seems to show ghosts, whether of Native Americans or of humanity in general, vanishing as they dance. In the mid-1890s when the canvas was painted, the term would recall the Ghost Dance of the Plains tribes, the millennial movement headed by prophet Wovoka which predicted a return of the original Native American way of life, the replenishing of the buffalo herds, the vanishing of the White Men and the return of the dead, who would arrive carried on a huge train. The dance that Wovoka taught the tribes took the form of a solemn circling motion lasting sometimes for days, designed to invoke visions and to generate the energy needed to bring the dead to life. The movement represented the last gasp of Native American resistance to White Manifest Destiny. The Federal Government responded brutally to the basically peaceful movement and in 1890 massacred over 150 Lakota men, women and children at Wounded Knee.[136]

Both Inness and Blakelock (who certainly knew each other, occasionally painting in the same studio buildings in New York City and living in the same area of northern New Jersey) were members of Swedenborgian congregations devoted to the teachings of the eighteenth-century Swedish visionary who exerted a profound influence on nineteenth-century American culture.[137] Both were also involved with the Spiritualist movement, that pervasive nineteenth-century attempt to found a new religion on communication with the dead (which may have influenced Wovoka as well). Inness was the more articulate both visually and verbally, and as DeLue shows, his experimental approach to landscapes derives from a desire to push vision beyond itself, '…endeavoring to give men sensuous apprehension of… that which is unseen – of that which the Spirit of God working in it reveals'.[138] He added in another instance: 'But God is always hidden, and beauty depends on the unseen, the visible upon the invisible.'[139]

As one of the culminating inventions of the later nineteenth century, the cinema emerges from a crisis in the conception of the visible and the invisible, a crisis provoked by progressive pressure placed on the technologies of sight, what film theorist Commolli called a 'frenzy of the visible', which took many forms, both physical and metaphysical.[140] Early cinema's most powerful landscape form, the phantom ride, grew out of a centuries-long process by which nature was turned into pictures, culminating in the concept of the picturesque. In America the encounter with a vast and virginal natural terrain provoked an ambivalent confluence of aesthetic appreciation with a technologically accelerated penetration of nature. American landscape painting charted a growing crisis inherent in a pastoral ideal achieved by technological means. New technologies in the representation of landscape, from the panorama to the motion pictures endeavoured to increase the sensation of immersion into a represented space, pursuing an almost obsessive goal of total spectator involvement. But the dialectic such systems set up between immersion and insulation created new paradoxes of spectatorship. As the phantom ride seemingly achieves a complete grasp and penetration of a landscape, this new technological sublime simultaneously encounters a sense of loss, of dissolution, a phantomization of the experience of self and world. Thus the dawn of cinema, rather than simply perfecting a new technology for the portrayal of landscapes, also inaugurates a new representation of loss in which the *pas de deux* of spectator and landscape becomes a ghostly dance of presence and absence, sensation and distance.

## Notes

1. Renzo Dubbini, *Geography of the Gaze : Urban and Rural Vision in Early Modern Europe* translated by Lydia G. Cochrane (Chicago : University of Chicago Press, 2002), p. 3.
2. Edgar Poe, 'The Domain of Arnheim', in *Poe: Poetry and Tales* (New York: Library of America, 1984), 859.
3. Descriptions of Claude's influential composition can be found in Kenneth Clark, *Landscape into Art* (New York: Harper and Row, 1976), 128, 139; Barbara Novak, *Nature and Culture: American Landscape and Painting 1825–1875* (revised ed.) (New York: Oxford University Press, 1995), 228 and Wilton and Barrington, *American Sublime: Landscape Painting in the United States 1820–1880* (Princeton: Princeton University Press, 2002), 13. A useful summary of the way

these conventions were understood in nineteenth-century America is offered by Rachael Ziady DeLue in *George Inness and the Science of Landscape* (Chicago: University of Chicago Press, 2005), 97–103, as well as the description of the Ideal Landscape offered by Stephan Oettermann in *The Panorama: History of a Mass Medium* (New York: Zone Books, 1997), trans. Deborah Lucas Schneider, 25–30.

4. Quoted in John Dixon Hunt, *Gardens and the Picturesque* (Cambridge: MIT Press, 1997), 106.
5. Allen S. Weiss, *Mirrors of Infinity: The French Formal Garden and Seventeenth Century Metaphysics* (Princeton: Princeton Architecture Press, 1995), 16.
6. Dubinni, 118–120; Hunt, 179.
7. Hunt, 174–179.
8. Ibid., 175.
9. Ibid., 178.
10. Arnaud Maillet, *The Claude Glass: Use and Meaning of the Black Mirror in Western Art* (New York: Zone Books, 2004), trans. Jeff Fort, 86.
11. Ibid., 110.
12. Ibid., 88.
13. Ibid., 96
14. Scott McDonald, *The Garden in the Machine; A Field Guide to Independent Films about Place* (Berkeley: University of California Press, 2001), 429, fn. 36.
15. Rachael Ziady DeLue, 102.
16. Leo Marx, *The Machine in the Garden: Technology and the Pastoral Ideal in America* (New York: Oxford University Press, 1964), 29.
17. Richard Grusin, *Culture, Technology and America's National Parks* (Cambridge: Cambridge University Press, 2004), 9–10.
18. Marx, 225.
19. Quoted in Marx, 249.
20. Marx uses the term 'technological sublime' on 195; he quotes Thoreau on 252. See, also, Allen S. Weiss' insightful essay 'No man's garden', in *Unnatural Horizons: Paradox and Contradiction in Landscape Architecture* (Princeton: Princeton Architectural Press, 1998), 84–107.
21. Diderot quoted in Bernard Comment, *The Painted Panorama* (New York: Harry Abrams, 1999), 78.
22. DeLue, 127.
23. This political aspect of American landscape painting as embodying manifest destiny and the drive towards expansion has been treated in depth and with insight by Novak, Angela Miller, *The Empire of the Eye: Landscape Representation and American Cultural Politics, 1825–1875* (Ithaca: Cornell University Press, 1993) and Albert Boime, *The Magisterial Gaze: Manifest Destiny and American Landscape Painting 1830–1865* (Washington DC: Smithsonian Institution Press, 1991). See also W. J. T. Mitchell's important essay 'Imperial Landscape', in W. J. T. Mitchell (ed.), *Landscape and Power* (Chicago: University of Chicago Press, 2002), 5–34.
24. Boime, 75–76.
25. Barbara Novak, 165. A similar point is made by Susan Danly in 'Introduction', in Susan Danly and Leo Marx (eds), *The Railway in American Art: Representations of Technological Change* (Cambridge: MIT Press, 1988), 13.
26. Novak, 170.
27. Leo Marx, 'The railroad-in-the-landscape: An iconological reading of a theme in American art', in Danly and Marx (eds).

28. Detailed reading of Cole's *Course of Empire* can be found in Novak, 10–14; Angela Miller, 21–37 and Andrew Wilton and Tim Barringer, *American Sublime: Landscape Painting in the United Sates 1820–1880* (Princeton: Princeton University Press, 2002), 95–109.

29. Novak, 172–174. Novak contrasts this expanse of stumps to the more limited and symbolic use of the tree stumps in such clearly celebratory paintings as Asher B. Durand's *Progress* from 1853. However, one could compare the stumps here to Sanford Robinson Gifford's *Hunter Mountain Twilight* from 1866 whose meaning is equally debated (see Wilton and Barringer, 120–121).

30. Inness quoted in DeLue, 117. See also the discussion of this painting in Boime, 125–127.

31. Boime, 128.

32. See Susan Danly in 'Introduction', *The Railway in American Art*, 1–50; Novak, 175–177.

33. See, for instance, the chromolithograph published by Rand McNally and Company of the Rock Island Route reproduced in *The Railway in American Art*, 31. The importance of guide books and their illustrations in the American landscape tradition is carefully developed in the fine dissertation by Matt Johnson, 'Surveying the Nation in Time: Landscape in Nineteenth-century Print Culture' (University of Chicago, Department of Art History, Autumn 2004) with great insight into the symbiosis between railway travel and landscape culture.

34. Danley, 13.

35. Novak, 176.

36. Wolfgang Schivelbusch, *The Railway Journey: Trains and Travel in the Nineteenth Century* (New York: Urizen Press, 1979), 62.

37. Ibid., 66.

38. Quoted in Dubbini, 135. Although dealing mainly with formal French gardens, Allen S. Weiss's discussion of Le Nôtre's seventeenth-century gardens at Vaux–le-Vicomte and Versailles provides a brilliant presentation of these gardens as a dramatic succession of views, *Mirrors of Infinity*, 39–61.

39. Quoted in Dixon, 179.

40. Stephan Oettermann, *The Panorama: History of a Mass Medium* (New York: Zone Books, 1997), trans. Deborah Lucas Schneider, 7.

41. Ibid., 15.

42. Comment, *Panorama*, 100.

43. Ibid., 77.

44. Ibid., 161.

45. Oettermann, 21.

46. Quoted in Comment, 97.

47. Oettermann, 22.

48. Ibid., 31.

49. Quoted in Novak, 71.

50. Oettermann, 105.

51. Ibid., 110.

52. On audiences for the panorama see Oettermann, 30–31, and Comment, 115–119.

53. See Comment's discussion of this debate, 84–88.

54. Quoted in Angela Miller, 'The panorama, the cinema and the emergence of the spectacular', *Wide Angle* 18(2) (1996), 35–69; 44.

55. Oettermann, 244. Emily Godbey's recent dissertation, 'Rubbernecking and the Business of Disaster' (Department of Art History, University of Chicago, Summer, 2005) presents an original and insightful discussion of the relation between the spectacle of sensation and the nineteenth century sublime.

56. Gunning, 'Animated pictures: Tales of cinema's forgotten future after 100 years of films', in Christine Geldhill and Linda Williams (eds), *Re-inventing Film Studies* (London: Arnold Press, 2000).
57. On the moving panorama see Oettermann, 323–342, Comment, 62–65.
58. Oettermann, 323.
59. Angela Miller, 87.
60. Iris Cahn, 'The changing landscape of modernity', *Wide Angle* 18(3), 1996, 85–100; 89.
61. Quoted in Wilton and Barringer, 13.
62. Quoted in ibid., 22.
63. McDonald, 23–30.
64. Wilton, 'The sublime in the old world and the new', in Wilton and Barringer, 17.
65. Quoted in Novak, 24.
66. Quoted in ibid., 27.
67. See, for instance, the comments of Heinrich von Kleist about a panorama of Rome and the description of the Mareorama in Comment ,104.
68. Kenneth Clarke repeats this anecdote in *Landscape into Art*, 187, without vouching for its reliability.
69. Emily Godbey, 'Rubbernecking'.
70. Schivelbusch, 66.
71. Quoted in Miller, 163.
72. Jules Verne, *Around the World in Eighty Days* (New York: William Morrow & Company, 1988), trans. George Makepeace Towle, 52.
73. Peter Galassi, *Before Photography: Painting and the Invention of Photography* (New York: Museum of Modern Art, 1981), 29.
74. Quoted in Comment, 99–100.
75. Galassi, 19.
76. *Cosmos: A Sketch of the Physical Description of the Universe* was the title of Alexander von Humboldt's magnum opus published in five volumes between 1845 and 1862. See the two-volume reprint edition by John Hopkins University Press, 1997. It greatly influenced American landscapists, especially Frederic Church.
77. Comment, 86.
78. On Muybridge's panorama, see: David Harris with Eric Sandweiss, *Eadweard Muybridge and the Photographic Panorama of San Francisco, 1850–1880.* (Montreal : Centre Canadien d'Architecture, 1993).
79. Evelyn Onnes-Fruiterma, 'Of panoramas old and new', in *The Magical Panorama* (The Hague: B.V Panorama Mesdag, 1996), 32–35; Comment, 242–245.
80. Comment, 138.
81. Ibid., 144.
82. Emmanuelle Toulet, 'Cinema at the Universal Exposition, Paris 1900', *Persistence of Vision* 9 (1991), 10–36.
83. Novak, 29.
84. Comment, 145.
85. Gunning, 'The cinema of attractions: Early film, its spectator and the avant-garde', in Thomas Elsaesser and Adam Barker (eds), *Early Film* (London: British Film Institute, 1989).
86. Gunning, 'Before documentary: Early non-fiction films and the "view" aesthetic', in Daan Hertogs and Nico De Klerk (eds), *Uncharted Territory: Essays on Early Nonfiction Film* (Amsterdam: Nederlands Filmmuseum, 1997).

87. On early travel cinema see Charles Musser's classic essay, 'The Travel Genre', *Iris* 2(1) (1984), 47–60: Jennifer Peterson's fine dissertation soon to be published in a greatly revised form as a book from Duke University Press and my own essay 'The view aesthetic', in Hertogs and De Klerck.

88. The classic pioneering work on the train and the cinema is Lynn Kirby's *Parallel Tracks: The Railroad and Silent Cinema* (New York: Duke University Press, 1997). My own essays on the relation between cinema and the railroad include: 'Systematizing the electric message', in Charlie Keil and Shelly Stamp (eds), *American Cinema's Transitional Era: Audiences, Institutions. Practices* (Berkeley: University of California Press, 2004), 15–50; 'The whole world within reach: Travel images without borders', in Roland Cosandey and Francois Albera (eds), *Cinema sans frontiers 1896–1918/ Images across Borders: Internationality in World Cinema: Representations, Markets, Influences and Reception* (Editions Payot Lausanne (Switzerland), 1995) and 'An unseen energy swallows space: Early film and the avant-garde', in John Fell (ed.), *Film Before Griffith* (Berkeley: University of California Press, 1984).

89. Charles Musser points out this double rivalry of motion picture companies and railroads in *Edison Motion Pictures, 1890–1900: An Annotated Filmography* (Washington, DC: Smithsonian Institution Press, 1997), 260.

90. See my 'An aesthetic of astonishment: Early film and the [in]credulous spectator', in Linda Williams (ed.), *Viewing Positions* (New Brunswick: Rutgers, 1995). An argument for the possibility of such a confusion is made by Stephen Bottomore in 'The panicking audience? Early cinema and the train effect', *Historical Journal of Film Radio and Television*, 19(2) (1999), 189–190.

91. The reviews from the *New York Telegraph* for 15 October and then 17 October 1896 are reprinted in Kemp Niver, *Biograph Bulletins 1896–1908* (Los Angeles: Locare Research Group, 1971), 14.

92. Comment, 103. Yuri Tsivian supplies a masterful reading of films of the arrival of a train genre in Russia, in *Early Cinema in Russia and its Cultural Reception* (Chicago: University of Chicago Press, 1998), 135–147.

93. Klaus-Jurgen Sembach, *Art Nouveau: Utopia: Reconciling the Irreconcilable* (Köln: Taschen, 1996), 9.

94. O. Winter, *New Review* Feb. 1896, reprinted in Colin Harding and Simon Popple, *In the Kingdom of Shadows: A Companion to Early Cinema* (London Cygnus Arts), 1996) 13.

95. Maxim Gorky reprinted in Jay Leyda, *Kino: A History of the Russian and Soviet Film* (London: Unwin, 1960), pp. 407–409.

96. Tsivian, 146–147.

97. Review from *The New York Mail and Express*, 13 October 1896, reprinted in Niver, 2.

98. As I have indicated elsewhere, this experience of startling emergence of figures from a screen had also appeared in a visual entertainment of the early nineteenth century, although one rarely associated with landscape painting, The Phantasmagoria of Philipstahl and Robertson. See Gunning, 'Phantasmagoria and the manufacturing of illusions and wonder: Towards a cultural optics of the cinematic apparatus', in Andre Gaudreault, Catherine Russell and Pierre Veronneau (eds), *The Cinema, A New Technology for the 20th Century* (Editions Payot Lausanne (Switzerland), 2004), 31–44.

99. Barry Salt, *Film Style and Technology History and Analysis* (London: Starwood, 1983), 42.

100. Cahn, 98.

101. Quoted in Musser, *Edison Motion Pictures*, 208.

102. Musser, 'Travel film genre', in Musser, *The Emergence of Cinema: The American Screen to 1907* (New York: Charles Scribner's' Sons, 1990), 429.

103. Edison Catalogue 1903.

104. Emmanuelle Toulet, *Persistence of Vision*.

105. Reprinted in Musser, *Edison Motion Pictures*, 511.

106. Edison Catalogue 1902.

107. See my discussion of such thrills in relation to early cinema in: 'An Aesthetic of Astonishment: Early Film and the [In]Credulous Spectator' in *Viewing Positions*, ed. Linda Williams (New Brunswick: Rutgers, 1995).

108. Novak, 175; Danly, 7.

109. Hales Tours are described in Musser, *The Emergence of Cinema*, 429–431. Raymond Fielding's pioneering essay, 'Hale's Tours: Ultrarealism In the Pre-1910 Motion Picture', in *Cinema Journal*, Vol 10, No. 1, (Autumn, 1970), pp. 34–47, provided the first scholarly account of this phenomenon, although he errs is claiming it began at the 1903 St. Louis Fair.

110. Comment, 130.

111. Gunning, 'An unseen energy swallows space: Early film and the avant-garde', in John Fell (ed.), *Film Before Griffith* (Berkeley: University of California Press, 1984) and 'The whole town's gawking: Early cinema and the visual experience of modernity', *Yale Journal of Criticism*, 7(2) (1994). Charles Musser in his article on the 'Travel genre' cites another account of the same film written around the same time, published in *The Phonoscope*. It reads, in part: 'He was a passenger on a phantom train ride that whirled him through space at nearly a mile a minute…There was nothing to indicate motion save that shining vista of track that was eaten up irresistibly, rapidly and the disappearing panorama of banks and fences. The train was invisible…and faraway… was the mouth of the tunnel and toward it the spectator was hurled as if a fate was behind him and the spectator being flung through the cavern with the demoniac energy behind him. The shadows, the rush of invisible force and the uncertainty of the issue made one instinctively hold his breath as when on the edge of a crisis that might become a catastrophe.' Musser, 'Travel genre', 53–54. The similarities between the two descriptions are striking, and either indicates a broadly common mode of experiencing this film, or less excitingly, a single author. I suspect the former, but can't rule out the latter.

112. *New York Mail and Express*, 25 September 1897, reprinted in Niver, 29.

113. Christian Metz, *The Imaginary Signifier: Psychoanalysis and the Cinema* (Bloomington: Indiana University Press, 1982), 96.

114. Ralph Waldo Emerson, 'Nature', in *Nature: Addresses and Lectures* (Philadelphia: David McKay Publisher, n.d), 14. See Novak, 197.

115. Walter Benjamin, 'On some motifs in Baudelaire', in Howard Eiland and Michael Jennings (eds), *Selected Writings Vol. 4 1938–1940* (Cambridge: Harvard University Press, 2003), 341.

116. Noel Burch, *Life to Those Shadows* (Berkeley: University of California Press, 1990).

117. This thought, besides being prompted by the anonymous journalist and by Kant's concept of the sublime as an experience that makes us reflect ultimately on perception itself, is also inspired by Annette Michelson's pioneering essay, 'Towards snow', *Art Forum* 9(10) (1971), 30–37, in which Michael Snow's extraordinary film *Wavelength* is seen as a phenomenological reflection of consciousness. Thinking about Snow's film in relation to Poe's painting could be a fascinating exercise. It is no coincidence that Snow has made perhaps the greatest of all landscape films, *La Region Centrale*.

118. 'On beginning the treatment (further recommendations on the technique of psycho-analysis)', in *The Standard Edition of the Complete Psychological Works of Sigmund Freud* (London: The Hogarth Press, 1958), trans. James Strachey, Vol. XII, 135.

119. Edgar Allan Poe, 'The Fall of the House of Usher', in *Poe: Poetry and Tales* (New York: Library of America, 1984), 325.

120. Charles Olson, *Call Me Ishmael* (San Francisco: City Lights Books, 1947) p.12.

121. Charles Olson, *Call Me Ishmael: A Study of Melville* (San Francisco: City Lights Books, 1947), 12.
122. Walter Benjamin, 'The Paris of the Second Empire in Baudelaire', in Walter Benjamin, *Selected Writings*, vol. 4, 27.
123. Inness's criticism of the Impressionists is quoted by DeLue on 205.
124. DeLue, 32.
125. Ibid., 11.
126. Ibid., 55.
127. Ibid., 79.
128. Ibid., 116; 193.
129. Ibid., 108.
130. Ibid., 82.
131. Ibid., 215.
132. The major accounts of Ralph Blakelock's life and painting are: Abraham A. Davidson, *Ralph Albert Blakelock* (University Park: Pennsylvania State Press, 1996) and Glyn Vincent, *The Unknown Night: The Genius and Madness of R. A. Blakelock, An American Painter* (New York: Grove Press, 2003).
133. Davidson discusses Blakelock's Indian paintings, 43–80.
134. Description of Blakelock's technique can be found in Davidson, 202–205.
135. Davidson, 79.
136. See Davidson 77–78. The classic account of the Ghost Dance is James Mooney, *The Ghost Dance Religion and the Sioux Outbreak of 1890* (Chicago: University of Chicago, 1965).
137. Vincent has done important research on Blakelock's Swedenborgian background and his relation to Inness 150–154; 161; 195–196; see also Davidson 130–133. Inness's Swedenborgian background forms an important them in DeLue, especially 42–50.
138. DeLue, 21.
139. Ibid.
140. Jean Louis Comolli, « The Frenzy of the Visible », in The Cinematic Apparatus, ed. Teresa de Lauretis and Stephen Heath, New York, St. Martins Press, 1980.

# PART II

Mapping Cinematic Landscapes

# Chapter 3

## 'One Foot in the Air?' Landscape in the Soviet and Russian Road Movie

Emma Widdis

In a key scene of Andrei Tarkovskii's *Mirror* (1974), the young protagonist comes across two mysterious women in his deserted apartment.[1] They hand him a dusty volume and tell him to read aloud from a marked page. As he does so, the words of the poet Alexander Pushkin (1799–1837) ring around the echoing chambers and peeling walls of the empty space. The text is a letter, written by Pushkin to Count Petr Chaadaev in 1836.[2] It is one of the best-known discussions of the 'problem' of Russian national identity – and specifically, of its relationship with the landscape. The scene acts as a key to the film and, more broadly, to the myth of the Russian landscape or space – the *prostor* (expanse) – and its role in cinema.

Pushkin's letter was written in response to a famous pamphlet or 'philosophical letter', published by Petr Chaadaev in 1836, in which he described Russia as backward, as Europe's 'illegitimate child', mired in the obscurantist traditions of Orthodoxy and Byzantium, with no civilization of its own.[3] In reply, Pushkin did not defend Russia's sorry political state, nor did he deny its separation from the main course of European history, but he did emphasize its greatness. That greatness, he wrote, was rooted in the space itself: 'It was Russia, its immense expanse, that repelled the invasion of the Mongol horde [in the fourteenth century]. The Tatars did not dare to cross our Western boundaries…They withdrew to their deserts, and Christian civilization was saved.'[4] It was this same expanse, Pushkin affirmed, that separated Orthodox Russia irrevocably from Catholic Western Europe and its civilization. But where Chaadaev saw this separateness and difference as the source of Russia's problems, Pushkin saw it as her destiny – and, in a sense, her salvation: 'We have had our own mission.'

Tarkovskii's inclusion of this letter makes Russia, and specifically the Russian space, into a character in the film. In the kaleidoscope of memory and interwoven narratives that make up *Mirror*, the Russian landscape is the only constant, and it returns, vivid and alive, as a kind of refrain. There are two principle landscape images in *Mirror*, and together they provide an instructive introduction to the significance of natural imagery in Soviet cinema more generally. The first, and most frequent, is that of the pastoral, wooded space that surrounds the family's country house (*dacha*) in the protagonist's childhood. This is the landscape of memory: vivid, lush, beautiful – and profoundly subjective. The second appears in an extended sequence near the middle of the film, and pictures the Russian territory more clearly according to the terms of the Pushkin text. Here, we see real documentary footage of soldiers struggling across the mud of the Sivash gorge in the Crimea during the Second World War. In real time, the sheer intractability and hostility of the natural world is vivid and tangible: feet in close up sink into the sodden earth, in a journey that seems to have neither end nor beginning. Minutes later, and now in colour, Tarkovskii pictures a Brueghelian landscape, vast and snow-covered, in which people appear as tiny, irrelevant dots. A young boy, alone, climbs a hill and stands for a long moment, silhouetted against this enormous and indifferent scene which extends in extraordinary depth behind him, before continuing his journey. As documentary and staged footage blur into one, they create a vision of a natural world that both challenges and contains all human experience. Landscape and history are intertwined, man is shown subject to forces far greater than himself, and those forces represent, for a moment, Russia itself – abstracted into a vision of the landscape.

The significance of these visions of intractable nature in Tarkovskii's film is better understood within the specifics of the Soviet context of which he was so much a part. At root, the Soviet utopian dream was a technological one, founded on the ideal of the human conquest of nature, its subjugation to the higher powers of enlightenment reason. Lenin's famous project, announced in 1921, for the 'Electrification of the Soviet Union' was a graphic illustration of this dream, an attempt to incorporate the vast territory of the Soviet Union within a single network. The geographical and geological reality of Russia, however – its scale, its inhospitable Siberian taiga, its endless steppe – made such 'domestication' of nature a particularly challenging, or even impossible, project. Can man control the natural world, Tarkovskii seems to ask, or is it the other way around? What is the relationship between the individual, the collective (Russia, the State) and the physical environment? Situating the intensely personal landscape of the dacha, and of memory, alongside a picture of nature as a vast and indifferent force, Tarkovskii constructs a vision of the natural world which is explicitly non-political, and which cannot be appropriated to the cause of state or collective. His landscapes create a dual image of the natural world, at once protective, private and subjective, and vast, intractable and impersonal. This apparent dichotomy is not unique to this film. It lies, in fact, at the root of representations of landscape in Soviet and Russian cinema, particularly since the Stalin period.

This essay will examine how this dual image of the landscape has emerged in various incarnations of what could be described as Russian 'road movies' or 'travel adventures' since 1930. The 'boundless' territory (so large that, as the poet Tiutchev expressed it, 'it cannot be understood by mind / Cannot be measured by common means'[5]), offers a rich space for exploration, and the motif of travel has been used in differing but consistent ways throughout a century of Soviet and post-Soviet cinema. It begins, indeed, before the age of cinema as a recurrent trope in literary descriptions of the landscape, and even in discussions of Russian national identity. From Nikolai Gogol's famous exclamation in *Dead Souls*: 'Is there a Russian who does not like fast travel?', to the poet Aleksandr Blok's revolutionary poem 'The Scythians' (1918), in which he pictures the destiny of Bolshevik Russia as a 'journey through the steppe', characterized by extraordinary energy and dynamism, one response to the sheer size of the Russian territory has been to formulate images, both real and metaphorical, of travel through it.[6] Pushkin's correspondent, Chaadaev, described Russia as a country of 'nomads':

Don't we all have one foot in the air? We all look as though we are travelling. No one has a definite sphere of existence; no one has proper habits; there are no rules for anything, there is no home base, everything passes, leaving no trace either outside or within us. In our home we are like visitors, among our families we are like strangers, in our cities we are like nomads, more nomadic than those whose animals graze on our steppes, for they are more attached to their deserts than we are to our cities.[7]

For Chaadaev, of course, this was a metaphor for Russia's lack of development; for Blok, however, such nomadism was a symbol of vital revolutionary power. However it is used, the image is resonant – and remains so today.

What, then, of the landscape of the Russian 'travel film'? The Western 'road movie' is a narrative of personal development, expressed through the metaphor of a journey. Particularly associated with the vast spaces of the United States, and with travel by car along its endless highways, it (in contrast to that other product of America's vast terrain, the Western) is premised on technology – the automobile or the motorcycle – as a means of personal escape or liberation.[8] As a genre, loosely understood, the road movie is structured around a relationship between the viewing and experiencing subject (the traveller) and the landscape. In Russia, of course, the scale of territorial expanse is equal or greater to that of the United States, and it is certainly the case that technology – the train and the plane in particular – plays a key role in Soviet travel narratives. In the Soviet case, however, evolutions of the landscape as seen through the gaze of the traveller are inevitably more closely tied to the shifting ideological field with which filmmakers were forced to engage. There will be three main stops on our own journey through Soviet film history, a sketch of the representation of landscape since 1917. Travel films of the Stalin period and the Thaw (1956–1968) will provide a framework through which to understand two more recent Russian films which have had significant impact on the international scene: Andrei Zviagintsev's *The Return* (Vozvrashchenie, 2003) and Boris Khlebnikov and Andrei Popogrebskii's *Koktebel* (2003). Both of these films can be described as post-Soviet road movies, and both, I will suggest, show a 'return' of landscape, but picture the Russian and post-Soviet landscape in new terms.

## Collective landscapes

In the early Soviet period, the question of how to represent the natural world was complex. This, after all, was the age of technology, the age of cities (the urban proletariat was the supposed force behind Marxist revolution). It was the age that saw the transformation of the Russian agricultural system, based on peasant farming, into vast, mechanized collective farms – agricultural factories. The 'conquest' of the vast territory – by railways, hydroelectric power stations, canal systems, etc. – was a clearly stated political aim. In this context, landscape assumed a new role: it was not something to be viewed, or admired, but something to be changed, and the task of revolutionary filmmakers was to echo this transformation. Film, indeed, was itself part of the re-making of the physical world: like man, it could cut up the world and put it back together in revolutionary form. Sergei Eisenstein's 1929 *The Old and the New* or The General Line (General'naia liniia), for example, pictured the real Russian landscape of wooden huts and peasant farming as something to be eliminated, a symbol of the country's economic backwardness, to be overcome by Soviet modernization. At the end of the film, Eisenstein created a model collective farm of the future – white, shining and modern as a symbol of things to come. Another 'classic' of the period, however, Alexander Dovzhenko's *Earth* (Zemlia, 1930) adopted a more lyrical approach to the representation of rural space; it was accused of 'pantheism', of showing *too much* nature. One thing was certain: landscape was ideological.

In the Stalinist 1930s, a new vision of the Soviet countryside began to emerge. As the revolutionary avant-garde gave way to the conservatism of Socialist Realism, Soviet artists were called on to tell simple stories of ordinary men and women, to convey a clear political message: that all was well in the Soviet Union under Stalin. In somewhat paradoxical parallel with the mechanization of the countryside under collectivization (initiated in 1929), a genre that we may term the 'collective farm musical' emerged, and pastoral landscapes appeared in Soviet cinema. Films such as Grigorii Alexandrov's *The Happy Guys* (Veselye rebiata, 1934), Alexander Medvedkin's *The Miracle Worker* (Chudesnitsa, 1937), and Ivan Pyr'ev's *The Rich Bride* (Bogataia nevesta, 1937) and later *Cossacks of the Kuban* (Kubanskie kazaki, 1949), pictured the Soviet countryside as a lush idyll in which man and machine worked in harmony. If, in some of these films, technology is paradoxically absent from the film's visual surface, it is present as the ideological subtext of the genre's celebration of Stalinist Collectivization. Notably, these pastoral cinematic landscapes were marked by explicit visual quotation from the well-loved landscape paintings of a group of nineteenth-century artists known as the Itinerants (*peredvizhniki*), which included Isaac Levitan and Ivan Shishkin.[9] Thus they filtered their 'nature' through ideologically acceptable cultural frameworks. As Evgenii Margolit suggests: 'Even in those instants when an image of nature appeared on the screen, it was always framed as merely a sign of nature – nature that had been "acculturated".[10] Thus domesticated and benign, these landscapes posed no threat to the Soviet project of re-making the natural world. Drawing on the traditions of nineteenth-century visual art, they were crucial to the consolidation of the new vision of Russo-Soviet identity that emerged under Stalin, symbols of continuity and tradition. The world may be transformed by collectivization and industrialization, they implied, but it remains Mother Russia all the same – timeless, eternal and unchanging.

Hand in hand with the emergence of the Soviet pastoral, however, came a parallel trope of conquest and adventure, evident in the Stalinist 'travel film'. In real terms, the massive infrastructural projects associated with Stalin's rapid industrialization sent a clear, if utopian, message: the vast 'boundless' space could be tamed and domesticated by Soviet power, transformed from the mysterious *prostor* into the benign provider of the raw materials out of which Soviet civilization was to be built. The task of the Soviet citizen was to participate in this project. Filmic narratives and landscapes were shaped by ideological imperative, and a genre best described as the 'adventure film' proliferated. Heroes such as electrical engineers, geologists, cartographers, set out to pit their wits and strength against the might of the territory. Sergei Gerasimov's *Seven of the Brave* (Semero smelykh, 1937), for example, followed a group of young adventurers on a journey to the hostile reaches of the Arctic North. Its grand panoramas emphasized the sheer force of nature against which its young heroes were pitted. Snow storms, crashing waves and monumental mountainous landscapes predominated, and the human body was shown pointedly diminished against them. The majesty of nature was emphasized, however, only in order to make clear the human achievement in 'taming' and domesticating it, rendering the uninhabitable habitable. The Arctic was 'conquered'.[11]

The dynamic of such Stalinist travel films was that of construction and transformation. In Gerasimov's next film *Komsomolsk* (1939) for example, the heroine heads off by train on a momentous journey that takes her to the Far East; there she joins a band of young pioneers whose task it is to build a new city out of nothing, to foster Soviet civilization at the edges of the empire. In Dovzhenko's *Aerograd* (1935), a similar bunch of enthusiasts aim to build a city on the banks of the Pacific Ocean. Cinematographically, both films use images of the landscape to ideological effect: the scale of their heroes' courage and achievement is in implicit proportion to the scale of the territory that they seek to 'conquer'. In *Aerograd* in particular, long aerial panning shots of the vast territory, across Siberia to the Far East, act as a metaphor for conquest – the seamless cinematic 'eye' is able to encompass, to 'read' and implicitly to *control* the formerly 'ungraspable' expanses of the territory. Travel is a metaphor for conquest.

So the Stalinist 'road' (or train or plane) movie had an ending – and that ending was spatial, temporal and metaphorical: the transformation of the landscape, the creation of the Soviet Utopia in the here-and-now. Its travellers must, by definition, *arrive*. Their journey was, moreover, a collective one: the experience of the individual was of value only as part of the shared endeavour; their personal achievement was a symbol of the achievement of the Soviet state. If the Western road movie can be accused of 'romanticizing alienation', its Soviet version romanticized *participation*: the narrative of personal change became a narrative of *national* self-determination. And although such films were based around travel and forward movement, they pictured the natural world – the landscape – as fundamentally static, a monumental space framed by the film just as it was to be conquered by man. This was nature, as Margolit has suggested, fundamentally 'disconnected from the [human] character'.[12] In contrast to the subjective gaze afforded by the automobile, the train and the plane presented shared views. There were few intimate landscapes in Stalinist cinema; vast panoramas and sweeping aerial views offered a gaze that was implicitly collective.

## Subjective landscapes

After the death of Stalin in 1953, and in particular after Nikita Krushchev's famous 'secret' speech of 1956, in which he denounced Stalin's cult of personality and set in train the period known as the Thaw, landscape assumed a different significance. As Margolit points out, the very term used to describe this period of relative cultural openness is one drawn from nature: the metaphor of spring, of an un-freezing of the static and sterile climate of Stalinism, was evident in many of the first films of the Thaw period.[13] In Felix Mironer and Marlen Khutsiev's *Spring on Zarechnaia Street* (Vesna na Zarechnoi ulitse, 1956), for example, the spring wind acts as a symbol of change. Broadly speaking, the films of the Thaw period are marked by a liberation of landscape. The natural world, with all its seasonal and meteorological change, emerges as more than simply an object to be transformed or conquered; its force is not subject to man. If anything, indeed, that force is appropriated in cinema as a symbol of an emerging conception of individuality – a rejection of the dominant ideal of the collective in official Soviet culture. There is an implied kinship between the unpredictable, uncontrollable natural world and the world of human feelings.

One of the best-known of the Thaw-period films is Grigorii Chukhrai's *Ballad of a Soldier* (Ballada o soldate, 1959), which was awarded the Golden Palm at the Cannes Film Festival in 1960. Despite its focus on a train journey, *Ballad of a Soldier* can be described as closer to the archetype of the 'road movie'. In flash-back, it follows the journey of young Alesha, who sets off for his home village, on short leave from the Front, to help his mother mend her roof. His journey is continually interrupted and profoundly frustrating, and Alesha ultimately arrives home with time only to embrace his mother before rushing back to the Front. Its purpose thus displaced, however, the journey acts as a path to self-knowledge or consciousness for the young protagonist. It presents him with a series of trials and encounters (including a romance) through which he grows in self-awareness. In parallel with this nascent subjectivity, landscape appears as a largely personal and lyrical frame to action. Views of forests from the train window provide, for example, the background that frames Alesha's near-kiss with his new love, Shura. The open Russian plain is the site of his final and emotional encounter with his mother, implicitly the source of his authenticity, and of his 'natural' goodness. Often viewed in close up, his face lit from below, Alesha himself appears as a force of nature – a hero who is instinctively, rather than consciously good – who acts not for any abstract notion of the collective, but for 'others' who are real and tangible. He is part of a contingent natural landscape very different from that of the Stalinist adventure movie.

In Sergei Bondarchuk's *Fate of a Man* (Sud'ba cheloveka, 1959, an adaptation of the short story of the same name by Mikhail Sholokhov), landscape appears in two, or even three different guises. On the one hand there is the world of the hero Sokolov's pre-war past, the memory of which is marked by an apparently organic unity with nature. These memory sequences are often signalled in the film by close ups of leaves, which fade into images of his former life. Despite the limitations of Bondarchuk's black and white stock, these sections are distinguished by brighter light, and by a landscape that is pastoral and lyrical in emphasis. Close ups articulate a relationship between the individual and the natural world: human bodies are frequently brushed by branches; Sokolov and his wife touch leaves as they walk through the countryside around their village. In contrast to this vision of a nurturing earth, when Soklov is taken prisoner the landscape of war is barren, even hostile. The film hints, however, at a redemptive possibility, located in nature: in a dramatic escape scene, Sokolov runs through a forest of birch trees before emerging into a corn field where he takes refuge, crouched and hiding between the towering sheaves of grain. Momentarily protected by nature, he lies flat and stares up, through the corn, towards the sky. This physical contact with the earth enables an apprehension of freedom that is so absolute that he is able to sleep – and he awakens with a jolt to find himself caught by German sniffer-dogs and returned to camp.

In a sense, *Fate of a Man* is a road movie: a man leaves his home (though not by choice) and embarks on a journey of suffering and loss, but ultimately also of reconciliation. The third landscape of the film is that of the present, and the film's flashback structure means that it both begins and ends the narrative. This landscape is, in fact, the same rural Russia that we have seen in Sokolov's past, but changed by war almost beyond recognition. Sokolov's family has been killed, his home destroyed, and he has become a rootless wanderer. He is not alone, however: he has become the adoptive father of a boy who has lost his parents to the war. Together they travel and, the film implies, have the potential to rebuild their world. This space, then, lacks the romanticized lyricism of the landscape of the past, but nor is it the sterile, hostile world of the war. Rather, we sense a new, fragile and transient relationship between the characters and the physical world. Nature is pictured not in soft close ups of the pre-war pastoral, or in the vast intractable panoramas of the war, but in medium-range.

In the subtle gradations of Bondarchuk's natural imagery, we can see how the very representation of landscape in Soviet cinema was ideological. Film offered not just views of the territory, but ways of looking at it (and living it), and defined particular relationships with the territory. The sweeping panoramas of Stalinist cinema were implicitly the gaze of the collective; by contrast, films of the Thaw period offered the subjective close up, a new sensory proximity between man and nature. These small-scale landscapes were a pointed rejoinder to the grand scale of Stalinist cinema. They refused shared meaning. For the group of writers know as the 'village prose' movement (including Fedor Abramov, Valentin Rasputin and Vasilii Belov), rural Russia was a symbol of so-called 'real' Russia, the source of an authentic, pre-Soviet way of life, and form of identity, that might offer a way out of the perceived problems of Stalinism. Turning their gaze away from the city, these writers looked to the village, and to the landscape, to renew Soviet culture. In Alexander Solzhenitsyn's short story, 'Matrena's Home' ('Matrenin Dvor', 1964), for example, the rural space was co-opted as a symbol of a new kind of freedom and continuity – one that had been lost, but which could perhaps be regained.

One of the best-known authors of the 'village prose' movement was also a film director and actor: Vasilii Shukshin. His 1973 film, *Kalina krasnaia* (Snowball Cherry Red) in which he also played the lead role, was adapted from a short story of the same name. Its protagonist, Egor, is an ex-convict, who leaves prison determined to start a new life. Where does he go for that new life? To the countryside, of course. In one scene, as Egor travels to his new world of freedom and purity, he asks his taxi to stop for a moment, jumps out and heads to a roadside birch copse. There, he looks up at the rooks nesting in the tree (a symbol of Russia, of spring and of hope, since Alexei Savrasov's reowned, 'The Rooks Have Returned', of 1871), caresses the tree's bark and embraces it: 'My mother…You've waited for me', he sighs. For Egor, the landscape represents the homeland. But it is a homeland that has nothing to do with the political state of Soviet Russia. It remains unchanging in the face of a difficult history, and as such it contains his hope for the future.

## The new Russian road movie

*Kalina krasnaia* was finished in 1973, in political conditions different from those of the Thaw that had given birth to the original Village Prose movement. Nikita Krushchev had been ousted from power in 1964, and by the beginning of the 1970s the more restrictive political climate now known as 'Stagnation' had begun to take hold. It is therefore perhaps appropriate that Egor's apparently simple equation between nature and purity fails; the rootless ex-convict, who has lived all his life in towns, is unable to settle, even in his pastoral paradise, and eventually dies. The countryside, thus, holds no easy solutions to Russia's ills.

Egor is rootless and restless; as such, he is one of the same nomadic Russians, their 'feet in the air', unable to settle, that Chaadaev described some 150 years earlier. This image continues to have resonance to the present day. In the cinema of the Glasnost and early post-Soviet period (which we may categorize approximately as 1986–1996), in particular, one cinematic response to the break-up of the Soviet Union and the associated collapse of ideological certainties was the representation of spatial disorientation. In 1997, Oksana Bulgakowa described post-Soviet cinema as characterized by 'homelessness':

> The post-Soviet film-hero has no house to live in – that is the statement that the film throws at us – so he finds a refuge for a night or a week in the monument, in the museum, in the zoo or in a strange apartment that belongs to nobody (in any case, not the hero), a permanent temporary state, where the protagonist is a fugitive, an alien. This state of being an 'alien at home' or even 'homeless at home' is the leitmotiv of most urban films of the recent time.[14]

In parallel with this urban 'rootlessness', 'landscape', as either background or protagonist, more or less disappeared. True, Dostal's *Cloud Paradise* (Oblako rai, 1991) shows the protagonist, Kolia, abandon his Petrozavodsk housing estate for a journey to Siberia in a quest for a 'better life'. The film focuses, however, not on the journey and its landscapes, but on his departure. Neither subjective nor collective, nurturing nor hostile, the natural world was often simply absent from early post-Soviet cinema.[15]

The early twenty-first century, however, has seen the emergence of a new type of Russian road movie, and the tentative contours of a new landscape. Parallels between Zviaginstev's *The Return* and Khlebnikov and Popogrebskii's *Koktebel* are easy to find: both feature a journey undertaken by a father and son (or, in the case of *The Return*, two sons) – a journey that is as much psychological as physical. Both journeys are paradigmatic and highly stylized, with understated aesthetics, which offer a radical re-picturing of the Russian space.

*Koktebel* is a film constructed as a journey. But this is a journey with a symbolic end that is always out of sight. It opens *in medias res*, with little explanation of either narrative or location. The nameless father and son at the centre of the film are travellers. They have left their Moscow lives entirely behind them and are headed to Koktebel – a holiday resort on the Crimean Riviera. After the tragic loss of wife and mother, and home, they are on a journey to find happiness, and, as such, their story can be linked to the Russian folk tale (*skazka*), traditionally structured around a similar journey in search of a distant kingdom or better life.[16] As in a folktale, it is journey rather than destination that occupies the body of the film. The imaginary space of the Crimea (a site of exotic landscapes, seaside, sunshine) is juxtaposed with the real space through which the protagonists travel, and until the very last moments, it is the latter that offers the only tangible landscape in the film: the placeless Russian *prostor,* flat, empty and anonymous. Khlebnikov and Popogrebskii take the symbol of Russia's 'boundless' landscape and picture it as lived reality, creating spaces that appear, literally, 'in the middle of nowhere'. The nomadic state of father and son is echoed in the apparent transience and liminality of the 'homes' where they take up temporary residence. Their loneliness and fragility is expressed by the vast, featureless landscapes through which they move.

Following the folkloric tradition, the travellers have three 'encounters', which shape the progress of their journey. The first is with a benign signal-man and railway worker, who finds them stowed illegally on a train, throws them off, but then offers them food and shelter in his own home. Second, they come across a tumbledown house, a parody of the idealized dachas of Chekhov's plays. The father offers labour in exchange for shelter, and works for a while on the owner's roof. Gradually, he is drawn into alcohol-induced bonhomie with their strange, solitary and unsympathetic landlord, until a violent argument forces them to move on, after a violent argument in which the father is shot. This is an encounter with a putative domesticity, as the father enters a relationship with the woman. As the camera lingers on the woman's domestic space (on her hairbrush, cards, photographs, books), its solidity is in pointed contrast to the life of impermanence and transience that father and son have. Yet these symbols of domesticity are not unambiguously positive. For the father, perhaps, they represent a possible future. For the son, on the other hand, they represent a barrier to his dream, and he finally runs away to travel alone to Koktebel. He hitches a lift from a lorry driver, and eventually finds his way to the sea. There, as he sits lonely on a jetty looking out to sea, his father joins him.

*Koktebel* pictures the Russian landscape in early winter, with trees bare of leaves, the earth brown, the sky drained of colour and the first traces of snow on the ground. As such it rejects more stereotyped images of lush summer landscapes or romantic snowbound plains. Father and son's journey is a difficult odyssey, and the landscape through which they move pointedly offers nothing to console. It is devoid of meaning. The film largely lacks either establishing shots or subjective views. As such, it rejects the dual categories of Soviet landscape imagery, and creates instead a symbolically empty space. Frequently interrupted with long darkened frames, which only gradually become light, and force the spectator into a process of spatial orientation, the film makes the landscape physically unwelcoming. Its camera is often static, allowing its human protagonists to move out of the frame, hovering at disconcerting length over empty vistas. In this vision of Russia, telegraph wires and pylons figure as much as birch trees; one pointedly stylized, and unusually colorful, scene shows a mass of denuded birch trunks, darkness behind them, and a wan green grass in front, marked by the stumps of trees that have been felled. Although Koktebel, dream destination, is eventually reached, the future remains uncertain.

Zviagintsev's *The Return* tells the story of two brothers, Andrei (fifteen) and Ivan (twelve), whose father returns after an unexplained absence of twelve years, and who takes them on a journey that is ostensibly a fishing trip, but turns out to be something altogether more mysterious and sinister. The journey takes them to a number of haunting and empty spaces, before ending up on a deserted island in the Lake District north of St Petersburg. The relationship between father and sons is fraught, even violent, wracked with unexpressed questions and answers, and on the island it ends in tragedy. The father is killed trying to reach his son, who has climbed a look-out tower; the two boys load his body onto a boat, row back to land, and then leave, apparently to return home, as the boat-coffin sinks into the water.

The landscape of *The Return* is disconcertingly pared-down and stylized.[17] From the opening sequences, however, nature is clearly a force to be reckoned with: as Ivan stands petrified at the top of an observation tower unable to jump, the water below stretches out, indifferent and immutable, in front of him. Throughout the film, the human body is subject to the moods of the natural world: the narrative is interrupted by a series of sudden storms – leaving Ivan soaked by the roadside, their car caught in the mud, forcing them to run for shelter on the island. Just as *Koktebel* opens to a darkened frame and the sound of pouring water, here nature is alive: water moves, and wind blows through trees, and the film makes such phenomena almost preternaturally tangible. This emphasis on the power of nature is part of the film's stylized, almost mythological narrative and mood, in which the landscape plays an important role. Frames are carefully and consciously composed. In particular, Zviagintsev's cameraman, Mikhail Krichman, makes powerful use of the horizon, which frequently bisects the frame, dividing it into dramatic swathes of light and dark. In much of the film, nature is drained of colour. Elsewhere, as in the sequence which shows father and sons briefly at peace by a lake, the aim of the 'fishing trip' momentarily realized, it is lush and peaceful, saturated with dense green.

Like *Koktebel*, *The Return* pictures essentially static landscapes, which appear out of place within the road movie genre, lacking the momentum and continuity that the genre would suggest.[18] It operates rather as a series of disconnected scenes and encounters, in spaces that are unmapped. Only one section uses the classic road movie trope of the car journey, with familiar shots of apparently endless highways and telegraph poles, and of characters staring out of windows at the passing landscape. Even here, however, Zviagintsev is determined to use space to disconcert, rather than to console, so that the generic views are visually defamiliarized. The first road shot is a static view, with the camera positioned immobile at a distance, watching as the car approaches from afar. Similarly, as the youngest brother Ivan stares vacantly out of the car window, we stare *at* him, but do not share his view. In another shot, the camera hangs back, as the car moves forwards into the distance, hovering over the image of the receding vehicle for a little too long. Later, when Ivan is abandoned on the roadside by his brutal father, the sheer emptiness of the road, and the vast flat spaces around it, create a liminal space in which no-one and nothing is visible. An approaching truck seems to promise narrative development, but simply moves past, its vast size diminishing Ivan's small frame even further, and leaves him to his isolation. Above the flat and low horizon the sky hangs heavy.

For all its familiar scale and flatness, this is a Russian landscape that is almost entirely lacking in traditional signs. In an early scene where the two brothers chase one another home, for example, we pass through an old provincial town, but see its buildings truncated, only at ground level, as the camera determinedly follows the boys' chase. They run alongside a river, on the other side of which we glimpse the tantalizing base of what appears to be an old Russian church, but we are never permitted to see the totality of the view. It is no accident that when they finally arrive at their home, it turns out to be a vast, inexplicably isolated and almost entirely empty building, a curious mix between an elegant, once-grand mansion and former factory. This withdrawal from recognizable space is typical of the film as a whole. Throughout, Zviagintsev rejects the traditional symbols of provincial Russia. In its place, he offers a series of curious landscapes without markers or points of orientation, and entirely un-peopled.

Locating his film in the northern Lake District, Zviagintsev pointedly chooses a landscape that is different from the 'classic' views of Russia. Here we see neither the wide expanses of the agricultural regions south of Moscow, nor the vast scale of the steppe; we see pine forests rather than birch, vast lakes rather than rivers. Water, indeed, plays a key role in the film, with underwater shots providing both a beginning and an end. Like *Koktebel*'s final expanse of sea, *The Return* finishes with a long view of water. Both films use water as metaphor of freedom, which they then set out to interrogate. Indeed, the island in *The Return*, indeed, and the waters that surround it, become a kind of prison, the apotheosis of the film's reduction of landscape to liminal space. Isolated, with its sandy beaches and empty interior, the island is an archetypal adventure space, a kind of Treasure Island of the north. Yet it is also a stark, pared down landscape, which becomes a psychological space. Within it, nothing is explained; the world of questions that the father carries with him (why has he returned, why did he leave in the first place?) assumes physical proportions, most overt in the deserted ruin where he unearths a hidden chest (the significance of which is never revealed), but also in the collage of spatial 'moments' which make up the island's landscape. At one point, on a walk, the boys walk through a forest scene which appears almost enchanted, as sunlight glimmers through its leaves, dappling the ground. Then they emerge into an apparently pastoral landscape of open fields. They find ruins; they camp on white sand beaches; they row around a cove to discover a deserted military base. Simply put, the space doesn't add up. It exists as a composite rather than a whole. As such, its geographical (un)mapping echoes the secret at the heart of the film. Like the narrative, this landscape pointedly eludes signification.

## Landscapes without meaning

The history of representations of the Soviet and Russian landscape is one of ideological imperative. The vast *prostor* has been appropriated, variously, as a symbol of economic backwardness, of pastoral harmony and continuity, of collective courage and power, of individual freedom and subjectivity. It has been called on to represent 'Russia' in all its complexity. The struggle between individual and collective – between visions of the natural world as an index of subjectivity, and its symbolization as a force of history – lies at the root of filmic representations of the Russian landscape, and is particularly clear in images of travel.

There is another kind of landscape available, however. In the final scene of Tarkovskii's *Mirror*, we find ourselves back in the country house where the film first begins. In a remarkably extended panning shot, the camera creates a natural world that is intensely alive: the moss on trees, the green of grass, all emerge with vivid physicality. Finally, as the film ends, the camera draws away into the wood, retreating into the permanence of nature. Ultimately, for Tarkovskii, the natural world transcends the human, evades control. The final scenes of *Mirror* picture a world in which politics are absent – or, at the very least, irrelevant – and in which nature has the last word.

This, in a sense, is what we see in *Koktebel* and *The Return*. In these films, nature is no benign index of subjectivity, no symbol of regrowth and purity as it was in the films of the Thaw period. It is pointedly empty, both physically and metaphorically. It is neither intimate nor grand, subjective nor collective. Yet this anti-symbolic landscape conveys no negative message. It is, instead, part of a long process in post-Soviet culture of *reclaiming* the physical world. After a century in which images were never just images, the attempt to frustrate signification, to picture landscapes which cannot be co-opted to meaning, either personal or universal, but which simply *are*, is an important one. At the beginning of Russian cinema's second century, these films represented a genuinely new departure – a new journey.

## Notes

1. This essay was written in 2003. Due to the length of time that has elapsed between conception and publication, some of my claims regarding Russian cinema that was then 'new' have acquired a historical dimension; likewise, further secondary literature has been published that is not referenced here.
2. Aleksandr Pushkin, Letter to P. Y. Chaadaev, 19 October 1836, in *Sobranie sochinenii v desiati tomakh* (Moscow: Gosudarstvennyoe izdatel'stvo khudozhestvennoi literatury, 1959–62) X (1962): 305–306. All translations are mine unless otherwise stated.

3. P. Y. Chaadaev, 'Letters on the philosophy of history', in W. J. Leatherbarrow and D. C. Offord (trans and eds), *A Documentary History of Russian Thought from the Enlightenment to Marxism* (Ardis, 1987), 67–79 (69).

4. Pushkin, Letter to Chaadaev, 36.

5. F. I. Tiutchev, *Polnoe sobranie stikhotvorenii* (Leningrad: Biblioteka poeta, 1987), 229.

6. Nikolai Gogol, *Sobranie sochinenii v vos'mi tomakh* (Moscow, 1984) v, 248; A. A. Blok, *Stikhotvoreniia*. 3 vols (St Petersburg, 1995) III, 286.

7. Chaadaev, 68.

8. See *The Road Movie Book*, edited by Steven Cohan and Ina Rae Hark (London: Routledge, 1997), 1–2.

9. Medvedkin, indeed, made this visual intertext explicit when he wrote in his notes towards the film: 'I can't do it better than Levitan!'

10. Margolit, 'Landscape, with Hero', in Alexander Prokhorov (ed.), *Springtime for Soviet Cinema: Re/Viewing the 1960s* (Pittsburgh Russian Film Symposium, 2001), trans. Dawn Seckler, 29–41 (31).

11. See John McCannon, 'Tabula rasa in the north: The Soviet arctic and mythic landscapes in Stalinist popular culture', in Evgeny Dobrenko and Eric Naiman (eds), *The Landscape of Stalinism: The Art and Ideology of Soviet Space* (Seattle: Washington University Press, 2003), 241–261. My own *Visions of a New Land: Soviet Cinema from the Revolution to the Second War* (New Haven: Yale University Press, 2003) discusses these issues in more detail.

12. Margolit, 31.

13. Margolit, 33.

14. Oksana Bulgakova, 'Constructing the past in contemporary Russian cinema: images of architecture, or where the Russians live in Russian films', in Gregory Freidin, *Russia at the End of the Century: Culture and its Horizons in Politics and Society* (Online volume of conference papers. Stanford University, 2000: http://www.stanford.edu/group/Russia20/volumepdf/bulgakowa.pdf), 6.

15. This account is not complete, of course. The films of Nikita Mikhalkov are a notable, and important, exception. Mikhalkov exploits the myth of the Russian landscape as a site of authenticity untainted by politics and history. As such, he answers a popular demand for historical continuity. From a different perspective, might also consider *Rogozhkin's Peculiarites of the National Hunt* (Osobennosti natsional'noi okhoty, 1995).

16. See Vladimir Propp, *Morphology of the Folktale* (Austin: University of Texas Press, 1994).

17. Ziaginstev also makes interesting symbolic use of landscape in his more recent *The Banishment* (Izgnanie, 2007).

18. Vladimir Padunov, Review of *Koktebel* (2003), (http://www.kinokultura.com/reviews/R103 koktebel.html).

# Chapter 4

Landscape of the Mind: The Indifferent Earth in Werner Herzog's Films

Brad Prager

T he German director Werner Herzog is a frequent champion of the visual over the verbal. While a preference for images is nothing unusual for filmmakers, Herzog spends more time than most explicitly theorizing about their importance. In Les Blank's documentary *Werner Herzog Eats His Shoe* (1980), Herzog asserts that we will become extinct as a civilization if we fail to produce 'adequate images'. He pleads:

> Our civilization doesn't have adequate images, and I think a civilization is doomed or is going to die out like dinosaurs if it does not develop an adequate language or adequate images. I see it as a very, very dramatic situation. For example, we have found out that there are serious problems facing our civilization, like energy problems, or environmental problems, or nuclear power and all this, or over-population of the world. But generally it is not understood yet that a problem of the same magnitude is that we do not have adequate images, and that's what I'm working on – a new grammar of images.

More recently, Herzog has added:

> We need images in accordance with our civilization and our innermost conditioning, and this is the reason why I like any film that searches for new images no matter in what direction it moves or what story it tells. One must dig like an archaeologist and search our violated landscape to find anything new. It can sometimes be a struggle to find unprocessed and fresh images.[1]

In his search through 'violated' terrain in pursuit of something new, Herzog has presented viewers with an endless variety of landscapes. There are Alaskan, Swiss and Bavarian ones in *Heart of Glass* (1976), South American ones in *Scream of Stone* (1991), *Aguirre* (1972) and *Fitzcarraldo* (1982), Pakistani ones in *The Dark Glow of the Mountains* (1984) and Kuwaiti ones in *Lessons of Darkness* (1992), to name a few. In the following chapter, I attempt to elucidate the goal of Herzog's archaeological quest, paying specific attention to his depiction of landscapes. I first ground my observations in a national and historical context, describing how Herzog's work can be seen to represent certain specifically Germanic tendencies, and I then draw conclusions concerning the nature of the existential and philosophical concerns that suffuse his cinematic preoccupations.

Herzog's camera studies and surveys landscapes in order to act on two related agendas. On the one hand, he wants to show us the world in ways that we have not seen before, or provide us with 'fresh images'. With the intention of privileging his own cinematic aesthetics over the reifying effects of capitalism, Herzog rejects the kind of processed images that have become symptomatic of US advertising or of cable news. According to him, such images plague us as would a disease. In *Werner Herzog Eats His Shoe*, he explains that television 'is just ridiculous and destructive'. He adds,

> It kills us. And talk shows will kill us. They kill our language, so we have to declare holy war against what we see every single day on television commercials…I think there should be real war against commercials, real war against talk shows, real war against 'Bonanza', and 'Rawhide.'

But secondly, and perhaps more significantly, Herzog wants us to resist viewing the world and his films through the lens of our rational tendencies, and view them sensually instead. To cite one example, in *Fata Morgana* (1970), Herzog includes a high-angle shot taken from a helicopter of thousands of flamingos moving swiftly across the Kenyan landscape. From that distance and at that speed, the birds are hardly recognizable as flamingos, and on the director's commentary that accompanies the DVD, Herzog explains that he wants it that way. He says that these images should not resemble images that one would find on the *Discovery Channel*; the sequence is only supposed to wash over the viewer, making the same strange and sensual impression that it would on a visitor from outer space seeing Earth for the first time, one who has no categories with which to define the colours and shapes of the planet. In this way, one can understand his often repeated statements that the films *Fata Morgana* and *Lessons of Darkness* were really intended to be works of science fiction more than anything else.[2]

While Herzog has an overall resistance to putting things into conventional language, he has a particularly strong aversion to the academic and alienated grammar of philosophers. There are numerous instances in his films in which such rhetoric itself is ridiculed. The figure of the philosopher in *The Enigma of Kaspar Hauser* (1974), for example, is made laughable, as are the 'scientific' pursuits of the manipulative doctor in Herzog's *Woyzeck* (1979). Even though the prose of his screenplays often tends towards poetry – especially in the cases of the narration accompanying *Lessons of Darkness* and *Fata Morgana* – Herzog works against any overtly rational articulations that would interfere with what he generally describes as the 'ecstatic' experience of viewing his films. The director explains:

> I have never set out to imbue my films with literary or philosophical references. Film should be looked at straight on, it's not the art of scholars but of illiterates. You could even argue that I am illiterate. I have never read a lot or thought about philosophical themes that I could then shoot through these stories I tell. For me it is much more about real life than about philosophy. All my films have been made without this kind of contemplation.[3]

Herzog's attitude stems from a distrust of cognitive categories of perception as they are given to us through language. Yet insofar as he has an enthusiasm for poetic expression, it is clear that he does not distrust all forms of language. In comparing his work with other directors with a similar interest in cinematic landscapes (primarily Terence Malick and Stan Brakhage), the critic Noël Carroll explains:

> it is not just language, literally construed, that these filmmakers distrust, but everything that language – conceived of as a socially inculcated filter of experience – can, in a rather broad sense, be made to stand for. And that can be quite a lot.[4]

Of course one should not seek to make Herzog's philosophical aesthetics consistent through and through. Although one hears the distinctively Germanic echo of Heidegger's discussion of 'chatter' (*Gerede*), and even of Adorno's contempt for 'jargon' in Herzog's views, his statements have only the rigour required of practitioners of the visual arts, rather than that which would be appropriate to the sphere of the dialectician. Herzog's main goal is to defamiliarize us from our own landscapes in the hope of providing a sensual experience that stands apart from conventional and academic ways of thinking. Hence he is not only waging a holy war against television, as he declares in *Werner Herzog Eats His Shoe*, but also against rhetoric, in the name of experience, or 'real life'.

Despite his intention to provide us with new images, and with geographies so strikingly unfamiliar that we cannot help but look at them with alien eyes, there is no guarantee that Herzog's landscapes fall beyond the scope of material that has been previously processed. His ravishingly filmed images import their own art historical baggage, and often run the risk of losing their impact, or becoming what Carroll refers to as 'icons of the sublime'.[5] In that the fog covered mountaintops in the film *Heart of Glass*, or the high waterfalls in *Nosferatu* (1979) may call to mind the weighty philosophical suggestion of sublimity, resonances with the history of painting can be a virtue. At the same time, however, such images also risk becoming clichés. Throughout *Heart of Glass*, *Nosferatu* and *Scream of Stone*, Herzog's compositions undeniably recall the work of that sublime German romantic artist Caspar David Friedrich, and in this sense the images cannot be said to be entirely 'new' or 'fresh'. Many of Herzog's shots are composed in a style that resonates with Friedrich's early nineteenth-century works, including *Traveller Overlooking a Sea of Fog* (1818), *Two Men Contemplating the Moon* (1819) and *Morning* (1820–21), to name a few. Herzog openly acknowledges that Friedrich is one among many of his art historical influences, and he also mentions painters associated with the Northern Renaissance such as Matthias Grünewald and Hans Baldung Grien.[6]

Numerous critics such as Christopher Wickham and Lotte Eisner have elaborated on Herzog's association with Friedrich, and in *Herzog on Herzog*, the director explains why he returns to Friedrich and the German Romantic tradition. He says:

> For me a true landscape is not just a representation of a desert or a forest. It shows an inner state of mind, literally inner landscapes, and it is the human soul that is visible through the landscapes presented in my films…This is my real connection to Caspar

David Friedrich, a man who never wanted to paint landscapes *per se*, but wanted to explore and show inner landscapes.[7]

The prevalence of fog and waterfalls, the diminutive human figures and compositions that deny the spectator a point of access where their eye might easily 'enter' the frame, are all echoes of Friedrich's style. However, it is important to point out that Herzog draws not merely upon specific, recurring icons of the sublime, but also upon Friedrich's characteristically romantic inclination to use the landscape as an external representation of the complexities of internal psychology. The aim of such work is to make the fog that dominates our inner lives manifest upon the canvas, or in Herzog's case, upon the screen. With respect to the overgrown jungle in *Aguirre*, for example, Herzog explains: '[it] is really all about our dreams, our deepest emotions, our nightmares. It is not just a location, it is a state of our mind. It has almost human qualities. It is a vital part of the characters' inner landscapes'. He adds, 'The question I asked myself when first confronted by the jungle was "How can I use this terrain to portray landscapes of the mind?"'[8]

Yet while those sequences that linger on Herzog's strange and beautiful landscapes are among the director's most stunning and evocative ones, they sometimes awaken the spectres of German nationalism, and of filmmaking during the Third Reich. Of Herzog's film *Heart of Glass*, for example, Eric Rentschler notes that:

*The Blue Light*, [Leni] Riefenstahl's directorial debut, and *Heart of Glass* bear striking resemblances, in a number of ways. Both films are dramas set in a pre-modern world of pastoral landscapes and sweeping mountains. The iconography in each case draws heavily on nineteenth century German painting. Riefenstahl's film quite explicitly underlines this tradition by having an artist from Vienna journey to the Alpine location: an early shot in fact has him pose as Caspar David Friedrich's *Traveller Overlooking a Sea of Fog*. The final sequence likewise borrows freely from Friedrich's work, especially as the painter strolls through the woods in the morning fog. Herzog just as strikingly evokes this painterly heritage.[9]

While Rentschler does not mean to read Herzog's film, made in an entirely different decade and context, as he would a work by Riefenstahl, such observations confirm that there is an inescapably Germanic element in Herzog's work.

Whether it is the history of German Romanticism, Fascism or even Heideggerian philosophy, one may be inclined to ask whether Herzog's films can be wholly defined by his German identity. Of the desolate landscapes in *Fata Morgana*, the filmmaker's friend Amos Vogel concludes that that work 'could only have emerged from a country ravaged by two world wars, total fascism, the traumas of scientific genocide and saturation bombings'.[10] Likewise, a film such as *Little Dieter Needs to Fly* (1997) can be said to be a working through of the German past in that the first memories of Herzog's pilot-protagonist Dieter Dengler are of the Allies destroying his small Black Forest village from the air. Even Herzog's short film *Ballad of the Little Soldier* (1984), which was filmed in Nicaragua and Honduras, can be said to deal implicitly with the militarization of German youth under Hitler. While this line of criticism may occasion some heated debate, it is undeniable that many specifically Germanic themes emerge in his work, and especially that work that focuses on the landscape. *Heart of Glass*, for example, is a reckoning with the German *Heimat* film, and Herzog himself has enigmatically remarked that even though some of the film was shot in Alaska, and some in Switzerland, it is a film in which he declares all landscapes to be Bavarian, that region of southern Germany in which he grew up.[11]

While some critics dwell on the Romanticism of Friedrich, and others on the politics of Riefenstahl, one cannot argue that the numerous and varied sequences in Herzog's films in which the landscape takes centre stage have a singular and unambiguous meaning. As the critic Jürgen Theobaldy points out: 'In contrast to *Fata Morgana*, the images of *Heart of Glass* do not stand in juxtaposition to the text (the pronouncements of the seer Hias), they illustrate it.'[12] It is often the case that his more Friedrich-inspired compositions reinforce the themes of his films, while his more alien landscapes run against the grain of the narrative voice. In *Nosferatu*, for example, as Jonathan Harker heads toward the vampire's castle, the scenic cliffs and waterfalls of the Borgo pass (which are actually the Tatra Mountains of the former Czechoslovakia), reflect the mystery of a journey into unknown and foreboding territory. Sometimes, however, the text and the images undermine one another, as in *Fata Morgana*, which depicts the impact of oil drilling and other forms of industrialization on the African landscape. In that film, Lotte Eisner's voice-over narration is taken from the creation myth of the Mayan text of the Popol Vuh, and as Eisner reads the part that instructs man to be fruitful and multiply, Herzog shows footage of decomposing animal cadavers strewn about the desert sands. While he insists in the director's commentary accompanying the DVD that the text and images are only opposed to one another 'on the surface', it is hard to argue that these scarred and desolate landscapes serve a function identical to the romantic and aestheticized ones in *Nosferatu*.

Still another symptomatic example of Herzog's use of landscape is in his film *Signs of Life* (1968), based on the literary fairy tale *The Madman of Fort Ratonneau* by Achim von Arnim. Herzog adapted this romantic story quite freely, setting its events in the twentieth century, during the Nazi occupation of Greece. The film's protagonist, a German soldier named Stroszek, is quietly healing from a battle injury at an abandoned fort on the Greek island of Kos, where he has been given little to do and is growing mad with boredom. A combination of factors ultimately pushes him over the edge, including the unexpected sight of a landscape populated by dozens of spinning windmills, a sight that Herzog says inspired his film.[13] Similarly, the opening shot is quite unusual. From a great height, the camera looks down on a curvaceous country road while a truck wends its way around and eventually disappears. This Greek landscape seems to extend well beyond the borders of the frame, and Herzog holds our gaze there, not zooming one bit closer. The shot maintains its position long after the credits have ended. Herzog himself explains:

In *Signs of Life* there are long shots of the incredible landscapes of Crete. The opening credits, for example, hold for an unusually long time with a single shot of a mountain valley. It gives you time to really climb deep inside the landscapes, and for them to climb inside you. It shows that these are not just literal landscapes you are looking at, but landscapes of the mind too.[14]

The image Herzog employs here, that of climbing into the landscape while the landscape climbs into you, is indeed evocative. This uniquely long establishing shot forces the viewer into a reverie, relying on the fact that we are prisoners of the cinema in order to compel a sensation of solitude. In its steadfastness, the camera refuses to explore the landscape for the viewer, and in this way Herzog addresses issues similar to those addressed by Friedrich with respect to prior styles and conventions of landscape painting. Traditionally, in the work of French painters such as Claude-Joseph Vernet, for example, it was expected that painted landscapes would provide an opening through which the viewer's gaze could enter and wander from place to place. Paintings were to be appreciated over time, like a walk in the countryside. In Friedrich's compositions, however, one's desire to enter the frame was frequently frustrated by the lack of a clear point of entry. Friedrich was alternately lauded and lambasted for the absence of markers that traditionally defined the borders of paintings. His works were said to produce the vertiginous sensation that there is no stage upon which one can tread. The same can be said of many of Herzog's shots, which hold the viewer's gaze at a disconcerting height or distance from landscapes that apparently extend beyond the borders of the screen. They refuse to provide the illusion that we are seeing a stage onto which we might wander.

Understood from this perspective, it is no coincidence that Herzog has placed an emphasis on walking in countless interviews and commentaries. He treats travelling on foot as a guiding principle of existence, urging everyone to walk as often as possible. Herzog describes every journey on foot as a pilgrimage, and even believes that a journey he once made on foot from Munich to Paris helped save Lotte Eisner's life when she was dying. In an interview, Herzog tells Lawrence O'Toole that if he could not make films, he would like to spend his life walking, and adds:

I would not like to live a life in the ordinary sense. I would like to live an *existence* – and walking on foot brings you down to the stark naked core of existence. You should walk more on foot. We travel too much in airplanes and cars. It's an existential quality that we are losing. It's almost like a credo of religion that we should walk.[15]

In this way, the landscapes in Herzog's films are part of an overall existential position, an effort to force us to find a point of entry and to prevent our reliance on the camera to do the labour for us. The protracted opening shot of *Signs of Life* can thus be seen as an attempt to recreate the solitude of a long walk, by virtue of its formal refusal of the probing zoom and rapid cuts that are the stock and trade of commercial cinema.

The fact that Herzog keeps the viewer at a constant remove from the landscape is by no means to suggest that he always holds his camera static. Although Herzog rarely zooms and probes with his lens, he frequently pans along the landscape, as is the case in many sequences in *Fata Morgana*. Additionally, much of *Lessons of Darkness*, which documents the oil fires in Kuwait following the first Gulf War in 1991 – a film that can be seen as a re-visitation of the themes first introduced in *Fata Morgana* – was shot from a moving helicopter. In both of these two films, Herzog's intention was to alienate the viewer from ways of seeing landscapes to which they had grown desensitized or inured. He wanted to present images of burning oil fields in Kuwait so that we see them anew. In his words, he wanted 'to penetrate deeper than CNN ever could'.[16]

As in the case of those travelling shots in *Lessons of Darkness*, one sequence towards the beginning of *Fata Morgana* has the camera hover low over mountains of sand in the desert. At first glance, the mountainous landscape might be mistaken for a close up of a nude body. As John Sandford points out, in *Fata Morgana*,

Herzog dwells on the patterns, form and feel of the desert and the villages, often using camera movements to create extra effect, as in a particularly beautiful sequence where the traveling camera makes sculpted sand dunes cross and sway like a human body.[17]

Such anthropomorphism is hardly rare in Herzog's work, and for the most part we are expected to project the physical characteristics of human forms and faces upon the surface of the Earth. Similarly, in the film, *My Best Fiend* (1999), Herzog's documentary about his relationship with Klaus Kinski, the director explains that he wanted the opening shot of *Aguirre*, in which a colonial expedition moves along the mountainside appearing as tiny flecks on a giant physiognomy, to be a scene in which the mountain speaks its drama and pathos to the viewer. He says he wanted 'to film a landscape with almost human qualities'. Herzog here engages in what could be described as a *prosopopeia*, from the Greek word for face, *prosopon*. It means the conferral of face and a voice upon an inanimate object.

In this early sequence in *Aguirre*, the mountain is huge, but man is minute. These relative proportions are reproduced throughout Herzog's work, but especially in his mountain climbing films, *Scream of Stone* and *The Dark Glow of the Mountains*. This latter film documents the German climber Reinhold Messner's obsession with climbing, a fascination that has cost him his brother's life as well as several of his toes. In that film, Herzog follows Messner and his companion, Hans Kammerlander, to the Gasherbrum Mountains, each 8,000 metres high. After accompanying them and their many sherpas to a base camp, the two climbers set out on their own. As Scott Watson writes eloquently and rhapsodically about this film:

Herzog's image of two tiny figures embarking on their lonely ascent, barely visible, now almost lost, finally completely gone in a vast snowy white field, a white field that virtually fills the screen, is the central image of the expedition…Though the camera was there because of and for the departure and return of the two humans and though the film viewers are ostensibly looking at the image trying to hold the impression of two receding human figures until the last possible moment and later searching for the first sighting of two returning adventurers, the snow covered mountain slopes are overwhelming and it is clear that the two humans are at their mercy.[18]

Once they begin their journey away from Herzog's camera, where he can no longer follow them, the two mountain climbing protagonists grow smaller and smaller until the lens loses them on the vast snowy slopes. They vanish up until the point when Herzog edits in footage shot by Messner himself. The sequence in which the climbers disappear is similar to the very last shot of *Scream of Stone* in which the camera moves farther and farther away from the mountain climber who stands at the top of the mountain Cerro Torre, becoming smaller and smaller, ultimately reduced to a microscopic and irrelevant detail at the top of an enormous mountain.

The most defining characteristic of such landscape images is their enormity relative to the humans who populate them. These proportions do not encourage us to identify with commanding figures that dominate the natural world, but rather draw our attention to the almost irrelevant dimensions of the human body with respect to nature, and to the landscape's overall indifference to our presence. Such scenes, as with others from *Fata Morgana* and *Heart of Glass*, recall the scale of Friedrich's well-known work *Monk by the Sea* (1808), but also recall the work of another one of Herzog's key influences, Hercules Segers. Segers was a Dutch artist, who was born in 1612, and died anonymously after a fall down a flight of stairs. Many of his prints were wasted, having been used as scrap paper before his importance was finally discovered. Of Segers' work, Herzog says:

> encountering Segers was as if someone had reached out with his hand across time and touched my shoulders. His landscapes are not landscapes at all; they are states of mind, full of angst, desolation, solitude, a state of dreamlike vision.[19]

Through his use of coarse lines and brownish tones, Segers turned picturesque Dutch landscapes into ruined deserts, and his paintings such as *Landscape with City on a River* (1627–29) share much in common with the desolate Greek landscape in *Signs of Life*, where Herzog's Stroszek begins to lose his mind. *Signs of Life* contains a number of compositions that could have been inspired by Segers, as in the scene in which Stroszek and his fellow soldier Meinhard are sent on an expedition outside of the fortress. The two men appear small against the large, arid landscape. Relative to the overall scope of his images, Segers' paintings generally contain only the tiniest of figures. His work *Mountainous Landscape* (1633), for example, may include a figure in the foreground, but the figure is so small and undefined – like that of Friedrich's famous monk – that one can barely say with certainty that it is a figure at all.

At no point does Herzog hold such desolate and lonely landscapes in contempt. He seems to suggest instead that they are quite beautiful. In this regard he is not so far from other post-war European filmmakers such as Antonioni, who has a similar love–hate relationship with the modern landscape (as evinced in films such as *The Red Desert* (1964) and *Zabriskie Point* (1970)). Despite the fact that Herzog repeats over and over again that we have 'embarrassed' our landscapes, he encourages us to see these embarrassed landscapes as something beautiful.[20] Until he arrives at decomposing animal corpses in *Fata Morgana*, his portraits of the African desert, despite (and sometimes even owing to) the intrusion of the machinery of the oil industry, appear uncontestably beautiful. Additionally, whether the non-diegetic music is by Mozart, Handel, Blind Faith or Leonard Cohen, it does little to interfere with, and generally underscores, the ecstatic qualities of his cinematography.

The film theorist Jan-Christopher Horak notes that in *Signs of Life* and *Aguirre*, 'the landscape is a dangerous force, threatening by the very nature of its cosmic indifference to man'.[21] His statement applies equally well to *Lessons of Darkness*, *Fata Morgana* and numerous other Herzog films. Precisely these themes appear in a prose text Herzog once wrote, inspired by photos by Jean Renoir, entitled 'Why is there "Being" at all, rather than Nothing?' In that text, Herzog placed words in the mouth of Renoir's aging father, and has the old man, Auguste, say: 'If the sky were compassionate, it too would grow old.' In Herzog's films, the sky does not suffer with us, but rather abandons us to our mortal fate. In his view, we would like the landscapes to impart something to us or to show compassion, but they do not. These sentiments may contribute to explaining those vexing words with which the film *The Enigma of Kaspar Hauser* begins: 'Don't you hear the horrible screaming all around us, the screaming that men usually call silence?' This epigraph either bespeaks the knowledge that there is a language of nature that we are prevented from interpreting, or that nature simply has nothing to say to us. In either event, the screaming in Herzog's film seems to take place in the minds of his frustrated figures – in the psyches of Stroszek, Kaspar Hauser, Roccia and Aguirre – but it does not emanate from the indifferent fields or from the dispassionate peaks.

In 1999, Herzog wrote 'The Minnesota Declaration', a statement of principles that he has said was directed against the false truths of *cinéma vérité*.[22] In it, Herzog writes: 'Mother Nature doesn't call, doesn't speak to you, although a glacier eventually farts. And don't you listen to the song of life.' In explaining the origin of this statement, he says that he was watching a film about the American actress Katherine Hepburn, and when she was asked what advice she had to pass along to young people, her reply was that they should 'listen to the song of life'. Herzog recalls: 'I was cringing it hurt so much. I still smart just thinking about it.'[23] As a response, Herzog asserts that it is a mistake to think that one can comprehend the language of nature, or that one has any access to it at all. He reminds us that the belief that one can understand Mother Nature's call is a ruse, and his words should give pause to anyone who would mistake him for a naïve Romantic, who is engaged in a love affair with the beauty of the landscape. Although he gives his landscapes a face and a voice – a *prosopon* – it is a face and a voice that have nothing to say to us, and they say it resolutely. Elsewhere in that same declaration, Herzog continues:

Life in the oceans must be sheer hell. A vast, merciless hell of permanent and immediate danger. So much of a hell that during evolution some species – including man – crawled, fled onto some small continents of solid land, where the Lessons of Darkness continue.[24]

This hell, life both in the oceans and out of the oceans, is a teacher, but it teaches us only about its indifference. This sentiment lies behind even the title of *Signs of Life*, and in that case signals Stroszek's attempt to get the universe to talk back or evince some kind of reaction. To prove his own existence in the face of the boring vacuum that his life has become, he fires a wealth of firecrackers into the sky, staging, in the words of the film's narration, 'a titanic revolt' against what is in the end an insurmountably strong opponent.

In his interviews with Paul Cronin, Herzog makes a revealing remark about the filmmaker Ingmar Bergman. He says:

> Though I don't like most of his films, it seems that for Ingmar Bergman his starting point is a human face. The starting point for my films is a landscape, whether it be a real place or an imaginary or hallucinatory one from a dream, and when I write a script I often describe landscapes that I have never seen.[25]

Herzog wants his landscapes to talk back to us and to the figures that populate them, yet from his point of view, they have nothing to express but their wholesale indifference. In Bergman's most famous work, *The Seventh Seal* (1957), Max von Sydow's character, Antonius Block, is disheartened to discover that Death knows nothing, that there may be only emptiness beyond human existence, and this is a hard pill for even a brave knight to swallow. In that film, Bergman gives death a face, and one certainly sees the relationship between his messenger of death, one who has neither knowledge nor comfort to offer, and the landscapes in Herzog's films. They both speak to the figures and to the viewer, but only of their impotence, and of the irrelevance of our plight.

The vast indifference of the universe is a crucial theme in Herzog's work, yet it should also be made clear that this is as much part of a fantasy as it is a fear. In *La Soufrière* (1977), a documentary filmed at the base of the eponymous volcano in Guadeloupe while it was about to explode, it becomes clear that Herzog has engaged in a wildly risky documentary project because he desires to see total devastation, or because he hopes for what Kraft Wetzel describes as a 'massive obliteration' (*großes Weltabräumen*).[26] Likewise, in *The Dark Glow of the Mountains*, Reinhold Messner explains that he does not climb because he wants to die, but that he views his courtship of death as a life-affirming act. This is, of course, the paradox of such activity: he seeks a confrontation with death because it makes him want to live. Messner explains that if someone went on foot to the top of a high mountain in order to leap off, they would not be able to do it; the encounter with death fuels the passion for life. This truism applies not only to the extreme type of sports in which Messner is engaged, but also to Herzog's own principles of filmmaking. Without exception, by every film that Herzog has made hangs a tale of a close encounter with death. Freud would describe this type of obsession as a death drive, or a desire to return to the state of tranquillity that preceded our births. It represents a striving toward an original unity, a longing to undo the trauma of coming into the world, the trauma that Herzog's Kaspar Hauser describes as a 'painful blow'.

It is no coincidence that Reinhold Messner, like Herzog, portrays himself as an impassioned walker. He says that he would gladly walk continuously until the world came to a stop. Herzog commiserates, explaining that he too would walk until there is nothing left. His images of mountainous landscapes can be seen as the representation of just such an imagined apocalypse. In *The Dark Glow of the Mountains*, the portrait of Gasherbrum One enveloped in a snowstorm, could have come directly from out of Friedrich's *oeuvre*. It resembles his numerous Riesengebirge paintings, in which the peaks disappear beneath a cloak of fog. Given the fantasy about the end of the world and the wish to walk until there is nothing left, such images suggest a dream of endless obliteration, or a desire to see the world in ruins. The final image of that film, one in which the mountain peaks are wholly enveloped in mist, bespeaks a fantasy that even these most massive of objects will disappear. Herzog's urge to make man irreducibly small and ultimately cloak the mountains beneath curtains of fog is a part of the director's courtship of annihilation. For him, however, this encounter is vitiating; it is one and the same as a courtship of life.

## Notes

1. Paul Cronin (ed.), *Herzog on Herzog* (London: Faber and Faber, 2002), 66–67.
2. *Fata Morgana* was originally meant to be set on the planet Uxmal, its name taken from a Mayan archaeological site in the Yucatan. The name means 'thrice built', which perhaps corresponds to the film's three stages: 'creation', 'paradise' and 'the golden age'.
3. Cronin, 70.
4. Noël Carroll, *Interpreting the Moving Image* (Cambridge: Cambridge University Press, 1998), 287.
5. Ibid., 295.
6. For Herzog's comment on this, see Hans Günther Pflaum, 'Interview', *Werner Herzog*, Reihe Film 22 (Munich: Hanser, 1979), 59–60.
7. Cronin, 136.
8. Ibid., 81.
9. Eric Rentschler, 'The politics of vision: Herzog's *Heart of Glass*', in Timothy Corrigan (ed.), *The Films of Werner Herzog: Between Mirage and History* (New York: Methuen, 1986), 170.
10. Amos Vogel, 'On seeing a mirage', in Corrigan, 45.
11. Cronin, 132.
12. The original sentence reads: 'Im Gegensatz zu *Fata Morgana* stehen die Bilder [von *Herz aus Glas*] nicht kontrapunktisch zum Text, den Weissagungen Hias'; sie illustrieren ihn' (31). On this point, see also Ruth Perlmutter, 'The Cinema of the grotesque', *Georgia Review* 33 (1979), 169–193. She writes: 'The camera tracks laterally, without comment, sylleptically connecting the exquisite desert landscape with its living and dead skeletons – a lifeless society, rusted machines,

and the remains of dead animals. The harsh realities are in ironic counterpoint with the sound track, where the narration of an ancient legend about Creation is juxtaposed with the grandeur of a choral symphony, American folk songs of the sixties, and a tacky Oriental music hall re-creation of popular music from the 1940s.' (181)

13. Cronin, 39.
14. Ibid.
15. Lawrence O'Toole, 'I feel that I'm close to the center of things', *Film Comment* 15 (1979), 48.
16. Cronin, 245.
17. John Sandford, *The New German Cinema* (New York: Da Capo Press, 1982), 51.
18. Scott B. Watson, 'Herzog's healing images: Mountain climbing and mankind's degeneration', *Aethlon* 10 (1992), 178.
19. Cronin, 137.
20. Cronin, 47, 66; O'Toole, 48.
21. Jan-Christopher Horak, 'Werner Herzog's *Écran Absurde*', *Literature/Film Quarterly* 7 (1979), 226.
22. Cronin, 239.
23. Ibid., 300.
24. Ibid., 302.
25. Ibid., 83.
26. Kraft Wetzel, 'kommentierte Filmographie', *Werner Herzog*, Reihe Film 22 (Munich: Hanser, 1979), 123.

# Chapter 5

Visions of Italy: The Sublime, the Postmodern and the Apocalyptic

William Hope

D uring the last two decades of the twentieth century, industrialized society had evolved to a point where it attracted the nebulous label of 'postmodern', predominantly in socio-economic and cultural contexts.[1] A self-perpetuating materialism, fuelled by 'the continual circulation of commodified fantasies stressing erotic beauty, wealth, masculinity, achievement, happiness, successful love relationships and joyous, free selfhood', created societies that were stratified, increasingly fragmented and distinguished by 'postmodern' emotions such as 'anger and fear, coupled with existential anxiety' and a sense of being 'threatened by a postmodern world that promises more than it can deliver'.[2] These societies were and continue to be dominated by the media and characterized by a present that is multi-faceted, globalized and commodified, a culturally eclectic, shifting reality which combines what Jameson describes as a nostalgic and conservative longing for the past with the erasure of the boundaries that separate past and present.[3] Baudrillard's dystopic vision of a society ravaged by the excesses of capitalism and the mass media is typified by what he termed 'a pornography of the visible' – a constant sense of display and iconization particularly within the televisual medium, with streams of aestheticized advertisements and carefully edited 'reality television'.[4] Also, what is exhibited is often not authentic but simulated, as industry attempts to mass (re)produce everything from works of art to Parma ham.

The plight of individuals whose value systems and backgrounds problematize their integration into today's postmodern societies – characters who find themselves exposed to, exploited, and ultimately abandoned by the political and economic ruthlessness of late capitalism – was explored in two Italian films made in the mid-1990s. *Caro diario* (Dear Diary, Nanni Moretti, 1994) and *Lo zio di Brooklyn* (The Uncle from Brooklyn, Daniele Ciprì and Franco Maresco, 1995) are films which, despite their different aesthetic and subjective approaches, are linked by several themes. They explore the tribulations of individuals who experience varying degrees of estrangement from the societies in which they live; they inhabit landscapes which range from the ostensibly postmodern to what may perhaps be termed the post-postmodern, given the surreal and desolate *mise-en-scène* deployed in *Lo zio di Brooklyn*. Ciprì and Maresco's representation of the stagnant socio-economic plight of Sicily is a powerful indictment of the treatment of an area ignored by successive generations of politicians and largely bypassed by industrial and technological advances. By comparison, Moretti, in his semi-autobiographical *Caro diario*, discovers that despite their remoteness, the Aeolian Islands off the coast of Sicily are falling victim to market forces, economic exploitation and globalization, but in the film's opening episode, *In vespa* (On My

Vespa), the actor-director at least manages to achieve an idiosyncratic symbiotic rapport with Rome, his personal environment.

## Rome: The personalization of urban space

An air of restlessness, both physical and existential, pervades *In vespa*, and it is typified by the numerous forward tracking shots of Moretti on his scooter as he weaves his way through Rome's neighbourhoods, introducing them by means of a voice-over. Moretti comes across as a detached figure, isolated within his surroundings, and sidelined from the capitalist structures and mass mainstream culture to which he comically subjects himself in sequences such as his cinema visit to see *Henry, Portrait of a Serial Killer*.[5] His assumption of the role of outsider is a device which taps into most viewers' individualism and secret feelings of detachment from society, thereby creating a sense of alignment from the outset. Moretti's sense of malaise can be attributed to his difficulty in reconciling his intellectual engagement with the world around him – his standoffish, elitist impulses towards self-exclusion from society – with a more spontaneously emotional, affective desire to express himself and interact with others at a lower cultural level, illustrated by his self-conscious participation in a dance event, and by his gushing admiration for Jennifer Beals, the star of what was the epitome of mass appeal, postmodern, rags-to-riches 1980s films, *Flashdance*.

These contradictory impulses towards the popular and the elitist emerge in Moretti's guided tour of Rome and its residential areas. On the one hand, there are sequences such as Moretti's farcical visit to the modern quarter Spinaceto, the camera tracking him from behind as he ventures into its grey, characterless depths, musing on what he avers to be the area's undeservedly poor reputation. Reaching a cul-de-sac, he ascertains from a resident that the neighbourhood 'isn't bad at all' – a view which coincides with his own predetermined judgement of the place. He wheels away on the vespa, satisfied with this superficial corroboration which, however, is wholly insufficient to outweigh the impact of the long duration, panoramic shots of the grim surroundings that accompanied his arrival. On the other hand, he also remonstrates with a resident of the affluent Casal Palocco suburb, criticizing the bemused man for buying property in this exclusive area of the city decades ago – and therefore contributing to Rome's economic stratification – in a period when most of the city was 'wonderful' to live in. Significantly, Moretti's visit to Via Dandolo, punctuated by covetous point-of-view shots as the camera's upward pan from street level reproduces his gaze when it wanders up to a penthouse that he has had his eye on for some time, implies that he would not be averse to owning an apartment in a desirable area himself. Pointedly though, Moretti comments that the apartment's owner attributed its exorbitant price not just to its pleasant location, but also to the location's historical significance ('Garibaldi fought there'). The scene portrays Moretti's exposure to a value system that has become predominant in an age of postmodern simulacra, or reproductions of the authentic – an era in which the present fuses with the past or erases it altogether. The attraction of possessing such a property is comprehensible – a piece of history with an intrinsic sense of reassuring permanence in the midst of socio-economic change – and this is what drives the apartment's price up.

Rome itself, or what might be termed Moretti's sense of 'ownership' of the city – being one of its residents – goes some way towards mollifying the frustration he feels over issues ranging from the pseudo-intellectualization of low culture, to the way in which his revolutionary generation has sold out to the Establishment that they initially detested. Patricia Kruth has explored a similar theme regarding Woody Allen's affinity with New York – particularly Manhattan – recognizing that 'however distressing the situation, the stability of the relationship between the Woody Allen protagonist and his familiar surroundings is never at stake; the city is his'.[6] Both directors subjectivize their cities with personal choices of soundtrack music – often jazz in Allen's case, while in *Caro diario*, Moretti uses music as an emotional amplifier to convey his state of mind, ranging from the upbeat world music which denotes his exhilaration while riding his vespa, to Leonard Cohen's *I'm Your Man*, which follows a sombre meditation on the way he has attempted to remain true to his values. Music, together with frequent voice-overs, serves to exclude Rome's noise and to replace it with an externalized form of Moretti's identity. Filming the *In vespa* sequence in summer when Rome is deserted also helps the director to customize the city, by transforming empty urban space into a personalized place through his presence. Even Moretti's choice of architecture as depicted by the panoramic camera shots is personal to him. He eschews tourist landmarks that are familiar to and 'owned' by millions through their personal experience of them, in favour of an idiosyncratic selection of apartment blocks which illustrate how Rome's topography has been structured by successive political and economic forces.

During Moretti's exploration of the city's topography, restlessly traversing Rome like one of Pasolini's protagonists, it is no coincidence that he gravitates towards the monument that was built in remembrance of the director in the Ostia district after his murder in 1975. This sequence is characterized by an extremely long take which features the standard set-up of a tracking shot following Moretti's vespa at a distance of around 40 feet. The length and monotony of the take as he travels to Rome's hinterland is designed to convey the marginalization not only of Pasolini's monument, but also of his values, and its sheer duration allows Moretti's excursion to coalesce with Pasolini's last ill-fated journey in the minds of viewers. This pilgrimage to Ostia, at the city's margins, underlines the monument's negligible importance in Rome's layout, remote from its political and economic centre, and abandoned as illustrated in an image of it overgrown with grass, the state of the memorial constituting a forceful condemnation of the city council and its values. Like Pasolini's protagonists themselves – 'the pimp, the whore, the savage' – this is evidently an area 'despised by capitalism…useless to it and at its geographical and social periphery'.[7] It is here that Moretti and the camera linger, finally outside the loop of capitalism and materialism that has characterized much of the urban space traversed by the actor-director, and in a place symbolizing political and artistic values that have proved elusive to him thus far in the film.

## The Aeolian Islands: Utopia/dystopia

Although the Aeolian Islands are renowned for their natural beauty and for their remote location off the northern coast of Sicily, the second episode of *Caro diario* – *Isole* – paradoxically illustrates their growing economic importance as terrain for exploitation within the tourist sector. The narrative thread of the episode is inconsequential, a travelogue tracing the attempts of Moretti and his friend Gerardo to locate a tranquil spot so that Moretti might develop ideas for a film script. As in the best comic traditions, these intentions are doomed from the outset, since within seconds of Moretti disembarking on the largest island, Lipari, it is evident that the traffic chaos of Rome – strangely absent from the preceding episode in *In vespa* – has simply transferred itself to this Italian outpost. Through the noise of horns and klaxons that is mixed high into the soundtrack, and careful depth of field framing that depicts cars inching through the masses of tourists on Lipari's main street, viewers glimpse a nightmare scenario of a barrage of noise, pollution and human anxiety in constant circulation from urban to rural areas and back again, according to the season.

Venturing out to the volcanic island of Stromboli in search of some peace, the two protagonists' chastening encounter with the island's mayor indicates the fate that awaits the island. As with politicians the world over, the mayor is driven by a desire to implement change to justify his existence and to leave a tangible 'legacy' of some sort. Reflecting the unfettered Western capitalist ethos of the late twentieth century, he talks of the island and its inhabitants as 'material' ripe for development, and bemoans the area's 'wasted potential'.[8] Another archetypal symptom of nations in the throes of postmodernity is a propensity towards cultural eclecticism. David Bass identifies similarities between the visuals of what he terms the *film cartolina* (a 'tourist' or 'picture postcard' film which uses a city's landmarks to add local colour to a narrative) and discernible tendencies within contemporary town planning:

> The tourist movie treats the city as a museum and reconfigures its decontextualized contents at will. A similar practice can occur in the design of real cities. Seeing inspiration in other cities, the architect-tourist proposes fragments of them – souvenirs of their visit – to be built in his/her native city. Such is the (purely aesthetic) basis of much postmodern 'that's nice, I'll have one of those' design.[9]

The mayor reveals that he has discarded the idea of creating American-style tree-lined avenues on Stromboli, but enthusiastically outlines his forthcoming meeting with some Japanese agronomists, and also his vision of implementing a Storaro *mise-en-scène* for the island together with a specially written Morricone musical soundtrack that could be broadcast from loudspeakers at strategic points in the area. Although the mayor talks of giving the island back its identity, the danger is that by endowing Stromboli with a characterless, multicultural exoticism, its uniquely desolate, natural beauty will be lost. By wishing to 'enhance' the island with cinematic touches such as a *mise-en-scène* and an amplified soundtrack, the mayor envisages an aestheticized and synthetic tourist experience for future visitors – a postmodern form of interaction with a simulacrum rather than with the authentic, of engagement with a 'realistic' version of what the 'real-should-be' in Baudrillard's terms.[10] Appropriately, Moretti undercuts the mayor's lunatic ideas with a minimum of cinematic rhetoric, by using a series of lengthy takes and unelaborate long shots which frame Stromboli's volcanic slopes. Later, as Moretti departs at the end of the visit, a further extreme long shot of the island underlines its timeless and sublime qualities – its awesome propensity to overwhelm the senses with its rugged, imposing presence.[11]

The travellers' reluctant excursion to another island, Panarea, plunges them into an environment that has already fallen victim to capitalist exploitation, and which constitutes an epicentre of postmodernity. While metropolises such as Rome have gravitational poles in the form of historic city centres (which, through their architecture, provide a sense of tradition which stands firm even in the face of sweeping political and economic changes), landscapes such as those of the Aeolian Islands are more vulnerable to the insidiousness of market forces. In Italian metropolises, the varied styles of man-made constructions are the tangible heritage of successive epochs, and to erase them would be problematic; by contrast, regions such as the Aeolian Islands, although possessing an ineffable timeless beauty, are susceptible to losing their own pasts and to being condemned 'to live in a perpetual present and in a perpetual change that obliterates traditions', in Jameson's terms, precisely because they are virgin territory.[12] This has been the destiny of Panarea, and a panorama of cocktail-swilling tourists on the quayside greets Moretti and Gerardo as they arrive, as does a 'hostess' who corners them, promising a panoply of kitsch, multi-ethnic tat ('white elephants, watusi, Helmut Berger in his underwear') for the tourists' delight. Panarea has become an entertainment centre, which, through its dependence on tourism in a competitive marketplace, attempts to outdo its rivals by scheduling the greatest number of staged 'experiences' – layer upon layer of artifice – in the shortest possible time, to beguile the increasingly blasé traveller. A gloss of artifice has engulfed the island's characteristics, something which condemns visitors to interact with simulacra rather than with the authentic. The place has become a cultural hybrid – a 'global village' in some ways – with a multi-faceted (though inauthentic) present whose continual metamorphoses have become its only form of attraction, now that its natural heritage has been sullied. Predictably, Moretti and Gerardo turn on their heels and leap back on to the ferry that brought them to Panarea, just before it pulls away again.

A trip made by the pair to the craggy island of Alicudi finally provides them with the isolation that they profess to crave, but the sequence manoeuvres the film's focus back to the issue of the necessity of intellectuals like Moretti engaging to some extent with postmodern society, its mass media, technology and mass culture. Alicudi quickly reveals itself to be a place of inhospitable drudgery, underlined by an amusing high-angle camera shot looking down on Moretti, Gerardo and a member of a local religious order with his donkey, as they trudge up the island's slopes to their spartan accommodation. The character of Gerardo is a cypher for intellectuals in denial as regards their interaction with the mass media and culture

that surround them; he professes to have shunned television for the past eleven years in order to study Joyce's *Ulysses*, yet he is inexorably drawn – like a restless postmodern voyeur 'who sits and gazes, mesmerized or bored at the movie or the TV screen' – to any form of televisual entertainment.[13] At Gerardo's behest, during the Stromboli visit, Moretti is even forced to descend the slopes of a volcano to question a group of American tourists as to the latest developments in the soap *The Bold and the Beautiful*. The ascetic ambience of Alicudi finally takes its toll on Gerardo, who is last seen haring down the slope towards the harbour, screaming out the names of a range of mod cons of which he has been deprived and to which he needs urgent access. In this regard, viewers are invited to infer that it is Moretti's sense of equilibrium that represents an appropriate mindset for the postmodern age. Although he struggles to adapt to the changing environments in which he finds himself, and takes umbrage at the materialist excesses of Italian society, Moretti's *Caro diario* indicates that an ability to carve out a distinct space for oneself within urban or rural landscapes –
making them as far as possible personalized places in which to exist and circulate at one's ease – and also that of striking a balance between an austere, intellectual repudiation of mass culture and the media, and an undiscerning consumption of it, are indispensable tools to deal with life in the postmodern age and beyond.

## Palermo and peripheries: Construction and depersonalization

If Moretti's vision of the abusive development of the Aeolian Islands is disquieting, Ciprì and Maresco's stylized, apocalyptic portrait of Palermo's periphery is a numbing indictment of the plight of a region that has never been exploited by 'legitimate' capitalist enterprise, but which, instead, has remained in the hands of Mafia-run cartels, capitalism's mirror image. *Lo zio di Brooklyn* is a surreal tale relating how a local family – the Gemelli brothers – are 'invited' by the Mafia to accommodate a mysterious, elderly individual, a character who abruptly vanishes from the brothers' squalid apartment shortly afterwards. This, the flimsiest of plots, is an expedient to enable the directors to focus on their real agenda – the Italian state's neglect of southerners, particularly Sicilians, and the environments in which they eke out an existence.

The contrast between cinematic form and content in *Lo zio di Brooklyn* is abyssal. The directors' refined visual representations of characters within their surroundings is juxtaposed with the bewildering squalor of the environment itself, and a key element of the disorienting nature of the viewing experience lies in the disjunction created by the fact that abstract space is never effectively personalized into a human habitat. As David Forgacs has outlined, abstract space is transformed into social space through architecture, which 'provides the articulation, the "coupling" between mathematical or physical space and social space…mapping…the structures of social and economic life onto the physical world'.[14] In a cinematic context, shots of constructed areas possess several dramatic functions; Ian Wiblin notes that by implying a human presence, such sequences are imbued with narrative potential – the sensation that something has happened or is about to happen. He also posits that the style and condition of architecture can elicit affective responses from viewers:

> It is…architecture itself that has the stored potential to express human experience and emotion. In images of built space – whether still or moving – it is the discernible presence of humanity implied by the direct absence of people that is so moving.[15]

Forgacs, however, offers a different perspective, noting that cinematic shots of built space are normally justified by being linked to a character, or by having a specific narrative function; if, in due course, this space is not 'personalized' by the appearance of a character, it can become 'frighteningly vacuous' and cause tension.[16]

The viewing experience derived from *Lo zio di Brooklyn* is marked by precisely this sort of unease; using an approach reminiscent of the earliest screen representations of urban space – in which the Lumière brothers, Friese-Greene and others depicted segments of cities with a static, unrhetorical, almost scientific precision – Ciprì and Maresco open the film with a bleak visual document of the areas which serve as the film's diegesis.[17] The length of the takes, the number of them – linked together by unelaborate montage – and the absence of a human presence, apart from one shot of an area of scrubland in which a distant figure plaintively calls someone's name, immediately generate discomfort. A degree of disorientation is also caused by the landscapes themselves. Within the suburbs, angular apartment blocks located next to pristine, yet deserted roads convey a futuristic ambience, while the absence of historic monuments or buildings efface any sense of a past; the area is surrounded by desolate hills and moorland in which humanity does not appear to have set foot.[18] Wiblin's notion of a nuanced human presence applies even to this indefinable environment spanning past, present and future, but the paradoxes within the landscape's features invite all manner of inferences ranging from the presence of a race of übermenchen to that of semi-barbaric survivors of a nuclear disaster. Even when the film's late twentieth-century social misfits eventually materialize, there is no synergy between humanity and its surroundings, and no impression of any transformation of abstract, extrinsic spaces into personalized places. This is also implied in the circularity of the film's structure, its closing sequence featuring a further succession of empty panoramic shots.

Shot in black and white, *Lo zio di Brooklyn* is notable for its stylish camera set-ups and depth of field shots which, combined with the directors' propensity for centred, emphatic framings of figures, create an aestheticized, tableau effect. The screen space of external shots is invariably divided into three spatially distinct zones. Typically, there is a bleak stretch of road in the foreground, along which characters trudge, while the middle distance is occupied either by rows of ugly apartment blocks, or by barren hills and ridges. The upper third of the frame – a stylistic masterstroke – is dominated by a dark, glowering sky bordered by an incandescent light that hints at some form of impending celestial wrath. Society itself (the term is used loosely here) appears to be in a timeless vacuum with no discernible links to the age of industry, let alone technology, a space in which a few disembodied signifiers both of late capitalism and enduring Sicilian poverty float like archaeological artefacts.

## The void beyond postmodernity

A number of narrative elements imply that the film is set in an age situated beyond postmodernity. Early on, a local singer/guitarist, Lo Giudice, gives a tuneless street rendition of a song entitled *Playboy*, an evocation of the cultural logic of late capitalism – success, wealth and male charisma – but principally an unconvincing tribute to Lo Giudice's self-professed romantic values. After a close up of the singer, the directors switch to their standard external visual set-up, an extreme long shot of the environment which overwhelms and undermines Lo Giudice. The eye takes in piles of rubble strewn along the ground at the forefront of the frame, before passing upwards to the derelict building that forms the singer's backdrop. His words are an empty mantra, a hollow evocation of mythical values which no longer exist, and never existed in this part of the world. In the tradition of the musical genre, the song is a self-contained interlude to interrupt the film's negligible narrative momentum, and the length of the take forces viewers to register and reevaluate the scale of dilapidation within the *mise-en-scène*. Another lingering vestige of the postmodern emerges in the form of a cyclist who traverses the town in full cycling gear, his streams of consciousness lamenting the absence of womenfolk in the area and his inability to engage with the opposite sex. His fluorescent kit and racing bike are implausible fragments of late twentieth-century materialism in this surreal environment; they contrast with the poverty and semi-nudity of the other inhabitants, and the cyclist's anxieties are laden with the romantic nostalgia that critics such as Jameson and Denzin have identified as emerging in epochs where the past gradually recedes in favour of an ever-shifting present, and where love, families and religion have dwindled.[19]

The film also displays a subversive postmodernist streak in the way it deconstructs the simulacra created by both cinematic art and the media in general. The narrative is periodically interrupted by an inept television journalist, who, talking directly to camera, attempts to deliver vapid soundbites which constitute a clichéd defence of the region in the face of its grim reputation. These archetypal platitudes – the staple diet of Italian media reports in 'problem areas' – are demolished as the directors cut to an extreme long shot of an empty wilderness which appears to engulf the journalist, who flounders and forgets his lines. With its long duration takes, the camera lingering on deserted streets and areas of wasteland long after the film's assorted misfits and *mafiosi* have moved out of shot, *Lo zio di Brooklyn* reveals a strong documentary influence in its aesthetic construction. The use of these structures enables Ciprì and Maresco to remove the layers of artifice and manipulation inherent even in this, traditionally the most 'realistic' of genres. Reproducing the lengthy takes and emphatic framing of documentaries, the directors recreate the sense of pornographic excess that emerges in the way the more exploitative examples of the genre portray their subjects.

One such sequence features a documentary-style dialogue between two off-camera voices and Giordano – a destitute and truculent specimen of a character whom the directors often use to represent the worst excesses of the Sicilian psyche.[20] Wearing only his underpants, and standing on a pile of rubble, Giordano is questioned (and subtly goaded) by the voices as to how the film is going and how it is being received. He duly obliges with an inarticulate harangue of the film, its actors and its audience, before spitting contemptuously into the camera lens. The sequence serves to highlight the increasingly thin line between investigation and exploitation in modern documentaries, and the tendency to transmute the grim realities of vulnerable subjects into artifice through vicarious manipulation.

The deployment of Giordano, a number of musical turns by third-rate performers, a series of words and glances delivered directly to camera and, intriguingly, a use of ugly, semi-naked, live male statues to 'decorate' an already forbidding landscape, all create a sense of display and hint at the presence of an implied audience. Postmodern culture is very much a voyeuristic, 'looking' culture, and it is within this framework that *Lo zio di Brooklyn* ventures into the existential abyss that lies beyond the consumption of objectified images. The film's narrative is frequently interrupted by songs that are amateurishly delivered in the most incongruous of situations. As a religious procession snakes across an area of wasteland in familiar long shot, a youth appears and scuttles into centre frame. The procession halts as the performer delivers a song at breakneck speed, thanks the audience despite a complete absence of applause and remains rooted to the spot with an obsequious expression as the procession recommences behind him. Sung against a backdrop of crumbling buildings, and with a mechanical haste that never allows a fleeting impression of 'entertainment' to develop, the song is deprived of even the most basic sense of momentary diversion, and is exhibited as a numbing manifestation of time consumption. The interlude fails to emulate even the most vacuous of mainstream entertainment in whiling away a viewer's time, serving instead to generate a temporal and existential void by delivering nothing in return for watching it. With comic ruthlessness, the directors accentuate the viewer's discomfort by training the camera on the stationary singer for almost a minute after the procession has disappeared, and consequently the film passes beyond a subversive desecration of the experiences of viewers-consumers to confront them with the void that lies beyond the consumption of the simulacrum.

The same sense of an existential vacuum emerges in the directors' manipulation of the phenomenon of *veline*, women whose function is to decorate the sets of everything from quiz shows to variety programmes.[21] While their more politically correct British televisual equivalents sometimes use males to fulfil the same purpose, smirking with self-conscious, postmodern irony at their own objectification as they gesture at the available prizes, the Italian media have not yet reached this point of reflexivity. The female form is still exhibited gratuitously within televisual entertainment, with, at the most, a token veneer of arch self-awareness to justify it. The response of Ciprì and Maresco is to create a bleak diegetic film space devoid of all representations of authentic femininity – all female roles are played by men – and also to expose the void that lies behind the aestheticized, iconic simulacra of female beauty that are still used in advertisements to stimulate consumption, and within entertainment for the voyeur's ephemeral pleasure. Their tactic is to preserve the same structures of display and objectification, the essence of which is exposed and undermined by the substitution of nubile females with repellent, semi-naked males. These immobile figures frequently materialize within the *mise-en-scène*, sometimes positioned at road junctions to preserve the shot's symmetry, or framed by the doorways of derelict buildings. At an immediate, symbolic level, within the directors' extreme long shots, they embody the poverty and isolation of many Sicilians and the island itself, but the sheer duration of the takes forces viewers beyond this surface interpretation of their function. The figures' wretched appearance within dismal surroundings contrasts with the gratuitous, stylized sense of display with which they are presented, and the directors ensure that the sequences last long enough for viewers to perceive the vulnerability of the individual within these accentuated structures of exhibition and objectification, and to feel discomfort. Shorn of any aesthetic beauty, placed in barren locations and divested of any sense of irony and of the sensuality of *veline* which briefly allows voyeuristic viewers to transcend reality, these human statues lay bare the objectification of individuals for visual consumption by other individuals – the unpalatable truth lurking beyond facetious postmodern attitudes to such structures. Another more aggressive strategy by the directors to ensure an insidious viewing experience is elaborated when the camera enters a character's personal space within a living area. As it loiters there with documentary-style persistence, extreme reactions are often elicited from the subject. Once the camera's presence is invasive enough to constitute an exploitative objectification of the character (for example during the tragicomic death throes of the Gemelli brothers' father as he chokes on his dentures while eating), some form of bodily response from the character – who in this case vomits over the camera – serves to create an aggressive counter momentum from within the diegetic space. These abrasive responses from the objectified are another way of foregrounding the mechanisms of objectification, and countering them.

The film is characterized by an atmosphere of impending apocalypse, and it closes, appropriately, as the Gemelli brothers encounter a form of 'afterlife' which is located on some fields close to their suburb. The sequence reinforces the sense of stasis that has pervaded the film since its opening scenes, as, with their customary overexposed extreme long shots, the directors present a tableau of all the film's characters as they congregate to the strains of the tuneless municipal brass band. The local *mafiosi*, now dressed in white robes, cluster together as in their previous life, and other characters also repeat their behaviour patterns as mortals. While constituting a forceful visual metaphor implying that everyone will spend eternity in the same miserable way as they lived their lives (and their ancestors lived theirs), the *mise-en-scène* of the sequence gives a more tangible sense of the post-postmodern abyss that viewers have occasionally been forced to behold earlier in the film. At a certain point, an Elvis Presley lookalike emerges from a coffin, and launches into a substandard version of a rock and roll number; the lookalike – a relic of a postmodern simulacrum – is duly feted. Subsequently, a cut to a shot of the arid landscape gives it considerable depth of field, and in the middle ground of this ghostly yet strangely mortal hereafter stand a donkey, a patron saint who has been dragged from pillar to post during a never-ending procession, the ubiquitous semi-naked human statue, a couple of dwarf *mafiosi* and a cart with a coffin on it. These eternal signifiers of Sicilian life, now permanently detached from the signified, arguably constitute the last mirages of the real, immortalized against overexposed, empty nothingness.

## Notes

1. Dick Hebdige's article 'Postmodernism and "the other side"', *Journal of Communication Inquiry* 10 (1986), 78, lists an endless range of phenomena that have been branded as 'postmodern'. The list is reproduced in Anne Friedberg, *Window Shopping: Cinema and the Postmodern* (Berkeley: University of California Press, 1993), 10.
2. Norman K. Denzin, *Images of Postmodern Society: Social Theory and Contemporary Cinema* (London: Sage Publications, 1991), 54–55.
3. Fredric Jameson, 'Postmodernism and consumer society', in Hal Foster (ed.), *The Anti-Aesthetic* (Port Townsend: Bay Press, 1983); Denzin, vii.
4. Denzin contextualizes this concept from Baudrillard's *The Ecstasy of Communication*, 32.
5. *Henry, Portrait of a Serial Killer*, dir. John McNaughton, 1986.
6. Patricia Kruth, 'The color of New York: Places and spaces in the films of Martin Scorsese and Woody Allen', in Francois Penz and Maureen Thomas (eds), *Cinema and Architecture* (London: BFI, 1997), 72–73. Numerous parallels have been drawn between the comic neuroticism of Moretti and Allen.
7. Sam Rohdie, *The Passion of Pasolini* (London: BFI, 1995), 35.
8. Although the schemes described in *Caro diario* to develop the Aeolian Islands are grotesque inventions to emphasize a point, the danger posed to the islands by development is very real, as exemplified by proposals to construct hotel complexes in this protected area. Environmentalists helped to block these plans – at least temporarily – in the autumn of 2004.
9. David Bass, 'Insiders and outsiders: Latent urban thinking in movies of modern Rome', in Penz and Thomas (eds), *Cinema and Architecture* (London: BFI, 1997), 99 (88).
10. Denzin examines Baudrillard's ideas concerning the 'society of the spectacle' in the context of American society. Denzin, 140–141.
11. The cinematic sublime is outlined by William Hope in *Giuseppe Tornatore: Emotion, Cognition, Cinema* (Newcastle: Cambridge Scholars Press, 2006), 129–148.
12. Jameson, 125.
13. Denzin, 8–9 analyses the visual appeal of the postmodern.
14. David Forgacs, 'Antonioni: Space, place, sexuality', in M. Konstantarakos (ed.), *Spaces in European Cinema* (Exeter: Intellect, 2000), 101–111 (103).
15. Ian Wiblin, 'The space between: Photography, architecture and the presence of absence', in Penz and Thomas (eds), 112.
16. Forgacs, 104.
17. See Helmut Weihsmann, 'The city in twilight: Charting the genre of the city film 1900–1930', in Penz and Thomas (eds), 8–27.

18. These oases of the ultra modern (and unused), the derelict and the desolate typify certain urban agglomerations in southern Italy. They have evolved following sporadic state investment in, for example, new roads and characterless housing estates which have attracted few tenants, since many prefer to remain in the dilapidated older areas of cities. Illegal Mafia construction projects resulting in clusters of apartment blocks lacking basic amenities are also a problem.

19. Denzin discusses the film *Blade Runner* in the context of these themes, which also emerge in the work of Baudrillard. Denzin, 33.

20. For a résumé of Giordano's various incarnations in the television work of Ciprì and Maresco, see Ernest Hampson, 'Ciprì and Maresco: Uncompromising visions, aesthetics of the apocalypse', in William Hope (ed.), *Italian Cinema – New Directions* (Bern: Peter Lang, 2004), 131–150.

21. The *veline* phenomenon is showcased in a programme transmitted by Silvio Berlusconi's television network, in which women compete to win a 'residency' in another programme broadcast by the same network.

# Chapter 6

Landscape in Spanish Cinema

Marvin D'Lugo

## Cinematic ethnoscapes

The depiction of landscape in Spanish films is seldom a matter of a neutral cinematic-narrative setting. From as early as Eduardo Jimeno's actuality footage of parishioners leaving the Cathedral of Zaragoza after a midday mass in 1897, said to be the first Spanish film, background locale and *mise-en-scène* have carried an implicit charge of cultural meanings and values.[1] Depictions of folkloric traditions in both the silent and sound period, costumed dramas set in rural spaces, became stabilized in Spanish popular imagination as 'ethnoscapes', through which films portrayed 'the land as implicitly belonging to the people in the same way that the people belonged to the land'.[2] Integrated into larger spatial paradigms that eventually could 'stand in for the nation', landscapes as embodied in the seemingly neutral narrative settings of many Spanish films thus inevitably led to questions of national cinema.[3]

While often appearing to express only the aesthetic choices of individual filmmakers, these cinematic ethnoscapes over time came to embody competing ideologies that have shaped much of Spanish cultural history, the most prominent of these being the struggle for social and cultural modernization against the various expressions of traditionalism. Jesús González Requena notes how, for instance, cinematic depictions of rural spaces in particular became associated in the Spanish cultural imaginary with the faraway (tales of adventures), the exotic (tales of pre-capitalist society), borders (narratives fashioned after the Hollywood western, even spaghetti westerns filmed in southern Spain), finally, certain national historical scenarios.[4] The evocation of rural landscapes were often juxtaposed in audiences' minds against an opposing imagery, that of urban space and, consequently, modernity. Such a binarism was built upon a belief that local traditions, and by association the traditional community, were under siege by encroaching foreign culture and values, the latter often vaguely identified with European ideas, although expressing a more generalized pattern of xenophobia.

Such spatial binarisms are overly simplistic, of course, in that they do not take into account the intervention of the cinematic institution in landscape representations. González Requena notes how the cinematic apparatus itself is emblematic of the international modernizing process against which the ideology of traditionalism emerged. Historically, movie theatres were first located in urban centres and so, even as late as the 1930s and 1940s, the cinematic glorification of rural culture in Spanish film was almost always by way of nostalgic evocations of a world being erased in part by the mass media.[5] The image of popular culture, concretized in the ethnoscapes of Spanish films, thus become reified over time, transformed into mere cultural artifacts to be circulated and consumed as part of a cult of cultural nostalgia. To seriously explore the tension between rural and urban spaces in Spanish film, one needs to be mindful of the cinema itself as a set of signifying practices shaping the filmic message and the historicized patterns of reception of such images.

Despite such caveats, it is still possible to explore the Spanish cinematic treatment of landscape. Katherine Kovács has argued, for instance, that throughout the twentieth century the recurrent patterns of some landscapes have even formed the basis for a recognizable national film style.[6] The persistence of such associations as other film historians suggest, gives the impression of Spanish cinema's 'narrat[ing] the nation as just this finite limited space, inhabited by a tightly coherent and unified community, closed off from other identities besides national identity'.[7]

For Andrew Higson, the problem with the assertion of national cinema used implicitly in such arguments is that the 'imagined community', to use the popularized phrase from Benedict Anderson, is unable to account for the cultural difference and diversity that invariably mark both sides of a particular nation-state and the members of more geographically dispersed 'national' communities.[8] Higson's critique of 'the limiting imagination of national cinema' does not necessarily invalidate claims for a Spanish national film style approximating the condition of a national cinema.[9] Rather, it helps us to identify certain visual and pictorial styles as historical efforts, both conscious and unconscious, to use various spatialized narratives to forge notions of a national community. As we explore the varying cultural meanings inscribed in these landscapes, we acknowledge the temporal and spatial progression of a number of competing ideological projects as they valorize different cultural spaces that reinforce certain conceptions of the Spanish nation on film. At the same time, we are made aware in such an exploration of landscape imagery that many of these constructions inevitably result, as Higson argues, in the suppression of cultural difference and minority discourse as the price for securing such coherencies.

## Deep Spain

One of the earliest and most influential depictions of a simple Manichaean dichotomy between rural and urban culture and ideology is to be found in Florián Rey's *Aldea maldita* (Damned Village, 1930). As the last great epic of the silent period, the film appears to some critics as a hybrid text, a vivid picture of social conditions of rural Spain in the decade of the 1920s, and, as well, the narrative embodiment of the patriarchal values of traditionalist Spanish society that preceded the modern period.[10] These two sets of values are inscribed in the story of the forced exodus from his land of a rural Castilian farmer, Juan de Castilla, and his wife, Acacia. The failure of the crops over three years leads to what the intertitles liken to a biblical exodus. Juan is imprisoned for attacking the local usurer; Acacia is separated from him and joins her neighbour, Magdalena, who leads Acacia off to the city. Acacia's departure in a caravan of carts, as viewed by Juan from the window of his cell, underscores the negative values attached to migration and the consequent affirmation of rootedness, even in the face of entrapment, which is the economic lot of the Spanish peasant.

The Castilian landscape in Rey's film is figured along a moral axis that aligns the Manichaean structures of biblical good and bad spaces. Acacia is lured to the city by a character appropriately named Magdalena. This largely nostalgic evocation of rural landscapes encoded as patriarchal moral values became associated with the *españolada*, the popular folkloric cinematic genre of the 1930s and 1940s.[11] One of its most emblematic expressions is to be found in the multiple versions of *Nobleza baturra* (Rustic Chivalry), directed by Joaquín Dicenta in a silent version in 1925 and then in a sound remake by Florián Rey in 1935. Both versions deal with the concept of male honour and female probity as understood by rural communities. The 1935 film is set in a rural Aragón in which moral and ethical problems displace social and economic marginalization. John Hopewell notes, whether in folkloric song or in the communal harvest scene, Florián Rey's 'selective realism' serves to reinforce a 'mythicized vision of Aragón'.[12] By 1935, of course, the kind of world evoked in *Rustic Chivalry* only existed as a popular movie plot.[13]

The early sound period provided one notable refutation of the myth of the ennobling rustic world: Luis Buñuel's documentary, *Tierra sin pan* (Land without Bread, 1933). Based on an anthropological essay by Maurice Legendre on the rural society of the Spanish province of Salamanca, the film borrows Legende's subtitle, 'a human geography' to describe the abject poverty and institutional backwardness of the region's communities. As Buñuel's voice-over commentary notes, the rural regions of the northwest of the Iberian Peninsula were places of 'refuge from those authorities of church and state who had attempted to foster uniformity of religion and conformity to social mores'.[14] But, according to Kovács, the landscape of the region reveals that '[t]he Hurdanos are doubly imprisoned – by their environment and by an inappropriate system of values that only sinks them deeper into misery'.[15] Buñuel's evocation of the wretched social reality of rural Spain is, however, a rare disruption of the prevailing edenic portrait of folkloric Spanish culture evoked throughout the late silent period and much of the first two decades of sound cinema in Spain.

## Dystopian cityscapes

Because of the nature of the censorship process imposed on the film industry in the aftermath of the terrible Civil War, the landscapes of Spanish cinema were predominantly those of studio-generated genre films that perpetuated the fantasy of folkloric cinema. The dark side of Spain's cultural landscape, the city as 'the great bad place' in the Spanish cultural imaginary, only began to fill Spanish movie screens during the decade of the 1950s. From the style and strategies of Italian neorealism a younger generation of Spanish filmmakers discovered a way to circumvent the Franco government's film censors by underscoring a cinematic *mise-en-scène* of the urban underclass that was an implicit critique of the regime's failed economic policies. The earliest example of this embrace of the neorealist style was Antonio del Amo's *Día tras día* (Day after Day, 1951), a film that visually renders the city the site of the protracted struggle for survival by Spain's underclass. Shot on location in Madrid's Cascorro neighbourhood with a cast in which non-professional actors figured prominently, the film borrowed from neorealism's emphasis on the everyday actions of characters to tell the story of the destiny of two orphans, Anselmo and Ernesto. As José Enrique Monterde argues, however, the external elements of the neorealist *mise-en-scène* are counter-balanced by the regressive motifs of more doctrinaire Spanish films of the period: the presence of priests and the centreing of plots around photogenic little-boy actors, both elements of which were the source of melodramatic subgenres of the period.[16]

Also in 1951, a more powerful expression of Spanish neorealism, José Antonio Nieves Conde's *Surcos* (Furrows), focused on the struggle of a rural peasant family thrown off the land and forced to struggle for survival in the inhospitable environment of Madrid. Their arrival in the city exposes the father's economic impotence and the ascendancy of the children and, as in *Aldea maldita*, especially female characters, here mother and daughter. The view of grim urban slums is intended to update the vision of modernization having displaced the family and shattered the moral foundation of patriarchal order. The film ends with the father rising up against his wife and returning the family to the moral equilibrium of the country and of patriarchal power.[17]

The bleak narrative spaces of del Amo's and Nieves-Condes's films posed a tacit acknowledgement of the failure of the Franco government's economic stewardship. Such criticism could only be expressed opaquely since an elaborate state-run censorial apparatus was in place to promote the traditionalist narratives of the nation that suited the regime's own immediate political and long-range ideological interests. Thus, for instance, the censors insisted that the end of *Surcos* depict the family's return to the country.

In the 1950s implicit anti-Francoist resistance in cinema took form around that demonized space of the city, a cultural landscape that is shown continually to ensnare individuals precisely by their schemes to break out of it. As well, the influence of neorealism was to be found in a number of films set in rural spaces. Filmmakers sought to take what had largely been the clichéd landscape of folkloric comedies and traditionalist rural dramas and to connect them to the themes of contemporary social reality. Most noteworthy among these are Luis García Berlanga's *Bienvenido, Mister Marshall* (Welcome, Mister Marshall, 1952), and Juan Antonio Bardem's *Calle Mayor* (Main Street, 1956). Berlanga's film is set in the Castilian village of Villar del Río and depicts through a comedic plot the economic frustrations of rural inhabitants. The storyline, in which the rural community is transformed from a nondescript Castilian village into a more cinematically imageable Andalusian town, is an indictment of the cinematic falsifications of folkloric Spain and a critique of the imposed propaganda related to picturesque Spanish culture during the decade following the Civil War.

Bardem's *Calle Mayor* depicts a provincial cityscape in which social claustrophobia traps individuals within a pattern of behaviour that transforms provincial life into a psychological prison. The sense of the constricted spaces of social movement for Spaniards, whether living in towns or cities, is beautifully conveyed in the series of shots of the crowded thoroughfare of the title, a pillared promenade, the unnamed town's 'Main Street'. Shot in a number of Castilian cities to produce a generic view of provincial spaces, the reiterated sequences of the promenade suggest the ritual of surveillance and social control – seeing and being seen – that constitute the entrapment of Spaniards in an affective landscape of repressive social values.

Over the next decade, criticism of Francoist culture through a critique of the marginalized culture represented in cityscapes would come from a variety of sources. In addition to Bardem's *Muerte de un ciclista* (Death of a Cyclist, 1955), there were important films such as Marco Ferreri's *Los chicos* (The Kids, 1959), *El pisito* (The Little Flat, 1960) and *El cochecito* (The Little Car, 1961), all of which used the dreary cityscape to indict the regime's inept handling of the economy. This line is picked up and expanded in Carlos Saura's first feature, *Los golfos* (Hooligans, 1959), and Fernando Fernán Gómez's *La vida sigue* (Life Goes On, 1962).

Not coincidentally, the rise of a critical conception of cityscapes brought forth a generation of gifted cinematographers who were the creators of the politicized cityscapes we identify with the opposition cinema of the 1960s and later. Principal among these was José Juan Julio Baena (*Los golfos*, 1959; *El cochecito*, 1960) whose characterizations of the urban spaces of Madrid were those of a *mise-en-scène* teeming with people, quite different from the actuality footage seen in earlier Spanish films. Similarly, Luis Cuadrado (*La caza*/The Hunt, 1965; *Peppermint Frappé*, 1967; *El espíritu de la colmena*/Spirit of the Beehive, 1973; *Furtivos*/Poachers, 1975), shooting in rural and provincial settings, used the interplay of darkness and light to convey a series of landscapes that carried with them profound historical and political meaning.

## The landscapes of historical memory

Saura's 1965 film, *La caza*, may well be considered the beginning of Spanish cinema's transition to the post-Franco era. Though the film was made a decade before the death of the aging dictator, its formulation of historical material symbolically foretells the undoing of the old regime through petty rivalries complicated by the simple aging process of three men. The film follows four weekend hunters, three of whom were buddies during the Civil War, as they come together to hunt rabbits in a valley that was the site of a pitched battle during the war. By setting the action in that valley and supplying the three older men's personal history of what they did in the war, the film is able to bring characters and audience alike to discern signs of the past as preserved in landscape. The caves carved out of the hillside are, in reality, old bunkers; the rabbits under fire recall battle scenes. The idea of the hunt intensifies the mental and physical landscapes of entrapment and pursuit as they clearly evoke the memories of the war years.

Although *La caza* did not trigger many actual imitators, the film, which had been revised to meet the demands of the Spanish censors, did suggest to other directors and screenwriters a range of possibilities for serious films that might circumvent the censors and still challenge the image of the peaceful and prosperous Spain promoted by the government. Among these were three films of the 1970s that symbolically suggest the troubled landscape that is the legacy of the war and three decades of Francoism. All three films, Víctor Erice's *El espíritu de la colmena*, Ricardo Franco's *Pascual Duarte* (1975) and José Luis Borau's *Furtivos* (1975) were shot by Luis Cuadrado. In all three, the cinematographer's use of chiaoscuro, the definition of an empty *mise-en-scène* to accentuate individual isolation and tight close ups of the principal characters to intensify the appearance of the protagonists immobilized in confining spaces help to create a symbolic space of action that appears as the result of the ominous effects of the unseen dictatorship.

Each plot is structured around the eruption of violence in seemingly peaceful spaces. Though strikingly different in storyline and themes, all share the same intense construction of the remembered landscape of violence that harks back to the dictator. *Pascual Duarte* is a free adaptation of the acclaimed novel by Camilo José Cela as it recounts through flashback the troubled life of a peasant whose brutal acts seem to reflect the intensifying violence of the larger community leading up to the Civil War. *El espíritu de la colmena* is set in an unnamed Castilian village in 1940 and depicts the atomization of a family in the dreary post-Civil War period. Erice develops a treatment of landscape and *mise-en-scène* that becomes for many Spanish spectators the emblematic expression of the emotional disjunctions and lingering memories of the war that haunt recollections of life in the post-war decade. Santos Zunzunegui observes the way:

> *El espíritu de la colmena* maps out a universe of disconnected spaces…fragmentation is a mobilizing principle…each character will live isolated in his or her space…all the relations established among the figures are shown to be impossible; at stake are bodies (and spirits) that are at once proximate and profoundly foreign to one another.[18]

By contrast, *Furtivos* is a contemporary allegory of power structures set in the forest preserve of a northern Spanish province. The poachers of the title are trespassers on a game preserve, but their transgressions metaphorically expose the sexual and political poaching of Francoist society. *Furtivos* is perhaps the most explicit example of the deceptive veneer of normalcy and social stability that is hidden by the image of the peaceful forest. The forest that Borau evokes is a deceptive space of covert violence and transgression, thus providing another politically charged spatial metaphor for Spanish society.

Borau's script collaborator, Manuel Gutiérrez Aragón, expands that image in *El corazón del bosque* (The Heart of the Forest, 1979) to convey the historical traces of the war in the northern regions. The film tells the story of the maquis, the resistance fighters to the Franco regime, who survive in the forests and mountains of northeastern Spain. As in *Furtivos,* the forests afford clandestinity and resistance to the established order. This is really a double story: the first and more explicit narrative is that of Juan, who in the 1950s must search out the last maquis, El Andarín, to try to persuade him to give up the fight against the Franco regime. Over the years, Andarín's life in the forest has reduced him nearly to the level of an animal. The world of El Andarín suggests the landscape of persistent memories. Parallel to this political narrative is a fairy tale of the magical secrets of the forest.[19] As depicted in *El corazón del bosque,* the woods suggest the fertile, imaginative spaces of the north that are not so unlike the Castilian plains that similarly harbour harsh memories of fratricidal struggle, but which are, as well, endowed with the allure of magic. Thus the film may be read as a conceptual struggle between political disillusion of the past and the persistent magical appeal of the woods that may be a way through the unchartered terrain of post-Franco Spanish culture.

## Regional spaces; other spaces

With its focus on folklore linked to the landscapes of his native region of Santander in northern Spain, Gutiérrez Aragón's film becomes a useful stylistic bridge to the emergence of striking regional cinemas in Catalunya and later in the Basque Country, where territorial imagery and regional politics have been joined in recent decades. Though efforts at developing regional cinema are found in other parts of Spain, the Catalan and Basque experiences are instructive both for their sharp contrasts to the dominant *mise-en-scènes* of earlier Madrid-centred films and their crystallization of the two dominant ideological paradigms of spatial treatment in Spanish cinema: the *campo,* or countryside, and the city.

The new landscape of Catalan cinema was primarily the not-so-new cityscape of Barcelona. Prior to the Civil War, Catalunya had boasted its own brand of national cinema.[20] One of the distinctive features of its re-emergence was the cultivation of new images of modern cityscapes, principally those set in Barcelona, the regional capital, which had long vied for cultural supremacy over Madrid. The Barcelona of early films by Jaime Camino (*Los felices sesenta*/The Happy Sixties, 1964) and Vicente Aranda (*Fata Morgana*/Mirage, 1966) had been efforts to reject the arid and static *mise-en-scène* of films made in Madrid. With these and later 1970s films by José Juan Bigas Luna (*Bilbao,* 1978; *Caniche,* 1979), Ventura Pons (*Ocaña: retrato intermitent*/Ocaña, An Intermittent Portrait, 1979) and Francesc Bellmunt (*La orgía*/The Orgy, 1978; *La radio folla*/Radio Speed, 1984) there emerged a sense of an urban space equated with social and sexual liberation, an Iberian culture closer to Europe both in terms of its architecture and social customs.[21] This tendency has been picked up in more recent Catalan films by a younger generation, notably women filmmakers like Rosa Vergés (*Boom Boom,* 1990) and Marta Balletbò-Coll (*Costa Brava,* 1995). Through the interplay of their plots and settings, these films, as well as the intimate films by Ventura Pons (*El perqué de tot plegat*/What It's All About, 1994), normalize the image of urban comedy in which being Catalan is not any different from being European.

By contrast, emergent Basque cinema shows a freshness in its pictorial depiction of rural landscapes that had seldom been shown on screen before except in documentaries. Of special note is one of the earliest acclaimed Basque films of the post-Franco period, Montxo Armendáriz's *Tasio* (1984), a film whose story emphasizes Basque cultural traditionalism precisely through its focus on Navarrese landscapes. Narrating the story of generations of carbon workers who are deeply committed to their rural community, the film caused a sensation at various national and international film festivals, winning numerous awards. *Tasio* is distinctive in the way landscapes are used to define the regional character and shape the narrative. In a style that seemed both ethnographic and yet gripping as human drama, with *Tasio* and his second feature, *27 horas*/27 Hours (1986), Armendáriz ushered in a style of regional filmmaking in which the powerful visual treatment of Basque settings, both rural and urban, often appears to frame and enforce regional identity.

The motif of Basque rural space as the crucible of regional cultural identity seemed in large measure to borrow a page from earlier Castilian rural narratives of the 1930s. This is certainly true in some of the early films of Julio Medem, the most acclaimed of recent Basque regional filmmakers. In *Vacas* (Cows, 1992), and *Tierra* (Land, 1994), narrative emphasis is on the pre-eminence of location, especially the lush forests of the north in *Vacas*, made to seem all the more enchanting through Medem's signature use of eccentric camera angles and odd narrative points of view. In *Vacas*, for example, the story of three generations of family history is told from the eccentric point of view of cows, an emblematic figure that reaffirms Basque rural identity. Critics have suggested that the persistent images of cows are an intertextual evocation of Picasso's famed painting, 'Guernica'.[22] Indeed, the correspondences between the painting and the film's imagery is one pivotal way in which, even in his earliest work, Medem seeks to rethink the local imagery of the Basque Country in more universal terms.

Medem's most critically acclaimed film, *Amantes del círculo polar* (Lovers of the Arctic Circle, 1999) is arguably the quintessential expression of that process of shift from local to international contexts. The film's enunciative strategy of narrating the (Basque) nation through genealogical narratives breaks out of the confines of strictly Basque geography by following the movements of the title characters from the Basque Country to Madrid and, finally, Finland. The film links their identity and destiny to the past, the 1937 aerial bombing of Guernika when a fallen German pilot became the lover of a Basque woman. The strategy that informs this plot and, in many ways, the dominant feature of Medem's meditation on the nature of Spain's imagined communities, is the effort to erase confining borders and to break out of the old ideological traps that had positioned Spain, even in the minds of Spaniards, as exotic and different.

Medem's complex narrational style, employing markedly regional settings to tell stories that transcend the regional culture is a strategy mirrored in the best work of other filmmakers closely aligned with regional cinema, such as Eloy de la Iglesia (*El pico*/The Shoot-up, 1982; *El pico II*, 1983), Imanol Uribe (*La muerte de Mikel*/The Death of Mikel, 1983; *Los días contados*/Playing for Time, 1994) and Juanma Bajo Ulloa (Airbag, 1997).

## New and old spaces of modernity

The repositioning of Spanish cinema within the mainstream of international cultural movement through a re-imaging of the *mise-en-scène* of communal history is also expressed in the generation of filmmakers who, in the late 1970s and early 1980s, transformed the Madrid locale of an earlier generation's cinema into a new and youthful space of creativity. This group included Fernando Colomo (*Tigres de papel*/Paper Tigers, *1977, ¿Qué hace una chica como tú en un sitio como éste?*/What's a Girl Like You Doing in a Place like This?, 1979) and Fernando Trueba (*Opera Prima*/First Work, 1980; *Sal Gorda*/Coarse Salt, 1982 and *Sé infiel y no mires con quien*/Cheat on Your Partner with Anybody, 1985). The youthful actors and light, comic plots of these films were in the spirit of early Woody Allen movies, thereby suggesting a generational realignment of Spaniards with an international community.

The most notable of these younger filmmakers is Pedro Almodóvar, whose films throughout the 1980s used the urban settings of Madrid as the catalyst for his protagonists' creative self-affirmations. The plots of his early films, as well as their striking visual style, gave prominence to urban culture as the link to international modernity and thereby reflected the historical shift in the treatment of Spanish cinematic space and landscape. In his cross-over film, *¿Qué he hecho yo para merecer esto?* (What Have I Done to Deserve This?, 1985), and his Oscar-nominated comedy, *Mujeres al borde de un ataque de nervios* (Women on the Verge of a Nervous Breakdown, 1988) we see two striking examples of this development. *What Have I done…?* is, among other things, an ironic reworking of the neorealist tradition of narratives of migration to the cities that characterized a number of films of the 1950s and 1960s. Unlike the emblematic hero of Pedro Lazaga's 1966 comedy, *La ciudad no es para mí* (The City's Not for Me), who, like characters dating back to *La aldea maldita*, preferred the moral uplift of the countryside to the city,[23] Almodóvar's melodramatic heroine and her gay son discover personal liberation in Madrid. With *Women on the Verge*, Almodóvar breaks with nearly all the cinematic traditions of shaping cultural space of Spanish cinema by constructing a personal variation of the colorful cosmopolitical cityscape of Hollywood screwball comedies of the 1950s. Through a colourful new urban imageability, Madrid is seen as the site of the kind of antic comedy that previously had only been the domain of Hollywood screenwriters and set designers. The heroine Pepa's liberation from the designs of her philandering lover, Iván, not only signals her own emancipation from patriarchal control but reflects the self-confidence of a society now ready to become part of a more vibrant European culture.[24]

Another striking feature of Spanish cinema's modernized landscape is the increasing treatment of non-Spanish spaces on Spanish screens. From the 1980s onward, a series of Spanish filmmakers sought to shoot their films outside of Spain, most often in the US. With the exception of Fernando Trueba's *Too Much* (1995), all had been commercial failures. The source of these projects was a conspicuous effort to demarginalize Spanish cinema[25] and to acknowledge Spain's cultural heterogeneity. Growing out of a generational sense of cultural ties to Latin America, a series of notable co-productions with Cuba, Mexico and Argentina, began to transform the earlier provincialism of Spanish landscapes into spaces of reencounter between Spanish-speaking characters and audiences. Some films, like Colomo's *El cuarteto de La Habana* (Havana Quartet, 1999), were efforts to use cheaper production costs in Cuba while widening the appeal of Spanish films for Latin American audiences.

Others, like Adolfo Aristaráin's *Martín Hache* (1998) a co-production with Argentina, suggested the reciprocity that had grown and deepened between Spanish society and Spain's former colonies.

At the same time, a more complex ethnic image of Spain emerges in the 1990s due to migrations from Latin America (Manuel Gutiérrez Aragón's *Cosas que dejé en la Habana/Things I Left in Havana*, 1996; Icíar Bollaín's *Flores de otro mundo*/Flowers from Another World, 1999) and Africa (Montxo Armendáriz's *Cartas de Alou*/Letters from Alou, 1990; Imanol Uribe's *Bwana*, 1995; Carlos Saura's *Taxi*, 1996). These films are especially significant in that they suggest an ethnographic refiguring of Spanish urban and rural spaces that effectively dislodges the seemingly fixed milieus of a world previously treated as both ethnically homogenous and cultural eternal. A much less common, though nonetheless significant move are the rare examples of films that show Spaniards in Africa (Cecilia Batrolomé's *Lejos de Africa* (Far from Africa, 1996); Mariano Barroso's *Kasbah* (2000)), thus giving definitive end to the last great fiction of Spanish cinematic treatments of landscape: the myth of the Spaniard immobilized in a fixed *mise-en-scène* that defined national identity.

As these most recent developments suggest, the historically and culturally specific messages of Spanish cinematic landscapes have changed over the past century, with the cluster of related spatial markers in film, those of setting, topography, cityscapes and *mise-en-scène*, shifting meaning to reflect changes in the political, social and cultural communities that are its diverse national audience. Equally true is the corollary to that view, namely, that the struggle for modernization as reflected in so many Spanish cultural narratives has also changed. The idea of modernity has gone from a borrowed idea that was used to align Spain with Europe to the more recent recognition of the globalizing project within which Spanish cinema and Spain itself are part of a global network of cultural exchanges. The only constant in this rearrangement is the axiomatic principle that these depicted spaces continue to narrate the multiple facets of the evolving nation on screen.

## Notes

1. Núria Triana-Toribio, *Spanish National Cinema* (London and New York: Routledge, 2003), 164.
2. Anthony Smith, 'Images of the nation: Cinema, art and national identity', in Mette Hjorte and Scott Mackenzie, *Cinema and Nation* (London and New York: Routledge, 2000), 45–59 (55).
3. In his discussion of visual representations of national identity in painting and film, Anthony Smith notes the way in which 'ethnic atmosphere' in such visual representations is traditionally linked to the 'poetic landscapes of distinctive communities…or "ethnoscapes," within which the territory mirrors the ethnic community and is historicized by the communal events and processes whose relics and monuments dot the landscapes' (55).
4. González Requena, Jesús, 'Apuntes para una historia de lo rural en el cine español', *El campo en el cine español* (Valencia: Filmoteca Generalitat Valenciana, 1988), 13–27 (14).
5. Requena, 13.
6. Requena, 17.

7. Andrew Higson, 'The limiting imagination of national cinema', in Mette Hjorte and Scott Mackenzie, *Cinema and Nation* (London and New York: Routledge, 2000), 66.
8. Ibid.
9. Ibid., 67–69.
10. Agustin Sánchez Vidal, 'La aldea maldita', in Julio Pérez Perucha, *Antología crítica del cine español: 1906–1995* (Madrid: Cátedra, 1997), 84–85.
11. Jo Labanyi, *Constructing Identity in Contemporary Spain* (Oxford: Oxford University Press, 2002), 7; Triana-Toribio, 40.
12. John Hopewell, *Out of the Past: Spanish Cinema after Franco* (London: BFI, 1986), 9.
13. Though conceptually rooted in Castilian traditions of honour and probity among peasants, the folkloric space persistently evoked in Spanish cinema of this period collapsed distinctive regional specificities of Castile, Andalusia and Aragón into a general folkloric *mise-en-scène* populated by colourful folkloric types. Luis García Berlanga's 1952 political comedy, *Bienvenido Mister Marshall* (Welcome Mister Marshall) deploys that very conflation as the centrepiece of the film's parody of the Franco regime's cultural mythology (Hopewell, 48).
14. Katherine Kovács, 'The plain in Spain: Geography and national identity in Spanish cinema', *Quarterly Review of Film and Video* 13(4) (1991), 17– 46 (21).
15. Kovács, 21.
16. José Enrique Monterde, '*Día tras día*,' in Pérez Perucha: 290
17. Kinder, 53.
18. Santos Zunzunegui, 'Between history and dream: Víctor Erice's *El espíritu de la colmena*', in Jenaro Talensand and Santos Zunzunegui (eds), *Modes of Representation in Spanish Cinema* (Minneapolis and London: University of Minnesota Press, 1998), 145–146.
19. Kovács, 36.
20. J. M. Caparrós Lera, 'El cine catalán durante la Renaixença', in Sergei Alegre et al., *El cine en Cataluña: una aproximación história* (Barcelona: PPU, 1993), 22–31.
21. Marvin D'Lugo, 'Catalan Cinema: Historical experience and cinematic practice', *Quarterly Review of Film and Video* 13(1–3) (1991), 131–146 (144).
22. María Pilar Rodríguez, *Mundos en conflicto: Aproximaciones al cine vasco de los noventa* (San Sebastián: Universidad de Deusto/ Filmoteca Vasca, 2002), 88.
23. Triana-Toribio, 77.
24. Stuart Hall, 'European cinema on the verge of a nervous breakdown', in Duncan Petrie (ed.), *Screening Europe: Images and Identity in Contemporary European Cinema* (London: BFI Working Papers, 1992), 52.
25. Kinder, Marsha, *Blood Cinema: The Reconstruction of National Identity in Spain* (Berkeley: University of California Press, 1993), 8–9.

# Chapter 7

Landscape and Irish Cinema

Martin McLoone

In a tourism piece for the Guardian newspaper's 'Travel' section Tim Ecott extols the stark beauties and cerebral attractions of Connemara in the West of Ireland:

> At the seaward end of Killary is a tiny jetty, and a small hostel where the philosopher Ludwig Wittgenstein spent the summer of 1948, inspired by the solitude and proximity of the steep heather-clad slopes. And round the tip of the bay the beaches of Renvyle and Glassilaun are swathes of white sand, as perfect as any in the Western Isles. Places fit for thinking.[1]

This is a telling and persuasive mix of landscape and mindscape – a kind of 'outsider' romanticism where the natural beauty offers escape, creativity and philosophical truth. As such, it perfectly encapsulates the way in which the west of Ireland now exists as a kind of ideal regenerative environment for the troubled and worried mind of modernity. Ecott notes that the environs of Killary provided the locations for Jim Sheridan's *The Field* (1990), a film which explores another aspect of Connemara – history and myth – that holds special attraction for the contemporary tourist. Ecott is careful to tease out the ironies of history. Considering the landscape of nearby Cong, in Co. Mayo, the setting for John Ford's classic piece of Irish whimsy, *The Quiet Man* (1952) Ecott perceptively notes, 'This lush landscape is haunted by the ghosts of the victims of the great famine that sprang from the potato blight of 1845–1851'.[2] The vast and empty landscape of Ireland's western seaboard represents one of the least densely populated areas of Europe. The Famine decimated the population of the west and it is the memory of this catastrophe and the spectres of those dead that Ecott evokes here and which give this landscape a particular resonance.

The comic absurdities of *The Quiet Man* and the melodramatic excesses of *The Field* make for very different films but Ecott is right to see a central irony about both – '…the bitter irony of Irish Americans returning home, and using their cash to take property from those who stayed on the land'.[3]

In Jim Sheridan's *The Field* the eponymous piece of land is first revealed to the audience in a carefully composed shot that, in the Irish context, carries deep cultural significance. It follows an extended credit sequence (shot in the beach locations extolled by Ecott) in which we see Bull McCabe (Richard Harris) and his son Tadgh (Sean Bean) laboriously gathering seaweed from the shore and piling it into baskets which are then slung onto their backs. Father and son carry the seaweed up over the hills, disappearing into the mist and descending clouds. Surprisingly (and significantly, as we shall see) the younger man struggles to keep up with his elderly father, falling behind as his uncertain feet slip on the loose rocks. Eventually they reach their destination and pause on the hill to gaze down at the field which this seaweed will fertilize and sustain. 'God made the world', Bull says, 'and seaweed made that field, boy'. The camera cuts from a close up of Bull's admiring face to a high-angle panoramic shot of the landscape, the green lushness of the field standing out in stark contrast to the dull browns and greys of the bog land and hills that surround it. The field is the only evidence of cultivation in the midst of an otherwise wild and untamed landscape, literally a piece of culture hewn out of nature.

There is, however, more at stake in the Irish context than merely this contrast between culture and nature. The long shot of the field also shows a road winding past it and disappearing over the horizon to the hills beyond. This second contrast – between the cultivated field and the open road – lies at the heart of the film's meanings and visualizes a central historical and political reality about land in Ireland. If the field suggests home and rootedness then the road represents rootless wandering, a contrast between the settled community and the itinerant which figures as a considerable plot element in the film. However, in its political connotations this contrast between staying and going – between ownership and exile – conjures up the whole history of English colonization in Ireland and the consequent displacement of the native Irish through conquest, dispossession and emigration. This important historical context is captured melodramatically at the end of the scene. Bull plucks a dandelion and holds its white seed-head to his lips. 'This is what we'd be without the land, boy', he says and blows. The seeds scatter and disperse in the breeze.

A similar shot of the field is revealed later in the film, this time as Bull, Tadgh and their simple-minded minion Bird (John Hurt) travel back from the town. They have just had it confirmed that the field will be sold by public auction, thus opening up the possibility that it could be sold to a stranger. The camera again cuts from a close up of Bull's face to a crane shot view of the field in its majestic setting. Bull again offers his son instructional words of wisdom. 'Our father's father's father's father dug that soil with their bare hands, made those walls. Our soul's buried down there. And your son's son's son's sons will take care of it, boy. Do you get my meaning?' When Tadgh nods in response, Bull concludes, 'Guard it well.'

Bull's speech here elaborates on his comments of the earlier scene. As well as representing the rootedness of home, the field also represents for Bull immemorial tradition – stability and security rather than uncertainty and change. The field and the sacred duty to nourish and protect it is Bull's gift to his son.

There are echoes here of an earlier cinematic treatment of the land and rural life in Ireland, Robert Flaherty's 1934 documentary *Man of Aran*. Flaherty actually recreates the 'bare hands' toil that Bull refers to, showing in considerable detail the slow, grinding labour that goes into the making of a field amid the barren rocks of the Aran islands. Indeed, the original cinematic template for some of the imagery in Sheridan's credit sequences can be found in Flaherty's heroic posing of the Aran islanders against an elemental sky, the basket of seaweed on their backs. Bull's message about tradition and continuity is also rendered visually in a famous sequence from the earlier film.

Flaherty's Aran family has just rescued the fishing nets from the sea and the Man himself (Tiger King) has narrowly escaped drowning in the tempestuous waters. As the three characters (The Man, his wife and their young son) walk away from the shore, they pause on the edge of the cliff and look back at the crashing waves. Flaherty edits a series of low-angle shots of the human characters framed against the skyline with high-angle shots of the thunderous waves in such a way that a specific meaning emerges – one that Sheridan picks up on later in *The Field*. The sequence begins with a shot of all three characters framed on the cliff with the stormy skies behind them. This cuts to a shot of the raging sea and then back to a low-angle shot of the father himself. He turns his head slightly to offer a perfect profile of his chiselled good looks, framed against the skyline by his 'tam-o'-shanter' headgear. More shots of the crashing seas follow this stylized, monumental pose before another cut to a low-angle shot of the son framed in a similarly pensive pose. The sequence ends with a three-shot again of the family walking home against the majesty of the sky, fragile human beings tenuously holding on to a cultural space against the awesome power of nature. The main ideological impact of the sequence, however, is to suggest continuity between father and son – implying that the father's struggle will eventually become the son's and that this elemental existence is set to continue in an unending cycle. Flaherty here captures visually what Sheridan suggests through Bull's melodramatic words.

Flaherty's film is a romantic, stylized image of an elemental struggle – Man against the Sea, as the opening titles suggest – and its perspective on tradition and essentialist humanity makes its message a rather conservative one (and in the context of the politics of the 1930s, even downright reactionary). However, its evocation of an Ireland of harsh beauty and resilient peasants neatly encapsulated the ascetic nationalism that dominated political culture in Ireland at the time and its primitivist imagery was largely welcomed, even if the film stirred up much controversy and resistance elsewhere.[4]

If Sheridan's visualization of Ireland in the 1930s echoes aspects of Flaherty's style, *The Field* is, nonetheless, a very different piece of work. It is a film very much of the 1990s and this becomes clear in the way in which it explores the implications of land and tradition, in particular through the response of the son Tadgh to the burden of history which his father has bequeathed him. To return to the introductory shots of the field itself, the context of contemporary Ireland suggests another reading of the field/road dichotomy. For Tadgh, the road represents escape – the promise of freedom and opportunity and the chance to dream and to imagine – while the field, with its diurnal round of backbreaking toil, represents entrapment. For Tadgh, it is not so much a case of being rooted to the land as being chained to it in an unending cycle of duty and self-denial. As this aspect of the plot unwinds, the significance of Tadgh's inability to keep pace with his father in the opening sequences becomes clear. The younger man quite literally does not wish to follow in his father's (or his father's father's) footsteps. In this way, Sheridan's visualization of the field and its place in a wider landscape taps into the very heart of contemporary political and cultural debate in Ireland. In the generational conflict between father and son the film symbolizes a continuing cultural debate in Ireland – the relationship between a prosperous contemporary Ireland

and the memory of its oppressed and poverty-stricken past. This debate is multi-faceted and manifests itself variously as a clash between rootedness and transcendence and between home and exile; as an exploration of the cultural legacy of colonialism and nationalism and, most importantly, as a particularly Irish construction of the clash between tradition and modernity.

## Land, landscape and Irish nationalism

'Every mature nation has its symbolic landscapes', argued geographer D. W. Meinig. 'They are part of the iconography of nationhood, part of the shared set of ideas and memories and feelings which bind people together.'[5] If this is true for 'mature nations' it is even more so for a nation struggling into being from economic, political and cultural domination. In this case, the iconography becomes symbolic of *aspiring* nationhood and in the nineteenth century the west of Ireland landscape became a central part of Irish nationalism's developing iconography. To understand, therefore, the complexity of Sheridan's film (and the complexity of the original John B. Keane stage-play on which it is based) it is important to explore in a little more detail the political and cultural role of the land in Irish history.

In its simplest form, the field in Sheridan's film is a symbol of Ireland itself and Bull's desire to own and farm the field is a metaphor for the nationalist struggle in Ireland to reclaim the land from colonial appropriation. During the seventeenth century the English conquest of Ireland was completed (in the plantation of Ulster in 1609, the Cromwellian confiscations of the 1640s and the Williamite resettlements of the 1690s). These confiscation and resettlement policies meant that by 1703, only 14 per cent of the land remained in Irish Catholic ownership, a percentage that continued to decline well into the eighteenth century. By the 1840s, the Irish peasantry, huddled onto the poorest and most over-populated land, was wholly dependent on the potato crop for subsistence and when most of Europe was hit by potato blight in 1845, the failure of the crop impacted on Ireland more grievously than elsewhere. The devastation wrought by the resulting Great Famine of 1845–1850 is a shared subtext to both film and stage-play and Bull's warning to his son Tadgh at the beginning of the film resonates with this. 'Watch out for those tinkers, boy', he admonishes his son. 'They lost their footing on the land during the Famine and they'll never get it back.'

Many lost their footing on the land because, as the famine raged, the landlords responded by evicting their starving peasants, throwing them out to die by the roadside or to perish in disease-ridden overcrowded cities. By 1850, over 1 million had died, as much from disease as starvation. Many more attempted to escape the devastation by emigrating and this initiated a long, steady decline of the population so that by the mid-twentieth century it had almost halved from its pre-famine high of over 8 million. The west of Ireland bore the brunt of this tragedy and its population was systematically decimated.

Post-famine Irish nationalism, therefore, was built on a fundamental principle – the land of Ireland for the people of Ireland – and the struggle over land became the key element in the growth and spread of a nationalist consciousness from the 1850s on. The bitter legacy of the famine influenced the nature of this nationalism, imbuing it with a certain degree of anti-British feeling summed up in the famous dictum of radical nationalist John Mitchel: 'The Almighty, indeed, sent the potato blight, but the English created the Famine.' Irish nationalism was predicated on the desire for economic and political self-sufficiency (hence the name 'Sinn Féin', in Irish literally 'we ourselves'). Cultural nationalism was constructed around a sense of Irish difference to the imperial colonial power of Britain. Thus if Britain represented the high point of industrial urban development, Irish nationalism emphasized the rural and the demand for land ownership. In cultural terms, nationalism rejected English culture in favour of resurrecting (and re-inventing) Gaelic cultural traditions. One of the most crucial developments of the famine was that the Catholic Church in Ireland gave its support to the rising tide of Irish nationalism, cementing an alliance that was crucial for the nature of that nationalism. A certain type of 'rigorist' Catholicism, promoting a culture of self-denial and the surveillance of sexuality and the body, developed to meet the social needs of post-famine rural Ireland.[6] This rigorist culture became synonymous with Irish rural life (and for Tadgh is represented in his duties towards the field) and adherence to Catholicism became another marker of Irish identity in opposition to British Protestantism (and its Protestant unionist allies in Ireland).

If land was at the centre of Irish political nationalism, it is hardly surprising that the representation of land, landscape and rural life became a key element in cultural nationalism. In this regard, the western province of Connaught, its seaboard and its off-shore islands (the setting for both *Man of Aran* and *The Field*) became particularly important. The west, of course, was the part of Ireland furthest away from England and its very remoteness ensured that the area was the least integrated into colonial culture. It came to represent for Irish nationalists, therefore, the purest form of Gaelic Ireland, the unsullied expression of an ancient and proud culture that predated even Christianity. In the Cromwellian land confiscations of the 1640s, under the slogan 'To Hell or Connaught' the native Irish had been forcibly evicted onto the less fertile land of the west giving these claims of authenticity both a historical legitimacy and a contemporary political edge. In the flourishing cultural revival in Ireland that accompanied the growth of nationalist sentiment, the west became the focus for much literary and artistic creativity (the plays of J. M. Synge, the poetry of W. B. Yeats, the painting of Jack B. Yeats and Paul Henry). The writers of the late nineteenth-century literary revival were particularly interested in promoting, in Marianne Elliot's phrase, 'an image of an organic link between an ancient civilisation and a haunted landscape'.[7] These haunted landscapes became the symbols of Ireland's cultural awakening, the contours and trace memories of an ancient Irish nation. Thus Catherine Nash points out that for many of these nationalist writers the west came to signify 'the source for the revitalising of Ireland, a landscape of both personal and national regeneration'. She makes an important point about its status as national symbol: 'the West, in the sense of standing for the whole island and as a source of biological and physiological regeneration, could be seen as embodying the nation'.[8]

The landscape painter, Paul Henry, noted something similar in recounting his love of the west and his decision to live and paint there: 'I wanted if I could to get into my work the very soul of Ireland.'[9]

The west of Ireland landscape, in other words, came to symbolize the very essence of Irishness and its harsh beauty and traditional ways became a source of both escape and regeneration. For Paul Henry, the landscape and the people embodied an ideal. He describes his own life journey as 'an escape' – from childhood in industrial Belfast ('with its most narrow and arid religious atmosphere'), through a sojourn in 'London and its realities' to 'the new life' in the west of Ireland island of Achill. This is a classic romantic journey – from modernity to tradition, from the city to the country – and the romantic sensibility that it reveals infused his paintings of the landscapes and people of the west.

What is perhaps peculiar about Ireland is the way in which this sensibility also infused political culture. In writing about the inspiring images that life in Achill provided, Henry provides a vivid description of the women of Achill.

The women's dresses always supplied a rich note of colour; most of them wore flannel homespun. This course material dyed vermilion, after wear and weather and washing, turned to a variety of tones, and a group of women working in the fields with a background of rich brown earth, made the strip they were working on a riot of gay colour…The instinct for gaiety of colour to relieve the monotony of their lives always struck me as pathetic.[10]

Compare this to a passage from the political writings of Michael Collins, the military leader of the IRA during the War of Independence with Britain (1919–1921) and the subject of Neil Jordan's 1996 biopic:

impoverished as the people are, hard as their lives are, difficult as the struggle for existence is, the outward aspect is pageant. One may see processions of young women riding down on Island ponies to collect sand from the seashore or gathering turf, dressed in their shawls and in their brilliantly coloured skirts made of material spun, woven and dyed by themselves, as it has been spun, woven and dyed for over a thousand years. Their simple cottages are also little changed. They remain simple and picturesque. It is only in such places that one gets a glimpse of what Ireland may become again, when the beauty may be something more than pageant, will be the outward sign of a prosperous and happy Gaelic life.[11]

The similarity of these two passages is remarkable and given the fact that Henry, in his autobiography, eschewed political commitment and promoted a universal, apolitical conception of his art, it illustrates very well the unusually close relationship in Ireland at the time between the inspiration of its artists and the aspirations of its political activists. In this way, Henry's landscapes of the west, like Flaherty's film of Aran, came close to being, in the 1920s and 1930s, the 'official' image of the newly independent Ireland that Collins and his political generation helped to bring into being, so well did their elemental beauty capture prevailing nationalist orthodoxy. Henry's landscapes of thatched cottages in their west of Ireland setting were used for tourist purposes in the 1920s and 1930s and this quintessential image continues to operate as a marker for a general Irishness even today. Given the history of Ireland's colonial past and especially the memory of its famine trauma it is hardly surprising that the land and the landscape carried profound political, cultural and emotional resonances.

The landscape and the thatched cottage play an important political and ideological role in *The Wind that Shakes the Barley* (2006), Ken Loach's film about the War of Independence and the ensuing civil war. Loach sets his film among the IRA 'flying columns' of rural Cork and his cinematography of the Irish countryside is devised in such a way to show the 'insurgents' as native to these hills and fields while the British presence is literally a blot on the landscape. Early in the film, Loach establishes as a key location that emblematic symbol of rural Ireland, a white-walled, thatched cottage, the family home in this case to one of the IRA volunteers and a 'safe house' for the local insurgents generally. It is no surprise that later in the film the British (in the guise of the 'Black and Tans') evict the tenants from this cottage and set fire to the thatched roof. The destruction of the cottage becomes a metaphor for British military and cultural barbarism. It is a scenario that taps into the very heart of Irish nationalist discourse and Loach's radical anti-imperialist message is here inscribed into the very landscape that he recreates.

Loach's film is, in many ways, a riposte to Neil Jordan's earlier *Michael Collins* (1996). It is interesting that both films cover exactly the same years of armed insurrection and civil war (1916–1922) but for the most part, they actually look quite different. Jordan's *Michael Collins* is set mostly in Dublin (though important key scenes, as we shall see, take place in rural and small-town Ireland). The film's prevailing imagery consists of shadowy urban nightscapes – dark, misty-blue and subterranean, mirroring the underground world inhabited by Collins' secret army. It is in this nightmare urban landscape redolent of the film noir cityscapes that the fratricidal tragedy of the Irish civil war is played out as Collins launches his now official army against his former comrades, killing in the process his long-time friend and colleague, Harry Boland. The events leading up to the assassination of Collins himself, however, constitute one of the major rural sequences in Neil Jordan's film. The irony is that this killing is carried out by one the flying columns of Collins' native county Cork, the kind of rural guerrilla army that earlier in the film he is shown encouraging and instructing. In many ways this irony – the incorrigible Cork man Collins assassinated by one of his own brothers-in-arms – symbolizes the tragedy of the civil war.

In Loach's film the fratricide is literal – brother kills brother – and this again is played out against the beauty of the Cork hills and valleys. Both films use the historical events to address more contemporary issues, of course – in Jordan's case the film has resonances for the peace process in Northern Ireland as it was in the mid-1990s and in Loach's case, there are echoes of the British and American invasion of Iraq and the consequent war there against 'insurgents'. But the way in which the films use their landscape shots of Co. Cork suggests a surprisingly similar perspective on the course of the civil war. In Jordan's film, Collins' army – in its grey military uniforms and grey military vehicles – assumes the look of the interloper British forces it has displaced while the members of the flying column from the hills who ambush and kill Collins himself seem to emerge from and disappear back into the native landscape. Jordan's humanist message is that violence begets violence and there is always tragedy (and sacrifice) involved in stopping the cycle of conflict. Loach's conclusions are, of course, much more political than Jordan's. His class-based analysis of the civil war argues that ultimately the Irish people were betrayed by their own petty bourgeois leadership, content to take over the roles and functions of the departing British. For Loach, a foreign oppression was replaced by a native one (and by implication there is a critique here also of contemporary Ireland and its global economic success). However, the use of the Cork landscape in both films achieves a similar effect – that of establishing visually the right of the native population to the ownership and control of the native landscape and to establish the British (and their native supporters) as the aggressive interlopers. As Luke Gibbons has argued:

> The point of drawing attention to (the) interpretation of nature as a symbolic field is to underline the case for treating landscape in romantic images of Ireland not merely as a picturesque backdrop, but as a layer of meaning in its own right, a thematic element which may reinforce or cut across the other levels of meaning in the text.[12]

## Cinematic Ireland and its landscapes

For most of the twentieth century, Ireland had no developed film industry. Indigenous fiction filmmaking began in earnest only in the 1970s and it was not until the 1990s that a fully funded industry was consolidated, eventually establishing a production ratio of about ten feature films a year. However, cinematic Ireland certainly did exist in the representations of both the British and American film industries. Ireland has been an important source of material for both down the years, the result being that the cinematic image often dovetailed the dominant traditions and prejudices of these producing cultures. Most scholars have identified two traditions of representations within the cinemas of Britain and America – in one, Ireland is represented as a kind of rural utopia removed from the stresses of the modern world and in the other, as a site for an almost pre-modern religious bigotry and violence. If the latter, darker image has predominated in recent years, following the outbreak of the 'Troubles' in Northern Ireland, the cinematic tradition that has had the most enduring legacy has been that of rural Ireland and its wildly romantic landscapes.

These romantic images of landscape can be traced back at least as far as the one- and two-reelers made by Sidney Olcott's Kalem Company and shot in Killarney in three successive summers from 1910 (possibly the first US films to be shot on location outside of the United States itself). Kalem's films were designed to appeal to the large Irish-American audiences that made up a significant part of the east coast blue collar audience for early cinema. The films, therefore, carried a strong nationalist message. The 1910 film, *Rory O'More*, for example, offers a short narrative that is almost a perfect template of Irish cultural nationalism. The film is set in the past and concerns the heroic struggle of a small rural community fighting the might of the English Redcoats and coping with the treachery of an informer within. The hero, Rory O'More, played by the director Sidney Olcott, takes refuge from the English among the beautiful hills and lakes of the Killarney landscape which are lovingly composed and photographed for maximum effect. Strategically placed insert captions tell the audience where the location is – the Lakes of Killarney, the Gap of Dunloe – establishing a long tradition where cinema aesthetics, hard economic logic and tourism coalesce to produce the enduring images of rural Ireland. These shots of the landscape, many of them remarkable for their cinematic sophistication, intrude on the narrative to such an extent that it is difficult to decide which is the more important – the mere narrative or its splendid setting.

Such as it is, however, the narrative brings together the dominant stereotypes and motifs of Irish nationalism – rural life and the romantic landscape, the fight for freedom, the heroic freedom fighter and the beautiful colleen, the nasty Brits and the dedicated parish priest. The other intertitles dotted throughout the film tell the story well enough: 'If to love Ireland be a crime, then I am guilty', 'Fr O'Brien has a plan', 'The Priest's sacrifice', 'Escape to America'. This potent brew of nationalism and religion, laced with an element of anti-Britishness and nostalgia and sentimentality about the land and the landscape, became something of a template for cinematic Ireland. The cinema's greatest statement of this sentimental Irishness is John Ford's 1952 comedy, *The Quiet Man* which recreates the west of Ireland as a prelapserian paradise where amiable peasants and feisty colleens inhabit a culture of unending leisure and quaint traditions and in which the political and sectarian tensions of the real world and of colonial history are neatly side-stepped. The characters exist almost at one with nature, the landscape and the weather seemingly a mirror of character and emotion. *The Quiet Man* is the ultimate Irish-American dream of Ireland, even if some critics have argued that the film does exude a self-reflective awareness of its own romantic myth-making.[13] The whimsical and sentimental aspects of this cinematic tradition, however, are apt to emerge even in contemporary cinema, as the success in 1999 of Kirk Jones's *Waking Ned* (in America, *Waking Ned Devine*) attests.

The cumulative weight of years of representation has given Irish landscape a set of connotations that reflect not only native aspirations but also the prejudices of colonization, the nostalgic longings of exile and the more general romantic impulses of urban modernity. In general the films that mediated this complex of connotations were made outside of Ireland. But with the rise of indigenous filmmaking from the 1970s on, something has slowly begun to happen to cinematic portrayals of Irish landscape and especially to the deeply significant and haunted landscapes of the west.

## Indigenous Cinematic landscapes

There is one striking fantasy sequence in Neil Jordan's *The Butcher Boy* (1997) that illustrates in extreme form the way in which recent Irish cinema has begun to explore and re-imagine Ireland's cinematic landscapes. In narrative terms, the sequence represents the drug-induced hallucination of the film's protagonist, the abused and abandoned twelve-year-old Francie Brady who has just been given a sedative to calm him down. However, its symbolic meaning is more resonant. The scene is set against a panoramic view of Ireland's natural beauty – green hills in the background and below, a verdant valley and azure blue lake. This sequence was filmed in Glendalough in Co. Wicklow, one of Ireland's most famous beauty spots and an important destination on the tourist trail. It is a familiar image, in other words, of a romanticized and stylized rural Ireland, a picture postcard Ireland of a kind that has dominated cinematic representations for decades. The shot is held for a second as Francie's best friend, Joe, appears in the frame. 'Is that the lake?' the confused Francie asks him, drawing the audience's attention to the blue lake in the background. Then, behind Joe's smiling face, the lake suddenly erupts in the mushroom cloud of a nuclear explosion, literally blowing away the beauty, shattering the natural landscape.

In the scene that follows, Jordan recreates Francie's small rural hometown in the aftermath of the nuclear explosion, devastated and barren now, scattered with the charred heads of pigs and populated by mutant humans with the heads of insects. These images shatter audience expectations of rural Ireland and offer some of the most subversive representations of Ireland that the cinema has yet produced. Although set in the early 1960s, the film, like Sheridan's *The Field*, speaks to the Ireland of the 1990s. It is a complex exploration of a changing society in which old certainties of religion and family are blown away and anxiety and doubt replace them. The explosion and the abused child become extended metaphors for Ireland itself, traumatized by its colonial past and its religious/nationalist present and considerably shaken up by the cataclysmic influences of contemporary culture.

If *The Butcher Boy* represents the most dramatic revision of the landscape, it is, nonetheless, merely the most visually striking in a long line of indigenous films that have attempted to engage with the traditional representations of landscape and the west of Ireland.

One of the earliest films to explore the realities (and the downright misery) of rural life in 1950s Ireland was Pat O'Connor's breakthrough production, *The Ballroom of Romance* (1982). The west of Ireland settings are beautifully photographed, but the film also captures the lives of quiet desperation lived out in this visual splendour. The eponymous ballroom is cruelly and ironically named. There can be no romance or glamour in such a dying rural culture. This is a society populated by an assortment of aging men and women, the sons and daughters left behind (or abandoned) like so much human jetsam by successive waves of emigration. They grope blindly towards each other, desperately seeking marriage partners and enduring their social and sexual repression with a mixture of philosophical resignation and childish immaturity. The suffocating emptiness and sterility of such rural communities is a factor in many revisionist portrayals of rural Ireland. Thus as far back as 1978, Kieran Hickey's *Exposure* probed sexual repression, male bonding and Catholic guilt, the action taking place in a small hotel set in the bleak beauty of the west of Ireland. In the same year, Bob Quinn's *Poitín* offered a deliberately unromantic view of the west in a grimly realistic tale of endemic criminality, violence and murder (and incidentally the critical and artistic success of both confirmed the emergence at last of a real indigenous cinematic vision). In Kevin Liddy's short film *Horse*

(1992) and his feature film *Country* (2000), rural Ireland is represented as an emotionally stunted and cold world, devoid of love, sympathy, and basic human communication. A palpable sense of cruelty emanates from these films and a sense of suppressed male violence, fuelled by frustration and lack of opportunity, inhabits their bleak landscapes.

Thematically, these films considerably revise, interrogate or undermine the dominant romantic and nationalist conceptions of Irish landscape and rural life. Sometimes, though, indigenous filmmakers have attempted to re-imagine the landscape visually as well as thematically. One of the more interesting examples of this was Joe Comerford's *Reefer and the Model* (1987). Comerford peopled his west of Ireland landscapes with a disparate set of outsider characters, alienated from mainstream society and subsisting at the edge of criminality and a thwarted idealism. He introduces Theresa, the 'model' of the title, in a characteristically provocative manner. The film opens with establishing shots of the landscape, recognizable through countless representations as the west of Ireland. However, he cuts immediately to a low-angle mid-shot of a woman's legs, the suede mini-skirt and high boots connoting sex and female sexuality – the very opposite of the romantic asceticism and nationalist idealism normally associated with this landscape. It turns out that Theresa is a pregnant, drug-addict prostitute and her intrusion into the haunted landscapes of nationalist Ireland is a particularly telling challenge to dominant imagery. Irish cinema's first gay sex scene is also played out in the film, significantly located in a pub ('The American Bar') on the Aran island of Inis Mór, suggesting that the remoteness of the west cannot stop the intrusion of a modern sensibility.

Thaddeus O'Sullivan's *December Bride* (1989) is one of the most intensely cinematic of these films, reworking Catholic nationalist preconceptions by populating the Irish landscape with a staunchly Presbyterian community. The film is set and was largely shot in the Strangford Lough farmlands of Co. Antrim, close to Belfast and even though the green scenery and thatched cottages conjure up the dominant images of cinematic Ireland, this is a worked landscape as opposed to the wild, untamed landscapes of the West. O'Sullivan populates this landscape with a hard-working farmer community and establishes these people's mastery over both the landscape and the land in a series of carefully composed shots of a lambeg drummer beating out the message of Protestant conquest and control. Overall, the film's visualization of the landscape is a reminder that the industrial workers of Belfast are only part of the Protestant story and that the romantic nationalism of Catholic Ireland is only part of the story of Irish landscape.[14]

The tendency then in recent indigenous Irish filmmaking has been to challenge the romantic nationalist tradition of representing rural Ireland. This has been done both thematically and visually by exploring rural life through a realist aesthetic and by offering sometimes radical alternatives to the dominant traditions of representation. Crucially, Irish filmmakers have also been anxious to represent contemporary urban life, in many ways the missing discourse of Irish culture in general for most of the twentieth century – Joyce and O'Casey notwithstanding – and certainly the great absence in Irish visual culture, including the cinema. As the full extent of Ireland's economic boom manifested itself in the 1990s, an image of urban Ireland that was both celebratory and mildly utopian began to emerge. The most popular example of this significant subgenre was Gerry Stembridge's *About Adam* (2001), a film that celebrates the city's conspicuous affluence, consumption and sexual freedom with great visual flair and narrative invention. As Stembridge himself has argued, the film celebrates a liberal, guilt-free middle-class Dublin, 'a city that I have lived in for over twenty years and love living in and I have often wondered why it is not depicted in the way I see it'.[15] In the celebratory mood of these films, rural Ireland represented a sexually repressed past and the striking landscapes of cinematic Ireland were not so much systematically challenged as pointedly ignored.

However, not everyone is a winner in the affluent utopia of Celtic Tiger Ireland and not everyone welcomed Ireland's increasing wealth and consumerism with uncritical enthusiasm. In this regard, then, there is one final twist to the story of Irish cinematic landscapes that is worth noting.

## Back to the future: Restorative landscapes restored

In 1999, filmmaker Bob Quinn, director of 1978's *Poitín* among many other films, observed rather acerbically,

> Now that the country has shed its antediluvian religious beliefs, its national identity, its sense of personal and communal responsibility, its ethical inhibitions, its political sovereignty, even its own currency, all those things that retarded it for so long, the future glows with promise.[16]

Quinn's heavily ironic rhetoric may reflect underneath it a grudging acceptance of the scale of economic and social change in Ireland but his scepticism reflects a growing sense of unease as well. As Ireland embraces global capitalism and develops an increasingly consumer-led sense of identity, there is now growing evidence – in alarming levels of alcohol consumption, drug abuse and a high suicide rate among the young – that the decline of Catholicism (and of nationalism) has left a kind of moral and ideological vacuum that economic success alone does not fill. Quite simply, the Irish do not seem to believe in any 'grand narrative' at the moment, other than that of hedonism and consumption.

Tom Inglis characterizes this as a 'clash of cultures' – an unresolved tension between a generation (and a mindset) tutored in the culture of self-denial and self-deprecation and a younger generation (and mindset) nurtured to expect instant gratification. Ironically, however, as Inglis puts it,

> the rapid movement from a culture of self-denial to one of self-indulgence may have led to people not being able to cope with greater money and freedom and this has led to uncontrolled over-indulgence which in turn leads to a form of self-elimination.[17]

Many ideologies and politics in Ireland now compete to fill this vacuum of belief (including ironic and contradictory discourses such as 'new age' ancient Celtic spirituality or anti-immigrant racism in a country that itself endured almost two centuries of continuous emigration). In this vacuum, the haunted landscapes of rural Ireland are re-emerging to offer some kind of restorative relief.

In one sense, of course, they have never gone away and one of the ironies of the Irish 'economic miracle' is that it was built partially on a successful tourist industry selling Ireland's traditional landscapes to the troubled urban dwellers of global capitalism. Ireland joined the global economy by commodifying its past and the traumas of its history, and by offering to the global tourist an escape from the consequences of the global economy. In this way, tradition and modernity, the old and the new, the past and the present have always co-existed. However, when Irish culture reflected the values and aspirations of ascetic Catholic nationalism and its narrow rigorist ethos, the lure of the city (and the road out) was irresistible. Now that Irish culture reflects the dominant values of secular, consumer capitalism, the deep-lying romantic promise of the landscape now seem increasingly attractive. This tendency is evident in Jim Sheridan's script for *Into the West* (Mike Newell, 1992), an early indication that the myth of the west could still carry significant resonance for the Irish themselves. In 1994, John Sayles' *The Secret of Roan Inish* confirmed the potency of the west of Ireland myth and the enduring attraction of its regenerative potential, even for one of America's more radical independent filmmakers. Sheridan wrote the script for *Into the West* before he adapted *The Field* and it lay unproduced for a number of years before being picked up by a British/American/Irish consortium and directed by an English director. However, its appearance after *The Field* and in close proximity with Sayles' independent production merely indicates that the cultural climate in Ireland, Britain and the United States is always amenable to the evocative attractions of Irish myth and landscape. Both films work as forms of Irish 'magic realism', their denouements re-establishing narrative equilibrium by rescuing their dysfunctional families through the intercession, not of God and the Divine, but of magic and the supernatural. They stretch back beyond the recent past and appeal to a more ancient culture. The myth, like Wittgenstein's small hostel at the edge of the Western world, is always there – a local inflection of a more universal romantic response to modernity and its discontents.

Ireland's cinematic landscape, then, continues to offer escape and the promise of regenerative calm. That road wandering enticingly past the green field and on to a utopian future may very well, in the end, circle back in on itself.

**Note:** this chapter has appeared in a slightly different form in: Martin Mcloone, 'Film, Media and Popular Culture in Ireland: Cityscapes, Landscapes, Soundscapes' (Dublin: Irish Academic Press, 2008) as a chapter entitled 'Haunted Landscapes and the Irish West'.

# Notes

1. Tim Ecott, 'On location: West side stories', *Guardian,* Travel section, 23 September 2006, 3.
2. Ibid.
3. Ibid.
4. Martin McLoone, '*Man of Aran*', in Brian MacFarlane (ed.), *The Cinema of Britain and Ireland* (London: Wallflower Press, 2005), 41–51.
5. D. W. Meinig, 'Symbolic landscapes: Some idealizations of American communities', in D. W. Meinig (ed.), *The Interpretation of Ordinary Landscapes* (Oxford: Oxford University Press, 1979), 164.
6. Tom Inglis, *Moral Monopoly: The Catholic Church in Modern Irish Society* (Dublin: Gill and Macmillan, 1987), 138.
7. Marianne Elliot, *The Catholics of Ulster* (Harmondsworth: Allen Lane/The Penguin Press, 2000), 11.
8. Catherine Nash, '"Embodying the nation" – The west of Ireland landscape and Irish identity', in Barbara O'Connor and Michael Cronin (eds), *Tourism in Ireland: A Critical Analysis* (Cork: Cork University Press, 1993), 91.
9. Paul Henry, *An Irish Portrait* (London: Batsford, 1951), 93.
10. Henry, 51.
11. Michael Collins, *The Path to Freedom* (Dublin: Mercier Press, 1922/1968), 99.
12. Luke Gibbons, 'Romanticism, realism and Irish cinema', in Kevin Rockett, Luke Gibbons and John Hill, *Cinema and Ireland* (London: Routledge, 1988), 210.
13. Martin McLoone, *Irish Film: The Emergence of a Contemporary Cinema* (London: BFI, 2000); Luke Gibbons, *The Quiet Man* (Cork: Cork University Press, 2002).
14. Martin McLoone, 'December bride: A landscape peopled differently', in J. MacKillop (ed.), *Contemporary Irish Cinema* (New York: Syracuse University Press, 1999), 40–53; Lance Pettitt, *December Bride* (Cork: Cork University Press, 2001).
15. Michael Tierney, 'Minister for transport: Gerry Stembridge interview', *Film West* 43 (2001), 16.
16. Bob Quinn, 'Irish cinema at the crossroads: A filmmakers' symposium', *Cineaste* 24(2/3) (Contemporary Irish Cinema Supplement, 1999), 73.
17. Tom Inglis, 'From self-denial to self-indulgence: The clash of cultures in contemporary Ireland', *Irish Review* 34 (2006), 41.

# Chapter 8

The Ownership of Woods and Water: Landscapes in British Cinema 1930–1960

Sue Harper

The relationship between the natural landscape and cultural forms is complex. On the most primitive level, the natural world – the one which we inherit – provides the raw material of culture. The sights and sounds of nature are what human beings use to construct an _emotional ecology_. From these rocks, trees and water – from these deserts, winds and flowers – human beings construct systems of myth which enable them to discriminate between the pure and the impure, the sacred and profane. But cultural artefacts vary enormously in the manner in which they deal with these mythological systems. Formal differences in pastoral artworks are not the consequence of superficial developments in representational fashion; rather, they are the result of profound changes in economic and social arrangements, though indirectly expressed. And no period is homogenous in its pastoral iconography. Some non-Christian myths of origin and landscape – the Sacred Wood, the Green Man – appear sporadically throughout British culture, and it is possible to argue that pagan archetypes are consistently embedded in it from the Middle Ages to the present day. But on every level – mainstream Christian iconography, or unofficial culture – it is the transfer from the utilitarian _use_ of landscape to the aesthetic _appreciation_ of it which produces recurrent topoi.

Britain, as the first industrialized society, has had powerful pastoral myths, and these have been evoked by Raphael Samuel, David Matless and others.[1] Artists as distinctive as William Blake, Stanley Spencer and Eric Ravilious have been consistently preoccupied by the textures of the natural world. Novelists as far removed as Mary Webb, D. H. Lawrence and Iris Murdoch have included powerful symbolic evocations of landscape. Movements such as the Campaign for the Preservation of Rural England and the Ramblers' Association attest to the perennial appeal in British culture of the non-urban idyll. But the cinema is another matter. There is a relative paucity of landscape in British cinema; images of the countryside tend to be unevenly marked after the coming of sound, and their appearance is spasmodic. There is a clear disjunction between artistic forms here; pastoralism runs like a leitmotiv through most British cultural forms – except the cinema.

Why is this? It might be because British cinema audiences were predominantly urban, and that they chose films which confirmed their sense of their place. In the 1930s, taste among the working and lower middle classes (who constituted the majority of audiences) favoured cosmopolitan films. Evidence about bookings and attendance figures in the 1930s suggests that very few popular films could be classified as pastoral, or indeed contained extended landscape treatments.[2] Nor do extant oral testimonies indicate the presence of rural films in the pleasurable 'memory-horde' of respondents.[3] We can discern a similar pattern in the 1950s, where none of the popular films evoke pastoral imagery or celebrate the landscape.[4] It would clearly be foolish for commercial filmmakers to press ahead with projects that had no chance of success at the box office.

On another level, we need to be aware that film is the result of plural authorship. A book or a painting is filtered through the consciousness of an individual artist, and attests to his or her engagement with dominant or residual motifs in the culture; the cultural competence of the individual artist will shine through the work. But film texts are the result of plural agency, and of struggles for power which took place before production, during it and sometimes afterwards in the post-production phase. So the role which natural landscape may play in a film is determined by the negotiations which took place between the producer and director, or between the art director and the cinematographer. To examine this process of struggle will help us to establish the *means whereby* ideas about landscape actually get into film texts. This process can be well or badly described. For example, Stella Hockenhull demonstrates a clear similarity between the visual style of neo-Romantic painters such as Nash and Piper, and that of the 1940s films of Powell and Pressburger; she shows how, through the filmmakers' muscular engagement with contemporary motifs, new visual textures were forged.[5] On the other hand, David Matless describes the new ecologism of the 1940s and then presents a reading of *The Tawny Pipit* alongside it, as though the ideas filtered through into the text by a sort of fortuitous osmosis.[6] The first method is clearly superior to the second.

The other thing we need to recall is that film is an industrial product, and that production companies in Britain consistently favoured studio production from the early 1930s to the late 1950s. Producers disliked location shooting, because it meant that film practitioners were beyond the control of their paymasters. The major studios preferred sets to locations; sets are essentially a *built environment*, whether they signal plenitude or austerity. The bigger studios like Denham or Pinewood had back lots, where landscape could be presented, but they were controlled by management. A director who wished to break out of the studio and demonstrate a response to the natural world had to abrogate to himself the role of the art director. Those who wished to challenge the studio structure and its built geographies frequently espoused a realist ethic; they thought the 'real' world was worthier of their homage than a constructed one. Some realist filmmakers wanted to use the landscape as a provider of visual textures and to demonstrate the play of light and shade; but they also used it to frame and determine the protagonists within it.

The final general point we need to consider is that cinema is an art-form which is *habitually communicative*. Its currency is the look, and the returned look. Epistemologically speaking, cinema moves us by setting up a tension between that which gives and that which receives the gaze. People return looks in cinema, and if they evade them, that is meaningful. Even animals look. But the inanimate landscape can never interact, since it is by its very nature *outside humankind*. So the cinematographer is at a particular disadvantage with landscape. It is the sublime object, since it raises consciousness while being itself immovable.

## The 1930s

We can now assess the function of landscape in British cinema in a range of periods, having established that it is a minority subject and practice. The 1930s ('the Klondike era', as it was called) was characterized by flexibility, informality and financial crisis. Film companies flowered and faded with astonishing speed, and the whole period was marked by an extreme volatility of generic patterns. I have suggested above that films in the pastoral mode made little impact at the box office. Certainly the three big producers, Korda, Balcon and Wilcox, paid it little attention. To be sure, there were 'landscape' scenes during the hunting scene in *The Private Life of Henry VIII* (Alexander Korda, 1933), the journeys in *The Good Companions* (Victor Saville 1933) and *Victoria the Great* (Herbert Wilcox, 1937), but these are all incidental to the narratives, which are about human beings making their mark upon society. It looks as though John Betjeman was right when he noted that in mainstream British cinema, 'England's country when it appears has the atmosphere of the back-garden of a road-house'.[7] Rather, it is in the work of the minor (or ascendant) producers and directors that we find the symbolic resonance of landscape. Basil Dean, for example, made the landscape work extremely hard in a range of films: *The Water Gypsies* (Maurice Elvey, 1931) (on which Dean worked as writer and producer), *The Constant Nymph* (Basil Dean, 1933) and *The Mill on the Floss* (Tim Whelan, 1937) (for which, though he received no credit, the Dean Papers show he was very active in the planning stages and in production). Dean had a fondness for location shooting, and could indulge it since he was the financial backer of his own films. His most intense evocation of landscape is in *Lorna Doone* (1934), which gave prolonged attention to the Devon hills and clefts, which were treated as objects of more complexity and power than the protagonists. The publicity material for the film indicates Dean's extreme preoccupation with verisimilitude, and describes the hiring of local dialect coaches, and the painstaking reconstruction of contemporary landscapes and farming practice.[8] However, Dean's taste for realism had a specific gender spin: womanliness was symbolized by images of a duck with ducklings, and manliness by images of a sickle. And his interpretation of the social meaning of landscape had a political spin too. Dean had a close friendship with Sir Robert Vansittart, then Permanent Under-Secretary for Foreign Affairs, and he pressurized Vansittart to ease his films' paths through the market. He shared very many political views with Vansittart, including the innate superiority of the English way of life and the slipperiness of foreigners.[9] The function of landscape in Dean's films, therefore, was to be an index of sexual and social conservatism.

Landscape was made to operate strongly in some of the films of John Baxter, but from another political perspective. Baxter aimed to show the lives of the dispossessed, and his naturalistic focus on working-class lives in films such as *Doss House* (1933) rarely did well at the box office, though they gained powerful support from Grierson.[10] The landscape in some of Baxter's films is clearly intended to operate as the fulcrum of a glorious past in which the people existed in equality and organicism. Take the sublime *Song of the Road* (1937), which deals with a superannuated drover and his horse, who roam through the countryside in search of work. Once the boundaries of the town are breached, all is well. He finds his place: people are loving; nature is a bounteous mother. *Song of the Road* suggests that the countryside reveals the innocent life of society: creative and yet threatened, strong and yet pathetic. The drover knows that technology will destroy him and his kind, but he argues for a stay of execution, and the film celebrates this living archaism in a remarkable series of landscape shots. None of them, though, are without a human or equine inhabitant. Identical shots were the currency of other films, such as Victor Saville's *South Riding* (1938). But their meaning is different. In Saville's film, the landscape is there *in order to be reformed*.[11] In Baxter's, it is there to be loved and mourned, because it is the site of equalities which are no more.

The third landscape film operating 'from the edge' of British film culture is Michael Powell's 1936 *Edge of the World*. Powell had made a number of Quota films, and *Edge of the World* was his first independent venture. It was shot on Foula in the Shetlands, and was ostensibly the story of the St Kilda islanders, who asked to be evacuated from their lives of isolation. Powell, however, made a fictionalized film, which owed little to the ethnographical approach of Flaherty or other documentarists. He had a dynamic but symmetrical approach:

I took the simplest groundwork: two fathers and two sons. Each one took different sides. This gave conflict from the start in everything they said or did, like this:

| **FATHER I** | * | **FATHER II** |
|---|---|---|
| (Diehard, refuses to leave the island) | | (Far-seeing. Knows evacuation inevitable) |
| | | |
| **SON I** | * | **SON II** |
| (Rebel, wants to work and marry outside island) | | (Simple, strong, quite happy and in love with island girl).[12] |

The landscape was filmed so as to embody this principle of symmetry. Powell presented it as a sort of *perpetuum mobile*. It destroys: it brings to birth. It is beautiful: it is terrifying. It feeds its inhabitants: it starves them. These dialectical oppositions are resolved by the act of culture. The female protagonist gives birth to the dead son's child, and she expects the puritanical island community to reject her. But they celebrate her fecundity, and, in a profoundly moving scene, the whole community sits by the sea (on the only clement day in the whole film) and bless and serenade the child. The landscape for once provides a benison too.

## The Second World War

Landscape in 1930s films, then, only functioned powerfully when their progenitors were marginal in some way to the industry, which was chaotic in its structure. But from 1939 everything changed, when all film production came under the control of the Ministry of Information (MoI). It was its task to control the media, to monitor civilian morale and to encourage the production of texts which would usher audiences into a positive frame of mind. To this end, the MoI's Films Division and its attendant Ideas Committee either proposed or supported films which conformed to its policies (which changed radically throughout the war). Commercial film production went on as before, but the Films Division operated a kind of carrot-and-stick approach. Those films it approved were allowed a range of advantages and favours. Those films to which it was indifferent were offered no help, but were allowed to enter the market with the proviso that they conformed to new Ministry rules about censorship.

The MoI had its own documentary filmmaking body, the Crown Film Unit, which made documentaries and short films to inform the audience and bolster their morale. It also commissioned five-minute films from a range of small companies. It is significant that, although the MoI films clearly wished to enthuse audiences about the traditions for which they were fighting, rural imagery played a very minor role. *Miss Grant Goes to the Door* (1940) is set in a village, but is concerned with its resourceful inhabitants, and *Britain Can Take It* (1940) is focused on urban Britain and its survival. The MoI was really concerned with *contemporary* Britain, and the Crown Film Unit tended not to make films about rural landscapes or traditions because these were seen as the provenance of a backward-looking landed society.[13] In general, the Ministry favoured documentaries about the *transformation* of landscape by war, and the ways in which it could be made more productive. The one exception, of course, is the films of Humphrey Jennings, whose documentaries avoid linear narrative; they juxtapose contrasting visual textures and then weave them together. Jennings, who was influenced by the Surrealist movement and who eschewed the breezy pragmatism of other documentarists, directed a range of films in which the landscape symbolizes a set of values: common ownership, a sense of beauty, an organic relationship between mankind and nature. In *The Heart of Britain* (1941) and *Listen to Britain* (1942), Jennings forges a connection between the wild landscape (he rarely films cultivated ones) and highbrow musical culture. Neither seem to be anyone's property. A form of socialist patriotism runs through his films, which argue that all forms of national culture are of equal value. Jennings' examination of the relationship between political ideas and the visual textures of landscape are unique in Second World War documentary films.

The Films Division did not generally make its own feature films, although it did directly sponsor one, *The 49th Parallel*.[14] This was partly shot on location in Canada, and was directed by Michael Powell, who had already begun to develop his interpretation of landscape as an index of history and culture. The three groups who represent positive values in the film – the Hutterite community, the Eskimo tribe, the wilderness-dwelling intellectual – are all organically related to the land, and the film allows the landscapes to match the different characters. The problem is that the landscape is clearly intended to symbolize political values, but little space is provided for it to function with as much resonance as Powell would probably have liked. He appears to have been inhibited from a full-blown engagement with the poetic and social power of the landscapes by the propagandist desires of the Ministry of Information.

The MoI documentaries tended not to use the natural landscape in a particularly resonant way, but the feature films they promulgated were partially determined by the cultural capital of their producers or directors, and so there is a more mixed pattern of landscape symbolism. Ealing was the studio closest to the Ministry's policies, and after 1940, under the leadership of Michael Balcon, its films tended to comply with official attitudes. But even they gave greater emphasis to the rural ethos than the MoI did. In *Went the Day Well?* (Alberto Cavalcanti, 1942), there is a powerful desire to validate the village life and landscape, which is much less evident in the Graham Greene story on which the script is based. Other producers' films which had a close relationship with the Films Division were *Millions like Us* (Frank Launder and Sidney Gilliat, 1943), *The Demi-Paradise* (Anthony Asquith, 1943) and *Henry V* (Lawrence Olivier, 1945). In the first film, the one landscape shot – the hilltop scene between the middle-class heroine and the working-class overseer – is used as a backdrop to the debate about the most important issue in the film, that of class difference. The landscape is the only stable feature in the social revolution. In the second film, it is village life which matters above all, and in *Henry V*, the landscapes are there in order to look like paintings, to bear the signs of culture and to confer status on their consumers.

The films furthest removed from the propaganda canon make the most powerful use of landscape. The popular Gainsborough melodramas were made under a unique set of managerial circumstances during and after the war, and were aimed exclusively at female audiences. Both modern dress and costume melodramas evoked the landscape as the site and symbol of primal desires. In *Love Story* (Leslie Arliss, 1944), the composer heroine is artistically inspired by the Cornish landscape, whose wildness she emulates in her emotional life. In *Madonna of the Seven Moons* (Arthur Crabtree, 1944), the split-minded heroine consummates with her gypsy lover in a wild garden replete with pastoral and religious symbols of the rose and the lamb. The highwayman heroine of *The Wicked Lady* (Leslie Arliss, 1945) has her most intense love scenes by a picturesque river. And in *Caravan* (Arthur Crabtree, 1946), the heroine bathes naked in a mountain stream, before making love with her lover. In all these cases, the landscape operates as a stimulus to those 'natural' female desires which have been oppressed by social forces. It offers, through its wild beauty, an escape from the symmetry of the existing gender hierarchy.

Gainsborough melodramas operated a 'cheap and cheerful' form of expressionism in their landscapes. The films of Michael Powell and Emeric Pressburger deployed a more respectable and expensive expressionism. But they too placed a high premium on the values of landscape, and, like the Gainsborough melodramas, their wartime films (after *The 49th Parallel*) were in no way supported by the Ministry of Information. *A Canterbury Tale* (1944) and *I Know Where I'm Going!* (1945) are both utterly dominated by the filmmakers' desire to foreground natural forces and also to call to audiences' attention the traditions and innovations of landscape representation. *A Canterbury Tale* deals with the fallibility and power of Thomas Colpepper, a member of the landed gentry; he tries, through unconventional methods, to introduce newcomers to the beauties of the Kent landscape, which bears the signs of previous inhabitants. The film presents both the social and natural objects as saturated with meaning. Powell found locations such as the wheelwright's shop, and filmed them so as to intensify their link with the past.[15]

But more is at issue. Powell accorded great autonomy to his German cameraman Erwin Hillier, and allowed him time to select the right visual timbre and texture. Hillier noted:

> There are so many things in nature that are fascinating. When we used to go out to select locations I would spend hours by myself…I used to find out the time when everything looked most fascinating, when it has character and style, rather than shoot in a flat light.[16]

Hillier also photographed *I Know Where I'm Going!* This film deals with the mythical powers of the Western Isles of Scotland, and Hillier's subtle lighting techniques – graduated filters and small lamps at sunset – are the major determinant of the landscape imagery, which are the most sublime in the whole period. Hillier's visual sensibility operated as a kind of membrane through which a European sense of landscape could seep, and he had an individual 'landscape style', regardless of the director he worked for: consider the woodland scenes in *Great Day* (1945), directed by Lance Comfort. In this film, Hillier's landscapes evoke an other-worldly place, in which the aesthetic effects usher the viewer into the realm of the uncanny.

## The post-war period

It is now clear that landscape imagery functioned more powerfully from the *margins* of wartime cinema, and that much depended on the agency and autonomy of technical workers. After 1945, the demise of the Ministry of Information and its controls meant that a whole range of cinematic approaches were shaken loose. These fell into two main categories. The first were films which showed the landscape as a threat: beautiful but deadly. *Great Expectations* (David Lean, 1946) derived much of its Gothic frisson from the landscape shots, which, though they looked seamlessly threatening, were in fact composites: Robert Krasker lit and photographed the Romney Marsh shots, Guy Greene matched the textures in the studio exteriors and designer John Bryan exaggerated nature by painting clouds onto glass and constructing terrifying trees.[17] The landscape appears similarly in *Oliver Twist* (David Lean, 1948), as an index of pain. This type of landscape appears in very different films. In Ealing's *Scott of the Antarctic* (Charles Frend, 1948), it is a brooding presence, which dwarfs and destroys the human inhabitants, and even in *Whisky Galore!* (Alexander Mackendrick, 1948) it is a force which takes away more than it gives.

The second type of landscape function in this period is as a symbol of inequality and deprivation. The British landscape is dominated and partly created by enclosure, but economic issues are rarely foregrounded in film landscapes until the post-war period. In *Captain Boycott* (Frank Launder, 1947), for example, the landscape cannot be beautiful because it is owned by the wrong people; and in *Esther Waters* (Ian Dalrymple and Peter Proud, 1948) it is the same; only the naïve heroine is ignorant of the injustice the landscape symbolizes.

It looks as though landscape in post-war feature film is acting as a focus for contemporary anxieties about social space and class change, and alluding to them in a new way. But we also need to take account of the effect of technical innovation. In the more affluent post-war period, Technicolor became more widely available, and it had some advantages and some limitations in landscape photography. Three-strip Technicolor was unwieldy to use, since it was unblimped and dialogue had to be post-synched, and the camera itself was huge, making location shooting very difficult.

In the late 1940s, two conditions were necessary if Technicolor landscapes were to be innovatory. Firstly, a director had to give an experienced worker his head: Jack Cardiff noted that Powell, for example, was 'a cameraman's dream' when landscapes were prepared.[18] In *A Matter of Life and Death* (1946) Powell only interfered in the timing of the scene shot on Staunton Sands, when the 'dead' airman finds that he is alive. He allowed Cardiff and Geoffrey Unsworth complete freedom.[19] These landscape scenes, which are the most powerful of the period, usher the audience into an awareness of the miraculous aspect of the natural world. All Powell did was to insert a scene with a little naked boy 'playing on a reed pipe…while his goats cropped the sparse marram grass on the sand dunes. It looked charming, like a scene from Theocritus'.[20]

Secondly, a fluid interdependent relationship had to operate between the Technicolor cameraman and art director or designer. In *Black Narcissus* (Michael Powell and Emeric Pressburger, 1948), none of the 'Indian' landscapes were location shots; they were photographs, which were subsequently repainted. Jack Cardiff and Alfred Junge had to work together to produce a wild, sensual landscape which would destabilize the nuns.[21] Cardiff's account of the natural imagery is instructive. The final scene has raindrops falling on a huge gunnera leaf; the great rains have come, presaging a fertility from which the nuns are forever excluded. Cardiff made this 'natural' picture by sitting 'on a small ladder with a cupful of water, flicking drops onto the foreground leaf'.[22]

## The 1950s

During this period, the structure of the British film industry changed radically. As a consequence of the 1948 Cinematograph Films Act, economic power passed from the *producers* of film to its *distributors*. This meant that the old studio system came increasingly under pressure, and many of the creative decisions were taken by heads of distribution rather than production companies. The three largest distribution companies were the Rank Organization, Associated British Picture Company and British Lion. Because the administration of these companies was unwieldy, it was sometimes possible for dissident filmmakers to wriggle under or through the monolithic structures and make innovatory films. In addition, independent filmmaking began to flower in the second half of the decade.[23]

British cinema of the 1950s was primarily urban in orientation. Filmmakers were preoccupied by changes in the post-war social landscape, and a range of films were made which expressed an awareness of, and an anxiety about, the new gender and class arrangements. To be sure, the English landscape appeared in a range of films by different companies; but it was as a neutral background. Consider *Genevieve* (Henry Cornelius, 1953), a Rank subsidiary film: the landscape is something to drive through, bushes are something to urinate behind. Or consider Ealing's *The Titfield Thunderbolt* (Charles Crichton, 1953): the landscape is a backdrop for the train. Or ABPC's *Yield to the Night* (J. Lee Thompson, 1956): there are hardly any shots of natural objects, except for the single tree in the prison yard. To be sure, there is the odd film which foregrounds the landscape, its aesthetic effect and social meaning: *Laxdale Hall* (John Eldridge, 1952), and *Conflict of Wings* (John Eldridge, 1954). But the production background for these is telling. They were both made by Group 3, a short-lived organization set up with government money; it was a benighted attempt to encourage middle-budget pictures by young filmmakers. It was jointly run by John Grierson and John Baxter (who, we must remember, had a particular interest in landscape cinema), and lost a great deal of money.[24] In *Laxdale Hall*, the human inhabitants of the Hebridean landscape are judged by the intensity of their affection for it, and in *Conflict of Wings*, the bird-watching protagonists are inspired by the mystery enshrined in the landscape. But, to repeat, Group 3 productions were absolutely marginal to commercial film production as a whole, and indeed to patterns of popular taste.

A substantial part of 1950s British cinema displays natural settings which yield nothing and which are blank and featureless: the desert in *Ice Cold in Alex* (J. Lee Thompson, 1958), the Himalayan wastes in *The Abominable Snowman* (Val Guest, 1957), the watery vastness in *The Cruel Sea* (Charles Frend, 1953), the undistinguished marshland landscape in *The Long Memory* (Robert Hamer, 1953). These natural settings are unmarked, and are there to throw emphasis on to existential issues. But there is an important exception to this studied neutrality of landscape, and that resides in films made by the French director Jacques Tourneur, *Circle of Danger* (Jacques Tourneur, 1951) and *Night of the Demon* (Jacques Tourneur, 1957). In both these films, the landscape takes on a demonic life of its own, and its occult energies actively threaten the protagonists. In their use of landscape symbolism, these films are *legally* British (in terms of their registration ), but they are *culturally* other, and provide a stranger's perspective on the British landscape.[25]

One technological development in the early 1950s had serious consequences for landscape photography. Eastmancolor had single-strip technology, which meant that the camera could be much smaller, and the lighter Arriflex camera could be used. Colour films could thus be shot on location much more easily. Accordingly, a whole raft of films were made which exploited Commonwealth landscapes. Rank specialized in films of this type, and his 'Empire' films included *Simba* (1955, set in Kenya) and *The North West Frontier* (1959, set in India). But the landscapes in these films are inert, and have little emotional clout or aesthetic effect, because they are displayed as an exotic stimulus rather than a site of cultural value.

## Conclusion

This chapter has suggested that the most intense and resonant use of landscape tends to occur on the margins of mainstream British film production. From the 1930s to the 1950s, the studio system did not work to the advantage of those filmmakers who wanted to concentrate on the aesthetics of landscape. This was because those in positions of financial control wished to discourage forms which they perceived as elitist or old-fashioned. However, once the studio system went into serious decline in the 1960s, everything changed, and the ebb and flow of cinematic landscapes after that time became far more unpredictable. Suffice it to say for the moment that, with the rise in power of the independent director, it would be possible to categorize film landscapes according to his individual predilections – romantic and Lawrentian with Russell, cool and cerebral with Losey, darkly passionate with Jarman. What we should not forget too is that a new generation of designers and art directors came to maturity in the 1960s, and their training profoundly affected the way they selected, prepared or transformed landscapes. The work of John Box and Assheton Goreton are two cases in point.[26]

Finally, let us open up some broader issues, rather than concluding in a minor key. It might be suggestive to categorize film landscapes in terms of their interpretation of social space, and to ask ourselves whether the arrangement of natural objects in the landscape conforms to, or challenges, normative spatial relations: and for what reason? We might also consider the extent to which film landscapes deploy a sexual symbolism – whether the fertility or aridity in the landscapes are given a gendered meaning – and how this changes over time. I have considered the input of creative agency in landscape representation – the role of the producer, director or designer – but it might also be pertinent to consider the role which *visual fashion* plays. Visual textures and the modes of symbolization in film art are acutely predicated on cinema's relationship to painting, and a rigorous analysis of this relationship might valuably extend the parameters of the debate about landscape in film.

(The author wishes to record her thanks to Dr Mark Glancy and Professor Vincent Porter for their helpful comments on earlier drafts of this piece.)

## Notes

1. Raphael Samuel, *Theatres of Memory* (London: Verso, 1994); David Matless, *Landscape and Englishness* (London: Reaktion Books, 1998). See also Martin Wiener, *English Culture and the Decline of the Industrial Spirit 1850–1980* (Cambridge: Cambridge University Press, 1981).

2. John Sedgwick, *Popular Filmgoing in 1930s Britain: A Choice of Pleasures* (Exeter: Exeter University Press, 2000), 133–134 and Sue Harper, 'A lower-middle-class taste-community in the 1930s: Admissions figures at the Regent Cinema, Portsmouth, UK', *Historical Journal of Film, Radio and Television* 24 (2004), 565–587.

3. Annette Kuhn, *An Everyday Magic: Cinema and Cultural Memory* (London: I. B. Tauris, 2002).

4. Sue Harper and Vincent Porter, *British Cinema of the 1950s: The Decline of Deference* (Oxford: Oxford University Press, 2003), 249.

5. Stella Hockenhull, 'Romantic landscapes: Visual imagery in three films by Powell and Pressburger', *Journal of British Cinema and Television* 2 (2005), 52–66.

6. Matless, 224–225.

7. John Betjeman, 'Settings, costumes, background', in Charles Davy (ed.), *Footnotes to the Film* (London: Lovat Dickson, 1937), 95.

8. Publicity material for *Lorna Doone* in BFI library.

9. Sue Harper, *Picturing the Past: The Rise and Fall of the British Costume Film* (London: BFI, 1994), 45–48.

10. Jeffrey Richards, *The Age of the Dream Palace: Cinema and Society in Britain 1930–1939* (London: Routledge, 1984), 299.

11. Roy Moseley, *Evergreen: Victor Saville in His Own Words* (Carbondale: University of Illinois Press, 2000), 95–97.

12. Michael Powell, *Edge of the World: The Making of a Film* (London: Faber and Faber, 1990), 16.

13. There was a feud between the MoI and British Council, who wanted to make films about Olde England and its landscape: see *Picturing the Past*, 80–84.

14. For an account of this film's inception, see James Chapman, *The British at War: Cinema, State and Propaganda 1939–45* (London: I. B. Tauris, 1998), 70–74.

15. Michael Powell, *A Life in Movies* (London: Heinemann, 1986), 446–447.

16. Duncan Petrie, *The British Cinematographer* (London: BFI, 1996), 108.

17. Petrie, 98; Kevin Brownlow, *David Lean* (London: Faber and Faber, 1996), 213–214 (209).

18. Powell, 541–543.

19. Jack Cardiff, *The Magic Hour* (London: Faber and Faber, 1997), 85.

20. Powell, 543.

21. Cardiff, 88–89.

22. Ibid., 90.

23. This has been described in detail in Harper and Porter, *op. cit.*

24. See ibid., 185–188.

25. See Vincent Porter, 'Strangers on the shore: The contributions of French novelists and directors to British cinema, 1946–60', *Framework* 43 (2002), 105–126.

26. See Elizabeth-Marie Tuson, 'Interview with John Box' and 'Consumerism, the Swinging Sixties, and Assheton Gorton', *Journal of British Cinema and Television* 2 (2005), 137–147; 100–116.

**Chapter 9**

Filming the (Post-)Colonial Landscape: Claire Denis' *Chocolat* (1988) and *Beau travail* (1998)

Susan Hayward

# Introduction

L andscape within French cinema has been quite limited in terms of representation. There are the few 'Pagnol' films of the 1930s and 1950s set in Marseilles and the region of southern France, and their remakes or retakes (by Claude Berri) in the 1980s. Then there are Bresson's 1950s and 1960s austere portraits of rural life. But in general French films have focused on the city (in particular Paris) with landscape appearing as a mere dot on the French cinematic horizon. Although it might be foolish to claim a gender specificity here, if anything, women filmmakers have tended, since the 1970s, to give more space to the landscape as narrative than their male counterparts. This chapter does not propose to focus on the French landscape as narrative, however, but on the post-colonial landscape as narrative in the work of Claire Denis. *Chocolat* (1988) saw Denis attempting to come to terms filmically with France's colonial past. In *Beau travail* (1998), it is the inability of the West to understand the post-colonial moment that is under scrutiny. In her later film, Denis uses her portrayal of post-colonial landscapes to reveal the dislocated nature of the Western post-colonial body. In *Chocolat* she also uses landscape, but this time to question ideological positionings occupied by the colonizer and their effects upon the indigenous people. She shows, too, how positions of power are not always hierarchical and how resistances to hegemony can come from a multiplicity of spaces that are marked by gender as well as race. Her focus in *Chocolat* is western Africa (the former colony of the French Cameroon as it once was), whereas in *Beau travail* it is eastern Africa (Djibouti to be precise). Whichever landscape she employs, the socio-political messages are in evidence and tell us a great deal both about contemporary France and the legacy left behind some 80 to 100 years after France first set out to build her Empire. Thus Denis' work has a syncretism to it, produced from temporal and spatial discourses – what could be called filmic chronotopes. This chapter will focus in particular on these chronotopes – in relation to the two above-mentioned films – with a view to exploring how the landscape speaks. We must bear in mind, as does Denis herself, that it is a white-woman's camera that observes and that Denis occupies, as she must, the false position of the outsider as insider. A position which, nonetheless, she acknowledges, always.[1] But, first, a glance at the past is necessary.

## The legacy of French colonial and post-colonial cinema

France's colonizing history begins (as with Germany) in the mid- to late nineteenth century. France annexed Algeria in 1830, Senegal in 1850, Indochina in 1887, Djibouti (then French Somaliland) in 1862, the French Cameroon (formerly a German colony) as late as 1922 – as part of Germany's post-war settlement with France (north Cameroon went to France, south Cameroon to Great Britain). Surprisingly, given the national importance of colonization both as a nation-building practice (in terms of nationhood) and as a rich vein of visual 'exotica' to exploit, the colonial (fiction) film, where France is concerned, is very much a genre on the periphery. Interestingly, however, it appears and disappears at significant moments – tending to make an appearance at times of national crisis. Thus, in the 1920s, especially the early 1920s (when France was still expanding), colonialist films made a first significant appearance and were located mostly in north Africa. The emphasis was on the desert as a redemptive space for the male protagonist (the son of France, the mother nation) who had been sent 'away' to the colonies to expiate some sort of filial fault. The landscape becomes the background to the redemptive endeavours of the hero – testing his moral fibre through the landscape's own physical magnitude. Or, alternatively, the emphasis was on the pioneering spirit of the individual and France's role as 'la mère civilisatrice'. In the 1930s – the time of the greatest 'explosion' of the genre – colonialist films either showed the individual bravery of the ordinary man or the endeavours of France's great colonialists (mostly generals, etc.) to tame the territory. Either way, these films were very nationalistic, asserting France's greatness.

These two decades where France's political culture was concerned were times of great upheaval. The 1920s was a period of considerable civil unrest. Post-war France was in economic shambles. The lack of a labour force meant bringing in massive numbers of immigrant workers (3 million). The working class as an urban social group increased hugely. Factories were beginning to Taylorize, making working conditions worse than before the war. These factors and others (such as big increases in prices) caused mass protests to ensue which were brutally repressed. Against this background of civil unrest, the successive governments of the Right (predominantly led by the hard man of the Right Raymond Poincaré) called for national unity at the same time as it sought to contain forces of dissension. As for the 1930s, this was a period of mounting insecurity for France. By 1932, the effects of the depression were being strongly felt by all classes; the fear of Bolshevism was on the rise among the political classes of the Right, as was, among the political classes of the Left, the fear of Germany's new Fascist state and the very real threat of a new war; finally, the trends in demographic decline continued. In both these decades of crisis, France strengthened its economic links with its colonies, in an entirely exploitative way it has to be said – importing necessary materials and using the colonies as unimpeded dumping grounds for its own exports. Two huge colonial exhibitions were held – one in Marseilles in 1922 extolling the virtues of France's colonizing heroes and the other in Paris in 1931 with hundreds of pavilions that reconstructed aspects of France's great Empire.

Straightaway we can see how the colonial film genre fits into this call for national unity and functions thereby to disguise the colonizing nation's own sense of increasing insecurity (or crisis). What is so interesting is that the genre all but disappears until the 1980s. During the 1960s and 1970s a handful of political films were made, questioning France's role as a colonizer and primarily focused on Algeria (e.g. *La Bataille d'Algers*/Battle of Algiers, Pontecorvo, 1966; *Avoir 20 ans dans les Aurès*/Being 20 in the Aurès, Vautier, 1972). By the 1980s and early 1990s, this whole mood of questioning disappears and the colonialist film becomes a retro-mode genre. There are two dominant types. The first is somewhat reminiscent of the 1920s model where the landscape is the background to an individual's psychological state (e.g. Tavernier's *Coup de torchon*, 1981; Corneau's *Fort Saganne*, 1984). The second offers a visual tourism of an elective type of history. *L'Amant* (Annaud, 1991) and *Indochine* (Wargnier, 1992) are prime examples of making images that please (almost like the great colonial exhibitions before them). In this latter mode we are presented with the idea of screening history rather than criticizing it, in short, of offering images that deny the socio-political realities of the present by glorifying the past.

By the early 1980s, France was, for the first time in 45 years, under a socialist president, François Mitterrand (1981–1995) and government. In just one year, however, its politics of reform had to be abandoned in the light of global recession and, once again, the nation found itself experiencing a new economic decline and, with it, new types of social crises: heavy unemployment amongst the youth classes and a big rise in racism. Thus once more, whichever mode they were in, these retro-colonial films acted as a containment and displacement of the nation's sense of crisis. The latter, *Indochine*-mode, in its beautifying of the exotic past, barely disguises a mourning of history and thereby the loss of the Empire. A very odd post-colonial moment, it has to be said, given the political colour of the times as supposedly Socialist and of the Left. But of course it serves a function: the nation's own sense of crisis is replaced in these films with a nostalgic make-believe illusion of an 'unproblematic' colonial model which takes the form of looking at France's past in order to secure images that please (nice colonial homes, nice landscapes) or reassure because the hardships and squalor they show (respectively: the hero struggling in the desert sun and the poverty of shanty towns) are not those of the nation, but elsewhere. This cinema represents, therefore, an imagined, imaginary past, a mythical and unproblematic past, a celebration of nationhood rooted in a colonial Empire. As such it becomes a form of voyeurism that is scopophilicly driven (our spectatorial desires are fully satisfied). But there is a second form of voyeurism at work here also, this time with a more fetishistic drive: these self-serving aestheticized images turn the colonized nation into a spectacle that is often sexualized (the 'native' woman or 'native' man's nudity, etc.).

It is for this reason that Claire Denis's films set in colonial and post-colonial African nation states are important to investigate because they challenge, on so many levels, these a priori practices of the colonialist and post-colonialist cinema described above. In what follows, I shall examine her two films in turn in relation to questions of landscape and, thereby, detail the political cultural readings we can take from them.

## *Chocolat*

*Chocolat* is set in late colonial times, 1957 to be precise. The film's narration is related almost exclusively in a flashback (from the late 1980s back to this 1957 moment). The flashback is that of a woman in her 30s, France, who has returned to the Cameroon to meet up with her past. She accepts a lift from an Afro-American ex-patriot and it is during this ride that she flashes back to her childhood days (as a six year old) when she lived in the northern province with her parents Aimée and Marc – and was tended to by the house servant Protée. Her memories seem to focus on the spring months of that year – what few trees exist are barren, the land is extremely dry and dusty just as it is before the rains arrive. These memories constitute a patchwork of events that occurred at that time (which unbeknown to her as a child were the dying days of the nation's mandate of this country).

When, at the beginning of the film, we meet with the older France and the Afro-American and his son we are presently in the southern region of Cameroon between Douala and Limbé where France is headed to catch a bus to Yaoundé and there to fly – perhaps north to Garoua where she will need further transport to get her to Mindif, the place of her childhood (See Figure of Cameroon). Or maybe she will give up on the project and just fly home to France, because, just as the Afro-American says of himself: 'Here, I am nothing', i.e. 'I don't belong.'

This geographical placing is important for us to understand if we are going to be able to read what Denis is telling us via the spaces she visits within her film. The topography and climate change radically within this African state of 183,530 square miles (half the size of Nigeria and only slightly smaller than Great Britain). The southern province is the second wettest place on earth with its equatorial rain forests and savannas. It rains almost constantly until the dry season of November to February. Towards the end of the dry season, plants and crops turn rusty red, due to the fine red laterite dust that gets blown over them by the northerly *harmattan*. As one moves north and inland the tree-scattered savannas give way to mostly bush-lands, giant rock massifs and volcanic mountains. This is the terrain of Mindif, where the narrative of France's child-life is set. Mindif lies far north (in the northern province proper) near the fringes of the Sahara (see map for details). The volcanic Mandara mountains that lie due east from Mindif are undoubtedly the mountains that France's father, Marc, so painstakingly sketches into his book – sketches that could be read as his attempts to capture the landscape, as if seeking to mark them down, inscribe them into his colonial consciousness. Mindif itself has its own volcanic mountain: La Dent de Mindif/Mindif's Tooth which France's house looks out onto and behind which the plane falls (as France rightly declares, despite her father reasoning with her that it has gone over the horizon). The temperature inland – therefore in Mindif – reaches 40–42 degrees centigrade in the high season (April to May), thereafter the average is around 30 degrees. An oppressive heat which clearly distresses France's mother Aimée, and whose agent the sun, as the local black servants tell France, will undoubtedly burn her black if she does not stay out of it during the day.

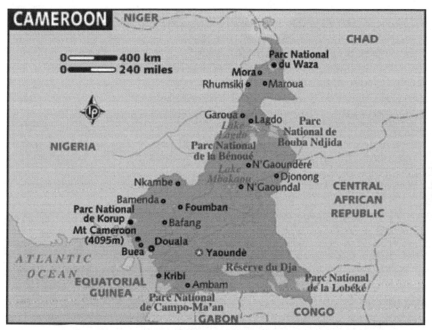

Reproduced with permission from lonelyplanet.com. © 2009 Lonely Planet.

This place of heat, dust and dark volcanic mountains is where France's father has been posted. And the question most assuredly is why? To ensure the communication lines are secure with neighbouring Chad? Certainly no crop growing is going on here – so it must be for security reasons? *Chocolat* is set in 1957; this is not an innocently chosen year. This was the year when, after considerable civil unrest, the Cameroonians obtained self-government, thanks in large part to the activities of the northern province-based party, the Union Camerounaise – becoming fully independent in 1960. We see the traces of this unrest in this film. When Marc runs to get the local Cameroonian doctor he finds him attending a political meeting – clearly a nod to the growing unrest that will lead in just a few months to self-governance. As Marc rightly remarks: 'They will chuck us out soon.' Interestingly he has no idea how soon it will be since he is still so focused on building roads! Furthermore, his liberal attitude towards the indigenous peoples brings out irate responses amongst several of the airplane crash victims to whom he gives shelter. 'So now it's the natives who control things' comments Delpich (the coffee plantation owner) sarcastically to Marc when he, Delpich, cannot enforce or bribe a village chief to give him a ride to the nearest town. Well yes, and soon.

When France took over the mandate of the German colony, in 1922, it put in place a large cultivation programme – producing mostly cocoa beans, palm oil and timber for export. Beyond building vast plantations and enlarging the port of Douala (for export purposes), it also established a huge infrastructure of roads. However, the means by which France implemented this massive building programme is already of interest to us here. The entire project was made possible by imposing heavy taxes on the indigenous peoples and, because they, for the most part, were unable to pay up, they had to pay in kind through enforced labour (which, technically speaking, was illegal since forced labour was forbidden under the regulations governing France's mandate). Nonetheless, France's building programme brought about an increase of wealth for the country (trade increased fivefold between 1922 and 1940). Several times in the film, France's father talks about enlarging the roads. So clearly he will be using this forced labour to implement this development. And lest we forget, in the film, at one point, we see him bringing in this enforced labour to help make a runway for the repaired airplane to make its getaway before the rainy season comes.

Already we can see how Denis' use of landscape gives us a considerable degree of information about the history of this colonized state. But the issues the film raises take us further into other arenas. What, one must ask, is Western domestic life as embodied by the two white females (France and her mother Aimée) doing in such an untamed, arid, burnt and unyielding space as Mindif? It is obvious that Aimée's relationship to the landscape is not one that produces knowledges about the country. She tends to a graveyard of German soldiers (killed in the First World War, one presumes) – a European space of death. Her crops (scrappy and pathetic things to behold) are tomatoes and lettuces – Western food that can hardly survive here in this heat and which would be destined for the salads she so desperately wishes to eat, but for the fact that her cook (an English-speaking British Cameroonian servant) refuses to prepare them, preferring to stick to his roast beef and Yorkshire puddings!

In fact, it is the ability to consume what is naturally provided that makes having knowledges possible and thereby the where-with-all to survive *in* this land (as opposed to surviving the ordeal of this land). Thus, the manservant Protée shares his knowledges with young France – always commencing this sharing with a riddle (just as his mythological namesake shared riddles in an endeavour to pass on knowledge) – and teaches her to consume ants on bread, shows her how tasty a night-moth is once you have removed the wings. But France is unable to sustain her desire to acquire knowledges. As she gradually acquires her mother's mannerisms so she too rejects what the land has to offer: 'You're disgusting' she retorts as she watches Protée eat the night-moths. Like his namesake, Protée will be driven to give up. Small wonder he turns to colonized (Western) technology in the form of the generator to signal his refusal to continue to share knowledge. In this painful scene, he answers France's question 'Will it burn?' by defiantly grasping the hot pipe of the generator, knowing that she will do the same. Having burnt the hand that represents the colonial indifference to the native dweller (as France by her namesake does), he turns away taking his own scorched hand away with him. A cruel metaphor for the vestiges of colonial oppression and rule.

Marc, France's father, although a considerate man, nonetheless works for the colonial administration. The first time we see him in relation to the land, we observe from France's point of view (in medium long shot) his pathetic yet masculine way of attempting to leave his mark. Standing with his back to us and staring out to the bush-land beyond, he declares to Protée – who is standing a few metres to his left also looking out into the distance – that he will enlarge this road. Protée says nothing. Both men are peeing. Two men, two different peoples; one indigenous, the other colonial; one discoursing about further appropriation, the other keeping his counsel. How in fact can he say anything? Why speak when it serves no function? At the close of the film we observe (again from France's point of view, this time the mature woman), in a long shot, one of the three baggage carriers working at the airport carrying out precisely the same gesture (peeing with his back to us). This time, however, he is surrounded by his two mates with whom he is joking and laughing. We have shifted from the silent one-way discourse of the colonizer (of the 1950s) who states in a series of un-echoing spaces his intention to control an uncontrollable landscape – uncontrollable because although Marc can drive roads through it, he cannot tame it (the rains and the dust will constantly erode these roads) – to the shared jocularity of three Cameroonians indifferent to the Western eye (the camera/France) that observes them from a distance (in this time of the 1980s), and whose exchanges she/we cannot hear. That is the ex-colonizer's place, the place of no meaning (of not belonging).

Sound and silence have a large part to play in this *mise-en-scène* of the landscape by Denis. We are made deeply aware of the natural ambient sounds of the bush, of the heat that crackles and the sound of human silence that has so little to say or whose own sounds get absorbed into this infinite landscape of heat and dust. The film is book-ended by the sound of water, the very commodity that the north and Mindif in particular so singularly lack. At the beginning, the sound of the ocean roars in our ears; at the end the torrential rain engulfs all other sounds. Already presented as a land of extremes, we are far from ready – much like the colonizers before us – for the barren yellow heat of the interior. Once inland and back in France's colonialist past, the natural sounds dominate: the deafening sound of the cicadas and other insects, the cries of the hyena and throaty roar of the lion at night, the vast oily sound of the vultures wings as they gather on top of the rock where France often perches herself to observe. The grand Imperial narrative, which seeks to temper, master and enslave the indigenous peoples, also seeks to master, by any means necessary, these natural elements that disturb. Thus, Aimée commands Protée to shoot the hyena – 'Dirty beast it can enter (the house) just as it pleases.' On one of his routine sorties out into the bush, Marc tells the local village leader he will organize a hunt to shoot the lions that are killing the sheep. In the first example, Protée does no such thing; rather he pops France on his shoulders and wanders out into the night brandishing his rifle and shouting out a cheery sound (that most likely will scare the hyena off). In the second example, the village chief snorts at Marc's idea ('The white man's system is no good, you have to kill the lion with a knife'). The natural precariousness of bush life is something the white man cannot tolerate. He has to wipe it out, control its threat. Aimée's words express fully the repressed fear in the colonial experiences of the dark continent (it, and too the dark indigenous body, can enter wherever and whenever it wants). Equally importantly, the indigenous response points to the ridicule of the white man's obsession to make the unseizable landscape and all that live in it an ordered, civilized (policed) space.

Two final interconnected examples serve to show how little comprehension there is in the white man's consciousness. The local Swedish missionary and his wife are feeling forced to leave and return home because their village has had their livestock devastated by a panther who noiselessly entered the village one night. The wife's nerves can no longer stand these unpredictable 'threats'. France and her parents, accompanied by Protée go to visit them after the devastation. France and Protée roam among the dead animals. Protée picks up a chicken's foot and places it next to France's hand (in close up); he then paints a mark on her arm from the blood of the dead chicken. While the missionary evangelizes – with the ostensible reason of civilizing the 'natives' – the true indigenous body (Protée) marks the inevitable but noteworthy fact that an animal has died (by tracing it in blood on France's skin). As we well know one of the hidden functions of the evangelical missionary work was to wipe out earlier 'heathen' cultures – such as the one just practised by Protée. When, at the end of the film, the missionary and his wife prepare to board the plane that will remove them from this inhospitable (to them) landscape, they try to load the missionary's portable organ onto the plane. But it is far too big and so has to be left behind. At which point the missionary exclaims 'I'll be back!' Apart from the obvious metaphoric value of the over-big organ that has to be left behind as some sort of white defiance to the black phallus, we should take careful note that, the missionary's zeal notwithstanding, the indigenous tribes were well able to resist any such idea of conquest or return. Today, only 15 per cent of the indigenous peoples are Christian, 20–25 per cent Muslim and the rest (the greater majority therefore) practice traditional animist religions.

We note however the rather anomalous situation of a Protestant (rather than a Catholic) missionary within a French mandate. This is but one instance of the way in which this landscape is criss-crossed by differing, trans-national, bodies. Nothing is fixed, as the colonial mentality would wish to believe it is. Even its own people, in the form of the administrators (religious or civil) show the cracks in this belief. We have already discussed the missionary and Marc, but there are others. Boothby may well don his dinner suit of the evening (and cause mayhem in the house as a result), he may well stick a picture of the Queen up in his bungalow, he may well insist on his tea; nonetheless, in his Britishness, he is just as transient and un-permanent in this landscape as are the rest of them. But how is it that his body crosses this French mandate? Because, in their wisdom of carving up the spoils of war in 1922 the British took south Cameroon. However, those working for the British colonial administration in southern Cameroon would still need to travel to northern posts in Nigeria which, although federated by 1954, was still part of the British colonies (becoming independent in 1960). Thus, Boothby is potentially the biggest traveller of them all (obviously the Black English-speaking cook got only as far as Mindif!), traversing hundreds if not thousands of miles to carry out his duties. But to what purpose? As the black woman servant's remark makes it clear, very little. Late at night after the dinner, she, along with France, observes Boothby being undressed by his servant. Her observations on his body fully sums up the meaning of his presence: 'You can tell that if he has hair on his shoulders he will have it on his bum.'

This criss-crossing of foreign bodies – even bodies that fall from the sky – across the landscape show how impermanent the concept of a unified state is. But they also show how colonialism and Empire-building, as a unifying principle for the nation, is a colossal myth since – as the evidence of this film makes clear – the land is shared or repartitioned like a whore, treated as a commodity of exchange and either hated, as some resisting temperamental (even demented) creature who will not do his/her master's will, or wistfully loved as some exotic mistress (as for Boothby and, to some degree, Marc).

## Beau travail

Ten years later, Denis is once again back in an African territory she knew as a child – Djibouti. But this time we do not flashback to a past colonial moment on the cusp of the post-colonial one; and, instead of using a little girl (who could well be a fictional version of Denis herself), Denis uses the French Foreign Legion as a corporeal means of speaking to this post-colonial space. The film is, however, once more narrated in the form of a flashback; this time that of one of the legionnaires, Galoup, who has been dishonourably discharged for attempting to cause the death of another legionnaire, Sentain, who he has perceived as a rival for the attention (affections) of their leader Forestier. It is a tale of jealousy, loosely based on Herman Melville's *Billy Budd* and partly scored by music from Benjamin Britten's opera of the same name. Denis transposes the tale to Djibouti and the contemporary. While the legionnaires are primarily on-land, the locations she has chosen to place them in are largely along the coastlines — almost as if the legionnaires are land-locked by the beautiful intensely turquoise blue sea (see Figure Djibouti).

In this film, then, we are in the contemporary – 1998–1999 – and in East Africa, a landscape of different histories. Djibouti was the last French colony to gain independence, in 1977. Indeed, in 1967, such was the climate of unrest between the indigenous inhabitants (especially the Afars and the Issas), when the Djiboutians had the chance to vote for independence, the majority Afar people voted to remain under French rule. Given the difficult climate of Djibouti and the fact that it has virtually no means of sustaining itself agriculturally, the desire to remain under the protection of the French and all that that can mean in terms of the provision of a reasonable infrastructure to support the indigenous peoples – to say nothing of military support – suggest that this resistance to independence can seem quite understandable. The arable land is a mere 0.4 per cent; there is no cultivation of permanent crops. In fact Djibouti's only wealth resides in its natural resources: gold, clay, granite, limestone, marble, salt, pumice and, finally, petrol. *Beau travail* gives us a very full sense of the inhospitable torrid climate and the hard materiality of its landscape – we see the men breaking up the volcanic ground, being made to march across granite territory that is so unyielding to their aching feet, the military cemetery with its white stains looks as if it is conjured out of limestone, and of course we see Sentain struggling to return to base across the salt lands of the Lac Assal.

The film proper opens with a train ride – the famous and only train track that runs between Addis-Ababa and Djibouti city (the Ethiopian-Djibouti line). A little later we move to shots of a boat that is transporting new Foreign Legion recruits to their camp somewhere outside Djibouti city. From here they look out to the sea towards Tadjoura – Djibouti's oldest town and originally an Afar village that traded slaves and which gave its name to the gulf that separates the Afar and Issa lands. Much later in the film, Galoup – who by now is so jealous of Sentain and covetous of the esteem Forestier holds him in – decides to take his men off for training 'to get Sentain away from Forestier', as he puts it. He takes them off to Lac Goubet, a seawater loch known locally as the 'Pit of Demons'. There, Galoup looks out to the three volcanic islands that stand luminously white and which he describes, interestingly, as sentinels. It is as if they stand as Galoup's projection of the legionnaire in his supremely white suit and cap; as projections of his ideal image – the one he so fervently believes in, but which he singularly fails to attain. Yet, at other times of the day these same islands are dark and menacing. Indeed, it is as if Galoup has fallen into the pit of demons, for it is here that he plots the destruction of his perceived rival Sentain – the legionnaire who refuses through his mutism to return or mirror back to Galoup the ideal image he so craves.[2] Galoup even goes as far as to acknowledge the correspondence between this pit of demons and his own inner turmoil over Sentain. We hear him in voice-over say: 'I looked out at the desolate Goubet, thinking my dark thoughts. People tell many stories about this terrible cul-de-sac: the devil, evil spirits, evil eye.' Once here, Sentain is doomed (or as he will say later 'lost'). Galoup sets out his trap and ensnares Sentain for insubordination. He then drives him off and deposits him away from the camp to find his way back. Unbeknown to Sentain, Galoup has provided him with a faulty compass. Instead of heading southwest back to the camp he goes northeast and ends up at Lac Assal, a salt lake and aquatic wilderness lying below sea level with brilliant white salt sulphur and halite crystals. A place of unremitting aridity in which Sentain lays down to die covering his head with his salt-stiffened shirt. He is however rescued by a nomadic tribe of Afars travelling with their camels.

Those who formerly, in bygone times, traded slaves now pick up the white man and save his life. This is but one of a series of reversals this film presents us with, played against the differing but relentlessly harsh landscape. The most significant one is the way in which indigenous peoples emerge from nowhere, in colorful clothing, and stand and watch the legionnaires as they slave away at seemingly useless tasks in the burning heat (breaking up volcanic rock, rushing around on a military exercise, painting rocks white and marking out spaces in the camp with them, and so on). The point is, in their colorful attire, the indigenous peoples stand out in their land whereas the legionnaires so evidently do not. Their clothing is a greeny-brown that matches the volcanic landscape they find themselves in. They too 'come from nowhere' – as legionnaires they have renounced their identity (Sentain is even more purely from nowhere since he is a foundling), but they disappear into the land, are absorbed into it – thus signifying the futility of what it is they do.

In historic terms, France's hold on Djibouti was primarily strategic: to keep an eye on the British on the other side of the gulf in Aden as well as keep a watch over the world's most important shipping lanes. And it is noteworthy that, since decolonization, France has never

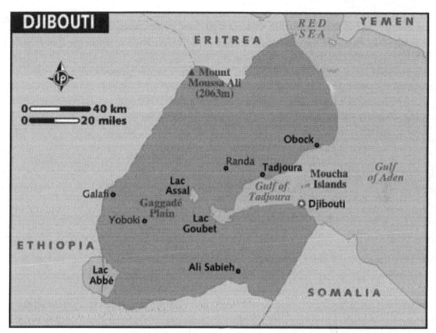

Reproduced with permission from lonelyplanet.com. © 2009 Lonely Planet.

ceased having a military presence of some order in Djibouti. During colonization, Djibouti was also a vital trade route for Ethiopia – and it still is today. As part of its strategic development, France built the important railway link between Addis-Ababa and Djibouti city. In *Beau travail*, Denis' first combination of shots tells us a great deal about these historic colonialist traces upon this land. First, the train ride: the camera is looking out to the landscape and we see in the sand the shadows of the men sitting on top of the train, then there is a cut and we see men in the carriages and a further cut to another carriage this time with women seated in it. The train moves on, the camera remains and cuts to a derelict tank. The two vestiges of France's colonialist past, therefore (later we will see a derelict plane – looking very similar to the one in *Chocolat* that fell over the horizon in Mindif). However, whereas colonialist history leaves its material traces (railtracks and armaments), the French Foreign Legion leaves none (note how their helicopter flips over and crashes into the sea). Almost as if to confirm this, the next shot is of the shadows in the sand of the legionnaires performing their exercises – in fact it is the first of their seven dances and scored to Britten's opening chorus ('O heave! O heave away, heave! O heave!').[3] Their shadows are as unsubstantial as those earlier shadows of the men on top of the train. And here is the extra twist in what Denis is showing us. In both instances, those shadows of men are the after effects of the colonial moment – a ghost-land that has first been exploited by its colonizing forces as a strategic base and which subsequently can give very little to its indigenous peoples since virtually no infrastructure

173

has been established during the century of colonial rule except for the building of Djibouti city and the railway. Two-thirds of Djiboutians live in the capital city, the rest are nomadic herders; 50 per cent of the nation is unemployed; nearly all food has to be imported. But the post-colonial moment never comes either, not completely. During the first Gulf War (and as it transpired during the second also, three years after this film's release) France and the allied forces used Djibouti as a strategic base. Are the Western military relics of the tank and the plane from that military engagement, one wonders? The women who dance in the disco are caught in their reflection, shadows and not physical beings – it is clear that their function is to service the legionnaires, that being their only source of income. There is so very little else to sell. Fresh 'qat' leaves (a mild drug, which Forestier loves to chew), but they too are not indigenous, coming as they do from Ethiopia. Even artisanal work fails to maintain a fair price. There is a telling moment when a woman comes to Djibouti city (who knows how far she has travelled?) to sell her hand-woven rugs: she is told the price has dropped massively since the celebrations – could they possibly be referring to the 1997 general elections which were supposed to put an end to ethnic hostilities?

## Conclusion

In both Denis' films we see how the landscape, for the most part quite silent landscape (apart from a few ambient sounds: the wind, the sea, the bells of goats, the call to prayers), is unyielding to those without knowledge. The arid landscape, hard-beaten as it is by the sun, will not embrace those who feel they can exploit or attempt to control it; it will stand by and watch, indeed, it will act as an unremitting foil to the unsubstantial, transcendent (lost) (post-)colonial body, becoming thereby a metaphor for its dislocation. Small wonder it is hard for this body to assert a clear sense of identity and sexuality in this terrain of dislocation. We recall how in *Chocolat*, Boothby tells Aimée how he slept with Marc, and how Luc, in order to fulfil his desire to be touched by Protée has to provoke him very hard (first he showers naked in front of him and when that fails he later taunts him into a fight – but even then that fails and it is a pitiful struggle that ensues and Protée chucks him out). In *Beau travail*, Galoup's obsession with both Forestier and Sentain pushes his homoerotic desire to the point of sadism; and although other legionnaires are more gentle with their desire (they bathe Sentain's bleeding foot, he gets carried tenderly on the left shoulder of one of his mates and so on), still the homoerotic desire does not dissipate. The clearest metaphor for not belonging is surely the planes or helicopters that fall out of the sky: Western Icarus has flown too close to the sun where he does not belong. Indeed, what the landscape yields is the incontrovertible proof on the one hand of the colonialist's folly and madness in the form of empty if brutal gestures of conquest, and, on the other, of the post-colonialist's inability to provide evidence that he has learnt anything from past history. Like Sentain's erratically swinging compass that returns to haunt Galoup, our location is just so many points on a compass but if we do not or cannot read it then we are truly lost.

## Notes

1. Claire Denis, 'Interview avec Claire Denis', *Première* 134 (1988), 123–125. For example, in relation to *Chocolat*, Denis readily acknowledged that as a white she could not adopt a black subjectivity. This is why she came up with the idea of using a little white girl (France) whose memories of those colonial times would constitute a point of view. Arguably she follows a similar procedure in *Beau travail* where it is a legionnaire's point of view (mainly Galoup's) we have of Djibouti (124).
2. As several critics have remarked Sentain could well mean 'sans tain' that is a mirror that can no longer reflect back because it has lost its silvering (see Cooper, Sarah, '"Je sais bien, mais quand même…" Fetishism, envy, and the queer pleasures of *Beau travail*', *Studies in French Cinema* 2(3) (2001), 174–182.
3. Denis wanted to use dance, and not war, to explore the myth of the French Foreign Legion (for a study of how she does this see Hayward, Susan, 'Claire Denis' films and the post-colonial body – with special reference to *Beau travail* (1999)', *Studies in French Cinema* 2(3) (2001), 159–165.

# Chapter 10

Landscaping the Revolution: The Political and Social Geography of Cuba Reflected in its Cinema

R. K. Britton

In film terms, unlike in painting or still photography which can be entirely different, a landscape, be it natural or urban, that is uninhabited or un-regarded, is generally without significant meaning. Landscape normally sets a scene, creates a context, establishes a mood, against or within which human agencies act out a narrative. But when the conduct and actions of the characters shown are shaped by a very particular set of historical, political, moral and artistic considerations that are universally shared by compatriot filmmakers, those functions may be altered. Indeed, they may even be reversed.

All countries have distinctive, often varied landscapes, within which the moods and contexts selected by film directors can be created. Cuba is no exception, though its variety is relatively limited. It is a small island in the Caribbean, some 800 miles long from east to west, and about a hundred at its widest point from north to south. Its natural flora is thick, tropical rain forest, with thickly wooded mountain ranges, while its northern coast boasts some of the finest beaches in the world and long sandy 'cays'. The Spanish colonists quickly depleted the forests to accommodate coffee and sugar plantations and ranching, and by 1550 had killed off most of the native Indian population, importing in their stead thousands of black slaves from West Africa to work the new plantations. Cuba's modern natural landscape is thus very much the creation of four centuries of colonial agriculture.

These facts are stated because they are important in understanding the Cuban national film industry since the 1959 Revolution. In the late 1950s, commercial filmmaking in Cuba was moribund, though the previous decade had seen a number of joint Mexican/Cuban productions, and the government offered a subsidy to filmmakers of up to 33 per cent of costs.[1] But only three months after the triumph of the Revolution, in March 1959, a new state-financed body, the Cuban Institute of Cinematic Arts and Industry (ICAIC) was set up by decree. It was designed to make, distribute and exhibit Cuban films, and to control the importation and showing of films from abroad for what had become, at least in Havana, a sophisticated cinema-going audience. Seldom can a national film industry have been given a more vital political, cultural, social and educational role. ICAIC was seen, and enthusiastically saw itself, as a standard bearer of the new society, whose job was to explain the Revolution to its own people and the outside world, on behalf of a country struggling to regain its self-respect, and to forge a new identity.

Of course, the phenomenon of a national film industry controlled and subsidized by the government of a single party state was hardly new. From the 1920s onward, filmmakers in Soviet Russia, Fascist Italy, Nazi Germany and Franco's Spain recognized the potential of film as an artistic mass medium that could be exploited for political and social purposes. But

179

equally significant was the global domination of Hollywood, and the ideological influence that it, and other national commercial cinemas that imitated it, exerted over public taste. Like other new and radical film movements, the new Cuban cinema set out to understand and oppose this model, both politically and artistically. In so doing, it also placed itself in the vanguard of a number of new and similarly motivated initiatives in Latin America, as part of what John King has called 'the Pan American movement of cultural and ideological liberation'.[2]

Despite a strong commitment to practice between the 1960s and 1980s, Cuban filmmakers were also prominent in producing essays that presented the issues faced by Cuban cinema in relation to continent-wide attempts to liberate filmmaking and establish a coherent alternative or 'Third' Cinema.[3] What all these have in common, particularly the pieces by the Cubans, Julio García Espinosa and Tomás Gutiérrez Alea, is the rejection of the mass commodification of cinema, and its consequent creation of a passive audience, as characterized by most of the expensive and technically 'perfect' products of Hollywood and its imitators.

Cuban filmmakers were neither isolated (despite the United State's boycotts and prohibitions) nor parochial in their outlook. Neither was the political cinema to which they aspired un-self-critical or dogmatic. Although ICAIC was involved in the debates that reflected the political shifts of the Revolution, particularly in the harder-line 1970s, it was never accepted that art should be subordinated to political or social doctrine. (Except in the broad sense that films could not condemn the Revolution as such, they have always been permitted to be critical of weaknesses within it.) It was also understood that if films were allowed to become political propaganda, they would lose their power to stimulate their audience to the level of moral and critical awareness that was the basis for revolutionary consciousness. Indeed, such films would simply become another type of commodity, creating a passive audience of a different kind.

Yet many of these assumptions arose also from technical and practical difficulties. In 1959, Cuba found itself with virtually no modern film equipment or film stock, and the annual budget for the whole of ICAIC's operation was less than a third of the cost of a single, middle-budget Hollywood feature film. For most of its first decade, ICAIC continued to use black and white photography, and the ambitions of filmmakers were both restricted and stimulated by these limitations. However, the need to record the realities of the Revolution had given ICAIC a first duty to produce newsreels and a range of documentaries to inform and educate the Cuban public.[4] ICAIC was also charged with taking films to the rural population in small towns and villages. Many stories are told of ancient projectors being loaded onto the back of borrowed Russian lorries to form mobile cinemas that toured the countryside.

The importance of documentary, and the creation of film styles that were based on documentary techniques, were to dominate the use of film in Cuba. All Cuban directors established themselves as makers of documentaries before they became known as makers of feature films. They took as their influences the work of Robert Flaherty and Dziga Vertov,

John Grierson, the Italian post-war neorealists and the French *nouvelle vague* of Jean-Luc Godard. Much was also learned from the Free Cinema of Tony Richardson and Lindsay Anderson. Despite this, classic films and technical innovations by the North American commercial industry were not ignored. Playful, admiring and often satirical references to great Hollywood screen moments and presences are frequent in Cuban films. The veteran Dutch documentarist, Joris Ivens, worked for some years in Cuba as a mentor to the new generation of filmmakers and technicians, and the French director, Chris Marker, directed *Cuba Sí* (1961) probably the outstanding Cuban documentary of the period.

The tumultuous nature of the early revolutionary years in Cuba and Latin America, meant that many young Cuban proponents of 'direct cinema' were, in Gutiérrez Alea's words, content to point a camera at the streets and trust to the results. Both Gutiérrez Alea and Julio García Espinosa were critical of the limitations of direct cinema, and it soon became apparent that this naïve realism was not enough. Michael Chanan comments on the emergence of Cuban documentary as follows:

> What is common to the approaches of Cuban documentary and direct cinema is the aim of *liberating documentary film from the conventions of commercial film* [my italics] such as insensitive but insistent background music, swish editing based on misplaced codes of fictional narrative, the alienation and paternalism of commentary…Crucially, there was also the aim of returning the documentary to the centre of attention in cinema – in which, by the end of the 1960s the Cubans had succeeded as no other cinema had done – with feature length documentaries becoming regular fare in Cuban cinemas.[5]

The techniques practiced in Cuban documentary film, including early Soviet-style montage using still photographs, historical footage and clever intercutting , elevated documentary to a prime place in Cuban cinema, and produced a fusion of reality and art that was to be the chief means of reflecting the Revolution to Cubans and the outside world. Inevitably it also set its stamp upon the fictional feature films that ICAIC began to produce by 1961. Cuban filmmakers were acutely conscious that cinema was able to occupy an immensely broad and diverse cultural space; one which, before the advent of moving pictures, had been shared among forms such as literature, painting, music and dance, theatre, journalism, historiography and even political and social movements. In fictional feature films, even more than in documentaries, the images of cinematographic art helped to create and define the concept of a people, their spiritual identity, their sense of moral and physical geography. All this was crucial to the aims of revolutionary cinema, and within it the presentation of landscape, whether rural or urban, was an essential element of that complex picture.

Landscape as a mediator or determinant of human action assumes major importance in most films. While a great deal of so-called natural landscape is man-made through agriculture or forestry, and urban landscape is entirely the creation of human kind, in fact both reflect the society by which they have been fashioned. As protagonists of revolutionary cinema, concerned primarily to portray human beings in a situation of struggle, change and self-realization, Cuban filmmakers felt obliged to show the country's landscapes as part of this particular process of portrayal. Thus the sceptical, uncommitted central figure of Gutiérrez Alea's 1968 classic *Memories of Underdevelopment* gazes down on the rooftops of Havana in the early days of the Revolution, questioning the nature of the change that is going on beneath them. Or, as in García Espinosa's early drama documentary *The Young Rebel* (1961) the forest is shown as a danger, but also and a place of concealment and safety for the groups of guerrilla fighters. Cuban feature films have, for example, rarely shown man in a symbiotic relationship with the natural world. Human beings are seldom shown to be reduced to a small element in a much greater natural picture, as they are in many films from the United States, Australia and Canada, which present the immensity of their natural space (forests, plains, mountains, rivers and lakes, deserts and snowy wastes) as a haunting or brooding presence, that dominates and shapes the actions played out against their imposing backdrop. Stimulated by the early documentaries of Robert Flaherty, and the backgrounds of Westerns by directors like John Ford and Howard Hawks, Hollywood had shown that black and white photography could capture certain types of landscape, particularly extremes, with great power.

On their small, mountainous island, with its vistas of tropical forest and cultivated savannah, Cuban directors had, prior to 1960, taken little account of these possibilities. Perhaps the pre-revolutionary decades, when Cuban landscape provided little more than decorative exoticism for screen romances made by Hollywood or Mexican companies, had left its mark upon them. But things were about to change. José Mansip, one of the film crew that worked with Joris Ivens in 1960–1961, kept a diary describing how Ivens taught Cubans to look afresh at their own countryside:

> This green, which is so beautiful to the human eye is not so to the mechanical eye of the photographic lens. With black and white film, the different shades of green are lost in a dark, undifferentiated mass. This means, for example, that if the dramatic quality of an action is accentuated in nature by the countryside behind it, this influence will be considerably reduced on the screen. The solution to this problem consists in finding an appropriate balance between the landscape and the sky. Cuba's sky could be the salvation of its countryside…Its astonishingly rich plasticity comes not only from its marvellous shade of blue, but above all from the extraordinarily varied shapes of the clouds. The sky, wisely included in a composition, can cancel the betrayal of the green.[6]

By 1987, ICAIC had produced 164 feature-length films, 112 of them fiction, 49 documentaries and 3 animated, of which 109 were in colour. In addition, to innumerable newsreels, 1,026 short films had been made (16 fiction and 1,010 documentary) of which 545 were also in colour.[7] Colour had gradually become the norm, and black and white photography was no longer a technological necessity.

These expanding technical possibilities saw the scope and subtlety of the portrayal of landscape, its inferred meanings and symbolism, develop considerably from the early practices of the documentary and direct cinema. They in turn complemented the changing approaches to the general themes which have preoccupied Cuban cinema over the past four decades. The most urgent and important of these was the political need to convey the nature of the Revolution, and the changes in social and moral outlook required of Cubans if its aims were to be realized. To its credit, ICAIC encouraged filmmakers to take a varied and sometimes complex approach to this most fundamental of concerns. The fictional feature films consequently produced offer simple but powerful lessons, from the kind found in García Espinosa's *The Young Rebel* (1961) and Humberto Solas's short film *Manuela* (1966) (both showing how uneducated *campesinos* learn to become revolutionary fighters), to Gutiérrez Alea's award-winning *Memories of Underdevelopment* (1968). Probably the most discussed film produced in Cuba, this work by the country's greatest and most versatile director examines the Revolution, through the eyes of Sergio, a bourgeois *rentier* and would-be writer. His family has left Cuba for the United States, while he remains in Havana, a disconnected and often self-deceiving observer of the new society in 1961, trying to make what sense of the changes he can.

The second theme was what was often referred to as the *rescate*, or rescuing of Cuban history, where filmmakers not only tried to reinterpret the record in ways that demonstrated the distortions and obfuscations of past accounts, but also attempted to reveal the complex truths about the state of colonial and post-colonial underdevelopment that had led (inevitably) to revolt and revolution.[8] The politically sensitive period of the late 1960s and 1970s saw a sharp debate within the Revolution, and a hardening neo-Soviet attitude towards the position of artists and intellectuals which came to a head over the Padilla affair.[9]

Consequently, ICAIC moved towards an oblique, historical examination of the Revolution, in place of the direct focus of works like *Memories of Underdevelopment*. Films like Jorge Fraga's *The Odyssey of General José* (1968) and Manuel Octavio Gómez's *The First Machete Charge* (1969), look back to Cuba's unsuccessful War of Independence against the Spanish in 1895. Interestingly, this was also the period in which Cuban film revisited its history as a slave-owning colony and the origins of its African past and present, in films like Sergio Giral's trilogy *The Other Francisco* (1974), *Rancheador* (1976) and *Mahuala* (1979), though the best and most politically revealing of the films on this theme is Gutiérrez Alea's *The Last Supper* (1979).

The third constantly recurring theme is that of women, their position in the Revolution and the struggle that many still experience as a result of the entrenched *machismo* within Cuban society, often shown as an undesirable legacy of underdevelopment.[10] Numerous films that examine this topic do so as part of a broader analysis of historic and contemporary social and moral conditions, particularly where they reveal different levels of female exploitation, and the struggle to escape from it. The film of this kind best known outside Cuba is Humberto Solas's *Lucía* (1968), a combination of three stories of young women from crucial periods in Cuba's past (the War of Independence of 1895, the fall of the dictator Machado in 1933 and the early years of the Revolution in the 1960s). Each 'Lucía' is also from a different class of society, an aristocratic *criolla* in 1895, a liberal *bourgeoise* in 1933 and a peasant girl in the early years of the 1960s, working on an agricultural cooperative. The resulting combination of historical portraits, pictures of political and social change, male attitudes and female psychology in the face of repression, places this film on a level with *Memories of Underdevelopment* as a landmark of the 'golden age' of Cuban cinema.

One of the last great black and white Cuban feature films, *Lucia* is also an exercise in the use of the natural and man-made landscape to reflect the mood and situation of the different female protagonists. The tragic powerlessness of the 1890s Lucia is echoed in the lush, grainy photography of the first part of the film, that makes it look like a product of early cinema, but is used to great effect to portray the soaking jungle and cane fields, and the decaying haciendas and sugar mills around which the savage hand-to-hand fighting of the second war of Cuban independence took place. By comparison, the sweat shop clothing factory in which the 1930s Lucia temporarily works symbolizes the protagonist's sense of limitation and frustration, using a hard-edged documentary camera style. But the country road along which the last Lucia, an agricultural worker freed by the Revolution, passes when she is given a lift by an interested lorry driver is a quite different environment. It is no longer a place of danger, decay and threat, but a tamed countryside in which all are working together for a common aim. Solas's pro-revolutionary note here may be a bit too simplistic and strident for the taste of some viewers, especially where the last Lucia rides off singing with a group of fellow female workers, but that does not alter the masterful way he has combined landscape, cityscape and narrative.

Although ICAIC managed to defend its artistic policies against opposition from certain elements in the party during the first half of the 1970s, its position on artistic freedom and pluralism of ideas and influences has, from time to time, been challenged by more orthodox Marxists. Towards the end of the decade, the cultural arena began to open up again, and some of the experimentation, humour and satirical exuberance of the 1960s (seen particularly in Gutiérrez Alea's surrealistic *Death of a Bureaucrat,* which achieved a considerable success in 1966) began to reappear. In 1979, the Latin New American Film Festival was established in Havana, and by the middle of the 1980s, words like *glasnost* and *perestroika*, though regarded with suspicion, were given a cautious welcome in the city.

But the changing mood also made it possible to explore new topics. In *Distance* (1985), Jesús Díaz confronted the hitherto 'off-limits' subject of the relationship between Cubans who stayed and the Cubans who had left for the United States, focusing on the gulf between generations in the same family and the human cost it entailed. In 1989, a fresh talent emerged when Orlando Rojas's *Secondary Roles* was exhibited, telling the story of a theatre company about to put on a performance of Carlos Felipe's play *Requiem for Yarini*, in which the generational difference and the actions of the actors, reflecting those of the characters they are playing, become a vehicle for a wider satirical reflection on Cuba in general. What Chanan has called the 'most carnivalesque' of this cycle of satirical films, *Alice in Wondertown* (1991) directed by Daniel Díaz Torres, was, however, banned in Cuba after winning an award at the Berlin Film Festival. Led by Alfredo Guzmán, who had returned to be its Director, ICAIC fought for the right to show the film and eventually won. But with

Cuba's economic position becoming highly precarious after the collapse of the Soviet Union, and the renewed blockade of the United States, ICAIC's position was also far from certain.

The ensuing 'special period' has seen Cuba regain some of its losses through the development of tourism, the creation of a new biotechnology capability and the diversification of food production. But in face of US opposition, the whole social fabric of the Revolution remains under threat. ICAIC has been obliged to depend more and more on co-productions with Spanish and Latin American companies to continue to make films. In this situation, films like Gutiérrez Alea's *Strawberry and Chocolate* (1993) – a Spanish/Cuban co-production – and his last film *Guantanamera* (1997), both co-directed with Juan Carlos Tabío, have emerged as works whose tolerance, humour and humanity expose the prejudice, hidebound thinking and inefficient bureaucracy of a system under stress. Yet contemporary works such as Leon Ichaso's *Bitter Sugar* (1996), where a doctor ceases to practice because he can earn twice as much playing the piano in a bar for tourists, and *Vertical Love* (1997), Arturo Sotto's surreal story of thwarted passion, seem to look impending failure and change more squarely in the eyes. This is the kind of pessimism, or *derrotismo* which Fidel Castro has criticized in the work of Cuban filmmakers.[11]

Looking back across this necessarily brief and selective account of the circumstances in which revolutionary cinema has flourished in Cuba, it is clear that the purposes and clarity of its themes, its social and political priorities and the artistic freedom it has enjoyed from commercial forces, have created unique values and criteria which it has consistently maintained. The presentation of landscape is not, generally speaking, subject to a different set of rules. It has been formed by the two contrasting techniques and styles the fictional feature films in Cuba have so often fused with astonishing results – experimentalism and surrealism on the one hand and documentary realism on the other. For the most part, particularly in the first twenty years of revolutionary cinema, the documentary presentation has predominated.

In 1959, the new generation of filmmakers had not only to assess the landscape of Cuba anew, but to decide what role it should play in their freshly conceived, historically urgent and politically committed aesthetic. On balance, landscape has tended to be shown as an objective reality, with, or against which, the human actors work or struggle in pursuit of their given collective or individual aims. Whether it consists of mountains, forest, a village, a street in Havana, the interior of a room or a view from a balcony, landscape has, generally speaking, been presented as an objective physical space where something happens, largely devoid of any wider or symbolic meanings. The early documentary and neorealist influences have tended to be enduring ones.

Both in the documentaries of the 1960s and in the fictional features of the next fifteen years, the countryside and the forest have been consistently portrayed as the world where human struggle or work takes place. This is illustrated in documentaries such as Gutiérrez Alea's *Histories of the Revolution* (1960) and Pastor Vega's *Men of Sugar* (1965), a study of a brigade of voluntary workers from the city at work in the cane fields. It is even more clearly evident in Gutiérrez Alea's fictional feature *Cumbite* (1964), and many of the historical films of the 1970s, including Sergio Giral's trilogy on Cuba's slave-owning past. However, Gutiérrez Alea's acclaimed *The Last Supper* (1975) shows a hint of significant change. The decade between the early 1960s and the early 1970s had made the wide-angle lens and coloured film stock available to Cuban directors for the first time. One of the earliest examples of the application of these new technical resources was Pastor Vega's short documentary *Song of the Tourist* (1967). Like the forest where García Espinosa's *The Young Rebel* is acted out, the portrayal of the countryside in *Cumbite*, bears striking comparison with the vision in *The Last Supper*, not least because of the technical differences between the films. *Cumbite* is set in Haiti (a number of Haitian immigrants to Cuba played supporting roles in the film). It tells the story of a Haitian who returns to his native village after some years spent in Cuba, and tries to persuade its inhabitants to build a well and permanent irrigation supply. In the film, shot in a sparse, economical style in black and white, and arguably the last of his films to employ neorealistic techniques, Gutiérrez Alea depicts the village and its surrounds in a studied, objective detail that provides a hard, unyielding backdrop to the story in which the main protagonist is killed by a jealous rival, and the irrigation system is not built.

In *The Last Supper* (shot in colour and wide screen), Gutiérrez Alea tells the story of an aristocratic slave owner, a Spanish Count who is introducing new machinery to the sugar mill on his Cuban estate. The camera picks out, monotonously, the buildings and surrounding land of the estate, which limit the horizons of the slaves and owners alike. The crucial scene is a long sequence in a dark, candlelit dining room, in which the Count reenacts the Last Supper, playing the role of Christ to twelve chosen slaves who represent the disciples. (It recalls the classic beggars' banquet sequence from Buñuel's 1960 Spanish classic *Viridiana*.) The message he preaches is one of acceptance of their lot and mutual love of master for slave. A slave rebellion follows, in which the mill is burnt down, and the brutal estate overseer is killed. The film ends with the hunting down of the rebellious slaves in the hills and forest around the estate. Only the determined and uncompromising Sebastián escapes. The final frames show him, a machete on his shoulder, running up a hill through the trees to emerge suddenly into the sunlight of freedom. The symbolism of the bright ending is as clear as that of the darkness in which the supper had taken place.

The 1980s and 1990s have seen a progressive return to contemporary urban settings from the rural backdrops of the historical films of the 1970s. Budgetary constraints have always forced Cuban directors to be bold and improvisatory in their efforts to overcome them. One of the outcomes of this has been the ability to manipulate long sequences of a fairly static kind, where dramatic tension and interest is generated between characters in a static – usually interior – setting. (It is a set of conventions with which British television, for example, is very familiar.) There are many outstanding examples of this use of interior and urban 'landscape' Striking examples are the effects of the inside of the family flat in Havana that constitutes most of the setting for Jesús Díaz's *Distance* (1985). The spatial confines of the flat and the occasional rooftop views from windows and balconies, are made to emphasize the alienation and the gap between the woman who has returned to Cuba from the United States on a visit, and the son and family she left behind years before.

In *Strawberry and Chocolate* (1997), Gutiérrez Alea employs the same strategy. The curiously ornamented and decorated room of the homosexual intellectual and artist Diego, in a nineteenth-century Havana tenement now dilapidated and crammed with families, is the location for much of the interaction of the film, with occasional forays out onto the narrow streets of the city, its parks, and the hostel where David, the young communist militant lives. At the end David and Diego walk together before Diego leaves Cuba for Paris, luxuriating in the sight of the skyline of Havana from the other side of the harbour. It is a sign that the sense of frustration that has, in different ways, oppressed them both has been lifted as a result of their friendship, but that the future will involve great change for both of them, and for Cuba.

Probably the most significant general and concluding observation that can be made about the portrayal of landscape in Cuban cinema since 1959 is that the commitment of filmmakers to mapping the cultural *terra nova* of the Revolution, has shaped this aspect of film and filmmaking, as it has all others. On the relatively few occasions when documentary and feature films have looked outside Cuba for their subject and material, invariably they have focused upon themes that have also illustrated some truth about the Revolution, or the circumstances leading up to it. ICAIC's creative policy, and collective way of working on new projects has not favoured the extremes of 'auteurism' possible in other national or state-controlled industries or independent production.

Thus the highly subjective or idiosyncratic vision that can emerge from an auteur's vision – that of a Andrei Tarkovsky or a Carlos Saura for example – with the obscurity that can often accompany it, has been largely avoided. Indeed, though no national cinema has been as resolutely and consistently willing to experiment as the Cuban industry, it has always sought a clarity of vision, and a scientific approach which, notwithstanding its experiments, has eschewed the distorting lens of subjectivism. The imposition of the 'neurotic gaze', or the distortion of reality through the eyes of an individual character, so frequently resorted to in Hollywood commercial melodrama, is not a major characteristic of Cuban film vocabulary. Thus until the present difficult juncture for filmmaking in Cuba, and even for the Revolution itself, the presentation of both rural and urban landscape in Cuban cinema has tended to go in the opposite direction from that followed by mainstream commercial cinema. Human endeavours and actions have tended to set the scene, with the landscape providing a space – sometimes neutral, sometimes with aspects that are emblematic or symbolic, but always objectively discerned – generally unshaped by the subjective eye, and subordinate to the interactions of the real or fictitious actors portrayed.

## Notes

1. A scholarly and perceptive account of Cuban cinema before 1959 is given in the first part of Michael Chanan's comprehensive study *Cuban Cinema* (Minneapolis and London: University of Minnesota Press, 2004), 25–116. This is a development of Chanan's earlier book *The Cuban Image: Cinema and Cultural Politics in Cuba* (London: BFI, 1985). The present brief study draws heavily upon Chanan's later work.

2. King, John, *Magical Reels: A History of Latin American Cinema* (London: Verso, 1990), 3.
3. See Martin, Michael (ed.), *New Latin American Cinema*, vol. 1 (Detroit: Wayne State University Press, 1997) which reproduces in translation a number of 'manifesto' and other essays by exponents of Latin American new cinema. These include: Solanas, Fernando and Getino, Octavio, 'Towards a Third Cinema: Notes and experiences for the development of a cinema of liberation in the Third World' (1965); Sanjinés, Jorge, 'Problems of form and content in revolutionary cinema' (first published in 1979 and expanded in 1989); García Espinosa, Julio, 'For an imperfect cinema' (1970) and Gutiérrez Alea, Tomás, 'The viewer's dialectic' (1989).
4. Only the National Literacy Campaign, begun in 1962, and itself the subject of numerous documentary and feature films, was given a bigger social priority in the first years of the Revolution. Within ten years, the campaign had raised literacy from 70 per cent of the population to 98 per cent.
5. Chanan, 194.
6. Quoted by Chanan, 199, and first published in *Cine Cubano* 3(24), under the title: 'Crónicas de un viaje: una lección de cine'.
7. Quoted by King, 146, from O. Getino's *Cine latinoamericano: economía y nuevas tecnologías audiovisuales* (Mérida: University of the Andes, 1987), 37.
8. This was a process that mirrored the much broader literary efforts of Latin American novelists to 're-create' Latin American history between the late 1940s and the mid-1970s. A leading figure in this tendency, and also a leading figure in the development of magical realism, was the Cuban novelist and musicologist Alejo Carpentier, who was accorded a privileged place among writers of the Revolution. Probably the best known Latin America writer, the Colombian Gabriel García Márquez, was similarly engaged in reexamining Latin American history through his fiction and journalism. His friendship with Fidel Castro, and his personal interest and investment in the Cuban Film School, makes him an important background influence on Cuban cinema, itself worthy of a separate study.
9. The crisis of cultural politics that followed the arrest of the poet Heberto Padilla in 1971 had far-reaching effects, though not directly upon ICAIC. For the next five years, an evident 'Sovietization' of Cuba's economic model and artistic policy was apparent, which lost Castro the support of a number of international artists and writers who had previously supported the Revolution (see Chanan, 312–313).
10. Marvin D'Lugo points out that the process was one of mobilizing female narratives on behalf of the nation, and was more than simply the structuring of stories about women and their experiences (see 'Transparent women: Gender and nation in Cuban film', in Martin (ed.), 155). He states: 'The underlying objective of such films was to develop a form of address to, and identification by, the Cuban audience through the mediation of a new revolutionary mythology rooted in the female figure.'
11. Officially the complaint was made by Fidel Castro in a speech at the National Assembly in early 1989. It centred on a report of the film *Guantanamera*, which Fidel had not seen, and which he did not realize was by the legendary Gutiérrez Alea, recently dead. At a subsequent meeting of UNEAC, the Union of the Cuban Artists and Writers, Fidel was faced with unanimous opposition to his criticism of the film, which he admitted he had not realized was by 'Titón' (Alea's nickname). He then retracted his criticism, but warned the ICAIC that it was being over-critical of things at a very difficult moment. (See Chanan, 1–2 for a more detailed account of the episode.)

# Chapter 11

Landscapes of Meaning in Cinema: Two Indian Examples

Wimal Dissanayake

The relationship between cinema and landscape is a complex and multifaceted one, generating issues of ontology, epistemology, aesthetics and forms of cultural representation. Most often, we tend to think of landscape in films as a provider of the requisite background for the unfolding of the narrative and a giver of greater visual density and cogency. This is indeed true so far as it goes; however, landscapes in cinema perform numerous other functions that are more subtle and more complex which invest the filmic experience with greater meaning and significance.

There are certain film directors like David Lean, Andre Tarkovsky or Chen Kaige who have earned a justifiable reputation as filmmakers preoccupied with the power and specularities of landscapes. Films such as *Dr Zhivago, Lawrence of Arabia, Yellow Earth* exemplify this fact. However, most gifted filmmakers are interested in landscape as a way of contributing to, and intensifying, the intended meaning of the film. Landscapes can operate in manifold ways in giving a greater depth to the projected filmic experience as is evidenced in the work of directors ranging from Orson Welles to Akira Kurosawa.

According to the Oxford English Dictionary, the term landscape was originally employed to signify a picture of natural land scenery, and later to mean a bird's-eye view, a plan, a sketch or map. It also came to mean the depiction or description of something in words. The study of landscape became popular because of painting and photography, and later cinema. The interesting developments in these fields of creative communication have had the salutary effect of forcing us to rethink the salience of landscapes in literature. To my mind, some of the most stimulating exegetical writings in this field have emerged in relation to Wordsworth's poetry. As we examine the growth of international cinema, we realize that landscapes can operate at a number of different levels of representational significance and enunciatory competence. Landscapes establish a sense of time, place and mood; they serve to punctuate the narrative and invest it with a more varied rhythm; they can intensify the pictoriality of films; they can enforce a sense of disjunction, an ironic juxtaposition; they can play on and manipulate our spatial consciousness; they open up new and interesting epistemological pathways to the meaning of a film; they can externalize inner dramas of characters; they act as visual analogies for complex psychologies of characters. These are but some of the ways in which landscapes function in cinema to forward the intentionalities of the director.

Landscapes, therefore, constitute a vital segment of the representational strategies deployed by filmmakers to communicate their experiences with the maximum effect. Let us, for example, consider the award-winning film, *Yellow Earth* (Hunag tudi, 1984) by the fifth generation Chinese filmmaker Chen Kaige. This movie retells a simple story. A soldier arrives at a desolate mountain village with the hope of gathering folk-songs. He decides to live in a house where a young girl is married to an old man. The soldier tells her how women are treated under the communist regime in the capital of Yan'an. Her mind is filled with hopes and desires. She sets out in search of the city of liberation. On the way, tragically, she drowns. Chen Kaige converts this simple story into a moving work of cinematic art. The landscape is central to the meaning of *Yellow Earth* as it projects visual similes and allegories that open up more interesting hermeneutical spaces. The vast landscape in which human beings are located reminds one of classical Chinese paintings. Clearly, Chen Kaige is paradoxically drawing on traditional Chinese aesthetics to infuse his text with newer resonances. But beyond this, one perceives how the director of the film is using the landscape – the vast barren earth, the rolling mountains, miniscule human beings moving across it – to make a political statement. What he is saying is that earlier, especially during the time of the Cultural Revolution, one did not have the luxury of portraying landscapes in films as directors were coerced into depicting workers and part officials busy marching forward toward socialism. Here, in a negative way, the landscape in *Yellow Earth* carries a vital freight of political meaning.[1]

In this chapter, I wish to focus on two films by two Indian directors who most discerning filmgoers regard as the two greatest Indian filmmakers. They are Satyajit Ray and Ritwik Ghatak. Ever since Ray made his epoch-making film *The Song of the Little Road* (*Pather Panchali*, 1955), his reputation has grown nationally and internationally as a gifted director imbued with a sense of humanism. Although Ghatak is a contemporary of Ray, and made his first film in 1952, it was only during the last two decades or so that Ghatak has begun to win national and international recognition largely due to the efforts of filmmakers such as Kumar Shahani and critics such as Ashish Rajadhyaksha and Paul Willemen. In this essay, my focus of interest will be on the two films *The Song of the Little Road* and *Cloud-capped Star* (Meghe dhaka tara, 1962). What is worthy of note at the very outset is that these are two film directors who were not primarily concerned with landscapes in the way, say, David Lean was. However, in my view, landscape is crucial to the meaning of both films, opening up interesting aesthetic and cognitive spaces. In a way, by focusing on two films that are not primarily and overtly preoccupied with landscape and picturesqueness, one can reinforce the centrality of landscape in cinematic meaning.

Satyajit Ray (1921–1992) is unarguably the greatest Indian film director. Internationally speaking, in any discussion of Indian cinema, his is the first name that springs to mind. His first film, *The Song of the Little Road* (*Pather Panchali*, 1955), inaugurated the tradition of art cinema in India, encouraging numerous other younger filmmakers to follow in his footsteps. As Adoor Gopalakrishnan, one of the leading Indian film directors remarked:

Pather Panchali, for me, marks the beginning of the true Indian cinema – a beginning for all of us. It was not only a total negation of the soulless and superficial all-India cinema indifferent to real people and issues, but also an affirmation of the emergence of the first consummate artist on the sub-continent's motion-picture scene. So, for us all – ardent lovers of the dynamic medium of art – in the beginning there was...Pather Panchali.[2]

Satyajit Ray gained wide international critical acclaim through his outstanding works of cinematic art such as *The Song of the Little Road*, *The Unvanquished* (Aparajito, 1956), *The World of Apu* (Apu sansar, 1959), *The Goddess* (Devi, 1960) and *Charulata* (1964). He is the author of over 35 films that carry the distinct stamp of his creativity. About two and a half decades after the showing of *The Song of the Little Road*, the great Japanese director, Akira Kurosawa remarked, 'I can never forget the excitement in my mind after seeing it. I have had several more opportunities to see the film and each time I feel more overwhelmed. It is the kind of cinema that flows with the serenity and nobility of a big river.'[3] Coming from Kurosawa, this is high praise indeed.

In this essay on landscapes of meaning in cinema, I wish to focus on two Indian films, namely, Ray's *The Song of the Little Road* and Ritwik Ghatak's *Cloud-capped Star*. Neither of these films deals with overt pictoriality or wide-angled panoramic visions of landscapes. They are not 'painterly' films that make a conscious effort to foreground the beauties of nature. However, despite the absence of extravagant landscapes, these two films, as indeed most well-crafted films by gifted filmmakers, make use of landscape to convey deeper artistic truths. The fact that the two films under scrutiny in this essay do not go out of their way to draw attention to the beauty and sublimity of the landscape is all the more significant in terms of the theme of this essay. What they underline is the centrality of landscape in cinematic communication.

The story of *The Song of the Little Road* thematizes the problems and hardships encountered by a Brahmin family living in a Bengali village at the opening of the twentieth century. The father (Harihar), the head of the family, is a poor priest and a poet who hardly earns enough money to support his family. The life of the mother (Sarbojaya) is typical of that of an Indian peasant woman – her life is an unending series of daily chores and privations. The daughter (Durga) is playful, mischievous and is depicted in the film as a daughter of nature. An old and feeble aunt of theirs lives with them, and one senses continuous tensions between Sarbojaya and the old aunt.

Into this family Apu is born, the protagonist of the trilogy comprising *The Song of the Little Road*, *The Unvanquished* and *The World of Apu*. Harihar talks optimistically of securing a job and ushering in a period of prosperity for the family. However, it does not come to pass. As Apu reaches six years of age, he is sent to a makeshift school run by the village grocer. Meanwhile, the animosities between Sarbojaya and the aunt deepen; the latter decides to leave. The old aunt, after a while, comes back and asks that she be allowed to live with the family. Sarbojaya turns down the request. The old woman departs, and Durga and Apu who are very fond of her, go in search of her. On a dark and windy night, as both of them run across the field having seen a train go by for the first time, they discover her dead body by the pathway.

Harihar, the father, has gone away to an adjoining village to officiate at an initiation ceremony. He writes home that the ceremony has been cancelled and that he plans to go to the city to earn some money. A few months later, he comes back with his meager earnings and a sari for his daughter only to learn that Durga has died. The family decides to leave their ancestral home and head for the city of Benares. The film concludes with a shot of them leaving the village in a cart. This, in brief, is the story of *The Song of the Little Road,* based on a popular novel by Bhibutibhushan Bannerji.

As I stated earlier, although this is not a film that deploys grand vistas of landscapes, nevertheless landscapes are central to the meaning of the film. One can, somewhat schematically, talk of natural landscapes and cultural landscapes. Natural landscapes refer to the hills and valleys and rivers – manifestations of nature. The term 'cultural landscape' signifies the way human beings have re-shaped the natural landscape into human settlements, investing it with the force of culture. In Ray's *The Song of the Little Road,* there is a close and mutually fecundating relationship between the natural and cultural landscapes. Let us, for example, consider the very opening scene of the film.

It is early morning in the village of Nishchindipur. A wealthy widowed matriarch of a household is standing besides the sacred 'tulsi' plant on the terraced roof of a spacious, brick house. She looks down and sees a young girl running away with a fruit in her hands. She complains about people plucking fruits from her trees. Durga conceals the stolen fruit in the folds of her sari. Her mother, Sarbojaya, passes by, carrying a pitcher and bucket; she is on her way to the village well. Durga hides behind a bush. After her mother is out of sight, Durga skips down the pathway through the bamboo grove; she walks speedily past the date palms and creepers, past a cow that is tethered to a tree, towards an old brick wall covered with creepers. Durga enters a courtyard through a wooden door in the wall, going past the tulsi plant that is located at the centre. She walks towards the section of the house where her old grand aunt normally lives. She climbs on to the elevated mud veranda and looks into the old woman's room. There is no-one. She says in a hushed tone, 'aunty'.

What we find here is the intersection of natural landscape and cultural landscape. To phrase it differently, we see how Ray has concerted space into place through poetically moving images. As the film progresses, we begin to realize that this place is both material and metaphoric. Ray is particularly cogent in the way he establishes relationships between place and identity; and this relationship is vitally connected to time. The transformation of space into place involves the interactions of peoples, routinized behaviours, rituals, etc. We see in this opening sequence how Ray fashions landscapes of meaning through symbiotic interplays between organic nature and collective social existence. Throughout *The Song of the Little Road* we see how the director has carefully created landscapes of meaning out of this conjunction between the natural and cultural settings.

Satyajit Ray, as he has stated in many interviews, was greatly influenced by the Italian neorealistic films, and most notably by the work of Vittorio De Sica. The neorealists sought to capture the misery and the hardships experienced by Italian people after the Second World War. They were interested in making documentary-like films using for the most part non-professional actors, deploying simple stories and shooting outside studios. This bent of mind appealed to Ray's cinematic imagination. He followed the neorealistic tradition, but sought to invigorate and extend its discursive boundaries through visual poetry, in a way that most neorealistic film directors did not. As a matter of fact when some of the artists associated with the neorealistic movement saw Ray's film, this was indeed their reaction. Let me illustrate this by focusing on a memorable scene from the film.

The candy seller has arrived. Durga wants Apu to go and ask their father for money. Sarbojaya shouts not to give them money. Harihar refuses. Durga says to Apu 'Let's follow him'. They go after him along the village path. A dog that was resting nearby runs after the two children. They go towards the edge of the pond. Next, we have a shot of their moving reflections in the pond. This is captured beautifully giving the whole sequence a sense of lyricism. Moreover, the moving reflection in the water, the candy seller followed by the two children and the dog, is emblematic of the impossibility and illusoriness of their childhood desires. Here we see how landscape is used both to introduce a lyrical quality and make a metaphorical enunciation.

One of the most memorable scenes in *The Song of the Little Road* is the one where Apu and Durga see a train speeding by for the first time in their lives. It illustrates the manifold ways in which landscape operates in cinema, infusing it with a multi-dimensionality of meaning. In the distance in a field full of white kaash flowers, we see Durga wandering by herself as the telegraph poles stand tall against the sky in the afternoon. One almost hears the low hum of the telegraph wires; Durga looks up; lowers her head; listens to the sound of the wires; walks away, searching for the origin of the unusual sound. Far away, we see Apu wading through some water; he walks towards Durga. By now, Durga has discovered that the sound is emanating from a telegraph pole. She places her ear against it and listens intently to the sound. Apu too has heard the sound. He looks upward; goes up to a telegraph pole; places his ear against it and runs after his sister. She runs deeper and deeper into the field, concealed in the tall grass. Apu feels lost. A sugar cane stick comes through the air and knocks him. Smilingly, he picks it up and walks up to Durga.

All of a sudden, Durga places her hand over Apu's mouth as if to silence him. She listens intently and says 'a train'. The two children spring to their feet in a moment and look around for the train. They see the top of an engine, with clouds of smoke billowing over the spread of white flowers. Apu and Durga dash across the field. The train is still away at a distance. While running, Durga falls down and rises again; Apu races ahead. The train appears in its majesty. Apu runs closer toward it. The engine rushes past, while we see and hear the wheels moving noisily. Apu clambers up to higher ground and keeps looking at the train as it begins to disappear. We see a long train of thick smoke hanging low over the clusters of white kaashi flowers.

This sequence of events is important on a number of accounts related to the investment of human meaning in the landscape. The arrival of the train on the landscape is a signifier of the inevitability of modernization and its effect on the village of Nishchindipur. For the most part, the village is depicted as a unified place; the train – a dominant symbol of modernity – will change things. It is not as if things have not begun to change that will impact the sense of place in the village. The reference to the 'Bioscope-wallah', and the fact of the father going to the city in search of work, are indices of it. The train sequence only serves to lend added weight to this inevitability of social change. The train sequence is important for another reason as well. It focuses on the sense of wonder that is crucial to the meaning of the film. As Apu grows up, he encounters the world around him, stirring within him a sense of wonder. In terms of traditional aesthetics, this sense of wonder, which is referred to as 'chamathkara' is of great importance as it forms the basis of the intended emotion generated by a work of art (rasa). Satyajit Ray has juxtaposed this scene, which evokes a sense of wonder in the two children, with the death of the old aunt in the following scene. This too generates a sense of wonder because Durga and Apu encounter death for the first time. One is a positive sense of wonder while the other is negative.

This scene, where the train intrudes into the tranquil landscape generating different layers of meaning, is vividly illustrative of the way Ray makes use of landscape to frame his meaning. It is in this sequence that we observe Apu realizing for the first time the emergence of his own individuality; it is evident that Ray is using nature and spatial consciousness to good effect. It is interesting to observe that towards the end of the film, after learning of Durga's death, Harihar lies awake at night staring at the ceiling. At that point, we hear on the soundtrack a train in the distance piercing the silence that has enveloped the night.

Another memorable scene in *The Song of the Little Road* is where young Durga dances gleefully in the rain. The way Ray has captured her emotions through the interplay of the semiotics of body and space is most interesting. Once again the landscape becomes a generator of human meaning. Apu and Durga are running across a field as threatening rain clouds gather overhead. The rain comes down torrentially. One sees a lonely kul tree, with its outstretched branches, in the centre of the field. Apu rushes there seeking shelter. He stands under the tree, shivering, calling out to Durga. The strong downpour drowns out his voice. Very quickly, ditches and ponds are overflowing with water. A dog dashes through the rain toward a house. Durga, in the meantime, experiencing a rare sense of freedom and self-celebration, dancing in the rain, poking fun at her brother, she runs across the field toward Apu, who is now shivering, draws him toward her and covers him with the end of her sari. In this scene, we see the way in which Satyajit Ray deploys the landscape as a way of giving greater definition to the personality of Durga, her experience of freedom, her enjoyment of the body, with hints of eroticism, underlining her sense of wonder that I referred to earlier. As with the train sequence, this scene gives way to the sad sequence of events leading to Durga's death through pneumonia, having being drenched in the rain. Once again, Apu experiences the sense of positive wonder and negative wonder I alluded to earlier.

Satyajit Ray is particularly good at capturing not only the larger, elemental forces of nature and landscape but also the telling details. He suggests that in the incessant and inexorable flow of life, we should be alert not only to the bigger events but also to little things; lilies blooming in a pond, raindrops hopping on leaves, grass swaying in the wind, a flock of birds rising up to the sky, water bugs flitting across the surface of a water pond, etc. Ray presents these little things in the spirit of reminding us that we should exult in the simple joys created by the landscape. In an interview, Ray remarked:

This is Indian tradition. It's very important. The presence of the essential thing in a very small detail, which you must catch in order to express larger things; and this is in Indian art, this is in Rajput miniatures, this is in Ajanta, this is in Ellors, this is in the classics, in Kalidasa, in Sakuntala, in folk-poetry, in folk-singing…[4]

It is interesting to observe the way in which Ray brings in classical Indian aesthetics to demonstrate his use of natural landscape in his films.

It is often said by art critics that when we appreciate a natural landscape or one represented through a painting or photograph, our attention is drawn to certain aspects of it more strongly than to others. Art critics designate this as the focal point in the landscape or painting. The meaning of the landscape, by and large, emanates from that focal point. It can be, and often is, interpreted from diverse hermeneutic vantage points, but the important point to bear in mind is that it is central to the intended or recognized meaning of the landscape. In the case of Satyajit Ray's cinematic landscapes, the focal point is always the young boy Apu who is beginning to experience the wonder of the world and is striving to make sense of it. The intent of *The Song of the Little Road* and the other two films that comprise the Apu trilogy is the growth of Apu into manhood. He is at the discursive centre of the trilogy. Hence, this privileged focal point is only to be expected.

On the basis of this discussion, one can make a number of observations regarding the way landscape is used in Ray's film. As I stated earlier, Ray was deeply influenced by Italian neorealism. However, he succeeded in going beyond the documentation of misery and hardships of people seeking to make a life for themselves, to invest his moving images with a sense of lyricism. Moreover, this lyricism is vitally imbricated with deeper layers of meaning. Let us consider the two sequences alluded to earlier – Apu's and Durga's first sighting of the train and Durga's dance in the rain. Both sequences generate a sense of wonder and celebrate a sense of freedom. And both these joyful sequences are followed by death. In the first, it is the death of the old aunt, and in the second that of Durga, who came down with pneumonia having been drenched in the rain. It is not merely a juxtaposition of the joyous and the melancholy; Satyajit Ray, being the gifted filmmaker he is, has been able to intimate that sense of mortality within the respective centres of the two scenes. In the train sequence, while we appreciate the sense of wonder experienced by the two children, we are overcome by a sense of foreboding, almost impending doom, as the train races across the field billowing black smoke. Similarly, while Durga is enjoying herself and bodily freedom in the rain, we feel the sinister power of rain as well. After all, in classical Indian mythology, rain spells the end of the eon.

Let us consider, next, the film *Cloud-capped Star* by Ritwik Ghatak. Ritwik Kumar Ghatak (1925–1976) is one of the most important, and until recent times, undervalued Indian film directors. He started off his artistic life as a poet and a playwright before turning to cinema. He was a socially engaged artist who realized the importance of art as a means of raising the consciousness of the vast mass of people in India. He completed eight films between the years 1953 and 1974, struggling against myriad obstacles. *Cloud-capped Star* is his fourth feature film and was made in 1966. Ghatak regarded it as his most favourite film, textualizing some of his deep-laid interests and preoccupations. This, like Ray's film, is not a work of cinematic art that deals explicitly with man and nature, beauties of natural scenery, etc.; however, the ways in which he has sought to portray landscapes, both natural and cultural, at different levels of visual and cognitive apprehension and in different visual and auditory registers, adds significantly to the weight of the film.

There are two important points that need to be made about Ghatak's films – one thematic and the other stylistic. He was a victim of the horrendous partitioning of India in 1947, and many of his movies bear the emotional scars of this traumatic event. Second, he was desirous of forging an indigenous art of cinematography that differentiated itself both from Hollywood and commercial Indian cinema. Ray once remarked, 'For him, Hollywood might not have existed at all.' He was one of the earliest Indian filmmakers with a serious bent of mind who was quick to discern the cinematic possibilities of melodrama. As he once observed, 'I think a truly national cinema will emerge from the much abused form of melodrama when truly serious and considerate artists bring the pressure of their intellect upon it.' *Cloud-capped Star* exemplifies the ways in which the inherent potentialities of melodrama can be quarried fruitfully to serve deep artistic ends.

Ritwik Ghatak was deeply influenced by the writings of the eminent psychologist Carl Jung. This is important in making sense of his films, including *Cloud-capped Star*, that I wish to discuss in this chapter, and the way he deploys landscapes. Commenting on Siegfried Kracáuer's celebrated work, *Theory of Film: Redemption of Physical Reality*, he made the comment that, 'Dr. Kracauer should have studied Jung's psychology of the unconscious'. Ghatak's interest in Jung serves to widen the discursive boundaries of the art of realism in cinema, and to invest his films with added layers of meaning. In my ensuing discussion of landscapes in *Cloud-capped Star*, I will expand on this point.

The story of *Cloud-capped Star* takes place in the 1950s in a suburb of Calcutta. The story centres on the character of Nita. She is the eldest daughter in a family that has been transplanted to Calcutta. Her aging father teaches in a small school and hardly earns enough money to support his family. Her elder brother, Shankar, wants to become a singer; he is self-centred and irresponsible, pursuing his career to the exclusion of everybody else. The mother is irritable and worn-down by household work. Her younger sister Gita and the younger brother Montu are both selfish and go their own way. Poor Nita has to carry the full burden of the family. She is in love with Sanat, who hopes to become a scientist. He is also dependent upon her for financial support. In the meantime, Sanat is increasingly attracted to Gita, Nita's younger sister, and their mother seems to encourage that move. Owing to the increasing demands placed on her, Nita decides give up her studies and takes up full employment in an office; she supplements her income by giving tuition. The father is compelled to give up his teaching job due to illness. Montu abandons his studies, and finds work in a factory. As if things were not bad enough already, Nita contracts tuberculosis; she isolates herself from the rest of the family for fear of infecting them. By now Shankar is a successful singer. He takes Nita to a sanatorium in the hills. The film ends with Nita sitting silently by herself surrounded by the mountains that she was always fond of. Overcome by a desire to live, she exclaims, 'I want to live.'

Ritwik Ghatak gives this contemporary story of self-sacrifice a mythic dimension by framing it in terms of classical Indian mythology. Commenting on the film, Ghatak remarked that:

The Great-Mother image that permeates classical and folk-literature is central to the meaning of the film. The great-other archetype is thus symbolized in various forms and shapes. The principal motif of Meghe Dhaka Tara is decidedly this, though a number of auxiliary themes have also been woven into the film. Hence my Nita is born on the auspicious day of the celebrations for the goddess jagatdhriti (the one who holds or contains the earth).[5]

Earlier on I alluded to the fact that Ghatak was deeply interested in the conceptualizations of Jung. His interest in Jung dovetails nicely with his fascination with Indian mythology. After all, Jung himself was fascinated by Indian mythology as evidenced in his writings. In his critique of Kracauer's book, he quotes with approval the following passage from Jung:

Man's need to understand the world and his experiences in it, symbolically as well as realistically, may be noted early in the lives of many children. The symbolic, imaginative view of the world is just as organic a part of a child's life as the view transmitted by the sense organs. It represents natural and spontaneous striving which adds to man's biological bond a parallel and equivalent psychic bond, thus enriching life by another dimension – and it is eminently this dimension that makes man what he is…[6]

It is against this background of thinking that I wish to comment on the function of landscape in Ghatak's *Cloud-capped Star*. Landscapes in cinema can be broadly classified into two groups – natural landscapes and cultural landscapes. Natural landscapes refer to hills and valleys and rivers and all other manifestations of nature while cultural landscapes refer to the landscapes built by human beings upon nature; cities and slums belong to this category. However, it is important to bear in mind the fact that there is a constant interaction between the two, one feeding the other.

There are three central landscapes in this film. The first is the shimmering waters at the opening of the film. And water figures prominently through the repeated shots of the pond by which Shankar practices his singing. Second, there are the spreading, majestic trees from whose shadows Nita first emerges in the film. And these trees are shown later. Third, there are the splendorous hills at the end of the film amid which Nita sits. All these three natural landscapes carry important symbolic meaning. As I stated earlier, the image of the mother, shaped by classical mythology is crucial to the meaning embedded in *Cloud-capped Star*. All these three symbols – water, trees and hills – are, in the opinion of Jung, vitally connected to the mother image. As Jung has pointed out, water and trees are maternal symbols. The hills are inextricably linked to the mother image.[7] It is also worth mentioning in this regard that in the Indian mythology water and trees and hills are associated with the mother image. In the Vedas, water is referred to as the 'most maternal' (matritamah).

What we find in Ghatak's films are landscapes invested with symbolic meaning and mythic depth. It is important to note, however, that Ghatak is not falling victim to a kind of essentialist fallacy purveying eternal and universal images of motherhood. His intention is to put into play, and bring to mutual crisis, two currents of thinking – the mythical and the historical, the idealistic and the materialistic, the idyllic and the realistic so as to generate a more complex and nuanced understanding of human thought, imagination and action. Ritwik Ghatak was a great admirer not only of Carl Jung but also of Karl Marx. He sought to combine Jungianism and Marxism, not an easy undertaking by any means, in his cinematic texts. Moreover, he does not use classical mythologies as framing devices mechanically or uncritically. Although he points out the nature of Nita as a sacrificing mother image, it is his contention that Nita represents only one aspect of the great-mother image. As the well-known filmmaker, and pupil of Ghatak, has rightly pointed out, the mother image is spread across three characters – Nita, Gita and the mother. If only Nita could have combined the other two aspects of motherhood represented in the characters of Gita and the mother, her life would have been less tragic. Ironically, although Nita is identified with the mother image, that is the very thing that she did not attain – maternality. Ghatak, therefore, uses landscapes very thoughtfully. He invests them with symbolic meaning derived from classical Indian mythology while bringing a historical and materialist perspective to the presence of mythology.

The way Ghatak plays off the natural landscape against the man-made landscape is indeed interesting, and opens up useful pathways to the inquiry into the use of landscape in cinema. Here man-made landscape refers to the house in which Nita and the family live, the all important courtyard, the grocery store, the school, etc. What we find is not a simple juxtaposition of the natural and cultural landscapes; there are interesting conjunctions and disjunctions between them. For instance the courtyard, which becomes the site of sacrifice (*yajna mandapa*) carries over the meaning from the natural landscape.[8] As Nita emerges from the shadows of trees, one gets the impression that she is coming out of the womb of nature itself. Moreover, the mythic associations of trees with motherhood and the Jungian glosses on them fortify our belief in the deification of Nita. As Jung once remarked:

> just as myths tell us that human beings were descended from trees, so there were burial customs where people were buried in hollow tree-trunks…if we remember that the tree is predominantly a mother-symbol, then the meaning of this mode of burial becomes clear.[9]

When she enters the house and the courtyard she is decidedly in the contingent world of material living. Even here, Ghatak brings in the ideas of myth in the way he converts the courtyard into a site of sacrifice.

In the natural landscapes in *Cloud-capped Star* that I have referred to, one sees the play of tension between the timeless and historical, the eternal and contingent. For Ghatak the only eternal truth of cinema is that there is no eternal truth; his focus is uncannily on the historical. However, to give it an ambiguous depth, he employs myths effectively. For Ghatak the maps of existence are illuminated by two beacons of light – the metaphysical and historical. They are both complementary and adversarial. It is the tension between these two that invests his landscapes with the power that they exercise in his films. His visual images of landscapes are historicized within a metaphysical frame. These landscapes carry with them an allegorical charge. If the desire to revitalize something of the past in terms of present preoccupations is a mark of allegory, Ghatak's landscapes can be productively read in terms of allegorical texualities. In *Cloud-capped Star*, one can discern an interesting interplay between Marxism and Jungianism. Ghatak has forced a tension between Marx and Jung in a way that opens up the filmic experience to deeper apprehensions of human being-in-the-world. Marx focused on the evolution of society in terms of man separated from nature, man against nature and interanimation of man with another mode of nature that he termed historical materialism. Jung pointed out the stages of man separating from the mother, man against woman and reunion with woman. These different stages in the understandings of man and nature and woman, as formulated by Marx and Jung, have deep implications for the comprehension of the meanings of cinematic landscape in Ghatak.

This discussion of the role of landscapes in Satyajit Ray's *The Song of the Little Road* and Ritwik Ghatak's *Cloud-capped Star* foregrounds, I believe, a number of important issues related to cinematic landscape. That the complex relationship between cinema and landscape has begun to attract increasing scholarly attention is indeed a welcome sign. In this regard, one should not undervalue the function of the spectator. A natural landscape, when we see it in the raw, is not something innocent and pure; it is always already shaped by our inherited cultural understandings and modes of perception. It is already an act of interpretation. As the German philosopher Martin Heidegger rightly pointed out:

> In interpretation, we do not, so to speak, throw a signification over some naked thing which is present-at-hand, we do not stick a value on it, but when something within-the-world is encountered as such, the thing already has an involvement which is disclosed in our understanding of the world, and the involvement is the one which gets laid out (made manifest) by the interpretation.[10]

Landscapes in films are doubly interpretive because we perceive the landscape as it has been reconfigured through the cinematic apparatus. The filmmaker encodes the landscape into the vocabulary of cinema, and we as spectators decode it in terms of our frames of cultural intelligibility and grids of recognition. These acts of encoding and decoding are not symmetrical, and there are gaps and slippages between them, making the reading of cinematic landscapes that much more challenging and exciting.

The theorist of art, W. J. T. Mitchell, once observed:

The commonplace of modern studies of images, in fact, is that they must be understood as a kind of language; instead of providing a transparent window on the world, images are now regarded as the sort of sign that presents a deceptive appearance of naturalness and transparence concealing an opaque, distorting, arbitrary mechanism of representation, a process of ideological mystification.[11]

Hence, we, as spectators, need to investigate cinematic landscapes, as indeed any other systems of visual signs, in the spirit of symptomatic reading. By so doing, we can locate film reading productively in the larger domain of visual culture.

## Notes

1. Kwok Kan-Tam and Wimal Dissanayake, *New Chinese Cinema* (Hong Kong: Oxford University Press, 1998).
2. Adoor Gopalakrishnan, 'In the beginning there was *Pather Panchali*', in Santi Das (ed.), *Satyajit Ray: An Intimate Master* (New Delhi: Allied Publishers, 1998).
3. Akira Kurosawa, quoted in Andrew Robinson, Satyajit Ray; *The Inner Eye* (Berkeley: University of California Press, 1989).
4. Satyajit Ray, 'Conversations with Satyajit Ray', *Sight and Sound* 39(3), 114–120.
5. Ritwik Ghatak, *Rows and Rows of Fences* (Calcutta: Segull, 2000).
6. Ritwik Ghatak, ibid.
7. Carl Jung, *Psychology of the Unconscious* (London: Kegan Paul, 1944).
8. Asish Rajadhyaksha and Ritwik Ghatak, *A Return to the Epic* (Bombay: Screen Unit, 1982).
9. Carl Jung, *op. cit.*
10. Martin Heidegger, *Being and Time* (New York: Harper and Row, 1962).
11. W. J. T. Mitchell, *Iconology; Image, Text, Ideology* (Chicago: Chicago University Press, 1986).

# Chapter 12

The Geography of Cinema – Zimbabwe

Martin Mhando

*Every man gotta right to decide his own destiny,*
*And in this judgement there is no impartiality.*
*So arm in arms, with arms, we'll fight this little struggle,*
*'Cause that's the only way we can overcome our little trouble.*

(Bob Marley – Zimbawe, 1980)

With this unofficial and pop-culture anthem of Zimbabwe Bob Marley characterizes the politics of geography that defines the contemporary representation of Zimbabwe in quite a substantial manner. It reflects a historical and ideological view that confers Zimbabwe a vital status over African identity and its representation. There is an argument here for the aspirational in cinema identity; that while socio-political aspirations are often based on ideology, they are also historically and sociologically contextualized positive characteristics.

I begin therefore with the following hypotheses:

1. To better understand the historical conditions for the development of cinema in the Southern African region, there is a need to transcend mainstream cinema traditions. Historical and cultural conditions in the Southern African region determine that national cinemas subsist under a regional one.
2. While recognizing the inadequacy of class and the national/territorial affiliation in determining cinematic identity, there is need to re-value the socio-political experiences of Southern Africa as an ideological and conscious 'other'. Under a regional approach the search for the roots of cinematic expressions in their socio-historical situation leads to the creation, growth and development of 'national' cinemas of the region. That is to say, here, the development of the 'nation' in cinema is determined to a great degree by regional dynamics.

Within the discourse of cinema in Africa, there are specific forces and institutions that have maintained or resisted the dominant and hegemonic socio-historical environment of post-colonial Southern Africa. I therefore use Zimbabwe as an example of such regionally ascribed narration of nations. Landscape is indeed a visual concept that proposes a perspective on social relationships based on notions of land use. As Daniel Trudeau suggests

Landscapes thus offer a perspective of a particular territory and the community relations and identity of the polity associated with that territory. Like Lefebvre's category of abstract space, landscapes offer a whole scene in which certain material and discursive boundaries are constructed and seem stable, such that power hierarchies are evident and are uncontested, and that particular arrangements of values, aesthetics and behaviour are considered normal or natural.[1]

In that way the term cultural geography in cinema proposes to explore the connections between identity and the geographical boundaries within a film and how they express the factor of belonging. A filmic concept however is not merely a representational device because it often attains the allegorical. The mental state that produces these representational discourses are often material thoughts inherent to cultural practices from and around which collective ideologies are constructed. However these states are not normative, since they project states of discursive affectations and are mostly constrained by space and time.[2] And as Robin Curtis argues in *Forgetting as a Representational Strategy: Erasing the past in Girl from Moush and Passing Drama*,

> The processes of collective memory and the experience of ethnicity are both shown to be processes of perception rather than means of accessing a symbolic and essential source (whether that be 'history' or 'identity'). *Girl from Moush* is an ersatz voyage to a country that is termed the 'homeland', but has never been visited in reality.[3]

Zimbabwe provides an excellent laboratory to test the many controversial aspects of belonging, of identity and more important of the creation of landscapes of memory. Zimbabwean cinematic landscapes and their notions of significance, demonstrate through textual analysis how a cinematic landscape reveals historico-cultural specificity. The significance of the national cinematic landscape here differs from the memorialization ascribed to physical components of landscapes or even the folk memory or ceremony that Schama's *Landscape and Memory* (1996) focuses on.[4]

Films produced in the Southern Africa region including Zimbabwe reconnaissance the 'landscape of memory' (an apt title for one of the series of documentaries produced in the region). The Landscape of Memory here is rather that of a cultural consciousness, which is essentially contextual as much as it is also a process of memorialization.

The power of the films produced here lies in the recreation of the traumatic harshness of contemporary Africa and its capacity to draw out of this historical environment a reading of the history of trauma expressed by generations of filmmakers from a whole region. What we see in these films is the capacity to create out of the images and sounds of geography and history a narrative of the human environment of suffering.

The cinematic milieu here is a set of challenges that have beset filmmakers themselves as characters, and to which they respond not only in a personal way but also towards the milieu that is constituted by their relationship to the present-past. Theirs are attempts at understanding the past and its significance in a manner that suggests a relation to an environmental social inheritance. Therefore through the filmmaker's words as much as images the public reconnaissance the nation as a landscape of complicity and denial, recognition and estrangement, crime and punishment, memorialization and recollection. The images allow the public to feel that they have participated in the past event and undertake a mourning of sorts, and imbue the filmic narrative with a socio-psychological status.

Finally, in many ways this discussion lends itself to a reflection on phenomenology and geography where we debate how environments, places, and creativity might have bearing on social identity and representation. One is immediately reminded of the works of Martin Heidegger (1962, 1971) Alexander (1987, 1993; Alexander, Ishikawa, and Silverstein, 1977), Casey (1993, 1997), Norberg-Schulz (1985, 1996), Paalasma (1996), Stefanovic (2000), and Thiis-Evensen (1987, 1999) where the concern lies with examining how nature, place, and creativity contribute to human experience and how it applies to meaning creation activities like film.

Cultural artefacts like film, indeed always create discursive spaces as well as dialogue about and within the nation. Film as a cultural phenomenon, especially during these early stages of nation-creation, becomes a dialogue; the discourse is often about identity and African filmmakers are themselves conscious purveyors of that nationalist dialogue about Africa. That is why one can see a clear difference between the views and visions of non-indigenous filmmakers (read 'White') and those of the indigenous (read 'Black') in the filmic landscapes constructed. All these filmmakers in fact reveal intents in the portrayal of landscapes. The intents encompassed are both moral and economic.

## Zimbabwe: History and film

As probably the most centrally located of Southern African countries, Zimbabwe is held up as a stronghold of regional indigenous pride. The proud focal point of the peoples of the region remains the major cultural manifestations such as the various kingdoms that rose and fell in that territorial surrounding the great lakes. Indeed archaeological and ethno-historical evidence proves that the16th century built Great Zimbabwe is a product of indigenous Africans – the Shona.[5]

The ethno-history of the region is a factor of importance in this discussion. Not only does ethno-historical knowledge cement the regional basis of my argument, but its perspectives also make one appreciate the intellectual heritage necessary to understanding indigenous knowledges.

A cursory study of film making in Zimbabwean reveals the usual fragmentation of history into pre-independence and post-independence periods that we find in most African countries. Pre-independence film making in Zimbabwe was essentially limited to the work of the Central African Film Unit (CAFU) and the government's Production Services, including Ian Smith regime's productions aimed at selling Zimbabwe as an exotic film set.[6]

Thomson Sodzo however, confirms the regional perspective active even at that stage when he writes of 'early film in Zimbabwe'.

> The very first films were simple instructions on issues as road safety, how to keep money wisely, hygiene and good farming methods. These films were made in Tanganyika (Tanzania) and sent to London for processing before they were distributed in East and Central Africa.[7]

This colonial outcome was essentially for administrative contingency but it also reflected the regional cultural landscape, defying national borders. If we define culture as active, collective and historical human interaction, cultural expression can only be historical and dynamic. The Southern African cinematic landscape assails the contradictions of nation as territory as well as nation as a temporal-cultural space. Here is a case for applying Gramscian concepts of hegemony in cultural expressions; the nation embodying specific and regionally defined hegemonic articulations.[8]

The region itself contains a myriad of imaginaries of cultural and environmental landscapes. Through the use of certain descriptive terms such as 'settler', 'tribal', 'development', 'front-line', 'liberation', 'Bantu', 'Black farmer', 'White farmer', 'Townships', 'Reserves' etc, the topographical imagery of Southern Africa is consciously and unconsciously endorsed as a cinematic space. Land myths abound in the West's view of Africa: Stories of travelling through Africa, battling the elements, of colonization, of exploration and settlement, stories of the environment and the people are the norm. Do the films evidence regional cinema culture beyond the sharing of similar thematic concerns, beyond reflections of the desire and need for reconciliation? Beyond structural readings that reveal conditions like the racial classifications and processes that have forged the living experiences of the region, what else is revealed?

## Zimbabwe as a regional cinematic landscape

Though a late entry into world indigenous films production circles, Zimbabwe has nonetheless developed an energetic film scene. Zimbabwean cinema provides the contexts for cinematic landscape discourse, not simply as 'universalized' images of regional societies but rather a reflection of the temporality of national spaces and how the films find links for cultural expression beyond national borders.

Zimbabwe has seen a dearth in feature film production since 2000 for many reasons including the insufferable environment of the Mugabe regime.[9] I shall therefore use four feature films produced in Zimbabwe Jit (Michael Raeburn, 1990), Neria (Godwin Mawuru, 1992) More Time (Isaac Mabhikwa, 1993) and Flame (Ingrid Sinclair, 1996) as my key texts in analysing the narration of the nation through regional cultural geography.

In the scheme of Southern African films Raeburn's film Jit is crucial. It combines the factors of popular memory and agency in a specifically Southern African context. The film presents a view of the past that forces us to look closely at the historical forces and value systems that suggest ways of producing meaning from the film. This theme of agency is also revealed in another Zimbabwean film, *Flame* (1996).

*Jit* tells the story of UK, a young man who comes to Harare to live with his Uncle Oliver, a Jit musician. Jit is an urban popular music genre in Zimbabwe.[10] UK helps his uncle deliver gramophone discs around the city and do household chores, as any young Zimbabwean, and for that matter, any African young man visiting a relative would do. In the meantime he falls in love with a beautiful girl, Sophie, and the film's story follows UK's endeavors in this boy-finds-his-girl comedy. His efforts are both hampered and advanced by his Jukwa. The Jukwa is an apparition or rather a guardian ancestor who follows him to the city to remind him of his duties to his family and himself. As he gets deeper and deeper into trouble, first with the girl's gangster boyfriend and then later with his family and that of the girl, he struggles to remain in the city as well as win his love. The combination of urbanity, music, and cinema culture makes this film a veritable representative of the cinema of the region.

Comedy is probably the best way to express the incomprehensible relations between a person and their belief systems. This genre is deployed effectively in *Jit*. Coupled with the romantic melodrama, the narrative develops in an inconsistent fashion with its rather episodic style. And yet these episodes are crucial texts for a cultural reading. Within these structural and cultural readings are revealed the ambiguities, inconsistencies and taboos of popular memory.

In *Jit*, good codified sequences include those in which the Jukwa pleads with UK to go back to the village. The concept of going back to the village is constantly harped on in the film and in many post-independence African states' political strategies. This is the post-independence cry of each political regime, which saw urbanization as a scourge (This is often referenced by the presence of the beggar in the street).

David Trend argues that '...identities defined purely on spatial terms fail to come to terms with the temporal character of culture'.[11] In *Jit* the identity of a Zimbabwean is represented as being produced by forces and relations of production that are consistent with post-*chimurenga* ideology. The middle class notion of popular memory that is being assumed in *Jit* seeks to replace the memory of popular struggle to White domination not only politically but culturally as well. This is done through a proposed concept of a collective care-freeness, common cultural values and the sharing of a sense of humor. Even the very sparse presence of the White settler community in *Jit* suggests certain homogenizing or at least the underplaying of the discordant presence of opposing cultures. This filial landscape proposes myriad implications.

In any case conventional narrative patterns would demand that a disrupted community be returned to sanity, to a more balanced relationship at the end, but not so in *Jit*. Apart from the boy-gets-girl resolve, the rest of society is left at the mercy of the open-ended way of returning to that equilibrium, if there was one to begin with anyway. This ambiguity and open ended-ness portrays an irresolvable situation for the individual. This suggests that the past has been eclipsed by time and that the landscape's social relations work only at the nostalgia level.

The social relations of the 'past' that are historical and are not imposed by the text (as these modern ones have been) are made to look finite, and that the only remaining reality is the reality of modernity. In this film, in which the past is the underlying discourse, history is not used to project popular memory. At the end of the film there is no clear comprehension of the historical conditions of the story. This is made abundantly clear through the use of the form (comedy) through which the director hopes he would be absolved from contextualization.

What is even more interesting in *Jit* is the deliberate proposal that some dominant positions of the past need to be challenged. One of the more clearly defined assertions with regard to 'tradition' is the position of women in society. However, the way that the narrative ends, with representing the modern woman (Sophie) as passive and subordinate, does not tell us much about how that desired change should happen.

Compare this treatment of popular memory, in a humorous way, in *Quartier Mozart* (1992, Cameroon). *Quartier Mozart* is the story of a working class neighborhood in Yaounde, the capital of Cameroon. It recounts the education of a young schoolgirl, Queen of the Hood where Maman Thekla, the local sorcerer, helps her enter the body of a young stud, My Guy, so she can understand the real 'sexual politics of the Quartier'. All in all *Quartier Mozart* contains more structured ambiguities than those in *Jit*. For all that, *Quartier Mozart's* narrative leaves us in no doubt as to how the audience could construct the possibility of representing modernity in a popularly memorable fashion. This opens up the readings of the texts rather than closing them as does *Jit*. In that way *Quartier Mozart* directs attention not only towards the past but more important towards the present and the absent-present which Gramsci suggests as one of the cornerstones of the national-popular narrative.[12] The desire for change is located within the popular memory discourse not outside it. For example, in *Neria*, while the text is clearly Zimbabwean the context needs to be slightly over-stretched for it to be located within the discourses of popular memory.[13] One of the areas that need this contextual elucidation is the woman's issue. As Mahoso says,

> In the Zimbabwean film *Neria*, we are assured that the oppression of women originates in Africa tradition and we become uncritical of the role of modern courts, even-though these were responsible for reducing the status of adult African women to that of perpetual minors.[14]

Here Mahoso does not criticize the women's perspective per se but identifies it as a 'voice' within the post-colonial landscape. He shows that what is important here is the underlying message transmitted through films like *Neria*; its failure to reveal the full significance of the conceptual space that Africans are yet to reclaim from the colonialist which lies in the effect of the narrow concept of development and traditional concepts in social engineering.

African body aesthetics on and in film reveal a very closed transnational gaze and are only particular to 'Africa' as they confront certain traditional concepts about women. Contemplations on women in African films are as contemporary as they could ever get. This is not an apologia for the supposed slow coming to terms with this abhorrent culture by Africans, but a positioning of the issue within its historical context and what I call the 'developmentalist' viewpoint. These are films that present the articulation of gendered issues as part of an internationalist imaginary landscape. Films like *Neria, Mama Tumaini, More Time, Jit, Wimbo wa Mianzi, Watoto Wana Haki, Consequences* all treat the issue of women's oppression in an overtly 'developmentalist' discourse. Here issues are being discussed because they in fact are made to overlap consciously with contemporary transnational positions.

*Jit, Neria* and *Flame* are the kind of representations that continue the legacies of agencies of European memorialization found in galleries, museums and the like where the emerging representations, even from well-intentioned sources, do not confront the dominant memory in order to insert in its place a populist one.

*Jit* was very well received in Zimbabwe when it opened in 1990 especially as it were the first full-length feature film produced by a Zimbabwean after the Chimurenga. According to Simon Bright, a Zimbabwe filmmaker, the film ran to full house attendance for two months in Harare.

The genuine laughter that came out of the recognition of locations, language, sayings, musical codes, actors and the like, made the film an immediate hit. Only a few months earlier Zimbabwe's first dramatic film *Consequences,* had been shown in the country and *Jit's* was a particularly strong showing since it pandered to the obvious cinematic tastes that audiences hungered for in the cinema. It however did not play to the 'empty pot' ('educational') pedagogical imperatives that colonial cinema had instilled in films produced for African audiences. This was left to films like *Neria* and *More Time* to fulfil.

To this day in every Zimbabwean village and indeed in all of Southern Africa, stories like Neria's are told and retold amid shaken heads and dumbfounded listeners. I myself have heard innumerable stories like it in Tanzania, some told by the victims of such traditions who were cowed to acceptance by the immoral and ineffectual tradition.

Godwin Mawuru, the director of the film, tells Neria's sad story with sensitivity and even candor. Through this film one also notes that melodramatic acting seems to be an endearing feature of African performance. This is because role-playing is an acceptable feature of the dramatic life of the society and believability is not sought for. It is in the nature of melodrama to make clear what the actor is saying. The extent to which an actor, with or without a mask, identifies with the character and the extent to which the audience would believe the actor to actually be the character is an unknown quantity. The audiences and the actors in the traditional theatre actually take on roles of actors and audiences interchangeably during performance thus revealing theatre to be a truly participatory event.[15] Therefore performance in African films needs also to be seen through this defining glass of theatrical experience if we are to understand the nature of interpretation in African drama.[16] This dramaturgical landscape reflects a core cultural code.

How that is translated in the cinema where realism is a cultural expedient is still questionable. Can this be another clear feature of cultural difference in cinematic appreciation? Could this also explain the continual 'chatter' amongst African (and Indian) audiences during film showings?

Just like with 'tradition', much passes for film language that is merely a reification of very recent codes that have no historical validity in the pre-colonial African landscape. This condition repeats itself often in the region given its colonial history and the racialized power structures. Mlama identifies the same tendency within popular theatre movements in Southern Africa where she argues: 'popular theatre forms are used to carry development messages to an audience, which is expected to translate those messages into action'.[17] The films of Apartheid produced for 'Blacks' played heavily upon such constructions. The opening chapter of Peter Davis's *In Darkest Hollywood* reveals the inscription of values upon African life, seen entirely from the Other.[18]

In *More Time*, the third feature film (fiction) to come out of Zimbabwe, a daring effort is made at discussing a very basic cultural weak link in the African edifice – that of sex education. While many people have often gone on to romanticize the sex education process in traditional society *More Time* criticizes it openly and dares say that may be it is not applicable in the urban conditions of today. This is a very serious statement indeed.

Traditionally in some Bantu groups discussions on sex between parents and children are not encouraged. It is believed that the language of sex is filled with metaphorical insinuations that are consciously left only to adults to divulge. Such discussions can be undertaken between the young and an aunt or uncle or even with a grandparent where pedagogical lines are already drawn in any dialogue between the parties. There is a clear demarcation and recognition of social function here, according to Bantu culture.

Therefore in *More Time*, when the mother decides that some form of pedagogical sex talk with her daughter is called for, she resorts to the traditional system of the aunt's role. The aunt categorically declines to help saying it is upon the mother so to do. This, of course maybe the reality in the European city. But one wonders if it is absolutely necessary to cut off all links with that particular tradition, in the African city landscape? It is well documented that African city dwellers rely on the rural areas for a stability of sorts and are totally unprepared for the cultural onslaught of the technological landscape of Western culture. It is even more ironic that in the film as soon as the 'auntie' has declined to help the mother, the family goes to their home village where we see a different form of sex education.

Zimbabwean cinema reflects the deeply laid social issues of post-colonial living. It is typical of many other countries of the region as well. As it expresses itself through the cinema we see Zimbabwean national concerns replicated elsewhere in the region. Many of the issues discussed in Zimbabwean cinema resonate well with other national narratives of the region. *More Time*, for example, has been distributed in the region with good audience reception in Botswana, Zambia, Uganda, Tanzania and South Africa. In Tanzania it was dubbed into Kiswahili and distributed under the title *Mambo Bado*, a contemporary Swahili urban idiom that further assisted its marketing. Despite criticism the film remains Zimbabwe's best-received film in Africa. It speaks to the urban, middle class youth whose aspirational values (modernist /developmentalist) are clearly reflected in the film. It compares well with films on HIV/AIDS from Tanzania (*Si Mungu Mtupu*, 1992), Uganda (*It's Not Easy*, 1992) and Cameroon (*Faces of Aids*, 1992).

In *Flame*, the didactic imagination employed in the film positions the viewer in a receptive mode and corresponds to the type of films produced during the colonial era. The first marker of this relationship in the film, is the 'documentary film' position that *Flame* locates us in. This makes us responsive to the narrative as 'reality' and 'historical' and offers the filmmaker a position of power as teacher and informed storyteller. To understand *Flame* one needs to deconstruct the discursive authority of the documentary genre as it is received by audiences in the region. The complacency of audiences in their comprehension of information reflects their familiarity with the documentary genre. This familiarity is used to its full advantage by the filmmaker, Ingrid Sinclair.[19]

The receptions of films amongst different audiences sometimes reflect the wide chasm in a given nation's cultural engineering. This is a prevalent feature of Southern Africa cinema culture. To attempt a cross-cultural reception of a film like *Flame* for example, requires a skilful portrayal of the everyday such that the ending does not simply say, 'here is a love story of the liberation movement that was wrong'. The people still want to celebrate liberation. As they watch *Flame* they ask themselves, 'Is fighting for liberation wrong?'

This is a theme that was taken up in a discussion at a social club Dar es Salaam where comparisons of the film with Hussein Ibrahim's *Kinjeketile* were brought forward. In his play *Kinjeketile*, the leader of the longest resistance to German rule in Tanzania is asked to renounce his use of the myth of Majimaji as being a lie. (During the war of liberation he had sprinkled people with water and made them believe they would be invincible to bullets). Kinjeketile did not renounce his use of magic-myth neither did he renounce his call to arms against the invader, explaining, 'If today I say that the water was a lie people would stop fighting. Is fighting for one's freedom wrong?'[20] He did not recant and was hanged. This shows that liberation is the narrational landscape espoused by the regional cultures.

The theme is taken up in the exceedingly beautiful short film, *After the Wax* (1991) by Chaz Maviyane-Davis. In *After the Wax* Chaz Maviyane-Davies uses the mythologizing qualities of film to highlight the poetic essence of nationalism. However with its poetic qualities, its pretty cinematography and symbolic lyricism the film celebrates the damning awareness of the nature of the nation in Africa. As an expression of the 'horizontal comradeship' indicated by Benedict Anderson, African 'nations' retain a skewed relationship.[21] The film basically discusses the place of the nation and the role of the media in representing identity in Southern Africa. It is in the film's process of signification that we find the discursive address that the 'nation' lays claim to but cannot fully reach. This film of extraordinary lyricism confronts the nation and makes a plea for liberation recognizing the limits of the national struggle without, however, necessarily aborting the national project.

In *After the Wax,* the metaphorical powers of all the representational imaginaries of the flagged faces, coca cola bottles, newspaper cuttings, bull-horns, water, shackles and the drum are used to ensure the continuity of key landscapes of cultural integrity. These structures indeed go beyond the current definitions of the nation and reveal the rise of African nations from the mess of capitalist consumption and the incessant cry for 'order, order, order'.

Although narrated at the national level these Zimbabwean films are first and foremost regionally oriented, and, as with the example of recent films coming out of Latin America, the films tend to 'defy rather than reinforce national category'.[22]

As social acts embedding the cultural processes of remembering, films have become statues of memorialization. Memorialization can be understood as the practice whereby individuals, communities, and societies, interact at sites of symbolically represented 'memory', deriving from, and impressing on, a item or act 'narratives about specific times, places, persons, and events laden with affective meaning'.[23] Through memorialization the cinematic landscape therefore becomes a rite of passage 'wherein trauma is expressed, processed and integrated. In this sense, memorialization is a therapeutic practice, wherein trauma is worked through, thus acting as a rite of passage, specifically for survivors.'[24]

Mostly this trauma is reflected through the victim's inability to integrate their experience, as well as to communicate the full catastrophic experience and knowledge coming from it to others. I view memorialization as a search for meaning through the performance of community rituals of mourning. Within this context there abounds a certain explosion of religious symbolisms from the many African traditional practices (such as spirit possession) that are indeed fundamental aspects of 'sites of memory' encapsulating notions of catharsis, loss, absence, and remembering.

What is necessary, important and indeed required by the victims is a facility whereby they can re-construct the trauma in a form through which they can negotiate the various meanings derived from the catastrophe, and be able to express it and convey meanings from and about it. The cinematic landscape fulfils that role as a site of memory. As a 'site of memory' a film becomes 'an active practice of remembering which takes an inquiring attitude toward the past and the activity of its (re)construction through memory… undercut[ing] assumptions about the transparency or the authenticity of what is remembered'.[25] Trauma is a veritable landscape of memorialization.

Finally a key aspect of this dialogue, however, is found in the process of selection. Forgetting is often part of the memorialization project. As Steele says, 'not simply because the project is often undertaken in opposition to forgetting, but also because in selecting what and how to represent, narrative itself "forgets"'.[26] This could be argued to be the unspoken purpose of films produced by some White filmmakers in Zimbabwe.

It is through such a spectrum that we may now see the contradictions of the Zimbabwe nation and its representation in the cinema. The Zimbabwean cinematic landscape has no totalizing vision: the individual subject finds containment within the cinema culture of the region. Through the regional communities, their history and futures, one envisions the subject's cultural landscape. Confining interpretation of the Zimbabwean cinema within local, class or ethnic paradigms is indeed limiting. There must, of necessity, be an ideological positioning to support any kind of self-analysis or representation.

Many of the feature films produced in Zimbabwe and in the region treat geographical landscapes in relation to ethnography and nationhood. The identity that is effected is a positivist one, the reifying effects of which remain at the crux both of life in the region and in cinema. Cinema has indeed become the model for the kind of ethnographic representation that has often called into question the ideals of scientific representation in film or anthropology. Memorialization acts show that cinematic landscapes need to be further exploited to inspire research on cinema and its spaces.

Many films by African filmmakers around issues of wars, gender oppression, racism and trauma in Africa, project not only confrontations of the individual filmmakers with the subjects but also of collective structures. However how these collective structures are foreground is an important aspect of the cinematic signification process. To understand the films we need to look at the relations between the individual, their community and society in general and how African cinemas reveal some formal signs conditioned by structures of social organization, of cultural affinity and immediate conditions of interaction.

Beyond those structural affectations can be seen cultural readings that pay attention to the way the films speak and represent the similarities of narratives. These readings are able to reveal cultural landscapes due to the dominant memory inflected in liberationist ideology. Any cultural reading of the series *Landscape of Memories,*(1999) for example, would have to take into account the place of history, language and kinship as determinants of regional cinema culture.

Beyond drawing stories from the past, regional narratives continue to use the present to discuss cultural experiences, as is shown in all the feature films discussed here. As much *as More Time* is a story about present day youth problems, with special reference to AIDS, it is still a story that demands examinations of familial ties that find their basis in traditional social values. *Flame* and *Neria* grapple with contemporary women's power struggles just as they subsume the indomitable spirit embodied by women like Mbuya Nehanda, the 19th century leader of the Zimbabwean resistance movement. In our readings the films create new ways of thinking about relationships between culture and power in the region.

While the look into the past is indeed a necessary and common feature of regional narratives, one needs also to note the growth of personal stories, symbolic landscapes and narratives in the form of proverbs, as further reflections of popular memory. Needless to say if the questioning of the nation has proposed a closer examination of the representation of cinematic landscapes, we need to look further into filmic perception and see if geography by nature embodies as well as displaces cultural landscapes.

## Notes

1. Daniel Trudeau, 'Politics of belonging in the construction of landscapes: placemaking, boundary-drawing, and exclusion', *Cultural Geographies* 13 (2006), 421–443.
2. Mookerjea Sourayan, 'Calendar's filmic concept of global flows', *Space and Culture* 5:2 (May 2002), 103–121.
3. Robin Curtis, 'Forgetting as a representational strategy: erasing the past in Girl from Moush and Passing Drama', *Screening the Past* (Electronic Journal) Issue 19 (March 2006). Accessed 24 September 2006 http://www.latrobe.edu.au/screeningthepast/firstrelease/fr1201/rcfr13b.htm

4. Simon Schama, *Landscape and Memory* (London, Vintage Books, 1996).
5. G. T. Mishambi) 'Before the predators', in J. R. Mlahagwa et al. (eds), *Landmarks in Southern African History* (Peramiho: Peramiho Press, 1989), 42–55.
6. Rosaleen Smyth, 'The Colonial Film Unit and Africa (1939–1955)', Paper presented at the Second History and Film Conference La Trobe University, Melbourne, Australia (1983), 1
7. Thompson Sodzo, 'Early Film in Zimbabwe', *Just For Me* (June 1991).
8. Geoffrey Nowell-Smith, 'Gramsci and the National Popular', *Screen Education* (Spring 1977), no. 22.
9. I have taken a conscious effort at not discussing the current political and economic situation in Zimbabwe because its discussion often leans towards discussing the regime of Robert Mugabe in its crass limitations. For an excellent discussion of the change in Mugabe from nationalist to dictator please read Stephen Chan's *Robert Mugabe: A Life of Power and Violence* (Michigan: University of Michigan Press, 2003).
10. Michael Raeburn explained the title thus: Jit is a term for Zimbabwean music. It is a mix of two Shona words, *jiti*, which means dancing in a ring, and *jikiti*, which means jumping up and landing with a bump.
11. David Trend, 'Nationalities, pedagogy and media', in Henry Giroux and Peter McLaren (eds), *Between Borders: Pedagogy and the Politics of Cultural Studies* (London/New York: Routledge, 1994), 229.
12. Nowell-Smith, 'Gramsci and the National Popular'.
13. In *Neria*, billed as a 'Women's Issues' film, we are told the story of Neria, a woman who upon losing her husband is pounced upon by her husband's brother and is divested of all their savings and property. 'Neria watches helplessly at first, believing there is no legal or moral recourse for her. But when Phineas (her brother-in-law) takes her children, Neria decides she must fight back. In desperation she seeks justice. Neria learns that law and tradition can both be on her side if she remains strong and intelligently fights for her rights.' (Taken from Neria's publicity blurb.)
14. Tafataona Mahoso, 'Audiences and the Critical Appreciation of Cinema in Africa', in June Givanni, *Symbolic Narratives: Audiences, Theory and the Moving Image* (London, BFI Publishing, 2000).
15. Penina Mlama, *Culture and Development: The Popular Theatre Approach in Africa* (Upsalla: Nordiska Afrikainstitutet, 1991), 80–90.
16. Joe Sanctus Chika Anyanwu, 'The image of Africa in African films: a critical perspective', in Peter F. Alexander, Ruth Hutchison and Deryck Schroeder (eds), *Africa Today* (Canberra, HRC: The Australian National University, 1996), 569.
17. Mlama, *Culture and Development*, 80, 90.
18. Peter Davies, *In Darkest Hollywood* (Athens: Ohio University Press, 1992), Chapter 1, 39.
19. In a flashback, *Flame* tells the story of two girls Florence (Flame) and Nyasha (Liberty) who, through a combination of factors decide to leave their village to join the liberation struggle for Zimbabwe (the Chimurenga). The film shows their time in the guerilla training camps where life was hard, what with the meagre food provisions that the camps received. The film portrays the harsh conditions specifically endured by women, including not being given any military training as well as being used as 'comfort women' by the guerilla commanders. Ultimately Flame is raped by one of the commanders called Che with whom she later has a child. The war is won but on returning to her village Flame rejoins the subservient position that women are held under. Finally she resolves to go to the city, Harare, to find her friend Liberty and to try a new life. As the country celebrates 'Heroes Day' the two women and other ex-combatants realize that they are not held in any respect and it looks like their sacrifice was for nothing.

20. Ibrahim Hussein, *Kinjeketile* (Dar es Salaam: Longmans, 1969) – translated from Swahili and paraphrased from the play Kinjeketile.
21. Benedict Anderson, *Imagined Communities: Reflections on the Origin and Spread of Nationalism* (London: Verso, 1983).
22. Anne-Marie Stock (ed.), *Framing Latin American Cinema* (Minneapolis: University of Minnesota Press, 1997), xxiii.
23. Bonnie Evans, 'Legacies: transforming memories into memorials (Thesis Summary, San José State University, 2002), 2. http://www.sjsu.edu/depts/anthropology/svcp/SVCPlega.html.
24. Sarah Louise Steele, 'Memorialisation and the Land of the Eternal Spring: performative practices of memory on the Rwandan genocide' (2006), http://www.google.com.au/search?q=MEMORIA LISATION+STEELE&ie=utf-8&oe=utf-8&aq=t&rls= Accessed on 30 July 2008.
25. Annette Kuhn, *Family Secrets: Acts of Memory and Imagination* (London: Verso, 2002), 157.
26. Steele, 'Memorialisation and the Land of the Eternal Spring'.

## Chapter 13

Crises, Economy and Landscape: The Modern Film Face of New China

Kate E. Taylor

We put thirty spokes together and call it a wheel;
But it is on the space where there is nothing
That the usefulness of the wheel depends.[1]

Planning and market forces are not the essential differences between socialism and capitalism. A planned economy is not the definition of socialism, and because there is planning under capitalism; the market economy happens under socialism, too. Planning and market forces are both ways of controlling economic activity.[2]

The physical landscape of China is changing. As the fastest growing economy in the world the country can be clearly seen as in the middle of a vast process of rapid modernization. This drive towards growth defined by the government as *Jùyǒu Zhōngguó tèsè de shèhuìzhǔyì* (Socialist market economy with Chinese characteristics), sees the landscape literally being transformed to promote the new Chinese economy. Whole areas of cities are re-built in incredibly short time periods: the 2008 Beijing Olympics saw mass building and development take place on an unprecedented scale to host the remarkable games. Whilst the Birds Nest stadium dominates the Beijing skyline, the construction of the vastly controversial Three Gorges Dam on the Yangtze River (which will become fully operational in 2011) will eventually raise the water level by 175 metres on a 400-mile stretch of the river. This process which has sought to control the Yangtze River (and ironically has now placed it in on UNESO's list of endangered rivers) has been achieved at the expense of dozens of towns, villages and cities which have been razed to the ground together with a forcible relocation of 700,000 citizens to other areas. This is not a new development: the Great Wall, Beijing's Forbidden City and the wonders of Xi'an's non-living army were all built to celebrate China's status as a world power and yet, rather than temples, there are now sky-scrapers and shopping malls, highways instead of fortifications: for the face of New China, economy and landscape go hand in hand.

Chinese cinemas have been generous in offering us a myriad of views on the land: from the early visions of Shang-hi in *The Goddess* (Shen nu, Yonggang Wu, 1934) and *Stage Sisters* (Wutai jimei, Xie Jin, 1965) to the modern visions of the urban in film such as *Beijing za zhong* (Beijing Bastards, Yuan Zhang, 1993) and the work of directors such as Wong Kar Wai and Jai Zhang-Ke. In *Yellow Earth* (Huang tu di, Kaige Chen, 1984), *Girl from Hunan* (Xiangnu ziaoxiao, Fei Xie, 1986) and *Tuya's Marriage* (Yuya de hun shi, Quanan Wang, 2006) the beautiful rural landscape is an environment that offers nothing but hardship and pain for the mainly female characters. However, in contrast, the splendour of the sweeping forests and hills in Chinese swordplay films adroitly personified in the recent worldwide blockbusters, *Hero* (Yingxiong, Zhang Yimou, 2002), *House of Flying Daggers* (Shi mian mai fu, Zhang Yimou, 2004) and *Crouching Tiger Hidden Dragon* (Cang long wo hu, Ang Lee, 2000), offers a different version of the Chinese countryside: one covered in the mythology, glamour and excitement of the *jianghu* or martial arts world.

Chinese cinemas are of course framed around the three elements of Hong Kong, Taiwan and mainland China.[3] In his summary on Chinese national cinema, Yangjin Zhang notes that, 'among all three Chinas, the mainland is the only place where the presence of national cinema is still accentuates in media coverage'.[4] With this in mind, can a difference in the representation of landscape be seen? This chapter will examine the difference in the representation of the landscape that exists in three films from China. It will question if the spaces that exist between the dualism of rural/urban, past/future, have, in the case of the two films from Taiwan and Hong Kong (long established centres of modernity), resulted in alienation of the individual from people, surroundings and ultimately from themselves. Yet, with the film to be examined from mainland China does the landscape, particularly the rural landscape, succeed in maintaining a much more positive placement in the cinematic imagination?

## Confessing in Hong Kong: *Confessions of Pain* (Seung sing, Wai Keung Lau and Siu Fai Mak, 2006)

For many, the cityscape of Hong Kong is the idealized image of economic success and ultimate modernity and is the setting for *Confessions of Pain* (Seung sing, Wai Keung Lau and Siu Fai Mak, 2006). The plot of *Confessions of Pain* is familiar territory for the successful directorial duo that is primarily famous for the incredible successful *Wu jian dao* (Infernal Affairs) trilogy. Nothing is all that is seems as a successful police chief Hei (played by Mak and Lau regular Tony Leung Chiu-Wai) is discovered to be a brutal and vengeful killer, and private detective Bong, the 'hero' (Takeshi Kenshiro), is an unhappy and tormented drunk forced to discover his friend and mentor is not who he seems. For the purpose of this chapter, and indeed arguably Lau and Mak's films as a whole, the plot is secondary to style. The Hong Kong setting dominates the narrative: from sweeping shots of cars racing through the maze of Hong Kong's streets and highways to visions of temples, luxury houses and dark apartments, all interdispersed with an occasional vista of the Hong Kong skyline.

*Confessions of Pain* opens on a vibrant New Year celebration; it seems to be a time of rejoicing and yet we discover that many of the celebrants are undercover police trying to catch a sadistic rapist and killer. The evening ends badly for all concerned: the criminal is beaten half to death by the vengeful Hei who seems to be attentive to punishing the man than comforting the female victim, and Bong returns home to lovingly kiss his sleeping girlfriend only to find she has slit her wrists. As the film fast-forwards three years we see he has become an alcoholic still morning her death while Hei is apparently happily married and a high-ranking member of the Hong Kong police department. When Hei's wife Susan asks Bong to investigate the brutal slaying of her wealthy father and his assistant, the landscape of Hong Kong becomes the setting for an almost oedipal murder narrative. Hei is in fact Keung, a Macau boy who witnesses the killing of his entire family at the hands of Susan's father and moves to Hong Kong to follow his family's killers and in fact marries Susan only to gain access to her father.

The landscape grants an ideal setting for the multiplicity of personality that both Hei and Bong demonstrate. The characters and the audience move from bright airy luxury buildings to dark, narrow corridors and apartments: this duality of landscape mirroring the confusion and ambivalence that is central to the narrative. The focus of the investigation becomes a Buddhist shrine where we learn Keung hid as a child and found his new name among the grave markers. This shrine becomes the site at which there is an eradication of the old in favour of the new. Hong Kong the colonial Westernized city becomes a part of China once more; the child Keung becomes Hei, a highly valued and respected police chief and husband of a wealthy beautiful women, in short an emblem of a modern Chinese success story. Yet, Hei is propelled by the history of Keung. He transports the violence he witnessed in Macau to Hong Kong and we come to realize that Hei and all that he initially stands for is an illusion. His commitment to the Buddhist temple (he gives them money) and his apparent commitment to family is undermined by his choice of a jade Buddhist statue to bludgeon his father-in-law to death with and his eventual murder of his wife via a house fire. Similarly, at the opening of the film, his commitment to helping the naked and bloody rape victim pales with his desire to beat the suspect close to death with a candlestick: a initial sign that the character of Hei is not as simple as initially presented.

Questions of monetary economy in the film (arguably one the main driving forces behind the creation of Hong Kong) is something that the film rejects as a positive: perhaps a nod towards the old Western adage 'money does not bring happiness'. Any hint of economic reasons behind the killings is quickly denounced; the usual desires of wealth have nothing to do with these murders. The inheritance of a large fortune means nothing to Hei/Keung, he just wants revenge for his family's death. His position as a police chief and his marriage mean everything to Hei (as he is presented) but nothing to Keung, the hidden element of Hei that drives the narrative. All the success that Hei has achieved is a method for Keung to enact his revenge. Rather than enhancing their placement as successful members of New China, all the economic transactions in the film are seen as methods by which the characters seek to alienate themselves even further from the city and those around them. Susan and Hei's purchase of their luxury apartment only offers Hei the perfect stage to torment and then kill Susan; Susan's farther is bludgeoned to death with the expensive Jade artefact and the only economic transactions Bong conducts are related to his alcoholism: he never buys food, only whisky, and pays a local waitress money to pass out on her floor (and possibly sex although this is never made clear) after his drunken binges. His drinking only serves to trap Bong in the continual process of mourning for his dead girlfriend and fuels his obsession with discovering all he can know about her last few hours. The city opens up easy opportunities for Bong to indulge his drinking and his relationship to the city streets is one that is nearly always conducted via alcohol as he is almost always weaving his way drunkenly through Hong Kong.

The film charts the 'process' as their personalities and identities become simultaneously more complex and in a similar fashion the landscape is a 'process' rather than a fixed entity. Hei's refusal to let go of the old past (personified in this case by Macau) results in his inability to ultimately engage with the future and eventually results in the final split between an individual and his surrounding – his death. The rupturing of the boundary between the old and new becomes polarized in one space/personality and this results in the suicide of Hei/Keung. Hei's remorse over Susan is compounded by the realization that although he has avenged the death of Keung's family the process has resulted ironically in Hei destroying his own. Bong's alcoholism, supported by the lifestyle the city affords him, results in not only his split from those around him on a personal and social level, but also between him and reality as he literally cannot longer trust his own memoirs. In their last conversation, Hei and he sit side by side gazing out over the city. For both, the city has becomes the site of their disenfranchisement from all aspects of their individual lives. At the beginning of the film, while chasing the rapist, the streets of Hong Kong offered the two policemen a map to follow in the form of the Hong Kong motorway network. The streets allowed them to find a conclusion to that particular crime narrative; however, at the end, Hong Kong resists offering a solution that is not death in reference to Hei, or alcohol in the case of Bong, when they are faced with their individual histories. Questions of the past need to be answered and when they are not the characters cannot face the present. Hei's need to avenge the past has destroyed his present and his future. Bong cannot come to terms with the history that surrounds him and also destroys his present via drink, and although we are given a glimpse of hope that he will form a relationship with the waitress he is still drinking heavily, which undermines a positive reading to the film's conclusion. In the *Infernal Affairs* trilogy the city of Hong Kong was awash with questions of dual identity and questions of belonging. In *Confessions of Pain*, the confusion remains but there is no hope of redemption; we are left instead with a vision of a city that offers no space for successful connection between past, present and future. The cityscape that the film ends on is dark and menacing and the characters seem inconsequential in the landscape that surrounds them.

## Rain and tears in Taipei: *Three Times* (Zui hao de shi guang, Hsiao-Hsien Hou, 2005)

If *Confessions of Pain* deals with questions of past versus present, Hsiao-Hsien Hou's *Three Times* questions the fixity of time and space and examines the void that appears to exist between individuals and their surroundings.

For many, Hou is one of the leading Chinese, or more specifically modern Taiwanese Cinema directors. *Three Times* is a rather confusing amalgamation of three different time periods: 1911, 1966 and 2005, in which various different characters are all played by the same actor (Chang Cheng) and actress (Shu Qi) as they move through what can only be seen as a series of vignettes focusing on questions of unfinished and unsatisfied love.

The various landscapes that exist in *Three Times* are juxtaposed within three time frames with three sets of relationships. The landscape adroitly frames feelings of loss and loneliness that the characters failure to find love exemplifies. The first vignette, set in 1966, is notable for the sheer amount of literal geographical movement around Taiwan that the characters enact. The man (Chang Chen), on leave from the army, tries to find a pool hall attendant (Shu Qi) that he has fallen in love with. This section follows the unnamed man as he travels around Taiwan (symbolized by the town signs as he passes through) until he eventually finds the woman – May. May is delighted to see him but since he has to return to the army base at 9 a.m. the next morning they eat cheap noodles and May holds his hand as they wait for his bus without any plans to meet again. For the characters in the next section love becomes a paid transaction. The man (Cheng) visits the women (Shu) in the brothel where she works. Although he is happy to help a fellow brothel member achieve her dream of becoming a second wife and it is made clear that both the man and woman maintain strong feelings for each other, he makes no effort to help his lover leave behind her former life and achieve a level of social respectability. He leaves to fight for Taiwanese independence and in his final letter, he states how he feels tears and sorrow for the fate of Taiwan but there is no comfort for his trapped lover who he has left with no money to pay her indenture. The final chapter moves to present day Taipei, where, although the intertitles announce 'a time for youth', there is no sense of vivacity or hope in the lives of the two characters. The woman is having an affair behind her lesbian lover's back with an attached male photographer. Although this is the only time we see the couple in the film's three time periods actually consummate the relationship, the end is shown as less than positive with all the characters still alienated from each other.

One of the most striking scenes from the film is the opening shot that makes up the beginning of the final section. Moving from the enclosed space of the 1911 brothel the camera cuts to a long single take of a motorbike speaking its way along the Taipei highway. The highway is backed by outlines of skyscrapers and various large buildings and it is this landscape, rather than the vehicle, that we initially follow. There is a couple on a motorbike (Chan and Shu) that we initially focus on but as the road divides, rather than remaining with the characters, the camera follows the flow of traffic on the highway. We are removed for a while from the figures we assume the narrative will follow and instead are presented with an everyday scene from the urban mass of Taipei: a busy highway, tall office buildings and no human element with which to make connection. This image of the urban space that the two will then inhabit becomes synonymous with isolation and alienation. After a while the motorbike rejoins the highway and it is then that the camera focuses in on the couple and we see the women is crying. The only way the women can communicate her distress above the noise of the traffic is to clasp her hands together until they are almost white and although the man notices this he does not make any effort to resolve the problem. This inability for individuals to communicate in an effective manner is a recurrent theme in the film.

For the first two sections the only real way the couple talk is via letter. The pool hall attendant in the first vignette receives letters from the man and yet when they are together they barely utter a word. Indeed, many of the emotions felt by the couple are not uttered by them but on the songs that are playing on the jukeboxes in the establishments that they frequent and in the non-diegetic soundtrack. At the end of the scene, as the couple forlornly wait for the bus *Aphrodite's Child*'s 'Rain and Tears' sounds, voicing what the couple cannot.

For the woman in the second section, when she makes attempts to talk to the man she loves about her position and her need for money in order to be able to leave the brothel, she is met with a wall of awkward silence. Yet, once he is no longer physically present, the man writes her a long letter detailing his beliefs and desires for the future of Taiwan. He makes no reference to her situation but conveys his desire for the freedom and happiness of Taiwan without seeing the irony, that he is making no effort to allow the woman he loves to escape from sexual and emotional slavery. Ideas of nationalism are shown as highly wanting as the man is willing to fight and discusses avidly abstract ideas but refuses to answer the woman's direct question about their future. The future of the land is tied to the future of the people that inhabit it and in his denial of the woman's future his desire for a national future seems idiosyncratic. In the final section letters have been replaced by mobile phone texts and emails. The man and the woman communicate with each other and their respective partners via a method that does not involve face-to-face contact and communication. When Shu's character suffers from an epileptic fit she notifies her friend of the fact via a text and then refuses to talk about it when her friend demands to know how she is. In return her friend leaves her a goodbye letter on her computer for her to read rather than speak to her in person. The man (Chen) takes endless photos of the woman but their verbal communication is very limited and relies on texts and emails and we are given the impressions that he actually met the women via the computer. In an image we see that she sends to him she is wearing a gag, a literal image of her inability to directly communicate to others. Even their physical contact is done without words and after their lovemaking they sit and stare at each other with, it seems, little to say. The woman has a yen (¥) symbol carved into her neck and she tells the man (via email) that the yen symbolizes 'no past, no future, just a greedy present'. Her body has become the ultimate symbol of urban economy: the past and future are subsumed in favour of a consumerist present.

This refusal to exist in the past or the future is a symptom of the woman's alienation and disenfranchisement from the world around her. The landscape of Taiwan that surrounds the characters in all three section seeks to keep the protagonists apart. Those in the modern section are kept apart by their inability to communicate; highways, office buildings and the trappings of modern existence. In the second section the woman is trapped in a single building while the literal land of Taiwan replaces her in her lover's affection. For the couple in 1966, the economic and cultural need to earn money and join the army respectively keep them apart except for a few precious moments.

## Re-viewing China: *Riding Alone for Thousands of Miles* (Qian li zou dan qi , Zhang Yimou, 2005)

If the two films that this chapter has examined offer a rather dismal vision of characters alienated from the landscape, there is hope in a film from mainland China. In Zhang Yimou's 2005 offering *Riding Alone for Thousands of Miles*, the Chinese landscape offers the chance for development of interpersonal connection and understanding rather than estrangement. *Riding Alone for Thousands of Miles* focuses on a Japanese father (Takakura Ken) as he struggles to be reconciled with his son. Dispute the fact father and son have not spoken in ten years, Takata (Ken Takakura), is invited to Tokyo by his daughter-in-law, Rie (Shinobu Terajima), when her husband, Kenichi (Kiichi Nakai), is hospitalized with liver cancer. After a rejection from his son, Rie hands her father-in-law a video tape of his sons attempt to document Chinese folk arts and the unsuccessful attempt by Kenichi to persuade the region's finest singer to perform a classic operatic song entitled *Riding Alone for Thousands of Miles*. The singer, Li Jiamin, won't comply but invites Takata to film him perform when he next visits. In order to make a link with his son, Takata decides to go to the Chinese province of Yunnan to film Li's performance himself despite the fact he has no knowledge of Chinese, Mandarin or indeed folk music. The film starts and ends on remarkable shots framed in a metallic blue/grey tone of the fishing village in which Takata resides. This landscape, then later that of Tokyo, is effective in conveying the man's sense of sorrow at the past and his past actions and decisions. China in contrast is shown as vibrant, colorful and hospitable when compared to the opening shots of Takata fishing village and the Tokyo hospital where the son lies dying. The visions of Yunnan, China that are offered hark back to Zhang's earlier work examining the rural landscape of China. Films such as *Red Sorghum* (Hong gao liang, 1987) and *Judo* (Ju-dou, 1990) rendered the land as an integral element to the characters sense of self and belonging. The female heroine of *Red Sorghum* dies defending her land and people from the Japanese invaders and her son, narrating from the future, connects his mother and father directly to the landscape of China in his placing them in a specific time and space. For the main protagonist of *Riding Alone for Thousands of Miles* the landscape of China will not provide any sense of home or belonging, indeed most of the film's humour and pathos comes from his attempts to deal with the alien language and culture; but for Takata, the folk songs of China will be the only way to communicate with his son. It is telling that when he arrives in China and discovers the singer Li is in prison so will be unable to perform, Takata rejects the option to film another singer even through the performance will be conducted wearing opera masks. Unlike in the other films, physical connection is important. Takata will not try to deceive his son by replacing one individual with another despite the fact his son may never realize. The bureaucratic difficulties of being allowed to film in prison are overcome with Takata's heartfelt videotaped plea to the appropriate officials. He uses the Chinese banners of thanks to convey to the officials that even though he is foreign and does not speak Chinese his need to film Li is one that is based on real human emotions and he makes a direct connection with the men watching the videotape.

Visiting Li in prison, Takata decides to unite Li and his illegitimate son in order that Li will perform the required song. The film then follows Takata travels to the remote Stone Village where Li's eight-year-old son resides. The landscape surrounding the stone village is some of the most striking in any of the three films. In one scene the boy Yang-Yang runs away and he and Takata spend the night in the harsh mountain regions surrounding Yuannan. But, as opposed to being a negative force, it is this sojourn in the mountains that allows Takata to realize all he missed by not showing his emotions to his own son, and to bond with Yang-Yang despite their inability to communicate via words. At the film's conclusion, even though he has learnt of his son's death, Takata films Li performing. Prior to this, he shows Li and the other prisoners photos that he had taken of Yang-Yang. These photos spark tears in not only Li but in many of the other prisoners and guards. Unlike in *Three Times* and *Confessions of Pain,* the relationships that are made between the characters in Zhang's film are marked by genuine emotional contact and the need to be understood as part of a community, be that the wider community of Stone Village or the smaller grouping of father and son.

*Riding Alone for Thousands of Miles* offers up the Chinese landscape as a space where positive change can occur. For *Three Times* and *Confessions of Pain* the alienation felt by the characters from the time and space that surround them results in the landscape offering nothing but loneliness and isolation. In *Riding Alone for Thousands of Miles*, the Chinese landscape opens up the possibility of connection between different cultures, languages, music (we see the classical Chinese opera interdispersed with a modern soundtrack) and ultimately families both Chinese and Japanese. Although the film ends with Takata staring out at the grey Japanese sea, his memories of the Chinese friends and the real human contact that the trip allowed him to gain with Yang-Yang, Yi and his own son Kenichi spark a small smile of recognition.

## Concluding remarks

Does the maintenance of an image of national cinema, encouraged actively in mainland China but suffering greatly in the more internationally focused cinemas of Hong Kong and Taiwan, result in the need to maintain a landscape that can be used as a positive and supportive cradle for the development of a new China? The urban/rural divide can be seen as caught up in the promotion of the New Chinese landscape; films by young directors such as Jia Zhangke, together with products from Hong Kong and Taiwan, seek to expose the 'underside of the glorious façade of economic reform buttressed by official rhetoric and commercial filmmaking'[5] and yet, the rural landscape of China as it has been recently presented in mainstream cinema (since the 1990s) has been a far more positive space of development when compared to the representations of urban city landscapes.

Many writers have examined how Hong Kong and to a lesser extent Taipei have come to be intricately bound in the questions and confusions surrounding globalization.[6] The increasingly large cities are formed as international focus points and the inhabitants of the global city are caught in the cusp of international/national identity questions. Perhaps the rural space is still one that can be marked as local, culturally informed and positive, as opposed to economically controlled, globally informed and ultimately negative spaces of the urban development. *Three Times* and *Confessions of Pain* are representative of the elements of Chinese cinema that question the drive towards growth at whatever cost and offer an image of individuals disconnected and disenfranchised from the landscape that surrounds them.

In Zhang's film, the landscape of China can even offer a Japanese man a chance at change, development, connection and re-integration. The question in terms of cinematic landscape that will arise with reference to mainland Chinese development policies is whether or not the feelings of alienation and separation that can be seen as marking the more urban cinema of Hong Kong and Taiwan continue to develop in the cinema of the PRC as literally the rural space of mainland China is consumed in the economic drive towards development. Taiwan and Hong Kong's economic and financial development has been taking place for several decades and the end result, in terms of cinema, has been a questioning about the downfall of the past/traditional in favour of a modern future. PRC blockbusters, as illustrated by the work of Zhang Yimou still maintain an image of rural traditions that the process of 'Socialist market economy with Chinese characteristics' may well eradicate in the near future, replacing this landscape with the traumatic urban landscapes that mark those filmmakers working in the modern cities. Whether or not the cinematic landscape will continue to move towards the urban isolation of Hong Kong and Taiwan as opposed to rural integration seen in films such as *Riding Alone for Thousands of Miles* remains to be seen.

## Notes

1. Lao Tzu, *Tao Te Ching* (London: Wordsworth Editions, 1997), 19.
2. John Gittings, *The Changing Face of China from Mao to Market* (Oxford: Oxford University Press, 2005), 2.
3. Yanjin Zhang, *Chinese National Cinema* (York and London: Routledge, 2004).
4. Zhang, 295.
5. Zhang, 271.
6. Abbas Ackbar, *Hong Kong: Culture and the Politics of Disappearance* (Indianapolis: University of Minnesota Press, 1997); Rob Wilson and Wimal Dissanayake, *Global/Local: Cultural Production and the Transnational Imaginary* (Durham: Duke University Press, 1996) and Steven Teo, *Hong Kong Cinema: The Extra Dimensions* (London: BFI, 1997).

# Chapter 14

Japanese Cinema and Landscape

Paul Spicer

A street of motion picture theatres in Asakusa Park, Tokyo, circa 1930. (Photo by Archive Photos/Getty Images)

If a national cinema identity is measured by how culture, traditions and societies' struggles are represented, then Japanese cinema could be one of the most truly self representative forms of art there has been. Throughout the history of filmmaking in Japan, directors have been, much like the country, on an ever-evolving journey of self-discovery. The Meiji restoration, through Taisho, nationalism, the Second World War and the rebuilding process, occupation, labour riots and the sexual revolution. All have been a cinematic canvas on which Japanese directors have crafted works of social, political, environmental and ideological importance. Ozu for example displayed, between scenes, images of Japan's industrialism through cityscapes, pollution belching from factory chimneys and steam trains, framing these images as if they were some huge monster dwarfing the cities and people that lived below. These images are then juxtaposed with shots of simplicity, washing hanging from lines and mass huddles of small houses, dwarfed by mountains, the old, the new and the mundane in harmony? Contemporary directors such as Kitano Takeshi and Miike Takashi continue this trend as a number of their key works are set in similar locations. However, unlike the directors before them, the Japan in which their films are set often represents confusion and violence, set in sprawling cities and dysfunctional suburbs, which are as uncomfortable as the people who inhabit them.

Above all, and arguably most important of all, it is the way in which all these directors have represented the changing face of Japan. The Japanese, in mannerisms have not swayed too far from the behaviour of their ancestors; however, it is the Japan in which they live which has become an ever-changing film set, one on which directors paint their stories.

In Japan, as in the rest of the world, the first films seen were projections of a collection of 1897 Lumière short films. The Japanese marvelled at these moving images. In the same year as the Lumière premiere, Asano Shiro and Kamada Koyo, employees at the Konishi camera shop, Tokyo, imported the first motion picture camera into Japan, 'La Cinematographie'. Asano and Komada were seen soon after, shooting everyday life in around Tokyo. During the same period, Shibata Tsunekichi and Shirai Kanzo of the camera department in the Mitsukoshi camera store began to shoot scenes of the red light district, the Ginza and the Geisha that worked there. Geisha were a popular subject for early Japanese films. As Richie notes, 'Geisha were chosen as subjects not because they were quintessentially Japanese but because their appeal was so strong'.[1] Indeed, even Asano and Kamada had noticed that among the postcards in their camera store, it was the Geisha images that outsold images of every other kind. The Geisha offered a traditional fascination to early Japanese cinemagoers and as Richie again points out, 'Geisha were [therefore] a commodity popular enough to warrant the necessary cinematic outlay'. By 1899, Kamada had earned enough money from film productions to leave the camera store and went on to create the Association of Japanese Motion Pictures. The AJMP sponsored entire Geisha dances held at the Tokyo Kabuki-za, charged hugely inflated admission prices and filmed everything, in focus, for show at the theatres that were beginning to appear in such cities as Tokyo, Osaka, Kyoto, Hiroshima and Yokohama.

It is around this time, the early 1900s, that the first evolution of Japanese cinema began as cameras moved from streets to stage as the art began to adapt, and the shots of street scenes and working Geisha began to disappear as Japanese filmmaking was growing, not from novels or short stories, but from the theatre. Traditional plays such as kabuki were the theme of much of the early Japanese works. The camera would film scenes from a position exactly as a watching theatre audience would see it, frontally. This is, of course, a cinema in its infancy but it is important to note how the Japanese were utilizing traditional theatre. Actors inhabited painted sets and performed their art on screen, just as it was on stage. With the advent of technical advancements in filmmaking, Japanese directors were becoming stifled with the rigid technical guidelines that this genre demanded and began to experiment by fusing new American styles with traditional Japanese. Although still regarded as kabuki cinema, it was inevitable that as more Western cinema was seen in Japan, with its outdoor action and scenes of high drama set to the huge backdrop of American scenery, traditionally represented kabuki cinema was destined to change as directors became more interested in portrayal of narrative and location. The first indication of change was in-part due to the Japanese love of Western techniques such as the close-up and the cross-cut chase sequence, hugely influenced by Victorin-Hippolyte Jasset's 1911 detective film, *Zigomar*, scenes that would have been impossible to recreate on a painted stage. The film was a huge success in Japan and caused an excitement among young Japanese audiences but a deep concern within the authorities, who saw *Zigomar*, a film where the debonair villain and master of disguise, 'Zigomar', continually clashes with the forces of law and order, as a threat to the very existence of Japaneseness. Indeed, the film, released in Japan by the Fukuhodo Company of Tokyo, created such a sensation that it defined the way that Japanese filmmakers would create, produce and discuss film thereafter. The frustration felt by directors of this period would have been high, but with the advent of the Shinpa directors, cinema began to explore the huge landscapes that Japan had to offer with films such as Tanaka's, *Ikeru shikabane* (The Living Corpse, 1918), Kurihara's *Amachua kurabu,* (Amateur Club, 1920) and Osanai and Murata's, *Rojou no reikon* (Souls on the Road, 1921). With films such as these, Japanese cinema was able to escape from the shackles of tradition and ideology and portray the foundations of Japan in its natural setting.

Although the directors had now moved away from the traditional confines of the theatre, the new challenge was in how they would frame their films in this new, pre-made set, Japan. It has been noted by scholars of Japanese film, that the art owes a huge debt to landscape painting, print-making and architecture. In *Ugetsu monogatari*, it can be seen that landscape influences originate from the Japanese *kakejiku*. These are hanging scroll paintings that were developed from China during the Kamakura period and were created within the arts of early Zen Buddhism. These *kakejiku* were black and white landscape paintings, depicting *sansui* (mountains and water). During the Kamakura period, *shoinzukuri* (a Japanese-style house) were built for the first time and within contained an area where the *kakejiku* could be hung, called a *tokonoma*. This assisted in the popularity of the *kakejiku*, as every *shoinzukuri* contained a *tokonoma*.

As mentioned, the first *kakejiku* depicted *sansui*, however this developed and soon *tokonoma* consisted of *kakejiku* which displayed Buddhist sutras and teachings, letters, autographs and portraits. It is interesting to note that these paintings initially represented landscapes and then developed into paintings of people and script, whereas cinema's journey started with people and moved onto landscapes. Indeed as far as cinema is concerned, the art of the *kakejiro* relates heavily to how early Japanese cinema was framing their landscapes and also highlighted the direction that new Japanese directors were heading as many such as Mizoguchi and Kurosawa studied as painters in their pre-filmmaking days and were among many to realize not just the power of the Japanese landscape, but the stunning and visual effect on narrative that it can have.

Of course, Japan has changed as has its films and the following three case studies highlight the ways in which the cultural landscape of Japan has had an impact on its filmmakers. The first will examine the film *Ugetsu monogatari* by director Mizoguchi Kenji and look at the aforementioned effect that a landscape can have on narrative and the huge impact it can have on emotional response. The second study will examine Teshigahara Hiroshi's 1962 work, *Otoshiana* (The Pitfall), and its man-made, industrial landscape. The final study will look at Miyazaki's 1997 anime film *Mononoke hime* (Princess Mononoke). This final study takes a different form as it is entirely animation, but displays elements of those early *kakejiku* as well as providing a warning of the power of nature in a hostile and unforgiving environment.

*Ugetsu monogatari* remains a pivotal work in the continuing experimental and creative art of Japanese film. The film was critically acclaimed in the West and in 1953 won a Silver Lion at the Venice Film Festival. *Ugetsu* is set during civil war, is heavily character-based and combines folklore and classic literature with reality. *Ugetsu* contains striking and beautiful representations of the Japanese image. However, it is with these images that Mizoguchi paints a portrait of Japan as a place of unrest, of human greed, lust and desire, played out beneath backdrops of Japanese iconography. Mizoguchi utilizes the splendour of Japanese natural beauty to begin and end the film as at these points we are reminded that we, as humans are insignificant compared with the majesty of our surroundings, placing, 'all of the human events and emotions of the narrative in the subsuming context of nature'. As the opening credits are played, Mizoguchi uses painted representations of Japanese landscape; first as the film title is displayed, a background of rolling hills with small houses buried deep within them is shown, this then cuts to a selection of timed images all representing nature, such as *kiku*, *ume*, *tsubaki* before cutting back again to a mountain scene very much in relation to the first. As the film starts this mountain image is realized as Mizoguchi, using a slow purposeful right to left pan, displaying rolling hills with small houses in the foreground. The poignant image of a worker is buried deep in the shot as the camera continues behind a tree and into a village on the north shore of Biwako Lake. It is here that Mizoguchi allows us to see the film's protagonists, Miyagi, Genjuro, Tobei and Ohama, although still fresh in our minds are the preceding images that Mizoguchi has offered. This first shot of the mountains again is reminiscent of the *emakimono* paintings previously discussed and sets a scene for the relationship of image and narrative. This image, however, is also seen in the last scene, just as the camera pans across the mountains and into the village in the opening shot, the end scene sees the camera move in opposite, as it lifts from the village and above, framing the very image that was seen initially. Superficially everything appears the same, but as the film has expressed through its narrative, everything has drastically changed.

Mizoguchi took two tales from Ueda Akinari's nineteenth-century collection of ghost stories, *Ugetsu monogatari*. At first the film offers no reference of any supernatural or ghostly happenings as the story revolves around a potter and his wife; however it is the very nature of Mizoguchi's representation that invokes an uneasy response in *Ugetsu*. Hosaka Kazushi argues that Mizoguchi's scenery doesn't visually represent reality and has an element of supernatural about it, and although what is portrayed in *Ugetsu* is the *real* Japan these images do not live in the minds of everyday Japanese. It is an interesting point, considering the importance that Mizoguchi places on landscape scenery and its necessity to the narrative. For example, it is this very representation that first exposes the viewer to a supernatural element within *Ugetsu*. The lake scene, where the four main characters are heading to Omizo to sell their pottery, is infused with supernatural elements and first attunes the viewer's senses to the fact that all is not what it appears. This shot, long and purposeful, is key as the mist rolls from the lake and the clouds in the background are dark grey and menacing. Ohama steers the boat carrying the characters to their destination as it moves slowly from far right of the shot to front left, shrouded in fog. The tension is heightened by Ohama's rendition of Sendo-uta (a song sung by boatmen), and the eerie mysticism of the lake. Mizoguchi uses long takes and sparse cuts which seem to be in tune with the boats motion and the small waves on the lake. This section of the film uses the supernatural elements of nature that Hosaka mentions, as a narrative in itself. This is the turning point of the film, where what has been seen up to now as a standard *jidai geki* (period drama) narrative, is turned into something completely different.

The supernatural events that occur within *Ugetsu* are represented extensively through the cultural Japanese image that Mizoguchi portrays. There are graphical relationships to Noh drama, traditional behaviour and ceremony and of course through the setting and landscapes that provide a parallel narrative. However, it is the representation of religious imagery through this iconography that forms the final part of this study. Mizoguchi was a devout Nichiren Buddhist, but his films do not obviously express views of a religious ethic. On closer examination it can be argued that Mizoguchi does include moments that indicate religious *values*. There are sections in Mizoguchi's films where the director deliberately seems to locate a character in a setting that connects with the serious personal problems or issues that they face. This then provides a direct link within the relationship between the landscape and the emotional state of the character. This is exemplified in the rape scene in the film. Ohama stumbles onto a deserted waterfront; she is desperate to find her husband Tobei, who has disappeared to pursue his Samurai career. As she wearily treads onto the sand, she is surrounded by desolation. The tree is bare; the reeds look dry and withered and even the hills in the background, in their beauty, look menacing and uncomfortable. The viewer, by examining this frame, is left uneasy because of this relationship. These feelings are founded as Ohama is taken forcefully by Samurai foot soldiers into a nearby temple; the camera does not follow into the temple, letting the audience imagine what is going on inside.[2] The fact that Ohama was dragged into a Buddhist temple set on a desolate, lifeless waterfront certainly turns viewers thoughts to religion, and the disgust felt that such an act can be carried out in a sacred place. Do we as the audience feel sympathy, not just to Ohama, but to the religious building, which is also about to be violated? As Ohama is taken inside and the camera draws back, we have a cut to Ohama's discarded sandals on the beach, half buried in the sand. We can imagine at this time what is happening to Ohama, and the horror of it, but could this be a moment for reflection, of meditation? If so this would be unusual as the sect of Buddhism that Mizoguchi practised does not involve meditation; however it could be argued that this relates to the Japanese method of Zen Buddhism, a form of Buddhism that is closely tied to Japanese culture. That one shot of Ohama's sandals, all seven seconds of it, could be seen as Mizoguchi's Japanese values and expectations ruling his religious sensibilities.

As previously mentioned, the fusion between character and landscape is key in *Ugetsu monogatari*. Not only does the scenery represent setting, character emotion, audience response, environment and narrative, but the very essence and direction of this story is represented by the location that the characters inhabit. Decaying villages, mysterious lakes, desolate and dying shores, bustling market squares, haunted mansions, each location a huge influence on the film's aims and themes. Mizoguchi was a meticulous director and demanded high levels of perfection from his staff. Maybe however, it was this film in which Mizoguchi was attempting to do the same justice to his backdrop, a backdrop which has allowed *Ugetsu monogatari* to become the masterpiece that it is.

In terms of use of landscape, Teshigahara Hiroshi's 1962 film *Otoshiana* (The Pitfall) is in direct contrast to *Ugetsu,* both aesthetically and politically. Preferring a claustrophobic mining town to spatial elegance, this was the director's debut into fiction and the first of four films in collaboration with distinguished writer Abe Kobo. Teshigahara is a director who like Mizoguchi studied painting and again, the effect of this can be clearly seen in *Otoshiana.* Teshigahara's film is set on Kyushu, and revolves around the story of a miner and his son. The film does not reveal the miner's name and indeed it is not until the later stages of the film, when more educated characters are displayed, that we are introduced to named characters. It is important to explain that the man is a *yamano-zurakarimono,* meaning that he is a deserter; in this case, not from an army, but from an unregulated, un-unionized coal mine. We first see an insight into his past as the man reminisces about his work and the shot breaks to a series of documentary shorts, highlighting the condition of these places. The images are graphic as Teshigahara shows starving children, corpses of miners and severe injuries sustained in these pits. However, it is the last segment of this sequence that possibly has the most symbolism, the image of a huge *botayama* (slagheap), on fire, a representation of the hell that the previous images have set up. This man-made landscape is one of death and through this imagery our sympathies are immediately with the man and his decision to run from the mine. Teshigahara does not utilize landscape to convey narrative in the way that Mizoguchi does; there is, however, an artistic tendency in his use of backdrop which he uses to convey a continual reminder of depravity throughout. Teshigahara's idea 'was to match the allegorical plot, typical of Kobo Abe, against the deteriorated coal mine city as an extremely realistic background'.[3] Teshigahara uses locations of work, man-made, bustling and unrelenting. The seaport setting for instance where the coal is being loaded onto boats is an example of this, and again the setting leads to misery as a worker attempts to escape this place, only to be caught by officials.

It is here that the differences between *Otoshiana* and *Ugetsu monogatari* can be examined. Teshigahara does not focus upon the *natural* beauty of Japan, but the industrialized landscapes that economic progression has created, the same industrial images that Ozu featured, mentioned earlier in this chapter. Indeed, the similarities of the films are striking, both contain supernatural elements, but whereas in *Ugetsu* it is represented by the lake scene, in *Otoshiana* nothing changes, the scenery remains the same and it is the characters within the scene that are the cause of death although the landscape complements this perfectly.

Teshigahara and Abe were politically active left-wing artists. During the 1950s Teshigahara was involved with documentary-maker Kamei Fumio creating radical A-bomb documentaries such as *Ikiteite yokatta* (It Was Good to Live, 1956) and *Sekai wa kyoufusuru* (The World is Terrified, 1957). Both of these films were documentaries and focused on the nuclear issue, the first being Hiroshima A-bomb victims and the latter about A-bomb tests. Abe was an avant-garde novelist and playwright, writing a screenplay for Kobayashi Masaki's 1953 film, *Kabeatsuki heya* (The Thick-walled Room). The film was controversial as it was based on war criminals that, in Kobayashi's view, were vilified and punished after the war for obeying orders from superiors. The film caused so much revolt that its release was postponed by four years. Teshigahara and Abe met while both were members of Seiki no Kai (The Group of the Century), a collection of artists, poets, filmmakers and writers. Teshigahara was attracted to Abe artistically, 'not only because of the older man's firm political stance but because his own intuitions as a visual artist were often confirmed in Abe's literary works'.[4] *Otoshiana* was the first collaboration and maybe the most cutting-edge. The film was an independent production, a rare commodity within the Japanese film industry at this time. Because of this, Teshigahara had to employ actors from the theatre, especially from the Shingeki, (New Theatre), as all the major stars were contracted to the larger studios. Unlike Teshigahara's subsequent films which starred better-known actors and actresses, *Otoshiana* had a truly independent feel to it as it fused political ideology and proletarian independence with the avant-garde and the supernatural. Therefore, the landscape of the Kyushu mine and the ghost town that it shadows are essential to the auteurism that Teshigahara is portraying. The desolation, dirt, pollution, death, danger and bleakness are a metaphor for the suffering of most of the film's protagonists. In a way which is totally different from Mizoguchi, Teshigahara uses the landscape to assist his ideologies and to complement the story. Indeed, and as it turns out, the surroundings are a perfect accompaniment to the action and a stunning realism of Teshigahara's art ethic as he uses the topography of rock and slag, intensifying the setting by use of the landscape's sculptural aspect.

Previously we have examined representations of two types of setting, the natural and the man-made. However, the focus in the final section of this chapter will examine the animated landscapes of Hayao Miyazaki through his 1997 film, *Mononoke hime* (Princess Mononoke). Of course, it would be easy to dismiss animated films and Studio Ghibli's work as pure entertainment with little substance; however this could not be further from the truth. Many studies have been carried out on Miyazaki's work, including Seiji Kanou's *Hayao Miyazaki Treatise* (2006), Sasaki Takashi's *Miyazaki's Anime; Hidden Messages – From 'Nausicaa of the Valley of the Wind' to 'Howl's Moving Castle'* and Helen McCarthy's *Hayao Miyazaki – Master of Animation* (2002). Many Miyazaki's films portray a harsh reality, that although exhibited in animation, have recurring warnings on the failure of man to heed the warnings that nature has provided. *Mononoke hime* is a film that is such a warning, and deserves its place within this case study. This can be achieved by examining the work as not just a piece of animation but that of a living, breathing and dying landscape.

*Mononoke* is based in and represents two areas of Japan. The first, the Shishigami forest, is influenced by Yakushima Island in Kagoshima prefecture, an area that is protected by the United Nations Educational, Scientific and Cultural Organization (UNESCO) as a world heritage site. The second are the Shirakami mountains in Aomori prefecture, which is on the Northern tip of Honshu, the inspiration for the village of the film's hero, Ashitaka. The film's animators visited the locations to picture and film areas in preparation for the animation so although portrayed through animation and therefore deemed as unreal and fantastic, the truth is that parts of these locations were meticulously recreated for the film. *Mononoke* deals with issues of environmentalism and industrialism, the latter destroying the former as well as issues of nature fighting back. To this end it is important to briefly give an introductory synopsis of *Mononoke hime*.

The main character, Ashitaka is cursed by the god of a boar Inoshishigami. He kills the god to protect his village and within the corpse finds a bullet, an indication to the reason Inoshishigami attacked a human village. Ashitaka then embarks on a journey, not only in search of a way to lift the curse but to discover who shot the god, as he thinks this is the reason the god tried to kill humans. It is Ashitaka's idea that if he discovers who made and fired the bullet he will be able to find his cure. During this search he meets a girl who was raised by the wolf god Moro. The girl, San, was abandoned when she was a child and has spent her life as a wolf, living deep within natural surroundings. The name Mononoke is literally translated as beast, and although San is human, her hatred, distrust and contempt for humans is clearly visible, fuelled by the human destruction of the forest where she lives. Indeed, when Ashitaka first encounters San, she and her wolf brothers are involved in a fight with workers from the local *tataraba* (ironworks). Moro has been shot and Ashitaka's first sight of San is a stark representation of the violence of nature: her 'jaws' smothered in blood as she attempted to suck the bullet from her injured Mother, she is dressed in animal fur, has strange 'tribal' make-up; she is in essence a child of nature. This image is a clear indication of mankind at a primitive natural level and coupled with the surroundings allows an insight into Miyazaki's intentions.

There have been conflicting suggestions to the time period of this film; however it seems hugely probable that it is set during the industrial Muromachi period as the references to this era are strong. The *tataraba* is the biggest hint although Miyazaki has changed some characters' clothes and hairstyles, which are not strictly based on this period: for example Ashitaka's hairstyle and some female *tataraba* workers' clothing is not typical of the Muromachi era.

Miyazaki's films exude warnings of the destruction of nature, the forced change of landscape and human disregard for everything that nature has offered. It is quite an accomplishment and testament to nature's strength that it still survives. Miyazaki himself has commented on the changing Japanese landscape: 'The Japanese landscape, after humans have violated the forests and mountains, is the landscape we see today. We call this landscape natural.'[5] On this relationship between this comment and the film, Miyazaki goes on to say that he believes that nature is powerful and terrifying, and deep within the forests and mountains there are sacred places which have not yet been invaded. This belief is deep rooted within the core of Japanese culture, which is hugely influenced by Shinto, an ancient Japanese religion which originated around 500 BC. An element of Shinto is rooted in nature with the belief that it is sacred and pure. Stones, trees, mountains, lakes and animals are just a few examples that are believed to possess a spirit, and to be aware of the power that they possess is to be respectful to the gods. The film represents this notion with the portrayal of Shishigami forest, the home of Shishigami. Throughout *Mononoke* this sacred forest is under threat from humans. The workers of the *tataraba* want to cut trees and dig for minerals, and those from Samurai are in search of the deer god, Shishigami, believing a myth that his head will bring good fortune. From this we can see that there is a lack of respect for the spirits of the forest, industrialization is attempting to destroy and the intention of the most Japanese of icons, the Samurai, is to kill the god Shishigami, who in the film is a symbol of nature's cycle, life and death.

Although thus far we have examined San, Ashitaka and the various nature gods in *Mononoke*, it is important to finally look at the effect of the *tataraba* leader, Lady Eboshi. Miyazaki does not portray humans as inherently evil, nor nature as violent and protective, and it is also important to note that there is no right or wrong on either side. However, it is with Lady Eboshi where Miyazaki gives a sense of balance. Industrialization, and in *Mononoke* in particular, the *tataraba*, is the evil to which much of the blame of the destruction of nature lies. With Eboshi, Miyazaki has created a character that is representative of humankind. She has no sympathy for nature; she is ruthless and determined with no fear. Her opinion of nature is that it is there purely for the advancement of industrialization. She is a defender of the weak, with an equal outlook to both men and women but it is clear that her loyalties are with her fellow man and industrial creation: 'what Eboshi is trying to do is to build her idea of paradise. That makes her a twentieth-century person'.[6] Through the character Ashitaka, Miyazaki is portraying a sympathizer. He is in a position to view this battle between nature and industrialism from both sides, seeing the benefits of preserving both, and the main question that he constantly asks is one of independent rationality: is there any way that humans and nature can co-exist? Through the film's narrative and tragic finale, this question is one that Miyazaki leaves open, leaving it to the viewer to ponder.

*Ugetsu monogatari, Otoshiana* and *Monoke hime* are three important examples of natural, industrial and cultural landscape representation. Of course the films are different, not just in terms of narrative and genre, but most importantly in the way that beauty is portrayed and utilized. Through these films we have examined three stages of the progression and subsequent destruction of the Japanese landscape. In a symbolic twist, it is interesting to point out that *Ugetsu*'s natural setting and *Otoshiana*'s industrial wasteland, come together to form the very basis behind the film *Mononoke hime*. Mizoguchi did not have a problem with nature being destroyed; the landscape was not in jeopardy during the set period of Mizoguchi's film and was used as a marker for change, to indicate that whatever happens to the people in the environment, nature remains constant. Teshigahara portrays the plight of the proletariat, and this is represented by framing a coal-mine, a symbol of left-wing politics and unionism. This suffering is strikingly represented with the man's image of hell, the *botayama* on fire. This graphic representation comes as no surprise from a director whose films exhibit some cutting-edge filmmaking (the freeze frame, overlays and unconventional angled shots), but whose aim was to represent the struggles of the normal working man. The settings of his films, in the man-made industrial wastelands of Kyushu, are in direct contrast to *Mononoke*, which represents two of the most untouched areas of natural beauty in Japan, Yakushima Island and the Shirakami Mountains. By using these pure landscapes Miyazaki was portraying the reality of nature, powerful and terrifying, and the areas represented and destroyed in the film could be a landscape anywhere in the world.

Finally it is important to note the periods of time in which these films were made. When *Ugetsu* was released, Japan had been out of war for just eight years, and although re-building was taking place at an alarming rate, much of Japan was still recovering from damage. Mizoguchi's film reminded the Japanese that out of all this destruction and beyond the influence of man, there is beauty, a natural beauty that the Japanese landscape can provide. Of course within this there are humans, with faults and questionable morals and it is here the comparison is drawn with *Mononoke hime*. People have finally begun to encroach upon the natural landscape; we have to have progression, but at what cost? This cost is shown during *Otoshiana*, the huge slag heap, the dangers of the mine and the dead land that surrounds acting as a warning in regard to human interference with the natural landscape. Indeed this wasteland, dead and empty, has become like many of the miners that inhabit it: they have no future, no hope, and in the end the mine industry will also destroy them.

# Notes

1. Richie 2001, 17.
2. Keiko McDonald, *Ugetsu* (New Jersey: Rutgers University Press, 1993), 11.
3. Dore Ashton, *The Delicate Thread – Teshigahara's Life in Art* (Tokyo: Kodansha International, 1997), 87.
4. Ashton, 84.
5. Hayao Miyazaki, 'The forest and the human-being', *Analysing Princess Mononoke* 2 (1997), 74–81 (77).
6. Helen McCarthy, *Hayao Miyazaki – Master of Japanese Animation* (Berkeley: Stonebridge Press, 2002), 193.

# Chapter 15

A Version of Beauty and Terror: Australian Cinematic Landscapes

Graeme Harper

# Terra-Vision I?

European film viewer can frequently enter the Australian cinematic landscape and confront evidence of their Imperial past. In representations of rural Australia, this confrontation was once akin to being drawn into landscapes presented in similar ways to those seen in fiction films featuring interplanetary exploration. Comparisons with some of the depictions of planetary landscapes in the *Star Wars* saga would not be unfounded. The sunset of the two suns of Tatooine come to mind, from *Star Wars IV: A New Hope*, neither a recognizable sun for the Tatooine visitor, nor an inviting prospect for the visitor who perhaps can imagine what might lie ahead in the heart of the Tatooine midday. The rural landscape in these kinds of Australian films – of which *The Story of the Kelly Gang* (Charles Tait, 1906), *Jedda* (Charles Chauvel, 1955) and *Walkabout* (Nicolas Roeg, 1971) are good examples – is depicted as inaccessible, orbiting around some unfathomable alien, heated heart, often physically as well as culturally challenging.

Evidence of urban Australia, alternatively, has found its alien form in a lighter, if in some ways more unsettling, confrontation. The unstable placement of European culture, and largely European characters, in situations of local, non-European dimensions is common in the urban landscapes of Australian films. Thus, for example, the 'inappropriately dressed' European in the heat of an Australian summer city; the British Empire's soldiers in their weatherboard country towns of Imperial memorial and reverence; here, indeed, the motor vehicles of North American dimensions glimmering on neverending stretches of unforgiving bitumen. The films *They're a Weird Mob* (Michael Powell, 1966), *Don's Party* (Bruce Beresford, 1976), perhaps even *Romper Stomper* (Geoffrey Wright, 1992), fit this description.

The mere mention of *Romper Stomper*, indeed, raises some interesting questions. Questions, that is, about landscape and politics, about the relationship between overt use of landscape in the filmic arts and the inadvertent, or seemingly incidental, use of it. In this vein, it is possible to think of a well-known non-Australian film, such as *Braveheart* (Mel Gibson, 1995), and explore in such a film the meld of long, slow scenes of the Scottish countryside, and rapid-cut scenes of courtly intrigue, the relationship between form and style and politics depicted in film. Similarly, specific political questions about the relationship between rural and urban landscapes in the evolution of Australian cinematic representation arise. Barbara Ching and Gerald Creed, in their introduction to *Knowing Your Place: Rural Identity and Cultural Hierarchy* note, in relation to rural/urban relationships, that:

Given the pervasiveness of the rural/urban opposition and its related significance in the construction of identity, it is remarkable that the explosion of scholarly interest in identity politics has generally failed to address the rural/urban axis. The resulting representation of social distinctions primarily in terms of race, class and gender thus masks the extent to which these categories are inflected by place identification.[1]

The authors go on to differentiate between the 'urban-identified' and the 'rural-identified', making reference to the confidence of the urban-identified in relation to their cultural value. Comparatively, the Australian landscape depicted in films seems to reveal a greater confidence in those whose identification is with the rural – even in films largely produced and directed by Europeans or European settlers, and despite the relative alien aspects of this non-European environment. The landscapes of the first two Crocodile Dundee films, *Crocodile Dundee* (Peter Faiman, 1986) and *Crocodile Dundee II* (John Cornell, 1988) provide a useful case study.

In these two films, the eponymous Dundee lives and works in the Australian Outback. The Outback – a term meaning exactly what it says: the place 'out the back' of civilization – is depicted here as dangerous, starkly beautiful, a combination of non-European terrains, largely semi-desert and desert and, in keeping with the haunts of Dundee's crocodiles, sub-tropical. Dundee's lack of sophistication with regard to the ways of the corporate and, indeed, European world is matched by a deep knowledge of this non-European terrain, and his understanding takes on the appearance of an indigenous knowledge, founded on appreciation of, as well as a respect for, the dangers and opportunities this landscape affords.

It might seem that Dundee's attitude to his environment is one that could be described as that of the 'pioneer'. However, the pioneer must surely endeavour to impose on their environment far more than Dundee attempts to impose. A pioneer must, surely, be a marker of an outpost, a challenger of the landscape, whereas Dundee seems to be complicit with his landscape, taking it within, in terms of his ethics, his world view, and using it to redefine his relationship with his largely Western compatriots. Is this thus the work of the pioneer? Perhaps. Perhaps, alternatively, it is the work of an infiltrator – not in the more or less explicit infiltration of a culture, because Dundee sets himself apart frm the indigenous, Aboriginal culture that surrounds him – but an infiltrator of the non-European landscape. Dundee, from his crocodile-tooth festooned hat to his suntan is a product of the 'environmental', far more than it could be claimed he is a representative of another product grandly expressed as 'the cultural'. It is a theme that carries through much of settler cinema in Australia.

In this sense Ching and Creed's notion of 'place identification' works well; because, while Dundee is plain in representing himself as 'an Australian', it is the notion of place, defined by a largely raw, rural landscape, that strengthens his claim to uniqueness, and it is the uniqueness of his infiltration into the landscape that makes him iconic. Dundee, in effect, *becomes* an ideal of the European relationship with the Australian Outback; yet it is an ideal that fails to pervade the largely urban Australian population, and it is an ideal that leaves an indigenous relationship with that very landscape in a deferred position. Indigenity is re-interpreted in the Dundee films, and where it is visible it is merely observed, as the landscape becomes the home territory of the infiltrating Dundee, not of the original owners.

This, then, is the cinema of 'Terra-Australis', the Australia previously defined by European explorers of the seventeenth and eighteenth centuries. Here, the Great South Land, as it was once called by Europeans, is not a home of an alternate culture – the notion of culture, civilization, even of a 'branch of humanity' was missing from European ideas about Australia at that point – rather, it is a physical mass, an alien continent, an alternative, otherworldly existence in which the style and dimensions, the alterity, of the landscape emphasize the impossibility of creating a normal relationship with it. In this sense all these films and those like them from Australian cinematic history, present a different view of landscape to those produced by indigenous Australians.

## Terra Vision II?

*One Night the Moon* (2001) and *Radiance* (1998), two films directed by indigenous Australian filmmaker Rachel Perkins, present a somewhat different view of the Australian landscape to that noted above. In an interview, published in 2001, Perkins declares '*One Night The Moon* was so much about the landscape…it had to be worked in there in some sort of approach rather than just a "cut to" here and a "cut to" there'.[2] Indeed, it is not merely the prevalence of landscape that is distinctive; rather, it is the way landscape is considered and employed. In both films, what Perkins has declared is neither entirely an aesthetic devoted 'realism' (that is, for example, her working with cinematographer, Kim Batterham, to develop the more expressionist use of light that pervades *One Night the Moon*, picking up the themes of the film in relation to *loss*, but likewise seeming to relate to what can be *found* in the Australian landscape), nor entirely lacking in 'reality' (that is, for example, the stark interiors of the *Radiance*, where the presence of beautiful things would have been, Perkins believes, less real in terms of the Aboriginal interiors she was depicting).

The timing of their success places these Perkins films in juxtaposition to those of Ivan Sen, whose indigenous Australian background also informs his work, including *Beneath Clouds* (2002) and *Yellow Fella* (2005). *Beneath Clouds* tells the story of Lena, the daughter of an Aboriginal mother and a father of Irish decent, and Vaughn, a Murri boy (Murri being the traditional, indigenous inhabitants of much of the Australian State of Queensland). Lena, with an idealized view of her absent father, decides that circumstances suggest that she should leave her northwestern NSW town, where her life is leading to very little, and head toward Sydney, where she supposes her father lives. Along the way, inadvertently missing re-boarding the Sydney-bound bus at a rest stop, she meets up with Vaughn. Vaughn has escaped from a minimum security prison and is also on a personal journey – in his case, to see his dying mother.

*Beneath Clouds* is, in part, a love story – though a love story whose points of contact are those drawn from a shared adversity, and a shared vision, and strain the conventions of such a 'love story' definition by placing this personal story in the realm of a cultural tension, shared, but at odds with itself. Landscape features notably in this. Lena's idealization of her Irish father's existence is reflected in visions of the Australian landscape seemingly filtered through a pseudo-European point of view. At one point, the Australian landscape, through Lena's eyes, even takes on the characteristics of a misty Irish landscape; and, while this is entirely possible in some respects, its emergence more reflects Lena's own attempts to relate the European and the Australian indigenous in one vision. This then informs the film's depiction of Vaughn, whose 'criminality' bears the marks of a mismatch between European and indigenous Australian ideals, where physical location is paramount to versions of a battlefield. Thus Vaughn's personal story and demeanour seem to embed themselves in the explicit clashes between place and person; whereas, Lena's story seems to use landscape as an indicator of inner turmoil that cannot be resolved in view, but only through concealed psychological reconciliation. Neither vision seems settled, and the film's depiction of an indigenous viewpoint constantly at oblique angles to European settler viewpoints is at the core of its meaning. Sen himself, the son of an indigenous Australian mother and a German father, takes his personal circumstances here as a backdrop, much as Perkins has drawn down on her personal knowledge of her cultural background.

Both Sen and Perkins have endeavoured to find a way of using their depictions of the Australian landscape, as well as character and story, to explore the relationship between indigenous and European Australians, while neither has made that exploration the only story they wish to tell in their films. In both cases the use and depiction of landscape combines personal and political significance with a sense of delayed closure, contrasting with the European settler filmic depictions where narrative and a sense of closure seems far more stable. Sen's directing of the 2005 documentary, *Yellow Fella*, the story of Tom E. Lewis, the actor who played the title role in Fred Schepisi's 1977 film *The Chant of Jimmy Blacksmith*, adds further weight to the analysis, because Lewis's story – as the son of an indigenous woman of southern Arnhem Land and a Welsh stockman – mirrors Sen's indigenous-European heritage. Co-wrote by Lewis, *Yellow Fella*, like *Beneath Clouds*, is the story of a journey of discovery, discovery underpinned by a relationship with a landscape that is shown to both hold and unsettle the protagonist's place in the world.

## Rabbit-Proof Fence

Considering the similarities and differences between those Australian films that appear to utilize landscape from a European point of view, and those films that appear to utilize landscape from an indigenous Australian point of view, *Rabbit-Proof Fence* (2002) raises an important question about the relationship between landscape and film. Directed by Phillip Noyce, Australian director of such Hollywood films as *The Bone Collector* (1999), *The Saint*

(1997), *Clear and Present Danger* (1994) and *Sliver* (1993), *Rabbit-Proof Fence* is the story of three young indigenous Australian girls taken from their home to be 'trained' into domestic servitude at a government institution called the Moore River settlement. The girls escape and, following the State Barrier Fence of Western Australia, known as the rabbit-proof fence, a barrier initially constructed in the early twentieth century to keep rabbits and other agricultural pests out of Western Australian pastoral areas, find their way home to their mother at Jigalong, in the East Pilbara, on the rim of the Gibson desert.

Depicting the essence of white Australian government policy in action in the 1930s as well as the personal stories of the three girls – Molly Craig, Daisy Kadibill and Grace Fields – the film follows the kind of escape and journey narrative that might be expected from a Noyce thriller of his Hollywood 1990s. But in *Rabbit-Proof Fence*, it is not the Hollywood actor Harrison Ford, who stars in *Clear and Present Danger*, or Denzel Washington, who stars in *The Bone Collector*, who features; rather, it is three unknown indigenous Australian girls, sought out by Noyce and his team in the film casting process.

If *Rabbit-Proof Fence* cannot thus be carried by established central 'movie stars', then what lies at the heart of its construction must be some alternate audience draw-card and, indeed, both the adventurous story and declarations regarding the quality of truth contained in the depictions of the three girls features in that process. Similarly, the incorporation in the hinterland of the central story of actors of the stature of Academy Award Nominee Kenneth Branagh, who plays Mr A. O. Neville, 'Chief Protector of Aborigines', adds to the strength of the finished piece in ways that de-emphasize the newness of the three central child actors or, perhaps more accurately, use that newness to casting advantage. The daughter of the eldest girl, Molly Craig, Doris Pilkington Garimara, on whose book the film was based, acted as script consultant to the film, and brought to the film's production a connection with the original story that aimed to include an indigenous perspective, and protect an indigenous point of view. And yet, she reports, the film's demands meant that some elements of her book needed to be adjusted:

> I was so arrogant to believe that the film-makers would follow my book very very closely, as for the script, I was like 'Is this my story?', but it's a matter of knowing and seeing the point of view of the film-makers. I was coming from a writer's perspective so I had to shift a little too to realize how the book makes a good film, makes a good story.[3]

In addition, the original book was passed through the 'filtering' screen of being turned into a screenplay by another writer – in this case by writer/producer Christine Olsen, whose other producer credits include the documentaries *Hephzibah* (1998) and *My One-legged Dream Lover* (1998). The Director of Photography for *Rabbit-Proof Fence* was Christopher Doyle, whose films include a great number of Chinese-language films, particularly with the director Wong Kar-Wai, including *Buenos Aires Affair* (1997), *Fallen Angels* (1995) and *Chungking Express* (1994) and, more recently, with such directors as Zhang Yimou and his Jet Li's *Hero* (2002). Doyle was also the Director of Photography for Gus Van Sant's version of *Psycho* (1998). Having left Australia at the age of eighteen, by the time of the making of *Rabbit-Proof Fence* he had been away from Australia for over 30 years, spending most of his life in Asia – his Chinese name is Du Ke Fung, and he speaks Mandarin and Cantonese fluently – and he brought to *Rabbit-Proof Fence* a reputation as a cinematographer with a strong background as a Chinese-language filmmaker, an interest in music and movement in film, and a trademark use of vivid colours.

Doris Pilkington Garimara noticed the process of adaptation changed the depictions, even if not entirely changing the story, and it could well be wondered how much the filtering through the devising of a screenplay and then through the machinations of photography bring to *Rabbit-Proof Fence* a depiction of landscape that owes more to the interventions of Olsen and Doyle and less to those of Doris Pilkington Garimara. This is not to make any accusations related to cultural hegemony; rather, it is simply to begin to think how the depiction of landscape in film can easily be mistaken as an innocent *re*-collection when the process of its *collection* involves cultural as well as aesthetic interpretation and, in a film with the economic imperatives familiar to directors such as Noyce, economic demands. In *Rabbit-Proof Fence*, film itself, brought to the screen with the input of international filmmakers whose experience of the demands of Hollywood and, indeed, Hong Kong and, to a lesser extent, European filmmaking gives the Australian landscape here an internationalism not otherwise present. Doyle's atmospheric style invests both daylight and night shots with mystery, and the landscape takes on the strength of a key character in a film that matches children against the demands of environment and, in Hollywood terms, cries out for star quality while having little inherent opportunity for employing recognized stars.

*Rabbit-Proof Fence* thus raises an important question about landscape and film; namely, the question of whether films made by those of one cultural background, and with global filmic notions frequently at play, can do anything other than collect evidence of the evolution of culture from an indigenous past to a global present, even when consciously seeking not to do so. Film, in that sense, interprets and promotes stylized landscape representations. And yet, the sophistication of today's global media audiences suggests that a more extensive theorization might better explain this process.

### Culture, art and filmic landscapes: The case of Australia

Tom O'Regan, writing in *Australian National Cinema*, says this:

> Unequal cultural exchanges are the normal condition of most nations of the world (given that most are small- to medium-sized)…Australian cinema relies on innovation, through producers and audiences alike adjusting local cinema and cultural traditions to common international formats most evident in contemporaneous US and to lesser extent British imports. Australian cinema can simultaneously appear too 'American' by the fact of evident and imagined imitation and not 'American' enough in the textual and on-screen results.[4]

This would appear to fit the case of *Rabbit-Proof Fence*, relating directly to the way landscape is depicted in the film, and the aesthetics that inform the elevation of the largely rural landscape, in particular, to a character within a story. Its reference to 'local cinema and cultural traditions' would seem likewise to offer something for the indigenous interpretations of Perkins and Sen. And yet, O'Regan suggests that such exchanges are the product of 'innovation' and 'adjustment', as if in some way active involvement of largely settler Australians in the filmic interpretation of the country has been a product of a tension between 'Hollywoodization' and a local, Australian product, relatively congruous in attitude and inflection. What might be more accurate, however, is to suggest that a certain settler bond borne out of the Europeanization of Australian landscape lies behind the use of Australian landscape in international films produced by settler Australians, and that this settler bond is not dissimilar to that produced in Australian pioneer narratives represented in such terms as 'mateship', 'dinky-di' and even 'ANZAC'.[5] It has relatively little relevance for indigenous Australians, not least in the filmic representation of landscapes. An analogous situation exists in the landscapes of Australian fine art, as a short piece of Australian art history reveals.

In the nineteenth century a group of Australian artists, notably painting around the city of Melbourne, and often referred to as the 'Heidelberg School', after the rural suburb of Heidelberg (though the term later referred to a wider geographic range) exhibited paintings of the Australian landscape that showed a keen interest in the effects of light, and in the impact of differing brushstrokes. These artists – of which Arthur Streeton, Walter Withers, Tom Roberts, Frederick McCubbin and Charles Conder are notable names – often painted *en plein air* and often depicted scenes of rural life, some indeed in the heat of the midday sun, and some indeed featuring the colours of the Australian earth and the country's distinctive vegetation.

From this fact grew the idea that the 'Heidelberg School' was to be acknowledged as the first movement of largely landscape artists to depict the *real* Australia; that is, in opposition to the more European depictions from those who had come before them, artists such as John Glover, Eugene von Guérard, Conrad Martens and Nicholas Chevalier. The emphasis on their interest in capturing an *Australian* Australia critically overshadowed all else. The problem with this interpretation is that it assumes those identified with 'Heidelberg' had a singular purpose and, simultaneously, applied that purpose to nationalistic ends. In fact, the nationalism of the period – specifically the significance of the period in which these artists worked, a period leading up to Australian Federation in 1901, and later the importance of establishing national, heroic traditions at the time of the First World War – focused on those elements of landscape painting that best supported a nationalist cause. Similarly, the identification of the 'Heidelberg School' with French Impressionist techniques elevated notions of the group's political status, emphasizing their role as revolutionary artists and downplaying their connections with other modes of representation. Therefore, works in which artists identified with 'Heidelberg' painted dim city scenes or portraits of public figures, or even landscapes featuring rain or darkness were not critically accentuated. This use of landscape as tradable representation, politically charged and nationalistically toned, bears relevance to how Australian landscapes, filtered through non-indigenous eyes, have informed filmic culture. A comparative piece of Australian art history, that of Papunya Tula, adds important contrast.

The birth of the Papunya Tula indigenous Australian art movement owes something significant to the figure Geoffrey Bardon. Bardon, a white, Sydney-born art teacher who, having previously abandoned the study of law for the study of art, arrived at Papunya, a remote Aboriginal settlement 240 kilometres northwest of Alice Springs, in 1971. Over a period of around eighteen months Bardon, a graduate of the National Art School, worked closely with the indigenous painters who were to become founders of the Papunya Tula art movement. Some of this involvement meant encouraging the transposing of patterns created in sand and earth into works done in paint on board; other aspects included the encouragement of painting activity among a range of indigenous participants and, ultimately, the invigoration of a cultural sense borne out of independence from the European notions imposed in and around the remote settlement in which he was working. Finally, Bardon's involvement raised the value of the completed art-works, becoming the bridge to commercial recognition for the indigenous artists of Papunya, a commercial recognition which later amounted to a sizeable economic contribution.

What is notable, beyond Bardon's involvement, in the story of the indigenous Australian art of the Western Desert, or 'dot art' as it became known, is the way in which representations of indigenous Australian ideals were provided with a viable conduit at a point in history where such viability was very far from guaranteed in Australia's white political and economic agenda. Certainly, not all those works of dot art emerging from Papunya were landscape works – most certainly not in the sense of landscape borne out of a European tradition – but many depict the relationship between indigenous Australian ceremony and ritual and the landscape that incorporates elements of those aboriginal metaphysical relationships and, in depicting these, often through aspects of shape and story and colour in which journeys and characters have specific roles, these works declare a relationship with the environment that is dissimilar to that held by European settlers.

If the aesthetics of Australian filmic landscapes, similarly, tell us anything it is that it has taken some years for an indigenous viewpoint to emerge from within a European settler environment and to begin to use film as a mode of representation that can challenge as well as 'adjust', as Tom O'Regan might well describe it, the representations borne out of an alternate tradition. This, essentially post-colonial, analysis would seem to offer some sense of the way in which abrogation, appropriation and disempowerment have their own evolutionary mode. And yet, there remain questions, not least founded in such films as *Rabbit-Proof Fence*, about the relationship between this kind of analysis and a thorough theorization of the appearance of landscape in film.

## Suggestions for a theory of filmic landscapes

Much has been left out of the discussion so far. For example, what of those films made by a variety of Australian settlers whose backgrounds are not all to be summarily grouped under the term 'European' or, indeed, 'Asian' or any other continental grouping – none of these descriptions accurately describe the variety of cultural and personal heritages held in individual filmic depictions of Australian landscapes. How, equally, to subdivide an analysis between key personnel in the production of a film text, and to determine in whose realm the depiction of landscape most obviously falls? Thinking in auteurist terms it might seem logical to point to a film's director, but the nature of landscape representation is such that the director here is unlikely to be key to the representation, and perhaps not even as strongly involved as he or she might be in the choice and deployment of actors or the style and direction of a script. Thus more analysis might need to be undertaken with regard the role of cinematographers in the politics and aesthetics of filmic landscapes.

What to make, then, of a film such as Rolf de Heer and Peter Djigirr's film *Ten Canoes* (2006), which seems to bring together some elements of the European settler and indigenous viewpoints mentioned earlier, even to the extent of being promoted as 'A Film by Rolf de Heer and the People of Ramingining'? (The town of Ramingining, in the Arafura Swamp area of northern Australia, being traditional territory to indigenous Australian David Gulpilil, the actor who brought the story to de Heer's attention, when working with him on the film *The Tracker* (2002), a well-known Australian actor, having first appeared in Nicolas Roeg's *Walkabout* (1971).) The *Ten Canoes* press pack recalls:

> There are three versions of the film in existence so far: there's the version that has Yolngu languages dialogue with English subtitles and English storytelling by David Gulpilil; there's the version that has both Yolngu languages dialogue and storytelling in Mandalpingu by David, with English subtitles; and there's the Yolngu version, no subtitles, everything in the languages of the people whose film it is.[6]

So the languages of the film – indigenous languages contrasted with English – prove to be a point of emphasis, but what of the depiction of landscape. The cinematographer on *Ten Canoes* is Ian Jones, the second unit director on *Rabbit-Proof Fence*, a regular de Heer crew member, and the steadicam operator on Noyce's *Clear and Present Danger*. Thus the debate simply comes full circle. To suggest a mode of considering filmic landscapes – highlighted by the case of landscapes in Australian cinema – a set of theoretical positions might best be put forward:

First, that the depiction of landscape in film carries cultural and political significance; second, that film, with its naturally generative visual and aural qualities, is capable of utilizing depictions of landscapes to overlay, reinforce, destabilize or even challenge the conditions of story, theme and subject presented in film; third, that the control of the depiction of landscape is perhaps less centralized that the control of many other elements of film, and therefore requires greater attention to the influence and impact of crew members, especially those associated with the quality and style of cinematography; fourth, that consideration of filmic landscapes benefits from some comparative considerations, especially where landscapes can take on aspects of changing historical and cultural conditions; and, finally, that filmic landscapes are never neutral in depiction or impact.

## Notes

1. Barbara Ching and Gerald W. Creed, *Knowing Your Place: Rural Identity and Cultural Hierarchy* (London: Routledge, 1997), 3.
2. Kathryn Millard, 'Interview with Rachel Perkins', in *Senses of Cinema* (2001), http://esvc001106. wic016u.server-web.com/contents/01/17/moon_interview_perkins.html. Accessed June 2004.
3. 'Rabbit-Proof Fence', Internet Movie Database, http://www.imdb.com/title/tt0252444/. Accessed November 2003.
4. Tom O'Regan, *Australian National Cinema* (London: Routledge, 1996), 106.
5. 'Mateship', meaning the promotion of the virtues of egalitarianism, loyalty and friendship, but connected specifically with ideas of an Australian identity forged primarily in settler/pioneer environments and raised to the status defining myth in time of turmoil (e.g. the First and Second World Wars). 'Dinky-di', an Australian term, meaning 'genuine'. 'ANZAC': the Australian and New Zealand Army Corps; often also connected with the ethos of mateship.
6. *Ten Canoes* press pack, http://www.tencanoes.com.au/tencanoes/pdf/Background.pdf. Accessed June 2006.

# Chapter 16

Battlefields of Vision: New Zealand Filmscapes

Jonathan Rayner

'New Zealand' offers at best an integration model which ends up privileging the Pakeha over the Maori… 'Aotearoa' will most likely remain as a Maori version of the national historical romance along with its narratives of Utopia and Fall. However, Aotearoa does still reverse the New Zealand mythology by allowing the two cultures to occupy different spaces within the same land…In theory and practice there can be then a New Zealand and an Aotearoa, a national mythology and a bicultural mythology which relativizes it. Each other's Other. New Zealand/Aotearoa.[1]

Peter Jackson's stage management of New Zealand landscapes throughout the *Lord of the Rings* trilogy has resulted in their worldwide familiarity, in the guises of Tolkien's Shire, Mordor and Riddermark. That these features of recognition are simultaneously sources of dispute (as to their fidelity to the author's vision or their logic within the director's conception of it, quite apart from enduring controversies over land ownership) underlines the New Zealand landscape's problematic cultural status, as a point of pride nationally and internationally, and a site of division, even to the point of nomenclature, for specific groups of its inhabitants.[2] Discrete meanings attached to the land emanate from these groups, more as indicators of difference than unchanging terms of disagreement, for both internal and international consumption.

The contention in this chapter is not just that the cinematic New Zealand landscape is bipolar, bivalent or divided (between North and South Islands, Maori and Pakeha, men and women) but is actively modified and multiplied in its meanings and interpretations by a diverse, indigenous filmmaking community. The significance with which the represented landscape is invested is also reliant upon readerly and writerly perspectives: 'What you see depends on who you are.'[3] Since the end of the 1970s, landscape as filmscape in New Zealand has been aestheticized, indigenized and gendered, acculturated, digitized and internationalized as a key commercial and cultural resource for the renewed national cinema. Mapping this process across the generic formulae and aesthetic strategies of New Zealand filmmaking reveals the importance of the land in the iteration and integration of competing cultural discourses, and the mobilization of the country's varied and distinctive environments within the national and international cinematic project. The working-through of relationships with the land (with the environment serving as the location, articulation or symbol of social, familial and cultural discord), which underpins the use of landscape in New Zealand cinema, marks the country's natural and social geographies as sites of continuous conflict.

The divisions and distinctions marked by the duplication of the naming of New Zealand/ Aotearoa find their parallel in the ambiguous status of landscape as *mise-en-scène* in the cinema. Does the landscape appear as a realist record, the only authentic and unperformed element in the frame, or does its conspicuous and eloquent presence, as a foregrounded background, remind us insistently of an idiomatic and rhetorical address, a deliberately incorporated performance of acculturated meanings? In short, how does a geographical landscape become a filmscape? Through a survey of a series of examples, which will be used to illustrate five thematic clusters or concentrations within the output of the national cinema, the shifting status of the national landscape will be considered, in its manifestations as a realist presence, an emblematic expression and a malleable spectacle.

## Travellers and outcasts: Landscape as male arena

The first features that appeared during the filmmaking revival in the late 1970s were independent productions, or relied on support from the Arts Council or New Zealand Film Commission. Two early films that originated key aspects of theme and characterization were *Wild Man* (Geoff Murphy, 1977) and *Sleeping Dogs* (Roger Donaldson, 1977). Murphy's short feature drew inspiration from the American Western. The New Zealand setting became the most westerly of wild frontiers, and the most barbarous of Barbary coasts, giving scope for raucous, scandalous and illegal behaviour in its narrative of confidence men at large in nineteenth-century pioneer towns. Donaldson's film (on which Murphy also collaborated) imagined a totalitarian state of the near-future, in which the countryside becomes a battleground in the fight against political repression. Several influential characteristics can be discerned in these early examples: the male protagonists appear as ironic or non-committal heroes (or are actively anti-heroic); the males' oppositional stance is derived almost by default from an instinctive non-conformity; retreat to the rural environment provides the opportunity to contest societal convention, or overturn it in carnivalesque abandon and, relatedly, in these narratives, blackly comedic and tragic elements become inseparably intertwined. These elements, apparent in the joviality in scamming which hides betrayal in Murphy's film, and the laughable but lethal Boy-Scout resistance movement in Donaldson's, can be traced through the subsequent examples of dysfunctional homes and heroes, characterizations embracing immature and iconoclastic behaviour and narratives with fateful and farcical outcomes which emerged through the 1980s.

The landscape becomes a key component in the depiction of the New Zealand male's predisposition towards non-conformity and marginalization. John Mulgan's *Man Alone* (1939) is the literary precedent for the filmic representation of the Pakeha male's aggression towards and retreat from society, from *Sleeping Dogs* onwards. Marital failure, ostracism, sexual violence and innate hostility mark the behaviour of the male, and predetermine his tragic expulsion or willing exile from the nuclear family and civilized society in *Smash Palace* (Roger Donaldson, 1981), *Bad Blood* (Mike Newell, 1982) and *Heart of the Stag* (Michael

Firth, 1984). Even when withdrawal from the conventional social landscape is incomplete, the environment appears tarnished symbolically by the male's action. In Donaldson's film, the 'palace' of the title is a sprawling junkyard symbolic of the male's self-destructive tendencies: in *The Scarecrow* (Sam Pillsbury, 1982), the arrival of a murderous stranger draws investigators to the incongruous rubbish tip on the outskirts of a quaint country town. Instead of stasis, security and social responsibility, the males' existences are characterized by nomadic, hazardous and anti-social activities, which both exploit and emblematize a fluid, under-populated, frontier-like environment.

The social disengagement and antagonism of the Kiwi male reaches its comedic peak in *Goodbye Pork Pie* (Geoff Murphy, 1980). A pair of drop-outs, John (Tony Barry) and Gerry (Kelly Johnson) drive a stolen rental car from one end of the country to the other, causing chaos and committing minor crimes en route. Murphy's comic road movie became the highest grossing New Zealand film to date.[4] Its authentic illustration of landscapes and landmarks from Kaitaia to Invercargill offered a readily recognizable setting for home audiences, which was still a novelty at that time.[5] The odyssey becomes imbued with an undifferentiated aura of rebellion, because of the range of social and behavioural taboos infringed along the way. John and Gerry taunt and evade the police, shoplift and steal petrol, take drugs and have sex with a hitchhiker, establishing themselves as a 'gang' which resembles a mobile counter-cultural commune. However, their revelling in disruption and indulgence of the space and freedom offered by the country and its roads belies the restraint and conformity which gains upon them. While their car is stripped bare and its parts sold to buy and barter supplies to keep going, the gang is gradually dissolved by the arrest of their female companion, Gerry's death at the hands of the authorities and John's continuance of the journey at all costs. The trip which John seems to take on a whim and prolong as an obsession is in fact carrying him to his estranged girlfriend on the south coast: the final outcome of the gang's unconventional conduct is his reintegration in a highly conventional couple. The landscape, which can be celebrated as a non-judgmental arena for the men's antics, is also just a void to be traversed arbitrarily and heedlessly, for conservative as much as iconoclastic ends.

## Descent and disease: Landscape as spiritual determinant

In comparison with the frivolity and recklessness that marks the itinerant behaviour of the males in the films of Murphy and Donaldson, Vincent Ward's protagonists undertake tests and quests, crusades and pilgrimages, driven by fervour and faith. The landscapes they traverse appear as indifferent, unforgiving or malicious as the fates and deities which impel them. If the landscapes in the films of his contemporaries assume values derived from American generic cinema, as settings for the causes and effects of human action, the landscapes of Ward's spiritual mysteries are tracts of tribulation, and proving grounds for piety.

*Vigil* (1984) contrasts the portrayal of the harsh and brutal life to be endured on an isolated hill farm with the heightened subjective perceptions of a pre-pubescent girl. The barren hilltops where the characters eke out a tenuous existence appear almost monochromatic in the film's muted colour-scheme, and their amorphous, medieval costumes distance the action from any recognizable era. The onset of Toss's (Fiona Kay) sexual maturity coincides with her father's death, who falls from a precipice trying to rescue a ewe, and the appearance of Ethan (Frank Whitten), an inscrutable hunter who both befriends and menaces the daughter and her widowed mother. In the child's mind, the convergence of events is fated rather than coincidental, with one father figure guilty of the death of the other on the elemental battleground. By privileging the child's perception, *Vigil* undermines narrative coherence: in place of an unequivocal pattern of causes and effects, intuitive and oneiric associations link the characters to each other and to the blighted land.

As she seeks to understand and transcend her father's death, Toss engages in pseudo-spiritual rituals. In a natural amphitheatre formed by exposed roots and decaying branches, she plants a dead tree, buries a plate of food at its base and douses it in lamb's blood. Her sacrificial offering seems directed to a pantheistic spirit of the land rather than to an ethereal deity, suggesting an origin and responsibility for the traumatic events in the earth itself. However, the events following Toss's devotions are accompanied by a worsening of the weather and a further deterioration of the family. Storms uproot Toss's tree, her mother succumbs to Ethan and then decides to abandon the farm, as it appears impossible to thrive in the valley in the face of the ordeal of the elements. As Ethan supplants her father, Toss is afflicted by a series of visionary dreams. One of these shows Ethan and her father duelling to the death with farming tools; later she imagines herself sheared by Ethan in the sheep shed. The sexual inference of this sacrificial submission to Ethan connects with an earlier scene, when blood sprays on Toss's face during the docking of the lambs, and also a subsequent one, in the blood of her first period which coincides with her subjective visions. Rather than symbolizing the settler's appetite for territory, Ethan's rapaciousness seems to embody the land's adversarial character towards those seeking to exploit it. The ambiguous drawing of his character opens the film to post-colonial as well as spiritual or psychological interpretations. The valley which rebuffs the family's efforts at subsistence appears as an anti-Eden, or a post-lapsarian world abandoned by God. When Toss expresses her belief to Ethan, that 'God doesn't care', he qualifies or corrects her by retorting 'Does the sky care? Do the hills care?' Ethan, seen gazing down on the farm from his hut, with his face crossed by clouds reflected in its windows, remains as impassive and remote from the family's suffering as the land, though both are implicated in its tragedy.

The landscape contains trials of another sort for the pilgrims in *The Navigator: A Medieval Odyssey* (1988). The opposition between humanity and nature which drives *Vigil* is replaced by the barely contained extremes of the modern and medieval worlds, and northern and southern hemispheres in *The Navigator*. A group of peasants in medieval Cumbria embark on a journey to raise a cross on a distant cathedral, as an offering to save their village from the Black Death. They mine through the earth, and emerge in present-day Auckland, a city afflicted by a modern plague and endangered by nuclear war. In effect, the pilgrimage becomes a transmuted voyage of discovery and colonial settlement, and a contemplation of modernity and national identity linked to recognizable landscapes (the Southern Alps being used for scenes set in Cumbria, and the modern city in the film's second half).

The city of the present provides updated parallels to the fears of the Middle Ages. Bemused foundry workers cast the cross required by the pilgrims out of charity, since their livelihoods are threatened economically (through redundancy) rather than spiritually (through disease and judgment). The pestilence of the past is evoked by images of the modern scourge of Aids, viewed by the pilgrims on television screens accompanied by footage of nuclear submarines, debates on New Zealand's troubled membership of the ANZUS alliance and the untenable nature of the country's 'nuclear-free' stance in the political climate of the late 1980s. The apocalyptic threat contained in these images connects with the pilgrims' terrified reaction to a submarine surfacing in Auckland harbour. Their conviction that this must be the Leviathan expected on the Day of Judgement connects the religious turmoil of the past with contemporary global (but also in this case poignantly national) fears of Armageddon. Such temporal and interpretative leaps set Ward's films apart, treating landscape suggestively, allusively and enigmatically. This cinematic expression is as highly personalized for the director as it is subjectified by his protagonists, and yet it also remains specifically and pertinently national in its reference and relevance.

## Landscape and restitution

Europe might have Culture, but New Zealand has Nature – the bush, the sea, the fjords and the mountains. Behind what some might judge as an essentialist and romantic attachment lie important historical determinants. For Maori, the land is intricately tied up with *whakapapa* and *turangawaewae*, their family line, ancestry and their determination to 'have a place to stand.'[6]

The threat of displacement aimed at Maori culture, entailed by territorial dispossession and submergence within Pakeha geographies and ideologies, is encapsulated in one of New Zealand cinema's iconic illustrations of landscape manipulation: the picture of a stereotypical pastoral ideal, revealed to be an illusory advertising image overlooking an urban slum, which opens *Once Were Warriors* (Lee Tamahori, 1993). The social realism implied by this image of falsehood suggests few places for indigenous people to 'stand' in the contemporary urban environment, and like other Maori-produced and directed features, Tamahori's film portrays a retreat to rural settings with a concomitant return to traditional community values, as a balance is sought between modern urbanity and rural traditionalism.

*Mauri* (Life Force, Merata Mita, 1988) suggests a natural landscape into which human actions are absorbed, on which human emotion is reflected, and in which human fates are predicted. Like other films addressing Maori cultural concerns, the female director's debut feature appears to offer the promise of restitution and harmony between communities. As in *Ngati* (Barry Barclay, 1987), the physical illnesses and secrets of cultural identity harboured by individuals effect a pervasive influence on the social landscape of mixed Maori-Pakeha communities: as in *Te Rua* (The Store House, Barry Barclay, 1991), the revelation of secrets leads to a spiritual restoration within the communities, which also encompasses a recuperation of differences between races and generations.

As the tribal matriarch Kara (Eva Rickard) nears the end of her life, she worries about the mental and emotional health of Rewi (Anzac Wallace), the loner who returned to the remote North Island settlement after a long absence. Rewi vies with Pakeha landowner Steve (James Heyward) for the affection of Ramari (Susan D. Ramari Paul), but despite her reciprocation of his love he refuses to marry her because of his hidden past. Semmons, Steve's father (played by Geoff Murphy), who acquired his property dishonestly from Rewi's father, will not tolerate his son marrying a Maori woman: he believes Ramari merely wants to get the land back for the Maori community through marriage. From her privileged position, Kara offers advice to the troubled and alienated members of the community – Rewi and his cousin Willie (Willie Raana) – and passes on traditions to young Awatea (Rangimarie Delamere). On a picnic, Kara explains to Awatea how she will go over a nearby hill on her way to Hawaiki when she dies.

Rewi avoids contact with family members and retreats to the wilderness: he kills game and lives rough when he is sought in connection with Semmons' death after Ramari's and Steve's wedding. However, in contrast to the characterization of alienated white males, this withdrawal from society (or rather the attempted evasion of social censure for one's actions) is shown to be no cure for guilt and shame. The numerous parallels and balances evoked in the narrative between characters and the interrelated dilemmas seem to predict their resolution, with the landscape forming an integral part of the cyclical pattern. The death of Semmons answers that of Rewi's father in connection with possession of the land, and Steve raises his child with Ramari although he knows Rewi to be the father. Rewi admits to the dying Kara that he is an impostor. He took Rewi's identity following the latter's accidental death to escape a life of crime, but has been haunted by the memory ever since. Kara instructs him to ask forgiveness, and his release from guilt is accompanied by his apprehension by the police, and paired with Kara's passing. The birth of Hinemoa's (Ana Hine Aro Kura Thrupp) child during the title sequence connects with Kara's death at the end, which is also marked by Awatea's run up the hill to watch her departing spirit.

Natural metaphors punctuate and elucidate this narrative. Through her magnifying glass, Awatea studies a stick insect in the Semmons' garden, while father and son argue nearby; she looks at barbs on the wire marking the disputed territory as Willie returns to the settlement; and she examines a spider's web as the police search for Rewi. These symbols reinforce aspects of characterization (Semmons camouflages himself as a scarecrow in his own fields, to ward off the 'tar babies' and the Maori constable who aspires to trap Rewi is despised by the community) and accompany the most enigmatic, recurring natural image of the film: that of a seabird flying over the coast in slow-motion. This image appears when Kara buries Hinemoa's afterbirth (which is 'part of us, and must be returned to the land'), when she discusses her death with Awatea and lastly when Rewi is handcuffed on the shore. Rather than symbolizing defeat or loss, the bird acts as a metaphor for the aptness of natural cycles, completed as fittingly in Rewi's confession and remorse as in Kara's death.

A similar pattern of male retreat (either from responsibility or into hidebound tradition) being answered by female emancipation is present in *Whale Rider* (Niki Caro, 2002). Pai (Keisha Castle-Hughes) is ostracized by her grandfather Koro (Rawiri Paratene) the tribal leader, because her twin brother, destined to be the next chief, dies at birth. Pai's father exiles himself voluntarily from the family and community because of his father's unappeasable aspirations for his child and grandchild, leaving Pai to be raised and supported by her grandmother. Koro seeks the next leader, who will prove himself to be the descendant of their mythical ancestor Piakea the Whale Rider, among the boys of the tribe, and Pai provokes his wrath when she copies and learns the initiation rituals in secret. In his eyes, the threat posed by her transgression both causes and is encapsulated in the mass stranding of whales on the nearby beaches. However, Pai proves her loyalty to the tribe and the patriarch, as well as her destiny to supplant him, by guiding the leading bull whale back into the sea and saving the whole pod. The littoral zone of the coast assumes a symbolic significance, as an interstitial environment neither solely land or sea. The revelation of the burial site of a cultural transgressor on the shore in *Te Rua*, and the beach as the arena for the assumption and recognition of Pai's leadership, shows the tidal territory functioning as both a visualization of cultural change, and as a rhythmic indicator of traditional continuity. This capacity of the landscape to articulate divergence, if not outright contradiction, in the perception and expression of contemporary Maori culture, suggests its expressive potential and vindicates its aesthetic and symbolic inclusion in indigenous filmmaking.

## Outlandish behaviour

The recruitment of the landscape in the elucidation of indigenous culture on film is matched by its manipulation in the expression of gender-specific experience in films by female directors. The use of landscape in contemporary and period dramas (*Crush*, Alison Maclean, 1992 and *The Piano*, Jane Campion, 1993) can be contrasted with the manipulation (and even bypassing) of the physical environment in comparable films from male directors (*Desperate Remedies*, Peter Main and Stewart Wells, 1993 and *Heavenly Creatures*, Peter Jackson, 1994). The narratives of all four films pivot on sexual manipulation, repression and liberation, and use the diegetic environment for commentary on the vicissitudes of social containment.

Evoking Ward's allusive treatment of American antagonism, *Crush* depicts a lethal animosity between New Zealand and American women, embodied by the passive Christina (Donogh Rees) and sexualized Lane (Marcia Gay Harden), and played out across the natural landscape. While they are travelling to interview a novelist, Lane crashes their car, and while Christina recovers from her resulting paralysis, the American woman continues the assignment, penetrating the author's home and disrupting the lives and sexualities of its occupants. Prior to the accident, Christina has described the New Zealand landscape as 'totally benign', with a resultant mania of the inhabitants being to 'search for the snake' which is absent from the local fauna. The implication is that the American woman will play the serpent's role, tempting and corrupting the previously innocent locals.

Lane's androgynous appeal seduces both the author and his teenage daughter Angela (Caitlin Bossley). The repression her presence threatens to overpower is signalled in the title sequence by close ups of the geo-thermal springs at Rotorua, which Lane later visits with Angela. While it remains unclear whether Lane inspires the release of hidden passions or creates them where none previously existed, she is also endangered by them, as indicated by Angela's warning not to venture too near the boiling mud. First seen awaiting her lift by the roadside with an unsightly slagheap in the background, Lane is last seen as a broken and lifeless body at the bottom of a spectacular waterfall, her corpse both diminished to and distinguished by her artificially bright clothing, incongruous within the earth tones of the landscape. Angela and Christina, who have both attempted to curtail the American woman's influence, conspire in her removal from (and killing by) the landscape. Whether stimulated by jealousy, hatred or self-protection, Christina pushes Lane over the cliff, and Angela condones her eradication of the invading serpent.

The threat to the colonizer embodied in the landscape is conceived in equally complex terms in *The Piano*. The transportation of Ada (Holly Hunter) to colonial life and contracted marriage, and the bartering of her body and her musical instrument between male settlers, equates marriage and territorial acquisition. The land appears passively resistant to the colonizers' presence (vegetation snags clothing and blocks movement, while rain floods cleared ground), but a further analogy is made between the non-compliance of the land, the unfathomability of Maori 'neglect' of their territory (in contrast to its exploitation by the settlers) and Ada's circumvention of male desire and authority inflicted upon the female body.

The film's clichéd association between the natural landscape and an unfettered and liberating sexuality embodied by Ada and the Maori is a controversial feature of its characterization and ideology.[7] However, the critique of colonialism via feminism which it incorporates is more coherent than the mixed metaphors of sexuality and commodity which permeate *Desperate Remedies*' studio-bound vision of nineteenth-century settlement. While the artificiality of the port setting in *Desperate Remedies* (reminiscent of *The Blue Angel*, Josef von Sternberg, 1930 and *Querelle*, Rainer Werner Fassbinder, 1982) comments on the fragility of constructs of gender and sexuality, it depicts only fragmented and expressionistic spaces for action, in contrast to the filmically (rather than geographically) connected locations for commentary seen in *The Piano*.[8] The eloquent locations used in *The Piano*, like the allusive settings of *Crush* and abstract spaces of *Desperate Remedies*, anticipate the exclusive, additive landscapes of *Heavenly Creatures*, which also strive to communicate a subjective and gender-specific perception. Ironically, the oppositional landscapes augmented by private imagination and created to exclude reality, which offer a supplementary 'world' of escape in *Heavenly Creatures*, preview the shared, conservative pastoral and national fantasy which pervades the *Lord of the Rings* trilogy.

## The violence of fantasy

> Cinema is the very paradigm of an artificial, technological environment that has incorporated utopian fantasies of nature, kinetic power, spiritual truth and human connection.[9]

Peter Jackson's justifications for shooting the *Lord of the Rings* trilogy in New Zealand combined pragmatism with parochialism. In interview, he conceded that he preferred to make the films where he lived, obviating the need to leave his home country, but stressed the uniqueness of the varied and unspoiled New Zealand landscape, which permitted shooting in areas still unmarked by roads, habitation and human intervention.[10] The nostalgia of the pastoral, with an inherent yearning and lament for an idyllic past (both as physical place and idealized repository of values), inflects the trilogy from the first Elfish voice-over: 'The world is changed. I feel it in the water. I feel it in the earth…Much that once was is lost. For none now live who remember it.' A significant proportion of the trilogy's fantasy appeal lies in its evocation of this idyllic pastoralism. Ironically, but perhaps inevitably given the fundamental inability of historical or geographical reality to match the pastoral imagination, the vision of the innocent fantasy past which the trilogy offers cannot be furnished by even the pure New Zealand landscape. The chosen locations must be amended and augmented by special effects in order to play their roles.

Within the films' conceptualization of the conflict precipitated by the ring, a culture-nature opposition, which incorporates the literal and artificially enhanced landscape, comes to dominate the *mise-en-scène*. The characters, races and environments defending Middle Earth display the righteousness of their cause through their sympathy with the flora and fauna. Gandalf's staff is an unaltered branch, and his allies are horses, moths and eagles. Hobbiton is physically embedded in the turf of the Shire and the clasps of the Hobbits' cloaks, which reveal their whereabouts to their compatriots, echo the shape of leaves. Arwen (Liv Tyler) summons river waters to block the pursuit of the Nazgûl. The cities threatened by Mordor share a uniform white in their stonework, with the architecture of Rivendell attuned to the forests and waterfalls, and Helm's Deep and Minas Tirith appearing to be hewn from the valleys and mountains which surround them.

By comparison, Mordor is a blighted land of volcanoes and ash. The marsh which the heroes traverse to reach it is filled not with life, but with corpses. In place of the earth tones which distinguish the heroes' costumes, the Orcs and Uruk-Hai are clad in black and Sauron and the Balrog with volcanic and infernal flame. Saruman's pledging of Isengard to Sauron's cause leads to the rape of the landscape. His staff, in contrast to Gandalf's and mimicking the crowns of thorns which top the towers of Isengard and Mordor, is a crafted metal rod. The sequences representing the creation of the Uruk-Hai reinforce the distinction drawn between industry and empathy, culture and nature, as the trees are 'ripped down' to feed furnaces and forges. Saruman's voice-over at this point echoes the exposition: 'The world is changing. The Old World will burn in the fires of industry. The forests will fall…'. This ecological obscenity provokes a literalized environmental response, when the Ents (sentient, walking trees) attack and destroy Isengard, and an earthquake swallows Mordor and its armies at the saga's climax.

Clearly, the landscape and conventional, romantic readings of its beauty and diversity occupy crucial positions in the making and marketing of the trilogy. Locations bear a moral and narrative significance as well as a national signification. The pride involved in and invoked by the depiction of recognizable national landmarks touches local and international audiences, and turns the locations used (such as Tongariro National Park and the Waikato) into tourist attractions in their own right. Yet a concomitant pride in indigenous filmmaking must also encompass the New Zealand effects company (Wetta) tasked with transforming landscape into filmscape. The disingenuousness voice-over which opens the saga epitomizes the trilogy's ambiguous relationship to the landscape which it absorbs and re-expresses. The words hint at a mystery with which the sizeable Tolkien fan-base is already familiar, just as characters in the diegesis exhibit full knowledge of the ring, its power and those who desire it, despite its stated disappearance for thousands of years. Similarly, the foregrounding and recognition of New Zealand landscapes in the trilogy are based on an equal and opposite (mis-)recognition of them as Tolkien's fantasy realm. The alteration and amplification of the landscape with computer-generated imagery 'changes the world', entailing that as much is 'lost' from the reality of recognition, as is gained from the recognition of a geographical reality. Paradoxically, the trilogy's status as the greatest achievement of the New Zealand cinema and its propagation of images of a quintessential national landscape, is based on the realization of a filmscape which adjusts and surpasses the physical reality, in order to affirm its indivisibility from national and Tolkienesque ideals. The violence of the fantasy is wreaked upon the landscape as much as it is contained within it.

## Conclusion

The phantasmagoria of progress involves a sustained immersion within an artificial environment *that suggests technology's own ability to incorporate what it has generally excluded.* If the disappearance of nature is seen as a consequence of a burgeoning technosphere, then utopian technologies will incorporate Arcadia.[11]

In embracing a series of oppositional intensities in their narratives (North versus South, male versus female, Maori versus Pakeha), contemporary New Zealand cinema has engaged in the construction of a series of colloquial filmscapes from the national, natural environment. Paradoxically, in so doing it has foregrounded conflict not just in its treatment of national narrative (in portraying racial, sexual and international tension) but also in its handling of national territory, as a fluent cultural resource. This chapter's charting of the New Zealand landscape's cinematic appearance as a literal or figurative battlefield (grounding differences between sexes, generations, ethnicities and nationalities) implies not only conflict but potential territorial gain, and loss, in each depicted skirmish.

The addition of the Pakeha male to the natural landscape results in an anti-pastoral: a retreat from civilization which is brutalizing and regressive rather than pacifying and progressive. If films such as *Sleeping Dogs* and *Smash Palace*, which portray the experience of the Pakeha male fail to fortify his rightful place within the landscape, films such as *The Piano* and *Heavenly Creatures*, which emphasize an oppositional female subjectivity, seek to banish him from it altogether. Only in the films of indigenous filmmakers, such as *Mauri* and *Whale Rider*, are convergence and compromise reached between generations, genders and ethnicities. In what can be regarded as the ultimate project in the national cinema's utilization of the landscape, the *Lord of the Rings* trilogy proposes a consensual, pastoral (Pakeha?) definition of the national filmscape, which offers recognition and reassurance of the landscape's constant and conservative cultural value, for viewers both at home and abroad. The trilogy's wholesale augmentation of the landscape, in order to furnish the perfect filmscape for tourists and Tolkien fans alike, suggests the expenditure of the landscape as a national, cinematic artefact, but also perhaps its recyclability, as a renewable cultural resource, suitable for the articulation of conservative as well as oppositional messages.

## Notes

1. Martin Blythe, *Naming the Other: Images of the Maori in New Zealand Film and Television* (Metuchen: Scarecrow Press, 1994), 234–235.
2. Guy Keleny, 'The incredible shrinking Tolkien', *Independent Review*, 27 December 2002, 13.
3. This line is given to the character of Birdie, played by Bill Kerr, in *Vigil* (Vincent Ward, 1984).
4. Helen Martin and Sam Edwards, *New Zealand Film 1912–1996* (Auckland: Oxford University Press, 1997), 76, 88.
5. Robin Bromby, 'In the picture – New Zealand', *Sight and Sound* 50 (1981), 152.
6. Annie Goldson, 'Piano recital', *Screen* 38 (1997), 277.
7. John Izod, '*The Piano*, the animus, and colonial experience', in Harriet Margolis (ed.), *Jane Campion's The Piano* (Cambridge: Cambridge University Press, 2000), 91–94.
8. Disparate locations across both North and South Islands are melded arbitrarily in the editing of Campion's film. Margolis, 18.
9. Scott Bukatman, 'The artificial infinite: On special effects and the sublime', in John Orr and Olga Taxidou (eds), *Post-war Cinema and Modernity: A Film Reader* (Edinburgh: Edinburgh University Press, 2000), 222.
10. Peter Jackson interviewed on *The South Bank Show*, ITV, 16 December 2001. The purposeful depopulation of the environment as a treasured national symbol echoes the directive relating to documentary filming of landscapes from the Government Publicity Office during the 1920s. See Jonathan Dennis, 'Restoring history', *Film History* 6 (1994), 118.
11. Bukatman, 222.

**Chapter 17**

The Landscapes of Canada's Features: Articulating Nation and Nature

Jim Leach

In *La région centrale* (1971), Canadian artist and avant-garde filmmaker Michael Snow filmed a wilderness landscape in northern Quebec using a specially constructed camera that could be remote controlled to move in a complete sphere in any direction. The patterns of movement in this three-hour encounter with nature are designed to demonstrate the potential of the cinematic apparatus, freed from the conventions and constraints of narrative, but the film also calls into question the cultural practices of representing nature. Snow uses technology to expose what he sees as the ways in which Western culture has used technology to dominate nature, a project that implies mainstream cinema's complicity with a social order dedicated to 'finding a way to subject nature and other people to our will'.[1]

I referred to the subject of this film as a 'landscape', but, more accurately, Snow was trying to capture the experience of nature *before* it becomes landscape, before it is framed and made to serve aesthetic and cultural purposes. 'It's all in the framing' is the recurring refrain in Kevin McMahon's *The Falls* (1991), a film that explores changing perceptions of Niagara Falls, Canada's most famous natural landmark. The commentary quotes observers from different historical periods and shows how their ways of seeing the Falls correspond to the cultural ethos of each period. These observations are interspersed within a depiction of the present-day Falls as exploited by technology (producing electric power but also pollution) and the tourist industry.

The tension between the sublime and the abject in *The Falls* may reinforce the desire to break the frame that motivates *La région centrale*. However, frames are a necessary feature not just of art-works (such as landscapes) but also of the cultural processes whereby identities are constructed. The problem comes, as *The Falls* demonstrates, when the frames themselves come to seem natural and thus fixed. In Canada, the vexed problem of national identity can thus be addressed in terms of the difficulty of finding an appropriate frame. 'The Canadian sensibility', Northrop Frye famously argued, 'is less perplexed by the question "Who am I?" than by some such riddle as "Where is here?"'[2]

For Frye, 'the vast hinterland of the north, with its sense of mystery and fear of the unknown', defies the capacity of the human imagination and thus resists framing, becoming what he termed an 'obliterated environment'. However, he also complicated his account by using the same term to describe the modern development of 'a global civilization of jet planes, international hotels, and disappearing landmarks'.[3] Since Frye made this observation in 1971 (the same year as *La région centrale*), globalization has proceeded apace, and subsequent commentators have picked up on the implication that other countries now contend with the same kind of disorientation that has long shaped Canadian cultural traditions.

From Frye's perspective, the problem of national identity in Canada, and the consequent crises of national unity, are functions of the difficulty of translating space into place. In this essay, I will focus primarily on Canadian feature films and their representation of landscape – rural and urban – through visual and narrative conventions that frame it within discourses of national identity. Landscape interacts with narrative in these films to produce an often troubled and complicated relationship between nature and nation. If the landscape is an abiding core of the 'real' in Canadian experience, its imaginary manifestations are as fragmented and contested as the nation's cultural traditions. Canada's two official languages are often seen as producing cultures that have little in common with each other, but both have been deeply marked by the historical encounter with the environment.

One of the major defining features in Quebec culture until the 1950s was the ideology of *conservation* that stressed the importance of the land and the threat of modern urban life to Catholic and French traditions. The landscape paintings of the Group of Seven became something of a national icon in English Canada during the twentieth century. Although the ideas of the nation that lay behind these responses were very different, even opposed to each other, both involved a picturesque component that was more than outweighed by a stress on the vastness of the land and the harshness of the climate. Both traditions also depicted the landscape as a 'virgin' wilderness, thereby virtually writing Canada's native peoples out of the account.

In Quebec, the ideology of *conservation* dominated the only sustained production of feature films in Canada prior to the 1960s. Between 1944 and 1953, a cycle of films, made in local studios in Quebec, proved enormously popular with domestic audiences. In their plots and iconography, these films stressed the importance of the land as 'the only guarantee of the perpetuation of the Catholic faith and French culture, the city being a place of perdition and industry, an invention of the devil'.[4] They depicted rural communities established by settlers sent by the church into the remote areas of northern Quebec, where they struggled to clear the land of trees and to withstand the rigours of the climate.

This ideology had already been celebrated on film by the Abbé Maurice Proulx who documented the colonization of the Abitibi region in the 1930s, and the church now supported the production of feature films that reinforce its values. Yet, while the rural settings may look idyllic, the stories acted out within them reveal what Christiane Tremblay-Daviault calls a 'collective malaise'.[5] The twin pillars of *conservation*, the church and the family, usually fail to protect the innocent, and one critic has even claimed that they demonstrate 'the impossibility of life in the country'.[6] In the two most popular films, *Un Homme et son péché* (Paul Gury, 1948) and *La Petite Aurore, l'enfant martyre* (Yves Bigras, 1952), the narrative centres on monstrous figures – an old miser who makes the life of his young wife miserable, a stepmother who abuses a young girl until she dies – whose cruelty can be seen as either a product of the harshness of the natural conditions or as a symptom of an oppressed society turned in on itself (or both).

These films use location shots to create a specific sense of place, but they also rely heavily on studio sets and stereotyped characters. The way of life that they depict was, in any case, already under threat from the modernizing movement known as the Quiet Revolution, whose triumph is usually signified by the election of a liberal government in 1960. In the years that followed, there was a shift away from a sense of identity rooted in the land to an attempt to build a new sense of a Québécois identity capable of meeting the challenges of the modern world. However, for all its achievements, this endeavour found it difficult to define the extent to which it involved a break, or a continuity, with the past, and depictions of nature and rural life still find it difficult to shake off the old connotations.[7]

It was the landscape painting of the Group of Seven that came to define the image of the north in English Canada, and their representations of the landscape became so familiar that it is now difficult to make images of the northern landscape that do not evoke them.[8] However, while these paintings often came to serve as emblems of the national culture, the effect was very different from the ties between land and nation in Quebec. Whereas the emphasis in Quebec was on the human effort to occupy an inhospitable environment, the English-Canadian tradition stressed the emptiness of the land and the sublime grandeur of untamed nature.

One of the few films to address the implications of this tradition was *The Far Shore* (1976), the only feature film directed by Joyce Wieland, who was closely associated with Michael Snow and whose art-work and avant-garde films explored the role of the landscape in myths of national identity. Wieland created a fictional account of the events leading up to the death of Tom Thomson, a painter closely associated with the Group of Seven and whose disappearance in the backwoods remains an unsolved mystery. In the film, he is shot because of his affair with the Québécois wife of an English-Canadian engineer, who exploits the natural environment with which the artist and his lover wish to live in harmony.

One of the reasons why the paintings of the Group of Seven had relatively little impact on Canadian cinema is that, until the 1960s, the landscape had largely been framed on film through the documentary lens. Canada's small population in the early twentieth century, and its geographical proximity to the United States, meant that it was unable to develop a significant national cinema and that it became part of Hollywood's (North American) domestic market. Although the creation of the National Film Board of Canada in 1939 signalled the government's sense of the importance of cinema as a nation-building tool, it also ensured that the emphasis would be on the documentary tradition rather than on competing with Hollywood for the popular audience.[9]

Underlying this project was the documentary claim to 'authenticity', in which the use of actual locations became a prime signifier of the nation's existence. The locations of most interest to the documentary movement were primarily those of modern industrial and urban life, but two feature films, produced by the NFB in the early 1960s, used natural environments to develop arguments about national identity.

*Pour la suite du monde* (Pierre Perrault and Michel Brault, 1963) is a documentary in which Brault's stunning images of the Ile-aux-coudres in the St Lawrence river become the setting for the verbal testimony of the people of the remote island community. Starting from a project to revive the abandoned practice of trapping beluga whales, the film becomes a meditation on cultural community, with the language and accents of the islanders offering evidence of the historical roots of Quebec culture, uncontaminated by the increasingly 'global' influences on urban life. In particular, the figure of Alexis Tremblay, an islander with a lively memory of the old days, became an icon of the independence movement, although the film also sparked a debate about the relevance of its vision for contemporary Quebec.

The NFB's English-language equivalent was *Drylanders* (Don Haldane, 1964), a historical fiction film, shot on location to capture the vastness of the prairie landscape and to provide 'documentary' authenticity to the depiction of the hardships endured by the Greer family who move from Montreal to Saskatchewan in 1907. After struggling to establish a farm on the wind-swept prairies, they finally succeed in the 1920s, but drought and the Depression in the 1930s again threaten the survival of the farm. The film ends with the death of Dan Greer in 1938, just before the drought ends, but his work is seen to have helped create the grain farms that were vital to the growth of the nation.

Both films turned to the rural past to provide a basis for national identity at a time when there was increasing concern with the alienating effects of urbanization, the other kind of obliterated environment identified by Frye. It was this environment that became the main focus of a new wave of documentary filmmakers at the NFB in the late 1950s. Breaking with the classical documentary (associated with the Board's founder John Grierson), with its dependence on an authoritative 'voice-of-god' commentator, the 'direct cinema' filmmakers used new lightweight equipment to document urban life. Their innovations, in such films as *The Days before Christmas* (1958) and *La Lutte* (Wrestling, 1961),[10] inspired several young filmmakers to apply them to fiction film production.

The most influential were *Nobody Waved Goodbye* (Don Owen) and *Le Chat dans le sac* (Gilles Groulx), both produced at the NFB in 1964 using budgets intended for documentary shorts. In both films, the city (Toronto and Montreal, respectively) proves to be an alienating environment, although it is not demonized as in the post-war Quebec films. Their adolescent male protagonists, in search of a viable sense of identity, represent not just the disillusionment of modern youth but also the problems of defining a national identity in Canada. At the end of *Nobody Waved Goodbye*, Peter steals a car from the parking lot where he works as an attendant, abandons his girlfriend when she announces that she is pregnant and drives off into the void of a neon-lit urban expressway. In the final image of *Le Chat dans le sac*, Claude is also alone, having left the city and abandoned his anglophone girlfriend, and he stands in a snow-covered landscape watching a young woman skating on a frozen pond.

These films, and others like them, established location shooting as a key element in a realist tradition that resonated with Frye's insistence that 'identity is local and regional' and that the tension between the 'political sense of unity and the imaginative sense of locality is the essence of whatever the word "Canadian" means'.[11] They inspired a cycle of 'direct cinema' fiction films that place their stories within sharply observed regional settings. Yet, while their visual appeal stems from their attention to recognizable and distinctive locations, the narratives deal with characters who want to escape from them. The failure to integrate regional identity into a unifying idea of the nation is linked to the economic deprivation of local communities and the frustration of the (usually) male protagonists who live there.

The narrative emphasis on failure in these films, whatever other pleasures they may have to offer, became a major hindrance to commercial success in a film industry whose distribution system was dominated by the Hollywood studios. However, two films – *Goin' Down the Road* (Don Shebib, 1970) and *Mon oncle Antoine* (My Uncle Antoine, Claude Jutra, 1971) – did achieve critical recognition (indeed they were quickly acclaimed as classic Canadian films) and a modest commercial success.

*Goin' Down the Road* begins with an aerial shot of Cape Breton Island in Nova Scotia. The following shots emphasize the natural beauty of the landscape but gradually begin to include man-made ruins that testify to the economic decline that provides the motivation for the departure of Joey and Pete for Toronto. When they drive into the city, Joey shouts exuberantly, 'Look out Toronto, here we come', before Shebib cuts to another aerial shot in which their car is hardly visible among the high-rise buildings, foreshadowing the imminent collapse of their illusions. The film rarely involves us with their point of view, as in classical narrative cinema, but rather adopts the observational style of direct cinema, the architecture of the prosperous city providing an ironic context for the men's attempts to assert themselves. In the final sequence, they are once more on the road, heading west, in the hope of achieving a better life in Vancouver.

*Mon oncle Antoine* begins with a panning shot across a landscape dominated by a hill that turns out to be made of waste from an asbestos mine. Although a caption locates the action in 'the asbestos region of Quebec not so long ago', and it was indeed filmed on location in this region, the temporal reference is rather vague, apparently referring to the beginning of the Quiet Revolution that overthrew the conservative traditions of the past. Yet there is little sign of protest in the film, and the visual cues sometimes suggest either an earlier or more recent period.[12] Its central character is Benoît, an adolescent who critically observes the adult community and discovers the pettiness and despair beneath the picturesque surface of their traditional way of life. The temporal ambiguity thus raises questions about the extent to which modern Quebec differs from the downtrodden society depicted in the film.

*Mon oncle Antoine* was produced by the NFB, but most of the 'direct cinema' films were made possible by the Canadian Film Development Corporation, established by the federal government after the earlier films had raised hopes that a film industry in Canada might now be a viable proposition. To some degree, as a tool of Canadian nationalism, the CFDC (which began operations in 1969) inherited the NFB's mandate to 'interpret Canada to Canadians and other nations'.[13] Yet its main purpose was to act as an investment bank to support films that would make money and thus establish a self-sufficient industry. Whereas the cultural objectives required films that in some way represented the Canadian 'here', the economic drive was towards films that would succeed in the international market (an imperative shaped by the government's ongoing refusal, under pressure from the Hollywood studios, to enact quotas on distribution and exhibition).

Although *Goin' Down the Road* and *Mon oncle Antoine* encouraged those who thought the future of Canadian cinema depended on small-budget realist films with distinctive Canadian settings, the frequent failure of later films in this mode, many of which received little or no distribution, called this strategy into question. Many producers attributed the problem to the lack of interest of international (specifically American) audiences in films about Canadians, and they started to make films that disguised their national origins. Since this approach conflicted directly with the emphasis on cultural specificity in the direct cinema films, the debate on the future of Canadian cinema became centrally concerned with the politics of location.

The economic goals of Canadian film policy came to the fore in 1974 when the federal government enacted the Capital Cost Allowance Act, which allowed a 100 per cent tax write-off on investment in Canadian films and led to a short-lived production boom. Although the direct cinema films had rarely received strong support from Canadian critics, there was widespread dismay at the films funded under the CCA, most of which avoided specific Canadian settings. For those spectators who knew the region in which a film was shot, the setting would be readily apparent, and many CCA films operate on the principle of showing but not naming the location. Others went to great lengths to eliminate specific cultural markers such as car license plates, Canadian money or local brand names, and still others introduced signs that identified Canadian landscapes as US settings.

Many of the CCA films were undistinguished, and they often went unreleased. However, the Act did help to establish the career of David Cronenberg, whose 'body horror' films made him one of Canada's most commercially successful directors but often disturbed critics who objected to the lack of cultural specificity in his films. In his CCA-supported film *Scanners* (1980), for example, the settings are nondescript modern industrial landscapes in which a sinister corporation experiments in mind control. Even when the setting is explicitly Canadian, as in *Videodrome* (1982) in which an infection is spread by cross-border television signals, the urban settings are equally characterless. Cronenberg's more recent films continue his use of obliterated environments: in *Crash* (1996), car crashes become a perverse source of stimulation in a city defined by the patterns of speeding traffic, while in *eXistenZ* (1999), both urban and rural landscapes are swallowed up in a virtual reality game.

As Robert Fothergill was one of the few critics to acknowledge at the time of the CCA boom, 'concealment of the locale is not necessarily a crime', and 'certain kinds of fiction positively require a vague location, free of specific associations'.[14] Many genre films (including Cronenberg's) depend less on specific markers of place than on an iconography that locates them in relation to other films in the same genre. The mean streets of film noir, for example, evoke Frye's obliterated urban environments, and it often matters little whether they belong in a specific city. When such locations can be identified, the tension between genre space and local space becomes an important element in a film's meanings and effects.

Don Shebib's *Between Friends* and Peter Pearson's *Paperback Hero* (both 1973) depend on the tensions between generic narratives and their identifiable Canadian settings. *Between Friends* ends with a heist goes drastically wrong in the wasteland around a mine in northern Ontario, in contrast to the slick job in California with which the film opens, while the main character in *Paperback Hero* is a hockey player in a small Saskatchewan town who behaves as if he is the marshall in a Hollywood Western, with disastrous results. In Quebec, several crime films, notably *Pouvoir intime* (Yves Simoneau, 1986) and *Un Zoo la nuit* (Jean-Claude Lauzon, 1987), used the violent imagery of the genre to evoke the political tensions surrounding the separatist debate. Both of these films are set in the seedy urban environments basic to the genre's iconography but end in rural landscapes that evoke the equally recognizable iconography of *conservation*.

Quebec critics debated the implications of such strategies in the context of the idea of *Américanité*, a concept that involves the adaptation of French cultural traditions to the North American setting but also a concern with the possible erosion of those traditions (as exemplified by the pressure to make films in English during the CCA era). For such critics, English-Canadian culture was already virtually indistinguishable from that of the United States, and the many films shot in vaguely North American settings seemed to support this view. The tension between genre space and local space disappears in these films, a state of affairs that is critically examined in *I Love a Man in Uniform* (David Wellington, 1993). Its central character is an actor who plays a cop in a TV crime show made in Toronto but set in an anonymous North American city. Although the film is itself shot on location, when the actor starts to identify with his character and walks the streets in costume, he is immediately accepted as a real cop, even by other policemen who wear the same generic uniform.

In this film, the blurring of generic and local space parallels the blurring of media images and reality that is a characteristic of most theories of the postmodern condition (and both processes can be seen as the product of Frye's second kind of obliterated environment). As Geoff Pevere has noted, even after the CCA boom, many films made in Ontario exhibited 'a conspicuous sense of placelessness', with the result that 'Ontario often seems like it could either be anywhere in North America or, more unsettlingly, nowhere at all'.[15] The obliterated environments in these films – and, as we shall see, this trend is also found in films made elsewhere in Canada – imply a culture in which the loss of a sense of a 'home' environment is a common experience.

One of the filmmakers cited by Pevere is Atom Egoyan, who captures the effect of his own films – and other films from this period – when he suggests that they deal with characters who 'never quite feel that they have the right to be where they are'.[16] While Egoyan claims that his films are 'very much the result of the city I made them in', he also points out that 'places in my films are concepts without a specific reference'.[17] His early films explore the impact of modern image technology (video and television) on the cultural identity of characters who feel cut off from their ethnic traditions. Egoyan's own Armenian heritage comes to the fore in *Calendar* (1993) and *Ararat* (2002): in the former, a photographer visits the homeland, but his shots of churches become picturesque illustrations for a calendar for migrants, while Canada is represented only by the interior of his apartment after his return; in the latter Armenia exists only as a film set in a film-within-the-film being shot in Toronto. Even when he transferred the rural community in *The Sweet Hereafter* (1997), based on an American novel, from upstate New York to the Canadian Rockies, the cultural references are so indeterminate that Egoyan was taken to task for setting the film 'anywhere – yet nowhere'.[18]

The motif of the obliterated environment appears in ever more ingenious ways in recent Canadian cinema. Gary Burns's *waydowntown* (2000) is set in the 'Plus 15' system of walkways that link the buildings in downtown Calgary and concerns four office workers who make a bet on who can avoid going outside for the longest time. A few brief insert shots indicate the location, but the glass-and-concrete buildings, fully equipped with surveillance cameras, are familiar features of life in most major cities. Although the system was designed to protect people from the cold winters, the director felt that 'it's sort of against the Canadian character – you should just deal with the elements', and Katherine Monk suggests that, in this film, 'the characters are not oppressed by snow and death, but by mountains of paperwork and dead-end jobs'.[19] These comments suggest that Frye's modern urban obliterated environment is replacing the primal one, subjecting it to a more literal obliteration.

The films of Vincent Natali also present us with environments from which all landmarks have been removed. In *Cube* (1997), a group of characters find themselves trapped in a mysterious structure containing a succession of cubic rooms full of traps, and the entire film consists of their efforts to break down the system and find their way out. *Nothing* (2003) begins with (computer-generated) images that set it in Toronto, with the dilapidated house of the two main characters isolated beneath a network of highways with the CN Tower in the background. This (relatively) specific setting suddenly fades away, and the two friends find themselves literally in the middle of nowhere, where they fall out and start to 'wish away' each other's possessions and then their bodies, until they are left as disembodied heads still arguing in white space.

As might be expected, Quebec films are usually more culturally specific. Yet several films point to the erosion of this specificity as a result of global and multicultural influences. In Lauzon's *Un zoo la nuit*, the father's apartment is shrinking due to the expansion of the Italian restaurant next door, while in *Léolo* (1992), Lauzon's surreal autobiography, a young boy in Montreal in the 1960s imagines that he is not French-Canadian but Italian. Denis Villeneuve's *Maelström* (1999) is set in contemporary Montreal, but its narrator is a fish (or several fish) lying on a chopping block in a dark cellar. The opening caption is in Norwegian, and the score includes a cantata with lyrics in that language. As Brenda Longfellow suggests, 'situating Norway as the site of the romantic sublime and archaic pre-modern can only be ironic given the absolute irrelevance of both to everyday life in a post-modern Québec'.[20]

The idea of an obliterated environment takes on a new meaning in the many diasporic films that represent the experience of the displaced cultural groups that have established themselves in Canada, as in most Western industrial nations. Some key films from the 1990s were *Masala* (Srinivas Krishna, 1991), *Double Happiness* (Mina Shum, 1994) and *Rude* (Clement Virgo, 1995), exploring questions of identity from the perspective of the East Indian, Chinese and Caribbean communities, respectively. As Krishna puts it, these films deal with what happens when 'the home you thought was home only exists in memory'.[21] Their stories of uprooted cultures take place in Canadian settings represented with varying degrees of specificity, but in Deepa Mehta's *Bollywood/Hollywood* (2002), a celebration of new hybrid identities, Canada becomes the slash between two dominant film traditions from elsewhere.

It is rather less easy to welcome hybrid identities in Quebec, given the perceived threat to the distinct culture on which the case for sovereignty is based. After all, the term 'French-Canadian' was rejected because its hybridity seemed a sign of weakness. There have been films that deal with the experience of diasporic Canadians in Quebec, but the recent box-office success of Quebec cinema with domestic audiences has largely been due to films that deal with (and sometimes question) traditional forms of identity. Popular comedies, such as the *Les Boys* series and Pierre Falardeau's Elvis Gratton films, exploit the stereotypes of Quebec culture, reaffirming them in the first case and savagely attacking them in the second.[22]

The success of Quebec cinema has also encouraged the emergence of what might be called the Quebec heritage film. *Un Homme et son péché* (Charles Binamé, 2002), a re-make of the 1940s film, broke all box-office records in Quebec, offering an uninhibited melodrama in which the northern landscape plays a much greater, and more spectacular, role than it does in the original. *Aurore* (Luc Dionne, 2005) is also based on the earlier film about an abused child, although it also draws on the historical record of the actual case that inspired the original, and the land is again more visually prominent. These films, and others in the same vein, create the pleasure of recognition of the traditional settings and iconography even as they adopt an ambivalent perspective on them.

The idea of heritage is, of course, a response to the disorientation of an increasingly global society in which the experience of both nature and of distinctive cultures (and of the links between them) is being eroded. A film that encapsulates many of the issues at stake in this situation is *Atanarjuat the Fast Runner* (Zacharias Kunuk, 2000). The first feature film in the Inuktitut language, it tells a story derived from ancient myths, set in an Arctic landscape and made possible by the use of digital cameras that would not freeze up in the subzero temperatures. In the most striking sequence, the title character runs naked across the ice to escape after being ambushed in his sleep, and the mythic struggle of good and evil is vividly embodied in these elemental images of the naked man racing across the vast barren landscape.

For Inuit audiences, the film was a way to make contact with a cultural heritage previously only occasionally represented by white filmmakers, most famously by Robert Flaherty in *Nanook of the North* (1921). The film was also a response to the fear that this culture would be obliterated by technology and media imported from the south, even though the filmmakers appropriated these modern means to represent the past. For other audiences, the location shooting in the Arctic creates a strong sense of 'authenticity' (a word that occurred in many reviews) and gives the film its power, as opposed to Hollywood special effects that are a more prominent product of digital technology. The reception of this film thus points to the tensions and contradictions involved in the representation of landscape not just in Canadian cinema but in an emerging economic and technological order in which both nature and nation are increasingly experienced as obliterated.

## Notes

1. Bruce Elder, "The Cinema We Need," *The Canadian Forum* 64, no. 746 (February 1985), 32. Elder is himself an avant-garde filmmaker and develops this idea and his admiration for Snow at much greater length in his book *Image and Identity: Reflections on Canadian Film and Culture* (Waterloo: Wilfrid Laurier University Press, 1989).

2. Northrop Frye, *The Bush Garden: Essays on the Canadian Imagination* (Toronto: Anansi, 1971), 220. The essay in which he made this claim was first published in 1965.
3. *Ibid.*, iii.
4. Christiane Tremblay-Daviault, *Un Cinéma orphelin: Structures mentales et sociales du cinéma québécois* (Montreal: Québec/Amérique, 1981), 54.
5. *Ibid.*, 41.
6. Michel Brûlé, quoted in Yves Lever, *Histoire générale du cinéma au québec* (Montreal: Boréal, 1988), 482
7. See Peter Harcourt, "Images of the Rural: The Cinema of Quebec," *CineAction* 69 (2006), 2–11.
8. The Group was founded in 1920 by Franklin Carmichael, Lawren Harris, A.Y. Jackson, Frank Johnston, Arthur Lismer, J.E.H. MacDonald, and Frederick H. Varley.
9. The founding of the NFB was not the beginning of the documentary tradition in Canada, but it established the link between documentary and nation-building that dominated Canadian film culture for many years; see Jim Leach, *Film in Canada* (Toronto: Oxford University Press, 2006), 12–16.
10. Both films were collective projects using many filmmakers to explore urban experience. The main organizers of *The Days Before Christmas* were Terence Macartney-Filgate, Wolf Koenig, and Roman Kroitor, while Michel Brault, Claude Fournier, Claude Jutra and Marcel Carrière were mainly responsible for *La Lutte*.
11. Frye, *The Bush Garden*, ii–iii.
12. For a more detailed account of the film's treatment of history and the uncertainty of critical responses, see Jim Leach, *Claude Jutra Filmmaker* (Montreal: McGill-Queen's University Press, 1999), 137–41.
13. Peter Morris, *The Film Companion* (Toronto: Irwin Publishing, 1984), 283. These words are quoted from the 1950 renewal of the mandate, but they aptly describe the original purpose of the NFB.
14. Robert Fothergill, "A Place Like Home," in *Canadian Film Reader*, ed. Seth Feldman and Joyce Nelson (Toronto: Peter Martin Associates, 1977), 348.
15. Geoff Pevere, "Middle of Nowhere: Ontario Movies after 1980," *Post Script* 15, no. 1 (Fall 1995), 15.
16. Egoyan, quoted in Leslie Ellen Harris, "Atom Egoyan: Laughter in the Dark," *Canadian Forum* 70, no. 805 (December 1991), 17.
17. Egoyan, quoted in Jonathan Romney, *Atom Egoyan* (London: British Film Institute, 2003), 12.
18. Gerald Pratley, "Canadian Films: What Are We to Make of Them," http://arts.uwaterloo.ca/FINE/judhe/gp-ca981.htm, accessed 19 August 1998. The novel is by Russell Banks.
19. Burns, quoted in Mark Peranson, "Calgary Everyman: Gary Burns Works *waydowntown*," *Cinema Scope* 5 (Fall 2000), 6; Katherine Monk, *Weird Sex and Snow Shoes and Other Canadian Film Phenomena* (Vancouver: Raincoast Books, 2001), 79.
20. Brenda Longfellow, "Counter-Narratives, Class Politics and Metropolitan Dystopias in *Maelström*, *waydowntown* and *La Moitié gauche du frigo*," *Canadian Journal of Film Studies* 13, no. 1 (Spring 2004), 77.
21. Krishna, quoted in Cameron Bailey, "What the Story Is: An Interview with Srinivas Krishna," *CineAction* 28 (Spring 1992), 43.
22. *Les Boys* was a huge box-office hit in 1997 and was followed by two sequels in 1998 and 2003 (all directed by Louis Saia); the first Elvis Gratton film was a short made in 1981 that proved so successful that two more followed, edited together into a feature called *Elvis Gratton: Le King des Kings* (1985), followed in turn by two sequels, *Miracle à Memphis* (1999) and *Elvis Gratton XXX* (2004). Despite Falardeau's proclaimed satiric intent, the popularity of the figure of excess, played with gusto by Julien Poulin, suggests that many in the audience identified with him; see Leach, *Film in Canada*, 140–2.

# Chapter 18

Science Fiction/Fantasy Films, Fairy Tales and Control: Landscape Stereotypes on a Wilderness to Ultra-urban Continuum

Christina Kennedy, Tiànna Kennedy and Mélisa Kennedy

Geographic studies reveal that, in American film, the city is often represented as dystopia or as a setting for crime and violence, while the rural environment is most often portrayed positively.[1] We seek to broaden the discussion of landscape types and their associated values. We explore the relationship between the landscape as a 'where' the narrative takes place and landscape as a 'how' the narrative takes place – by touching on how values imbued in landscapes, via their historical contexts and current social contexts, intentionally and otherwise colour a film. To this end, we equate science fiction/fantasy films to fairy tales and consider landscapes, not as a *tabula rasa* over which a film takes place, but as an ideologically charged environment inextricably bound up in the narrative. We are not claiming any universal truths about 'landscape as character', or offering to construct a universally applicable map with which to navigate the landscape of film: we are investigating the use of landscape stereotypes and their associated values not in a city–rural dichotomy but along a wilderness to ultra-urban continuum.

## Modern fairy tales: Science fiction and fantasy films

Feature films are considered to reflect and reproduce the world of dominant ideology and are the child of a storytelling, narrative tradition.[2] Science fiction/fantasy can be equated to fairy tales. Fairy tales are direct, simple, complete and define universal themes or plots such as that of redemption and initiation.[3] Their comfortingly recognizable narratives present an opportunity to create a 'secondary world…that…is symbiotic with the real modern world'.[4] They stay anchored in the 'real', but transcend normal reality and challenge normative modes of thinking to highlight truths and assumptions we take for granted.[5] Although essentially optimistic, fairy tales may also draw on the transitory, demonic or chaotic elements of mythic discourse, elements that continually menace human endeavour.[6]

Science fiction, fantasy and/or fairy tales all 'take place'. They occur in, are derived from or are reflective of actual geographic space or place. In many fairy tales, the landscape, the ugly reality that the hero or heroine must struggle through, with, or overcome, can be seen as an antagonist. It is a place, at least potentially, outside the control of the protagonist. This antagonistic landscape is often a foil for the village, or another controlled or utopian space imbued with positive values representative of the positive characteristics the protagonist demonstrates.

Traditional fairy tales reflect medieval Europe's landscape and social order. This conceptual framework was transplanted in America early by European settlers, and is still a source of powerful images informing landscape stereotypes in modern fantasy films. For audiences seeking entertainment but also a fairy tale format through which they can make sense of, and critique, today's social order, landscapes reflective of not only our cultural past but also current societal realities and spatial relationships are used. These newer frameworks reflect both positive and negative, but usually simplified versions of today's America, whether it is Jefferson's vision of America as an agrarian society, or caricatured suburbs and cities. Any of these landscapes may be idealized, parodied or vilified: portrayed as an ugly reality or utopian dream.

## Approach

Within a transactional framework, it is accepted that an audience views film through multiple filters: past experience, expectations, mood and personality.[7] We do not claim objectivity. Our interpretation of films is based, largely, on our past primary and secondary experiences.[8] The films we have watched, our academic and non-academic reading and the types of landscapes and places we have lived in or encountered, as well as our predispositions and personalities, all inform our experience, and interpretation of, film.

In an attempt to mitigate individual biases, my daughters and I collaborated. Together, we have a wealth of experience with different landscapes. We lived in wilderness in the Sierra Nevada of California; had our stint of small town or rural living in California's Gold Country, on the Navajo Reservation and in the White Mountains of eastern Arizona; were suburbanites in Tucson, AZ, and explored urban life in California's Bay Area. At the time of our initial collaboration, Mélisa was living in community of 600 people on the eastside of the Sierra Nevada, Tiànna in Brooklyn and I in a small bedroom community seven miles from Flagstaff, a small metropolitan area of 63,000.

We chose science fiction/fantasy films because we enjoy them, and because we feel that they embody modern-day fairy tales. We selected the films almost randomly, with the constraint that the predominant landscape be American and fall somewhere on the wilderness to urban continuum. We each watched the films, and through an inductive process, looked for emerging patterns. Landscapes along the continuum represented in these films are as follows: 'traditional' wilderness – *The Blair Witch Project* (Daniel Myrick and Eduardo Sanchez, 1999), village or landschaft – *The Village* (M. Night Shyamalan, 2004); small town and agricultural area – *Phenomenon* (Jon Turteltaub, 1996); suburb – *Edward Scissorhands* (Tim Burton, 1990); the city – *Men in Black* (Barry Sonnenfeld, 1997) and *Men in Black II* (Barry Sonnenfeld, 2002); and the ultra-urban circa 2259 AD – *Fifth Element* (Luc Besson, 1997).

## Wilderness and village

Fairy tale landscapes of Perrault and the Brothers Grimm, derived from peasant oral folktales, were settings reminiscent of medieval Europe, a place of wylder-ness and small landschafts.[9] Wylder-ness, meaning the lair of the beast was '…the spatial correlation of unreason, or madness, of the unhuman anarchy that informs so many folktales emphasizing the ephemeral stability of Christianity, society, and agriculture'. Landschafts (small human settlements in the midst of forest, swamp or fen) were the antithesis of wilderness. These small settlements linked tenuously by path or road 'implied an agricultural community and a smallness of scale unknown in town' and were under the aegis of nobles.[10] Landschafts not only included structures, dwellings and people, but also the inhabitants' responsibilities to each other and to the land. Those failing or defying their responsibilities, and those crippled, mentally deficient or 'different' lost their place within acceptable social order because of their 'otherness' and were cast out into the wilderness…adding to the dangers 'normal' people might encounter there.[11]

European settlers brought these attitudes to the earliest colonial endeavours in the northeastern United States and they are reflected in American literature such as Hawthorne's *The Scarlet Letter*.[12] Romantic and transcendental concepts of wilderness as providing 'sanctuary, emotional catharsis, solitude, and means of reassuring ourselves of our sanity are recent, within the last 180 years'.[13] Two films using landscape stereotypes common in fairy tales derived from medieval Europe are *The Blair Witch Project* and *The Village*.

## Lost in the wilderness

The *Blair Witch Project*, a false documentary, is purportedly 'found' footage shot by three college students in search of the story behind legends of a witch, actual murders and missing children in the woods of western Maryland. The students

> can't find their way out of the woods, their planned overnight hike turns into days of hysteria in the wilderness, and something – something – begins to reveal itself to them… this [is] more than just a horror movie. It's a return to your childhood's starkest memories of abandonment and dread.[14]

Wilderness is clearly vilified in *Blair*. Despite current popular views of wilderness as a positive challenge, beauty or sanctuary, it is our opinion that the directors do not intend to deconstruct current landscape stereotypes, but rather to invoke the 'unreason, or madness, of the unhuman anarchy' of an archaic 'wylder-ness'. Interestingly, the landscape used so effectively to terrify the protagonists is merely a mild deciduous forest in Maryland. Other than the house and Coffin Rock, there are no remarkable features in the landscape. The Blair Witch, herself, is portrayed as a natural element. She is covered in fur 'like an animal' and manifests as a collection of rocks and stick figures rather than in a human form. The forest is reduced to the simplified mythic archetype of woods with streams. A stark palette of black and white acts as a further filter, symbolically reducing the complex life of the forest to a basic dichotomy of good and evil.

The film's three protagonists are upper-middle-class white kids from orderly suburbs incompatible with the demonic or chaotic woods. Here, they are no longer connected to the familiar. They are on foot, there are no phones, and their lost map, useless compass and unhelpful video equipment all reveal the uselessness of technology to protect them from nature, evil and themselves.

By capitalizing on the 'no-no-don't-go-in-there!!' horror motif and by vilifying wilderness, the filmmakers actually idealize the comforts of the familiar, humanized landscape, or the status quo. In this film, the darker forces found in mythic discourse, characteristics associated with the antagonist and the archetypical wilderness overwhelm the protagonists. The resulting text is representative of a normative work that reifies the European concepts of wylder-ness and benefits of human settlement – in this case, the suburb.

## The safety of a/the village?

A traditional stereotype of wilderness is also seen in *The Village*. However, an idealized view of landschaft, of community life, appears, by extension, to denounce modern urban life. The story ostensibly occurs in 1897 in an isolated community surrounded by a mild deciduous forest which the villagers dare not enter. This forest is home to 'Those we do not speak of '('those...') who dress in the forbidden colour, scarlet – the color of passion and blood, of knowledge and loss of innocence (Eve's apple). 'Those...' make their presence known at night by strewing skinned, blood-covered animals throughout the village, and painting red slashes on doors as children hide in terror in cellars.

The villagers are usually kept safe by yellow-cloaked watchers manning guard towers and maintaining yellow-flamed beacon fires along the clear demarcation between village and wilderness. In contrast to the forest, the village life appears ideal. There are feasts, festivals, hard work and wholesome entertainment. Elders rule through consensus, and are ever constrained and polite.

In *Blair* safety and control lie in the suburb. In *The Village*, we have expectations of the forest as the frightening place, but it is in the edenic life of the village where the initial act of 'evil', human violence, occurs. Ivy, facing the transition from childhood to adult love and responsibility, asks permission from her father (the head Elder) to go for medicine to save the victim, her betrothed; thus setting the context for the 'hero's journey' and an opportunity to learn the 'truth' about the village.[15]

Ivy's journey is a classic fairy tale journey of initiation. Dressed in a yellow (not red) cloak and hood, Ivy, who is blind, survives the physical hardships of travelling through a rainy, autumn forest. She escapes from a deep mud pit formed by the roots of a toppled tree. The only 'evil' found in the forest is the mentally deficient Noah, disguised in the costume of 'Those…'. When he attacks, she kills him in self-defense by stepping aside, causing him to fall into that same pit from which she earlier escaped. Ivy makes it through the fairy tale 'thicket of thorns' – a wall covered in vines – encounters kindness 'outside', and returns with needed medicines.

The secret is that the village exists today, not in 1897. 'Those…' are, in truth, elders wearing costumes. They strive to perpetuate a utopian society and the innocence of their children by maintaining a lifestyle from a 'mythical', more pure, past and through total isolation from today's world. Each has suffered a personal tragedy and loss 'outside' in the city. The village is located in a Pennsylvania wildlife sanctuary where no overhead flights are allowed, and that is surrounded by a tall, cement wall and guards. The forest, rather than an evil, uncontrolled space is being used as protective or isolating barrier.

On Ivy's return, the Elders reach a consensus to continue their community based on terror and on ignorance of 'reality' for their young as an alternative to the potential dangers and perceived evils of modern life. To us, their choice is more frightening than 'Those we do not speak of'. Landscape stereotypes are used – dangerous, evil forest; safe, wholesome village; and city full of greed and violence. However, because in *The Village* these stereotypes are used as a narrative device (as a means for the Elders to control the innocents), it is unclear whether those stereotypes are reinforced or subverted. Perhaps it is a case of both and neither.

## Small town

As America's wilderness was pushed westward and the United States was being born, Thomas Jefferson had a vision of the United States as an agrarian society. He saw farming and the associated small towns as wholesome alternatives to overcrowded, industrialized cities such as those in Europe. To Jefferson, European cities were breeding grounds for disease, vice and debauchery. Although he valued 'civilized', beautiful music and art, he believed America would be a stronger, healthier, more democratic nation if peopled by honest, yeoman farmers owning their own private piece of land. This conceit has informed intellectual attitudes towards cities throughout much of our nation's history.[16] Jefferson's dream has dramatically affected America's landscape and settlement patterns.[17] Along with romantic idealization of the pastoral, it still informs and influences popular culture and film. Rural life is still seen as having 'an elemental simplicity and truth'.[18] An idealization of nature, vilification of the urban and essentially positive portrayal of small town and rural life is found in *Phenomenon*.

## Small town intimacy

As an affirmation of life, possibilities, relationships, community and redemption, it is fitting that *Phenomenon* take place in rural California. The pastoral landscape of old farms and small towns symbolizes the virtues of the Jeffersonian agrarian dream. George Malley embodies idealized rural social values: humility, honesty, generosity and involvement in community.

After seeing a brilliant light and losing consciousness in the darkened streets of his small town, George becomes an insomniac with unbounded intellectual abilities and inexplicable psychokinetic powers. His new power and intelligence frightens many of the townspeople he has known his entire life. By predicting an earthquake and breaking a military code, George attracts attention from outside the small-town sphere: the military, FBI and scientists.

The landscape is one of rolling golden hills studded with gnarled oak with old, white two-storey farmhouses and outbuildings. Cattle graze contentedly, and in the hazy glow of dawn the only sound is birdsong. The town, location of Malley's auto-repair shop, is a service centre for an agricultural community and one of our symbolic landscapes.[19] The town is human scale with two-storey, false-front buildings. Doc's office is over a store. There is a bar where the locals meet. Past its prime, but before gentrification, boutiquing and ranchettes, the landscape is worn, known and comfortable.

The 'ugly realities' George has to traverse are mostly interior landscapes: exploring his new powers and what they mean, dealing with the fears of his lifelong acquaintances and then escaping the city and the consequences of big-city mentality. Unlike wilderness in *Blair* and *The Village*, in *Phenomenon*, nature is ultimate good. His ability to move objects is based on cooperation with (husbanding, not dominion over) both the animate and inanimate. He asks and hopes rather than demands. The same is true of his relationship with Lace, an urban refugee. However, it is only after accepting his connectedness to the forces underlying all things (embodied in wind gently swaying cypress trees and oaks as a mother soothes a child) however, that he finds peace and is able to truly relate to and help heal Lace and her children.

As in *Blair* and *The Village*, dramatic tension comes from issues of 'otherness': from changes in an individual to intrusive values from 'outside' entering the small town community. These are things that cannot be understood or controlled. Outside governmental and urban values represented by the FBI, military and brain surgeon are vilified. The FBI are 'bad' because they do not consider the individual, context or humanity but focus solely on issues of national security. The military's distortion of garden imagery by using a formal garden pattern for their missile silos is, within the context of the film, blasphemy. The big-city brain surgeon focuses on science and technology, not on the possibilities of the human spirit, and holds personal success and scientific knowledge as gods.

The townspeople are, within limits, changeable in their relationship with 'otherness' and outsiders. An altered George is feared by lifelong acquaintances in the community until after his death. However, because of his life, and an increased awareness of the healing powers of 'nature', those touched by George are able to change. An organic fertilizer developed by George restores productivity to a barren field. Lace embraces life, relationships and associated risks of loss and she and her children, 'outsiders', are finally accepted. Their 'otherness' is resolved by adoption into the community and a return to the status quo of an idealized mythic, cohesive, cooperative small-town society. They are redeemed. George and the community have escaped vilified governmental and big-city values.

## The suburb

In the early half of the nineteenth century, suburbs provided escape from the degraded physical and social conditions of the industrialized city of modernity – the perceived urban wilderness. The promotional image of suburbs initially was as 'a haven from the city's whirl'.[20] Low-density housing, closeness to nature, healthful living, emphasis on nuclear families and social status were all used to sell suburbs.[21] Rapid expansion of suburbs after the Second World War was fed not only by highway expansion, increased use of automobiles, improved communication networks and the technological ability to build standardized housing, but also by idealization of suburbs in Hollywood films of the late 1940s and1950s.[22] The Jeffersonian ideal morphed from family farm to single family home with a yard – a privately owned, controlled piece of nature.

Privacy and safety became paramount with patios and closed-in backyards providing a sense of social control.[23] However, due to frequent resident turnover and the subsequent lack of community relationships, there remains little that can be defined as 'social' to control. American suburban life has also been criticized for its 'conformity and sterility', the 'anomic life of the nuclear family', gendered space and undifferentiated cancerous sprawl.[24] Culturally, suburbs are often centres of consumption for the products of the city. *Edward Scissorhands* brings characteristics of a stereotypical suburban life into sharp relief.

## Model homes

'The noble-hearted outsider getting persecuted by society may be the oldest – and most touching – story in the book.'[25] A take on Shelley's *Frankenstein*, *Edward Scissorhands is* touching. Moreover, it is a biting parody of suburban life.[26]

The standardization and gendered space of the film's 1980s suburb is established early as Peg Boss, Avon lady, begins her rounds of pastel houses embodying the lyrics of Reynolds' protest song about suburbs, *Little Boxes*. The film's houses are 'green', 'pink', 'blue' and 'yellow', 'all made out of ticky tacky' and 'all look just the same.'[27] Only women are home, and are caricatures of suburban housewives: a sex-crazed redhead, a fat, boisterous woman with her hair in curlers and a religious freak ready to demonize anyone out of the norm. Men are only around at night, on weekends and holidays. The image of gendered space is emphasized in an aerial shot that shows all the automobiles simultaneously backing from their garages into the street and heading to the city on a workday morning.

Peg discovers Edward in her search for customers. She ventures from the safety of her suburb (read contemporary village) into a fairy tale wilderness – the haunted house on the hill at the end of the cul-de-sac. She enters through a broken, iron spiked gate in a high wall covered in dead vines and past dead trees and dying bushes. Once through the 'thorn thicket', she braves a topiary dragon, a topiary hand surrounded by petunias and gargoyles to enter the 'house'. The apparently abandoned space she enters resembles a medieval cathedral or enchanted castle. In the monochromatic, dark interior Peg, in lavender with a blue bag, is the only colour. She is alien, an invader. She is unself-conscious normalcy, in the face of an invented 'punk'-appearing creature with weapon-like scissors and shears in place of hands. Peg epitomizes, yet is also a parody of, the positive, nurturing, mothering qualities expected of suburban wives. Without thinking of possible consequences, she takes the abandoned Edward home, camouflages his black leather and metal studded body in grey pants and white shirt, and installs him as part of her nuclear family.

Initially, Edward is accepted by the outwardly friendly suburbanites because he is a novelty, provides interest for the neighbourhood's bored housewives and because of his abilities with topiary and haircutting. Topiary, aside from bonsai, is the ultimate art of 'control' and fits with the continual maintenance of yards, mowing and watering, shown in the film.

The materiality of the suburb and dependence on automobiles are emphasized. The manager of a generic 'BANK' refuses to lend money to Peg and Edward so that Edward can open a beauty salon. The manager tells him how to fit in, 'Get a social security card. Establish credit. Buy a car.' A teenager, the antagonist, is willing to resort to steal his father's 'toys' – stereo and TV equipment – for money to buy a van to have sex in. Edward participates in the attempted robbery, is caught, and neighbours begin to distrust and fear him as a threat to property.

On Christmas Eve, a time of supposed brotherhood and love, Edward saves Peg's son from being run over. Neighbours, however, mistakenly think he is attacking Kevin and see him as a threat to life and safety as well as property. He is perceived as 'out of control', topiary-be-damned, and no longer having a place in the ultra-controlled environment of the suburb. Edward is chased by an angry mob of red and green clothed suburbanites along a well-paved street, past clean sidewalks and meticulously rectangular lawns, past houses dressed in rolls of fake snow and bright Christmas lights. Expelled from 'society', he slices off his white shirt and grey slacks and seeks sanctuary in the wilderness and his 'castle/church' on the hill. The once friendly 'neighbours' are appeased and willing to return home only when they are convinced Edward is dead – no longer a threat.

Ironically, Edward Scissorhand's adventures could be viewed as a hero's journey in reverse. He ventures from a life of isolation into what is accepted as 'normalcy' but is rejected and, like outcasts in medieval times, returns to the 'wilderness', his only sanctuary outside of communal society. Still, in keeping with heroes, he leaves a gift to those in the suburb. His gift is snow, flecks of ice from his continuous carving of ice sculptures, a hint of creativity and beauty being created outside the sterility, materialism and narrow mindedness of a villainized suburb.

## The city

Warner claimed that Americans 'live in one of the world's most urbanized countries as if it were a wilderness'.[28] Cities are often seen as dystopias, as urban wildernesses or jungles, seldom as utopias. Perhaps this perspective is due to the fact that although markedly different from cities Jefferson knew in Europe, today's American cities are still symbolically linked to many of both the positive and negative values he associated with them. Cities are still seen as crowded, unhealthy, full of 'debauchery'; while simultaneously being centres of culture and personal freedom.

American cities are described as spheres of production and consumption.[29] They are, however, more than a physical manifestation of capitalism, in which physical and social stratification ensures unequal access to resources. As built environments, they are tangible expressions of religious, political, economic and social forces. They house a host of often contradictory activities and meanings in proximity to, or congruent with, one another in heterotopic space.[30] On the human level, the city is 'human habitat that allows people to form relations with others at various levels of intimacy while remaining entirely anonymous'.[31]

Clarke argues that the development of the modern American city and cinema are interrelated and layered.[32] According to Baudrillard, they 'seem to have stepped right out of the movies'.[33] Bachelard and Koolhaas would have us believe that the city is the ultimate manifestation of the material imagination.[34]

America's cities may have new forms and functions, yet they carry a heavy historical burden including freedoms associated with medieval cities, values associated with modernity and scepticism of values and structures associated with post-modernity. Additionally they are imbued with a physical legacy of industrialization and post-industrialization. Ultimately, when deconstructing urban stereotypes, we are always caught between the 'vitality of the city – what makes it go, and its deterioration and dereliction; and between street life and that of private spaces'.

As places and cityscapes, however, they retain an individuality. New York City is the ultimate symbolic city of America and is a critical character in the movies we discuss.

## Alien-nation

*Men in Black* focuses on 'the adventures of a couple of hard-working functionaries whose assignment is to keep tabs on the sizeable alien population of the United States' and to keep the public 'a gullible breed' in ignorance.[35] J and K, two of the always anonymous functionaries, are on an assignment of redemption, to save earth from destruction. In order to save the planet, they have to track down a stolen universe the size of a marble.

Their investigation takes them out of the city to a rural environment very different from that in *Phenomenon*. Here, the idealistic country scenes of *Phenomenon* take on an entirely different meaning. J and K arrive on the scene of a spacecraft crash landing to interview

Beatrice who claims an alien walked off in her husband's skin. The house is old and leans to one side. The paint is gray and peeling, and there is no sign of productive agriculture, just a dirt driveway, an overgrazed hill and skinny cow. In Beatrice, with her illiterate dialect and sloping shoulders, and in her now-dead abusive husband, with his shotgun and bad temper, we see the parody of the hard-working country folk of *Phenomenon*. The simple turns to simplistic and productive to destructive. The idealistic landscape of the farm peels away like old paint to reveal the ugliness underneath.

The city, in contrast, is clean and beautiful. The city escapes parody. We see quaint neighbourhoods, ethnically diverse restaurants and breathtaking cityscapes. Even crime takes a back seat in this environment. Although crime exists, MIB, the secret federal agency that monitors both human and alien activity, holds it at bay. They know about and control every aspect of crime, as shown in the pawn shop scene. J and K force the owner of the pawnshop to give them the information they want about an illegal gun by shooting off his head, which, fortunately, regenerates. Not only did they know exactly where to go for the information, but there is no question as to whether the owner of the pawn shop will obey their order to leave. Another modern-day demon, pollution, doesn't exist in this 'idealized' New York. The sky is always blue, the scenery always beautiful. Neither does poverty exist, nor problems generally associated with poverty in big cities. J sits on a bench next to the Hudson watching the scenery all night without being arrested for loitering, mugged or hassled for change.

*MIB*'s fanciful representation of New York leaves one with the sense that just as the villainous alien is hidden in the rancher's skin, suburban mores (and in particular control fetishism) are cloaked by the skin of a city which is simply too good to be true. Although on the surface the city is a place to live with equanimity, it is at the expense of ignorance of 'aliens' in our midst, at the expense of purposeful information suppression by a secret government agency. This reality is blatantly exposed when, in *MIB II*, the Statue of Liberty – the ultimate symbol of American freedom – is used as a giant neutralizer, cleansing citizens' minds of anything uncomfortably alien to their ordinary experiences.

## The manifestation of material imagination

*The Fifth Element*, in a mad rush, drags us through the city of the future. While the protagonists are trying to save the world, we are treated to some of the most fantastic futuristic scenery in a science fiction movie yet. An immediate comparison to the city of *Blade Runner* (Ridley Scott, 1982) is inevitable, but the audience soon realizes the director has gone way beyond paying tribute to Ridley Scott. 'The movie "moves so quickly you don't have time to think of words like larceny"'.[36] However, larceny is perhaps acceptable, since this city is all about unequal appropriation.

The landscape of New York City 2259 AD is immense and mesmerizing: 'The frenzied city-scape of New York, with its vibrant day-glo colored, tall buildings, penetrating high into the clouds, and the swarm of cars, cabs, and other vehicles flying through labryrinthine skyways, is absolutely breathtaking to behold.'[37] The city of *The Fifth Element* is, in all ways, an extension of the stereotypical city of today: a thoroughly complex and artificial environment, that maybe even despite all of its problems, can be stunningly beautiful.

Unlike the portrayal in *Men in Black*, the New York City of the future exhibits all the social and environmental problems afflicting contemporary conurbations. Pollution is extreme. The sky is always brown and hazy – a fact that Zorg, the villain, seems to enjoy out of the picture window of his spacious office. A foray down into the depths of the city in a fantastic flying car chase shows a city floor entirely filled with garbage. There is notable lack of public transit. Everyone still has their own car, and we can safely assume that traffic jams take on three dimensions. In another scene, when an airport flight attendant apologizes for the huge piles of refuse slowly taking over the hallways, it is plain that the other characters hadn't even noticed until she said something. Citizens are so accustomed to not only pollution but also crime that when a zany addict tries to mug Korben, the hero, in the doorway of his tiny living cubical, Korben doesn't even blink. He instead fools the would-be thief into disarming his weapon and then adds it to his own array of weapons. We are confronted with a future that has all of the problems of the present, only more so.

If the city is in any way a utopia, it is a capitalist's dream world – access to resources is dramatically unequal. Control of space is related to money and power. Everything in Korben's tiny living cubical comes prepackaged and disposable, including the bed. The Priest, better off, has a luxurious apartment, while Zorg controls vast amounts of space, capital and power. As a weapons manufacturer, Zorg lays off workers by the millions. There is extreme anomie. As in *MIB* the communities that exist are of those of congruent interests – e.g. the police, the military, scientists, taxi-cab drivers, musicians or artists. These communities rub against each other but often with fear. In *Fifth Element*, as in *Blade Runner*, the city, too has a wilderness represented by the 'streets' or the lower levels of the city. This wilderness offers spaces where deviants (Korben escaping with LeeLuu) can hide, and get off the 'radar' of the police.

A trip away from the city to 'Paradise' – an untrammelled, beautiful planet – is an extension of capitalism and a biting parody of tourism. The characters are surrounded by entertainment, pop culture and remain totally isolated from nature. It is in 'Paradise', paradoxically, that the majority of violent action occurs.

Again the story is one of redemption. The fifth element (love embodied as Leeloo) with Korben's help saves the world. Despite the immensity and mesmerizing beauty of the ultra-urban landscape, paradise is an illusion. The labyrinthine quality of the city as manifestation of material imagination has led us back to some characteristics of traditional wilderness. It appears to be beyond control, chaotic, ruled by demonic forces. These demonic forces are different from those of traditional wilderness. They are capitalism and the attempt at ultra-control by police and military. As in fairy tales, it is left to the iconoclast, the little guy (in this case, the outcast) to help save the world.

## Coda

Eighty per cent of Americans live either in cities or suburbs. Wilderness is a rare, especially in the lower 48 states, and that wilderness, it can be argued, is both a human construct and human controlled.[38] Still, symbolic-stereotypic landscapes from wilderness to ultra-urban retain power that infuses an unspoken set of values into modern fairy tales, like science fiction/fantasy films, and helps us create a 'symbiotic secondary world'.[39] The simple, direct fairy tale narratives combined with idealization, parody and villainization encourage reexamination of values and truths we take for granted in our daily 'reality'.

A continuum appears to be a more useful heuristic device than a dichotomy. And, a continuum is able, perhaps, to capture characteristics such as population density and physical forms of landscapes. However, what it is unable to adequately capture are interrelationships between people and landscape, including historical, social, political, psychological and economic factors. Rather than a landscape continuum reflecting actual geographic features, we find we are looking at shifting scales of controlled and uncontrolled spaces. We are seeing, perhaps, more a circle or collection of feedback loops concerning issues of representations of psychologically loaded space denoting: 'human unreason and anarchy', safety, control and community; or what aspects of the landscape, or portrayed spaces indicate 'otherness'.

Stereotypes and fairy tales fail to deal with the depth of complexity and interconnectedness of reality. Fairy tales and science fiction/fantasy films entertain and can help us look at our environments from a new perspective. They may suggest that in our search for safety and control, we are building ourselves thickets of thorn that keep us from experiencing the chaos, possibilities and creativity of accepting things alien, of integrating 'otherness'.

## Notes

1. Christina Kennedy and Christopher Lukinbeal, 'Towards a holistic approach to geographic research on film', *Progress in Human Geography* 21 (1997), 33–50 and Christina Kennedy and Christopher Lukinbeal, 'Dick Tracy's cityscape', *Association of Pacific Coast Geographers' Yearbook* 55 (1993), 76–96.
2. Brian Dunnigan, 'Storytelling and film fairy tales, myth and happy endings', *P.O.V. filmtidsskrift: A Danish Journal of Film Studies* 18 (2005), http://imv.au.dk/publikationer.
3. Ibid.
4. A. S. Byatt, 'Harry Potter and the childish adult', *New York Times*, 11 July 2003, http://www.counter currents.org/arts-byatt110703.htm, http://www.nytimes.com/2003/07/07/opinion/07BYAT.html.
5. Mark Heberle (quoting Martin), 'An inquiry into the purposes of speculative fiction – Fantasy and truth (review)', *Marvels & Tales* 19 (2005), 142–145, http://muse.jhu.edu/journals/marvels_ and_tales/v019/19.1haberle.html.
6. See note 2.
7. Leo Zonn, 'Tusayan, thetTraveler, and the IMAX theatre: An introduction to place images in media', in Leo Zonn (ed.), *Place Images in Media: Portrayal, Experience and Meaning* (Maryland:

Rowman and Littlefield Publishers, 1990), 1–8; Ervin Zube and Christina Kennedy, 'Changing Images of the Arizona Territory', in Zonn, 183–203.

8. Jacqueline Burgess and John Gold, 'Introduction', in Jacqueline Burgess and John Gold (eds), *Place the Media and Popular Culture* (New York: St Martin's Press, 1985), 1–32.

9. Jeanette Sky, 'Myths of innocence and imagination: The case of the fairy tale', *Literature and Theology* 16 (2002), 363–376.

10. John. R. Stilgoe, *Common Landscape of America, 1580–1845* (New Haven: Yale University Press, 1982), 11.

11. We use 'other' in the Hegelian sense that the 'other' is critical to human self-consciousness while it also objectifies and places the 'other' in a subservient position. Only through evolution of the self in ethical life, in personal strength and grounding can the 'other' move from the dichotomous unequal relationship, 'I'-'it', to an inclusive relationship of parity, 'I'-'Thou'.

12. Nathaniel Hawthorne, *The Scarlet Letter* (Boston: Ticknor, Reed & Fields, 1850).

13. Joseph Sax, *Mountains without Handrails: Reflections on the National Parks* (Ann Arbor: University of Michigan Press, 1980); Roderick Nash, *Wilderness and the American Mind*, 3rd ed. (New Haven: Yale University Press, 1982).

14. This 1999 review of *The Blair Witch Project* by Michael Atkinson is no longer available on the web.

15. Joseph Campbell, *The Hero with a Thousand Faces* (New Jersey: Princeton University Press; reprint edition 1972).

16. Morton Gabriel White and Lucia White, *Intellectual versus the City: From Thomas Jefferson to Frank Lloyd Wright* (Cambridge: Harvard University Press and The MIT Press, 1962).

17. John B. Jackson, 'The order of landscape: Reason and religion in Newtonian America', in Donald Meining (ed.), *The Interpretation of Ordinary Landscapes: Geographical Essays* (New York: Oxford University Press, 1979), 153–163.

18. John B. Jackson, 'An Eengineered environment', in Ervin Zube and Margaret Zube (eds), *Changing Rural Landscapes* (Amherst: The University of Massachusetts Press, 1977), 28.

19. Donald Meinig, 'Symbolic landscapes', in Donald Meining (ed.), *The Interpretation of Ordinary Landscapes: Geographical Essays* (New York: Oxford University Press, 1979), 164–192.

20. John Gold, ''A place of Delightful Prospects': Promotional imagery and the selling of suburbia', in Leo Zonn (ed.), *Place Images in Media: Portrayal, Experience and Meaning* (Maryland: Rowman and Littlefield Publishers, 1990), 159.

21. Ibid.

22. See note 28.

23. Richard H. Thomas, in Patrick Deneen, 'Awakening from the American dream: The end of escape in American cinema', *Perspectives on Political Science* 31 (2002), 96–103.

24. Ibid., 103.

25. Desson Howe, 1990, http://www.washingtonpost.com/wp-srv/style/longterm/movies/videos/edwardscissorhandspg13howe_a0b2c5.htm. Accessed October 2005.

26. Richard Schreib, review: '*Edward Scissorhands*' (1990), http://www.moria.co.nz/fantasy/edscissorhands.htm. Accessed October 2005.

27. Malvina Reynolds, *Little Boxes* (1962).

28. Sam Bass Warner, Jr, *Streetcar Suburbs, The Process of Growth in Boston 1870–1900* (Cambridge: Harvard University Press and MIT Press, 1962).

29. David Clarke, 'Introduction: Previewing the cinematic city', in *The Cinematic City* (New York: Routledge, 1997), 1–17.

30. Michael Foucault, 'Of other spaces, heterotopias' (1967), http://foucault.info/documents/heteroTopia/foucault.heteroTopia.en.html. Accessed October 2005.
31. Hillel Schocken, 'Intimate anonymity' (2001), http://www.cyburbia.org/forums/archive/index.php/t-20571.html. Accessed October 2005.
32. See note 38.
33. Jean Baudrillard, quoted in Clarke, 38.
34. Gaston Bachelard, *The Psychoanalysis of Fire* (Pittsburg: Beacon Press, 1987) and Rem Koolhaas, *Delirious New York: A Retroactive Manifesto for Manhattan* (New York: The Monacelli Press; reprint edition, 1997).
35. Roger Ebert, review of *Men in Black* (1997), http://rogerebert.suntimes.com/apps/pbcs.dll/article?AID=/19970701/REVIEWS/707010301/1023.
36. Tom Lyons, review of *The Fifth Element* (1997), http://www.eye.net/eye/issue/issue_05.08.97/film/onscreen.html.
37. Review is no longer on web.
38. Scott Smiley, 'Making Sense out of Chaos: Landscape Order in Two California Wilderness Areas' (An unpublished Masters Thesis for the Department of Geography and Environmental Studies, California State University, Hayward, CA, 1994).
39. See note 4.

# Filmography

*The Abominable Snowman* (Val Guest, 1957)
*About Adam* (Gerry Stembridge, 2001)
*Aerograd* (Alexander Dovzhenko, 1935)
*After the Wax* (Caz Maviyan-Davis, 1991)
*Aguirre: Wrath of God* (Werner Herzog, 1972)
*Airbag* (Juanma Bajo Ulloa, 1997)
*Aldea maldita* (Florián Rey, 1930)
*Alice in Wondertown* (Daniel Díaz Torres, 1991)
*Amachua kurabu,* (Kurihara Kisaburo, 1920)
*L'Amant* (Jean-Jacques Annaud, 1991)
*Amantes del círculo polar* (Julio Medem, 1999)
*Aparajito* (Satyajit Ray, 1956)
*A propos de Nice* (Jean Vigo, 1929)
*Ararat* (Atom Egoyan, 2002)
*Arrival of a Train at Ciotat* (Auguste Lumière and Louis Lumière, 1896)
*Atanarjuat the Fast Runner* (Zacharias Kunuk, 2000)
*Aurore* (Luc Dionne, 2005)
*Avoir 20 ans dans les Aurès* (René Vautier, 1972)
*Bad Blood* (Mike Newell, 1982)
*Ballad of a Soldier* (Grigorii Chukhrai, 1959)
*Ballad of the Little Soldier* (Werner Herzog, 1984)
*The Ballroom of Romance* (Pat O'Connor, 1982)
*La Bataille d'Algers* (Gillo Pontecorvo, 1966)
*Beau travail* (Claire Denis, 1998)
*Beijing Bastards* (Yuan Zhang, 1993)
*Beneath Clouds* (Ivan Sen, 2002)
*Berlin: Symphony of a Big City* (Walther Ruttman, 1927)
*Between Friends* (Don Shebib, 1973)
*Bienvenido, Mister Marshall* (Luis García Berlanga , 1952)
*Bilbao* (José Juan Bigas Luna, 1978)
*Bitter Sugar* (Leon Ichaso, 1996)
*Black Narcissus* (Michael Powell and Emeric Pressburger, 1948)
*Blade Runner* (Ridley Scott, 1982)
*The Blue Light* (Leni Riefenstahl, 1932)

*The Blair Witch Project* (Daniel Myrick and Eduardo Sanchez, 1999)
*The Blue Angel* (Josef von Sternberg, 1930)
*Bollywood/Hollywood* (Deepa Mehta, 2002)
*The Bone Collector* (Phillip Noyce, 1999)
*Boom Boom* (Rosa Vergés, 1990)
*Braveheart* (Mel Gibson, 1995)
*Britain Can Take It!* (Humphrey Jennings and Harry Watt, 1940)
*Buenos Aires Affair* (Wong Kar-Wai, 1997)
*The Butcher Boy* (Neil Jordan, 1997)
*Bwana* (Imanol Uribe, 1995)
*Calendar* (Atom Egoyan, 1993)
*Calle Mayor* (Juan Antonio Bardem, 1956)
*Caniche* (José Juan Bigas Luna, 1979)
*A Canterbury Tale* (Michael Powell and Emeric Pressburger, 1944)
*Captain Boycott* (Frank Launder, 1947)
*Caravan* (Arthur Crabtree, 1946)
*Caro Diario* (Nanni Moretti, 1994)
*Cartas de Alou* (Montxo Armendáriz, 1990)
*La caza* (Carlos Saura, 1965)
*The Chant of Jimmy Blacksmith* (Fred Schepisi, 1978)
*Charulata* (Satyajit Ray, 1964)
*Le Chat dans le sac* (Gilles Groulx, 1964)
*Los chicos* (Marco Ferreri, 1959)
*Chocolat* (Claire Denis, 1988)
*Chungking Express* (Wong Kar-Wai, 1994)
*Circle of Danger* (Jacques Tourneur, 1951)
*La ciudad no es para mí* (Pedro Lazaga, 1966)
*Clear and Present Danger* (Phillip Noyce, 1994)
*Cloud-capped Star* (Ritwik Ghatak, 1962)
*Cloud Paradise* (Nikolai Dostal, 1991)
*El cochecito* (Marco Ferreri, 1961)
*Confessions of Pain* (Wai Keung Lau and Siu Fai Mak, 2006)
*Conflict of Wings* (John Eldridge, 1954)
*Consequences* (Godwin Mawuru, 2000)
*The Constant Nymph* (Basil Dean, 1933)
*El corazón del bosque* (José Luis Borau, 1979)
*Cosas que dejé en la Habana* (Manuel Gutiérrez Aragón, 1996)
*Cossacks of the Kuban* (Ivan Pyr'ev, 1949)
*Costa Brava* (Marta Balletbò-Coll, 1995)
*Country* (Kevin Liddy, 2000)
*Coup de torchon* (Bertrand Tavernier, 1981)
*Crash* (David Cronenberg, 1996)
*Crocodile Dundee* (Peter Faiman, 1986)
*Crocodile Dundee II* (John Cornell, 1988)
*Crouching Tiger Hidden Dragon* (Ang Lee, 2000)
*The Cruel Sea* (Charles Frend, 1953)
*Crush* (Alison Maclean, 1992)

*El Cuarteto de La Habana* (Fernando Colomo, 1999)
*Cuba Sí* (Chris Marker, 1961)
*Cube* (Vincent Natali, 1997)
*Cumbite* (Tomás Gutiérrez Alea, 1964)
*The Dark Glow of the Mountains* (Werner Herzog, 1984)
*The Day After Tomorrow* (Roland Emmerich, 2004)
*The Days before Christmas* (Stanley Jackson, Wolf Koenig, Terrence McCartney Filgate, 1958)
*Death of a Bureaucrat* (Tomás Gutiérrez Alea, 1966)
*December Bride* (Thaddeus O'Sullivan, 1989)
*The Demi-Paradise* (Anthony Asquith, 1943)
*Desperate Remedies* (Peter Main and Stewart Wells, 1993)
*Día tras día* (Antonio del Amo, 1951)
*Los días contados* (Imanol Uribe, 1994)
*Distance* (Jesús Díaz, 1985)
*Diva* (Jean-Jacques Beineix, 1982)
*Dr Zhivago* (David Lean, 1965)
*Don's Party* (Bruce Beresford, 1976)
*Doss House* (John Baxter, 1933)
*Double Happiness* (Mina Shum, 1994)
*Drunken Angel* (Akira Kurosawa, 1948)
*Drylanders* (Don Haldane, 1964)
*Earth* (Alexander Dovzhenko, 1930)
*Edge of the World* (Michael Powell, 1936)
*Edward Scissorhands* (Tim Burton, 1990)
*The Enigma of Kaspar Hauser* (Werner Herzog, 1974)
*El espíritu de la colmena* (Víctor Erice, 1973)
*Elvis Gratton: Le King des Kings* (Pierre Falardeau, 1985)
*Esther Waters* (Ian Dalrymple and Peter Proud, 1948)
*eXistenZ* (David Cronenberg, 1999)
*Exposure* (Kieran Hickey, 1978)
*Fallen Angels* (Wong Kar-Wai, 1995)
*The Falls* (Kevin McMahon, 1991)
*The Far Shore* (Joyce Wieland, 1976)
*Fata Morgana* (Vicente Aranda, 1966)
*Fata Morgana* (Werner Herzog, 1970)
*Fate of a Man* (Sergei Bondarchuk, 1959)
*Los felices sesenta* (Jaime Camino, 1964)
*The Field* (Jim Sheridan, 1990)
*The Fifth Element* (Luc Besson, 1997)
*The First Machete Charge* (Manuel Octavio Gómez, 1969)
*Fitzcarraldo* (Werner Herzog, 1982)
*Flame* (Ingrid Sinclair, 1996)
*Flashdance* (Adrian Lyne, 1983)
*Flores de otro mundo* (Icíar Bollaín, 1999)
*Fort Saganne* (Alain Corneau, 1984)
*49th Parallel* (Michael Powell, 1941)
*Furtivos* (José Luis Borau, 1975)

*Genevieve* (Henry Cornelius, 1953)
*Girl from Hunan* (Fei Xie, 1986)
*The Goddess* (Satyajit Ray, 1960)
*The Goddess* (Yonggang Wu, 1934)
*Goin' Down the Road* (Don Shebib, 1970)
*Los golfos* (Carlos Saura, 1959)
*Goodbye Pork Pie* (Geoff Murphy, 1981)
*The Good Companions* (Victor Saville, 1933)
*Great Day* (Lance Comfort, 1945)
*Great Expectations* (David Lean, 1946)
*Guantanamera* (Gutiérrez Alea and Juan Carlos Tabío, 1997)
*La Haine* (Mathieu Kassovitz, 1995)
*The Happy Guys* (Grigorii Alexandrov, 1934)
*The Heart of Britain* (Humphrey Jennings, 1941)
*Heart of Glass* (Werner Herzog, 1976)
*Heart of the Stag* (Michael Firth, 1984)
*Heavenly Creatures* (Peter Jackson, 1994)
*Henry V* (Lawrence Olivier, 1944)
*Henry, Portrait of a Serial Killer* (John McHaughton, 1986)
*Hephzibah* (Curtis Levy, 1998)
*Hero* (Zhang Yimou, 2002)
*High and Low* (Akira Kurosawa,1963)
*Histories of the Revolution* (Gutiérrez Alea, 1960)
*The History of the Kelly Gang* (Charles Tait, 1906)
*Un Homme et son péché* (Paul Gury, 1948)
*Horse* (Kevin Liddy, 1992)
*House of Flying Daggers* (Zhang Yimou, 2004)
*How It Feels to Be Run Over* (Cecil Hepworth, 1900)
*Ice Cold in Alex* (J. Lee Thompson, 1958)
*Ikeru shikabane* (Eizo Tanaka, 1918)
*Ikiteite yokatta* (Kamei Fumio, 1956)
*I Know Where I'm Going!* (Michael Powell and Emeric Pressburger, 1945)
*Ikuru* (Akira Kurosawa,1952)
*I Love a Man in Uniform* (David Wellington, 1993)
*Indochine* (Régis Wargnier, 1992)
*Infernal Affairs* (Wai Keung Lau and Siu Fai Mak, 2002)
*Into the West* (Mike Newell, 1992)
*Jedda* (Charles Chauvel, 1955)
*Judo* (Zhang Yimou, 1990)
*Kabeatsuki heya* (Kobayashi Masaki, 1953)
*Kasbah* (Mariano Barroso, 2000)
*Koktebel* (Boris Khlebnikov and Aleksei Popogrebskii, 2003)
*Komsomolsk* (Sergei Gerasimov, 1939)
*Ladri di Biciclette* (Vittorio De Sica, 1948)
*The Last Supper* (Gutiérrez Alea, 1979)
*Lawrence of Arabia* (David Lean, 1962)
*Laxdale Hall* (John Eldridge, 1952)

*Lejos de Africa* (Cecilia Batrolomé, 1996)
*Léolo* (Jean-Claude Lauzon, 1992)
*Les Boys* (Louis Saia, 1997)
*Lessons of Darkness* (Werner Herzog, 1992)
*Listen to Britain* (Humphrey Jennings and Stewart McAllister, 1942)
*Little Dieter Needs to Fly* (Werner Herzog, 1997)
*The Long Memory* (Robert Hamer, 1953)
*The Lord of the Rings* (Peter Jackson, 2001–3)
*Lorna Doone* (Basil Dean, 1934)
*Love Story* (Leslie Arliss, 1944)
*Lucía* (Humberto Solas, 1968)
*La Lutte* (Michel Brault, Marcel Carrière, Claude Fournier, Claude Jutra, 1961)
*Madonna of the Seven Moons* (Arthur Crabtree, 1944)
*Maelström* (Denis Villeneuve, 1999)
*Mahuala* (Sergio Giral, 1979)
*Mama Tumaini* (Martin Mhando, 1987)
*Man of Aran* (Robert Flaherty, 1934)
*Manuela* (Humberto Solas, 1966)
*Man with a Movie Camera* (Dziga Vertov, 1929)
*Martín Hache* (Adolfo Aristaráin, 1998)
*Masala* (Srinivas Krishna, 1991)
*A Matter of Life and Death* (Michael Powell and Emeric Pressburger, 1946)
*Mauri* (Merata Mita, 1988)
*Memories of Underdevelopment* (Tomás Gutiérrez Alea, 1968)
*Men in Black* (Barry Sonnenfeld, 1997)
*Men in Black II* (Barry Sonnenfeld, 2002)
*Men of Sugar* (Pastor Vega, 1965)
*Michael Collins* (Neil Jordan, 1996)
*Millions like Us* (Frank Launder and Sidney Gilliat, 1943)
*The Mill on the Floss* (Tim Whelan, 1937)
*The Miracle Worker* (Alexander Medvedkin, 1937)
*Mirror* (Andrei Tarkovskii, 1974)
*Miss Grant Goes to the Door* (Brian Desmond Hurst, 1940)
*Mon oncle Antoine* (Claude Jutra, 1971)
*More Time* (Isaac Mabhikwa, 1993)
*Muerte de un ciclista* (Juan Antonio Bardem, 1955)
*La muerte de Mikel* (Imanol Uribe, 1983)
*Mujeres al borde de un ataque de nervios* (Pedro Almodóvar, 1988)
*My Best Fiend* (Werner Herzog, 1999)
*My One-legged Dream Lover* (Penny Fowler-Smith and Christine Olsen, 1998)
*Nanook of the North* (Robert Flaherty, 1921)
*The Navigator: A Medieval Odyssey* (Vincent Ward, 1988)
*Neria* (Godwin Mawuru, 1992)
*Ngati* (Barry Barclay, 1987)
*Night of the Demon* (Jacques Tourneur, 1957)
*Nobleza baturra* (Joaquín Dicenta,1925/Florián Rey, 1935)
*Nobody Waved Goodbye* (Don Owen, 1964)

*The North West Frontier* (J. Lee Thompson, 1959)
*Nosferatu* (Werner Herzog, 1979)
*Nothing* (Vincent Natali, 2003)
*Ocaña: retrato intermitent* (Ventura Pons, 1979)
*The Odyssey of General José* (Jorge Fraga, 1968)
*The Old and the New* (Sergei Eisenstein, 1929)
*Oliver Twist* (David Lean, 1948)
*Once Were Warriors* (Lee Tamahori, 1993)
*One Night the Moon* (Rachel Perkins, 2001)
*Opera Prima* (Fernando Trueba, 1980)
*La orgía* (Francesc Bellmunt, 1978)
*The Other Francisco* (Sergio Giral, 1974)
*Otoshiana* (Teshigahara Hiroshi, 1962)
*Paperback Hero* (Peter Pearson, 1973)
*Panorama from Incline Railway* (American Mutoscope and Biograph, 1902)
*Panorama of Susquehanna River Taken from the Black Diamond Express* (Edison Manufacturing Company, 1897)
*Panoramic Scene, Susquehanna River* (Edison Manufacturing Company, 1897)
*Panoramic View, Kicking Horse Canyon* (Edison Manufacturing Company, 1901)
*Panoramic View of Lower Kicking Horse Canyon* (Edison Manufacturing Company, 1902)
*Panoramic View of Mt. Tamalpais, Cal.* (Edison Manufacturing Company, 1902)
*Pascual Duarte* (Ricardo Franco, 1975)
*Pather Panchali* (Satyajit Ray, 1955)
*Peppermint Frappé* (Carlos Saura, 1967)
*El perqué de tot plegat* (Ventura Pons, 1994)
*La Petite Aurore, l'enfant martyre* (Yves Bigras, 1952)
*Phantom Ride on the Canadian Pacific* (Edison Manufacturing Company, 1903)
*Phenomenon* (Jon Turteltaub, 1996)
*The Piano* (Jane Campion, 1993)
*El pico* (Eloy de la Iglesia, 1982)
*El pico II* (Eloy de la Iglesia, 1983)
*El pisito* (Marco Ferreri, 1960)
*Playtime* (Jacques Tati, 1967)
*Poitín* (Bob Quinn, 1978)
*Pour la suite du monde* (Pierre Perrault and Michel Brault, 1963)
*Pouvoir intime* (Yves Simoneau, 1986)
*Princess Mononoke* (Miyazaki Hayao, 1997)
*Psycho* (Gus Van Sant, 1998)
*The Private Life of Henry VIII* (Alexander Korda, 1933)
*¿Qué hace una chica como tú en un sitio como este?* (Fernando Colomo, 1979)
*¿Qué he hecho yo para merecer esto?* (Pedro Almodóvar, 1985)
*Querelle* (Rainer Werner Fassbinder, 1982)
*The Quiet Man* (John Ford, 1952)
*Rabbit-Proof Fence* (Phillip Noyce, 2002)
*Radiance* (Rachel Perkins, 1998)
*La radio folla* (Francesc Bellmunt, 1986)
*Rancheador* (Sergio Giral, 1976)

*The Red Desert* (Michelangelo Antonioni, 1964)
*Red Sorghum* (Zhang Yimou, 1987)
*Reefer and the Model* (Joe Comerford, 1987)
*The Return* (Andrei Zviagintsev, 2003)
*The Rich Bride* (Ivan Pyr'ev, 1937)
*Riding Alone for Thousands of Miles* (Zhang Yimou, 2005)
*Rien que les heures* (Alberto Cavalcanti, 1926)
*Rojou no reikon* (Minoru Murata, 1921)
*Romper Stomper* (Geoffrey Wright, 1992)
*Rory O'More* (Sidney Olcott, 1910)
*Rude* (Clement Virgo, 1995)
*Sal Gorda* (Fernando Trueba, 1982)
*The Saint* (Phillip Noyce, 1997)
*Scanners* (David Cronenberg, 1980)
*The Scarecrow* (Sam Pillsbury, 1982)
*Scott of the Antarctic* (Charles Frend, 1948)
*Scream of Stone* (Werner Herzog, 1991)
*Secondary Roles* (Orlando Rojas ,1989)
*The Secret of Roan Inish* (John Sayles, 1994)
*Sé infiel y no mires con quien* (Fernando Trueba, 1985)
*Sekai wa kyoufusuru* (Kamei Fumio, 1957)
*Seven of the Brave* (Sergei Gerasimov, 1937)
*The Seventh Seal* (Ingmar Bergman, 1956)
*Signs of Life* (Werner Herzog, 1968)
*Simba* (Brian Desmond Hurst, 1955)
*Si Mungu Mtupu* (Hammie Rajab, 1999)
*Sleeping Dogs* (Roger Donaldson, 1977)
*Sliver* (Phillip Noyce, 1993)
*Smash Palace* (Roger Donaldson, 1981)
*Snowball Cherry Red* (Vasilii Shukshin, 1973)
*Sonatine* (Takeshi Kitano, 1993)
*Song of the Road* (John Baxter, 1937)
*Song of the Tourist* (Pastor Vega, 1967)
*La Soufrière* (Werner Herzog, 1977)
*South Riding* (Victor Saville, 1938)
*Spring on Zarechnaia Street* (Felix Miromer and Marlen Khutsiev, 1956)
*Stage Sisters* (Xie Jin, 1965)
*Star Wars* (George Lucas, 1977)
*Strawberry and Chocolate* (Tomás Gutiérrez Alea and Juan Carlos Tabío, 1993)
*Stray Dog* (Akira Kurosawa, 1949)
*Surcos* (José Antonio Nieves Conde, 1951)
*The Sweet Hereafter* (Atom Egoyan, 1997)
*Tampopo* (Juzo Itami, 1986)
*Tasio* (Montxo Armendáriz, 1984)
*Taxi* (Carlos Saura, 1996)
*Ten Canoes* (Rolf de Heer and Peter Djigirr, 2006)
*Te Rua* (Barry Barclay, 1991)

*They're a Weird Mob* (Michael Powell, 1966)
*Three Times* (Hsiao-Hsien Hou, 2005)
*Tierra* (Julio Medem, 1994)
*Tierra sin pan* (Luis Buñuel, 1933)
*Tigres de papel* (Fernando Colomo, 1977)
*The Titfield Thunderbolt* (Charles Crichton, 1953)
*Tokyo Story* (Yasujiro Ozu, 1953)
*Too Much* (Fernando Trueba, 1995)
*The Tracker* (Rolf de Heer, 2002)
*Tuya's Marriage* (Quanan Wang, 2006)
*27 horas* (Montxo Armendáriz, 1986)
*Ugetsu monogatari* (Mizoguchi Kenji, 1953)
*Vacas* (Julio Medem, 1992)
*Vertical Love* (Arturo Sotto,1997)
*Victoria the Great* (Herbert Wilcox, 1937)
*La vida sigue* (Fernando Fernán Gómez, 1962)
*Videodrome* (David Cronenberg, 1982)
*View from Gorge Railroad* (Thomas Edison, 1896)
*Vigil* (Vincent Ward, 1984)
*The Village* (M. Night Shyamalan, 2004)
*Violent Cop* (Takeshi Kitano, 1989)
*Viridiana* (Luis Buñuel, 1960)
*Waking Ned* (Kirk Jones, 1999)
*Walkabout* (Nicholas Roeg, 1971)
*The Water Gypsies* (Maurice Elvey, 1931)
*waydowntown* (Gary Burns, 2000)
*Went the Day Well?* (Alberto Cavalcanti, 1942)
*Werner Herzog Eats His Shoe* (Les Blank, 1980)
*Whale Rider* (Niki Caro, 2002)
*Whisky Galore!* (Alexander Mackendrick, 1948)
*The Wicked Lady* (Leslie Arliss, 1945)
*Wild Man* (Geoff Murphy, 1977)
*Wimbo wa Mianzi* (Yusuf Chuwa, 1985)
*The Wind that Shakes the Barley* (Ken Loach, 2006)
*The World of Apu* (Satyajit Ray, 1959)
*Woyzeck* (Werner Herzog, 1979)
*Yellow Earth* (Chen Kaige, 1984)
*Yellow Fella* (Ivan Sen, 2005)
*Yield to the Night* (J. Lee Thompson, 1956)
*The Young Rebel* (Julio García Espinosa, 1961)
*Zabriskie Point* (Michelangelo Antonioni, 1970)
*Zigomar* (Victorin-Hippolyte Jasset, 1911)
*Lo zio di Brooklyn* (Daniele Ciprì and Franco Maresco, 1995)
*Un Zoo la nuit* (Jean-Claude Lauzon, 1987)
*Zui hao de shi guang* (Hsiao-Hsien Hou, 2005)

# Contributors

**Robert Britton** graduated in Spanish and French from Nottingham University, and after some years as a teacher and aid worker abroad, entered university administration while also pursuing his interest in Hispanic studies. He obtained a doctorate at Kings College, London, specialising in Latin American poetry, and later worked in adult and continuing education. His publications include numerous articles and reviews on modern Latin American literature and ideas, and a translation and critical introduction to Francisco de Quevedo's *Los sueños*. He has just completed a literary and political biography of the poet César Vallejo. Since 1993 he has been an honorary research fellow of the Department of Hispanic Studies at Sheffield University, and is a part-time lecturer in the University's Institute for Lifelong Learning, where he teaches courses in modern Latin American and Spanish Golden Age literature and culture, including modules on Spanish and Cuban cinema.

**Professor Wimal Dissanayake** is Lecturer at the University of Hawaii at Manoa. He is an Honorary Professor at the University of Hong Kong and is on the Affiliate Faculty of the Department of Political Science, University of Hawaii. He has published a large number of books including *Melodrama and Asian Cinema* (Cambridge University Press), *New Chinese Cinema* (Oxford University Press), *Colonialism and Nationalism in Asian Cinema* (Indiana University Press), and *Indian Popular Cinema* (Trentham Publishers). He was the Founding Editor of the East-West Film Journal, and has served as editorial advisor to such prestigious publications as International Encyclopedia of Communication, *Journal of Communication*, *Communication Theory*, *Framework*, *Deep Focus*, *World Englishes*, and the *Journal of South Asian Popular Culture*.

**Marvin D'Lugo** is Professor of Spanish and Screen Studies at Clark University where he regularly teaches courses on Spanish and Spanish-American Cinemas. He is author of *The Films of Carlos Saura: The Practice of Seeing* (Princeton University Press, 1991), *Guide to the Cinema of Spain* (Greenwood Press, 1997) and *Pedro Almodóvar* (University of Illinois Press, 2006)(. He is principal editor of *Studies in Hispanic Cinemas*. His principal areas of research are film authorship and transnational film productions.

**Tom Gunning** is the Edwin A. and Betty L. Bergman Distinguished Service Professor in the Department on Cinema and Media at the University of Chicago. He is the author of *D.W. Griffith and the Origins of American Narrative Film* (University of Illinois Press) and *The Films of Fritz Lang; Allegories of Vision and Modernity* (British Film Institute), as well as over one hundred articles on early cinema, film history and theory, avant-garde film, film genre, and cinema and modernism.

**Sue Harper** is Emeritus professor of Film History at the University of Portsmouth. She has written a wide range of articles on British cinema, and her books include *Picturing the Past: the Rise and Fall of the British Costume Film* (1994), *Women in British Cinema: Mad, bad and Dangerous to Know* ( 2000), *British Cinema of the 1950s: the Decline of Deference* (2003, with Vincent Porter, and *The New Film History* (2007, with James Chapman and Mark Glancy). Sue was Principle Investigator of an Arts and Humanities Research Council project on British cinema of the 1970s, and her future publications will include reports on that project.

**Susan Hayward** is Professor of Cinema Studies at Exeter University. She is the author of several books (*French National Cinema, Luc Besson, Simone Signoret: The Star as Cultural Sign, Les Diaboliques, Cinema Studies: The Key Concepts*). Currently she is working on a book for Intellect Press on The French Costume Drama of the 1950s. She is the founder and co-editor with Phil Powrie of the specialised film journal *Studies in French Cinema* (with Intellect).

**William Hope** is Lecturer in Italian at the University of Salford. His main research areas are Modern Italian cinema, Marxism and cinema and Fascism and literature. His publications include monographs on aspects of the Italian cinema: *Giuseppe Tornatore: Emotion, Cognition, Cinema* (Cambridge Scholars Publishing, 2006); *Curzio Malaparte - The Narrative Contract Strained* (Troubador, 2000); and an edited volume: *Italian Cinema - New Directions* (Peter Lang, 2005).

**Christina Kennedy** is Professor of Geography at Northern Arizona University. Her research interests include landscape studies, media/film geography, resource management and tourism, and she has published extensively in these areas.

**Mélisa Kennedy** holds a Masters in Landscape Architecture from the University of Arizona. Her main interest and research area lies in exploring the advantages of applying sustainable planning theory to a revision of existing zoning codes in low-density exurbs and suburbs.

**Tianna Kennedy** has a Masters in Performance Studies from New York University. She is interested in live art and geography, and has written for *liveartmagazine, Reckless Sleepers,* and *Glowlab*. She has also taught Radio Culture and Sight, Sound and Motion at Brooklyn College in the department of Television and Radio. She was also project manager for swimming cities of Serenissima (swimmingcities.org), and is also a founding member of the Empty Vessel Project, an Action, Art and Design Center fostering projects focused on Sustainable Living in Urban Landscapes.

**Jim Leach** is a Professor in the Department of Communication, Popular Culture and Film at Brock University, St Catharines, Ontario. His research and teaching interests include Canadian cinema, British cinema, popular cinema, and film and cultural theory. He has published books on the films of Alain Tanner and Claude Jutra and on British cinema and Canadian cinema, co-edited a critical anthology on Canadian documentary films, and developed a Canadian edition of an introductory film studies textbook. His latest book is a monograph on *Doctor Who* for Wayne State University Press.

**Martin Mhando** is a senior lecturer in Media Studies at Murdoch University, where he teaches in the areas of screen production, documentary theory, and Third Cinema. He has directed three feature films and numerous documentaries. His most recent film *Maangamizi* (2000), a feature film shot in Africa, has won a number of awards and was selected by Tanzania as its 2002 Oscar entry for the Best Foreign Film. Martin comes from an industry background and now combines technical skills with aesthetic applications through his work at Murdoch University.

**Martin McLoone** is Professor of Media Studies (Film, Television & Photography) at the University of Ulster. He is the author of *Film, Media and Popular Culture in Ireland: Cityscapes, Landscapes, Soundscapes* (2007) and *Culture, Identity and Broadcasting: Local Issues, Global Perspectives* (1991).

**Brad Prager** is Associate Professor of German and a member of the Program in Film Studies at the University of Missouri. His areas of research include Film History, Contemporary German Cinema, Holocaust Studies, and German Romanticism. He is the author of *The Cinema of Werner Herzog: Aesthetic Ecstasy and Truth* (London, 2007) and *Aesthetic Vision and German Romanticism: Writing Images* (Rochester, 2007). He is the co-editor of a volume on Visual Studies and the Holocaust entitled *Visualizing the Holocaust: Documents, Aesthetics, Memory* (Rochester, 2008), and of a forthcoming volume on contemporary German cinema entitled *The Collapse of the Conventional: German Cinema and its Politics at the Turn of the Twenty-First Century* (Detroit, 2010).

**Paul Spicer** lectured in Film Studies at the University of Portsmouth. As well as teaching on various film related courses, he was also coordinator for the Japanese Cinema and Culture and East Asian Cinema Units. In February 2009, Paul moved to Japan to complete research for his doctoral thesis which amongst other issues, examines the mis-reading of Japanese texts through the works of Kenji Mizoguchi. As well as his thesis related research, Paul is also interested in Japanese Film History and Movements, Popular Culture and Theory and the Japanese Theatre.

**Kate Taylor** is Lecturer in Visual Culture at Bangor University. She teaches and publishes on a variety of topics including Japanese and South Korean visual arts, feminism and world cinema and the body in film and culture. She is the author of *Rising Sun, Divided Land: Japanese and Korean Cinema*, forthcoming from Wallflower Press.

**Emma Widdis** is Head of the Department of Slavonic Studies at the University of Cambridge, and a Fellow of Trinity College. She is the author of *Visions of a New Land: Soviet Film from the Revolution to the Second World War* (Yale University Press, 2003), and *Alexander Medvedkin* (IB Tauris, 2004), and editor, with Simon Franklin, of *National Identity in Russian Culture* (Cambridge, 2004). She is currently working on aultural history of the senses in Soviet Russia, with a particular focus on Touch.

# Index